How to Study in College

NINTH EDITION

Walter Pauk
Cornell University, Emeritus

Ross J. Q. Owens

Houghton Mifflin Company
Boston   New York

Executive Publisher: Patricia A. Coryell
Executive Editor: Mary Finch
Sponsoring Editor: Shani Fisher
Marketing Manager: Edwin Hill
Senior Project Editor: Margaret Park Bridges
Senior Art and Design Coordinator: Jill Haber
Cover Design Director: Tony Saizon
Composition Buyer: Chuck Dutton
New Title Project Manager: Susan Brooks-Peltier
Editorial Assistant: Amanda Nietzel
Marketing Assistant: Erin Timm

Cover image of books: © Veer Incorporated/Rubberball Photography
Cover image of dictionary page: © Robert Schoen Photography

Printed in the U.S.A.

Library of Congress Control Number: 2006928873

Instructor's examination copy
  ISBN-10: 0-618-83403-6
  ISBN-13: 978-0-618-83403-7
For orders, use student text ISBNs
  ISBN-10: 0-618-76645-6
  ISBN-13: 978-0-618-76645-1

2 3 4 5 6 7 8 9-CRW-11 10 09 08

Part III   Retaining Information   **197**

To the Instructor of the Ninth Edition

Students who are seeking help are not primarily interested in theory, and most of them have little patience with merely inspirational talk. They want practical instruction on how to succeed academically. They want something that they can readily understand and apply and that works. After a week of classes, they discover that the hit-or-miss tactics that got them through high school are grossly inadequate and inefficient at the competitive college level. So they turn to us for help.

Let's then teach these students proven techniques for studying and learning. *How to Study in College* is brimming with exciting techniques, based on widely tested educational and learning theory, that have already helped myriad students. But the tail of theory is never allowed to wag the practical, feet-on-the-ground dog. While theory is always implicit and is sometimes given in enough detail to explain the rationale behind a particular technique or reassure the skeptic, it is never presented without explicit applications and never used simply as exhortation. After all, the person who needs penicillin is hardly cured by learning the history of antibiotics!

Because it is so crucial that students learn for the long term, we are wholeheartedly against techniques that stress mere memorization. Such techniques fill the mind with "knowledge" that melts away after a test and leaves learning still to be done. The techniques presented in this book result in real learning. And real learning, like a real diamond, lasts.

Finally, no textbook—no matter how complete or current—is truly useful if it is boring, confusing, or excessively difficult to read. We have worked hard to keep this book well organized and clear, maintaining a conversational tone so that reading it is like having a sincere, person-to-person chat.

What's Different in the Ninth Edition?

Although most of the popular elements from the previous edition have been retained, some of the book's familiar material has been rearranged and enhanced to make it even better organized, more helpful, and more timely. In addition, chapters on cultivating critical thinking, adjusting to different teaching and learning styles, gaining the most from discussions, and writing research papers have been added to make the book even more comprehensive and complete.

New! It's Your Q

How to Study in College is unique among study skills textbooks for the way in which it uses its own design to reinforce a core study technique. The marginal questions that run throughout the book supply hundreds of concrete examples of how main ideas can be used to formulate questions. Students who may be struggling with the vital skill can turn to any page in the book to see just how it's done and are constantly reminded of the value and effectiveness of this method. What's new is that in each chapter of the ninth edition a few of those questions are deliberately missing, providing students with an opportunity to test out the technique for themselves by formulating questions of their own. An icon has been added in the margin to help guide students to this feature.

New! Simplified Organization

Following the model of the book's chapters, each of which provides an easy-to-follow organizational road map, the book as a whole now has a similarly succinct controlling idea: *Becoming a successful student involves building a strong study skills foundation before gaining, retaining, and ultimately explaining information.* All of the book's chapters have been clustered beneath these four basic steps.

New! Managing Time *and* Space

The longstanding chapter on managing time now has an extra dimension. In addition to providing valuable scheduling tips and techniques, Chapter 2, "Using Time and Space Effectively," incorporates some simple but powerful advice on getting better organized.

New! Consolidated Techniques for Taking Tests

Although tests generally fall into one of two basic categories—objective or essay—all tests share some important similarities when it comes to the way you prepare for them, move through them, and learn from them. In the ninth edition, the tips and techniques for taking objective and essay tests have been woven together to provide a simpler, more unified test-taking plan of attack in Chapter 12, "Performing Well on Tests and Quizzes."

New! Chapter on Critical Thinking

These days, being able to think critically is more than just an admirable quality; it's a skill that's absolutely essential to academic survival. Given the sheer volume of available information, no student can possibly be expected to hold on to everything. Chapter 7, "Zeroing In on Information That's Valuable," provides tips for separating the wheat from the chaff by determining what's relevant, important, and reliable.

New! Chapter on Learning Styles

The ways in which information is conveyed in college are surprisingly limited, while the ways in which students learn best can be remarkably diverse. How can students who are operating on one wavelength tune in to information that's coming in on an entirely different channel? Chapter 8, "Learning Through Multiple Channels," addresses the crucial issue of learning styles by providing strategies for dealing with the dominant verbal and visual channels and introducing options for changing those channels in order to pick up information more readily and clearly.

New! Chapter on Discussions

In-class or online, discussions are a valuable part of the learning experience and may be an integral element of a course grade as well. Yet all too frequently, students are given very little guidance on what to discuss, how to discuss, and, most importantly, what to take away from a discussion. As a result, a precious opportunity for truly interactive reflection is often squandered. Chapter 13, "Getting the Most Out of Discussions," takes the simple, systematic, and commonsense approach that characterizes the book as a whole and applies it to this vital student interaction, whether it's face to face or computer to computer.

New! Chapter on Research Papers

A staple of the supplemental chapters for some time, Chapter 14, "Writing a Research Paper," has been thoroughly updated and is again included in the main book, rounding out the trio of ways that students are traditionally expected to demonstrate their knowledge and earn their grades.

Other Helpful Additions

- **Note-Taking Tips for Electronic Texts.** Not all texts start out on paper. Although the Cornell System is as relevant in this century as it was in the past one, taking notes on material from websites, presentation slides, and word processing documents requires some commonsense adjustments.
- **Proven Method for Prioritizing To Do List Items.** The urgency-importance matrix offers a simple systematic way to distinguish essential tasks from frivolous diversions.
- **Updated Research on Reading and Memory.** Researchers are steadily learning more about how we read and remember. The ninth edition incorporates updated information on both.

Valuable Features Retained

- **Concept Maps.** Concept maps continue to provide a graphical means of summarizing chapter content. Before reading a chapter, the maps supply advance organizers, which, according to David P. Ausubel, make it easier to learn and remember material in the chapter itself. After reading the chapter, the concept maps provide a bird's-eye view of the entire chapter, showing the main concepts with linking lines that establish relationships.
- **Chapter Quizzes.** Each "Have You Missed Something?" chapter quiz includes questions to reinforce students' understanding of key concepts. As always, the rationale for these questions is not to test but to teach. Any student who has read the chapter with care and understanding should achieve a perfect score.
- **Vocabulary-Building Sections.** Both the "Word History System" and the "Words in Context" sections remain in this edition. Because words are the building blocks of thinking, it is essential that students be given a variety of opportunities to add to and strengthen their vocabularies. Unfortunately, not all students have an instant affinity for learning new words. As instructors know all too well, it is often the approach and not the ultimate goal that can lead to indifference and even resistance in some students. The "Word History System" bolsters the impact of each word with a fascinating explanation and a compelling image, while the "Words in Context" sections, by dissecting the remarks of modern thinkers and leaders, provide a level of relevance that makes learning words more meaningful.

Ancillary Materials

This edition is supported by several ancillaries that are designed to reinforce and enrich the basic book:

The **Online Study Center** and **Online Teaching Center (college.hmco .com/pic/pauk9e)** provide additional materials for students and teachers. The Online Study Center includes "ACE Quizzes," "Roots and Prefixes Flashcards," "Words of Wisdom," and more. Find these activities along with additional ways to *Improve Your Grade* and *Prepare for Class*. The Online Teaching Center equips instructors with the author's PowerPoint slides, digital Instructor's Resource Manual, and additional support materials for your course.

The downloadable **Instructor's Resource Manual** provides you with quick access to information on preparing your syllabus, extra multiple-choice questions for each chapter, questions for discussion, and reproducible masters relating to the concepts found in the text.

PowerPoint Slides for each chapter of the ninth edition are now accessible through the Online Teaching Center. Use these slides to enhance any classroom presentation.

The HM Assessment and Portfolio Builder Etoken provides your students with online access to a personal assessment tool that assists them in preparing for lifelong learning. Students build a portfolio by responding to questions about their skills, attitudes, values, and behaviors in three key life areas: **Personal Growth**, **Career Growth**, and **Community Growth**. Each of these modules asks students to provide supporting evidence for questions where they rate themselves as highly proficient—great practice for critical thinking skills, as well as creating a résumé or preparing for interviews. An **Accomplishments Report** summarizes the results of their responses. This tool also provides access to Houghton Mifflin's web-based **Career Resource Center**, which includes tips, exercises, articles, and ideas to help students succeed on their journey from college to career.

Equipped with the information from their assessment and portfolio, students can explore Houghton Mifflin's updated web-based **Career Resource Center** for more tips, exercises, articles, and ideas to help succeed on the journey from college to career. **The Bridge from College to Career** lets students practice new skills in college that can be applied as they enter the job market. **Finding the Perfect Job** will help fine-tune résumé writing and interviewing skills. And **Skills For Your Future** provides strategies in problem solving and decision making to help students learn how to work with others and communicate on the job. The HM Assessment and Portfolio Builder eToken, with access to the Career Resource Center, can be shrink wrapped with your textbook.

Acknowledgments

Sincere words of thanks go to those who are permanently linked to this book: the late Henry F. Thoma and Ian D. Elliot.

Sincere thanks also go to the contributors of material in previous editions: Professors Harrison A. Geiselmann, Kenneth A. Greisen, and Jane E. Hardy, all of Cornell University; Professor William G. Moulton of Princeton University; Professor James A. Wood and Dr. Nancy V. Wood, both of the University of Texas at El Paso.

In addition, Walter Pauk remembers the valuable contributions made by Professors Mike Radis and Ron Williams of Pennsylvania State University as well as Professor Carol Kanar of Valencia Community College.

Ross Owens is especially grateful to Gwinn Owens and to Joan Quirie Owens, who instilled in him at a very early age a thirst for knowledge and a genuine love of learning, and also to his favorite future college students, Rebecca, Rachel, Sarah, Meg, Hannah, and Jack. But above all, thanks go to Walter Pauk himself, a loyal friend and wonderful mentor, who truly is the embodiment of this book's plain-spoken, clear-thinking, well-meaning wisdom.

At Houghton Mifflin we would like to thank Shani Fisher, Amanda Nietzel, and Andrew Sylvester for their editorial support of our work. We would also like to thank Margaret Bridges and Nancy Benjamin for their time and contributions in seeing this new edition to its completion.

We would also like to thank the reviewers of previous editions, as well as these reviewers of the present ninth edition for their helpful suggestions:

Cecelia Brewer, University of Missouri–Kansas City
Dennis H. Congos, University of Central Florida
Kelly Cox, University of Nevada–Las Vegas
Azucena M. Endrinal, Houston Community College, TX
Karen Goode-Bartholomew, St. Norbert College, WI
Sis McManus, Whatcom Community College, WA
Nita McMillan, Southwest Tennessee Community College
Janet M. Zupan, University of Montana

And finally, in this edition, as in the eight previous ones, Walter Pauk offers very special thanks to his students:

"I am eternally grateful to my many students who have taught me much—so that I may pass on a little more to others."

W. P.
R. J. Q. O.

To the Student

The desire for learning and the thirst for self-improvement are incredibly powerful impulses. Time and again they have dramatically altered individual lives and even changed our collective history. Helen Keller was unable to hear or see and yet she still learned to read and to communicate with extraordinary eloquence. Booker T. Washington, born into slavery, made a five-hundred-mile trek to high school in order to get the education he craved. More recently, Ben Carson made a U-turn away from what seemed like a dead-end life in a poor Detroit neighborhood by reading two books a week and ultimately earning a scholarship to Yale before going on to medical school and becoming the head of pediatric neurosurgery at the prestigious Johns Hopkins Hospital. And finally, there's the well-known story of Abraham Lincoln, whose willingness to walk twenty miles to borrow a book eventually put him on a path to the U.S. presidency.

Maybe you know someone like Keller, Washington, Carson, or Lincoln. Perhaps their stories share some similarities with your own. If so, you know firsthand how the desire to learn can give you the strength to start projects and to steadfastly see them through to a fulfilling finish. In college, few qualities will serve you better than a deep-rooted will to succeed. After all, on a cold winter morning, it's far easier to get out of bed if you want to ace a mid-term than if you don't really care about your performance!

How This Book Is Organized

Becoming a successful student involves building a strong study skills foundation before gaining, retaining, and ultimately explaining information. All of the book's 14 chapters have been clustered beneath these basic steps.

Part I: Building a Foundation lays the groundwork for success by addressing skills that are essential in college and beyond. You don't need to be a student to benefit from learning how to set goals (Chapter 1), control your time and organize your space (Chapter 2), stay focused (Chapter 3), and manage stress (Chapter 4).

Part II: Gaining Information deals with ferreting out and understanding the most valuable facts, ideas, and concepts that you encounter in lectures and texts, on websites, in discussions, and even in images and firsthand observation. You can enrich your verbal skills by improving your reading (Chapter 5) and bolstering your vocabulary (Chapter 6). You can greatly enhance the efficiency of your learning by focusing in on the most valuable information in each class (Chapter 7). And finally, you can adapt to the predominant academic teaching styles and use your particular learning style to its best advantage (Chapter 8).

Part III: Retaining Information helps you to hold on to that valuable information by defending your memory against the powerful force of forgetfulness (Chapter 9), by taking notes systematically (Chapter 10), and by mastering those notes to ensure that they become a permanent part of your knowledge (Chapter 11).

Part IV: Explaining Information focuses on the payoff for all your academic efforts. Although there's a lot to be said for "learning for learning's sake," the reality is that most courses inevitably expect you to actually "show what you know." To demonstrate the level of your learning, the extent of your knowledge will typically be measured in terms of tests and quizzes (Chapter 12), class discussions (Chapter 13), and papers (Chapter 14). All three chapters provide valuable tips and techniques that encourage peak performance.

Using This Book

No matter what academic goals you've set for yourself, this book can help you achieve them. In theory, there is no limit to learning and no limit to how you can improve your natural abilities to understand the material you study. By applying the techniques presented here, you will quickly begin to improve as a student, making your college experience a rewarding one.

How to Use This Book's Marginal Questions

If you've already had an opportunity to flip through this book, then you have almost certainly noticed something a little unusual about it. Running along the outside of each page in the marginal area that is blank in most books is a series of questions, one for almost every paragraph.

No single academic skill is more important than the ability to ask and answer questions. Questions are what make learning come alive. They activate inert facts and turn them into vibrant ideas. If questions aren't a key component of your studying, there's a chance that you aren't truly learning. What should you do with these questions? As it happens, they have several potential uses.

Use them as examples. If asking questions is already a part of your learning process, then their importance is already clear to you. But for students who are new to asking questions, this approach may seem a little awkward and strange. We understand that. And that's one of the primary reasons we've included our own questions in the margins of this book: to provide you with real examples of the kinds of questions you'll want to be pondering as you're reading along.

Use them as motivators. As you move through each chapter assignment, how can you be sure you've actually understood what you've read? One way is by asking questions. Before you read each paragraph, ask yourself the question in the margin. Then make it a kind of mini-goal to see if you can answer it as you read. If you find it a struggle to answer the question, you may want to read the paragraph again. (If you still can't answer a question after additional tries, you may want to get help from your instructor.) If you find it easy to answer the question, then you're probably picking up the paragraph's important information. That realization should provide motivation to read on and unlock the meaning of each new paragraph in a similar fashion.

Use them as a reviewing aid. After you've finished a page or, if you prefer, the entire chapter, go back and cover up the text of each page with a blank sheet of paper, leaving only the marginal questions uncovered. Then systematically read each question and try to answer it from memory and in your own words. Either recite your answer out loud or jot it down on the blank sheet you're using to cover up the text. Once you've provided your answer, check your work by comparing your response to the actual text.

Use them as a navigational tool. If you're returning to a chapter to look up a specific passage or to confirm a particular fact, it helps to be able to go directly to the information you're seeking rather than having to reread large portions just to find what you're looking for. Chapter and section titles help you in this effort, but they only go so far. The marginal questions give you a quick sense of what each important paragraph is addressing.

Not all books have questions in the margins, of course. In fact, most don't. But the value of learning with a book that has the questions already supplied is that you can then apply this approach to your other textbooks. Your efforts should lead to true comprehension and mastery.

Use them as practice.   Although most of the marginal questions have been supplied for you, in each chapter a few questions have deliberately been left out. (See "How to Use the 'It's Your Q' Component" below.) Going back through a chapter and formulating your own question in those spots where the questions are missing will give you a chance to practice this vital part of the learning process.

How to Use the "Have You Missed Something?" Questions

The end-of-chapter questions are designed to teach, not test; you'll find no trick questions and no traps to lead you to an incorrect answer. Take each question at face value and answer it to the best of your ability. Use any incorrect answers you give as opportunities to reread the pertinent portion of the chapter. By re-reading and rethinking the question and answer, you will greatly strengthen your understanding of the entire concept. Answers to these questions are located in the appendix.

How to Use the "It's Your Q" Component

The Q System uses marginal questions to encourage active reading. In each chapter most but not all of the paragraphs are accompanied by marginal questions. At the end of each chapter, the "It's Your Q" component encourages you to go back and test your ability to come up with your own marginal questions for the chapter paragraphs that don't already have them. An icon has been added in the margin to help guide you to paragraphs that do not have marginal questions.

How to Use the Vocabulary-Building Components

The final pages of every chapter are devoted to vocabulary building. There you'll find "Words in Context," a series of quotations that can be instructive, inspiring, and sometimes even amusing. In each quotation, one or more words is italicized. You are asked to select from three options the word that most nearly reflects the meaning of the italicized word. This is not a test; rather, the purpose is to expose you to words in a real-world context. You may select unfamiliar words for further study. Familiar words will provide reinforcement for your existing vocabulary.

Finally, at the end of each chapter, a single word is pictorially presented in a way that is both highly interesting and incisively memorable. Without a historical background, a word, like a gas-filled balloon, usually floats freely out of sight and out of mind. But once it is anchored to its colorful origins, a word should always remain with you. For example, the history of the word *tantalize* at the end of Chapter 1 is portrayed by King Tantalus. Just out of reach of his parched lips is a pool of fresh water that recedes whenever he tilts his head to drink. Just out of his grasp is a branch of succulent fruit that draws back whenever he tries to pull it toward him. It's hard not to sense his profound frustration. The picture makes a memorable mental impression that the word *tantalize* means "to excite (another) by exposing something desirable while keeping it out of reach." The Chinese adage that "a picture is worth a thousand words" proves itself again.

A wide and precise vocabulary is really the main ingredient or quality that provides all of us with the endless ability for better thinking and judgment in all phases of life—personally, socially, and professionally.

Discover Your Own Resources

"Know thyself" is wise advice for a student poised at the path that leads to an academic goal. Development of your skills begins with understanding your personal learning style and study skills. By identifying your preferences and strengths, you can zero in on the best study skills techniques for you. The following list can help you identify your basic learning style. For each item, circle the letter that best matches your style. Keep your responses in mind as you read this book.

Learning Styles Self-Assessment
1. I study better (a) by myself; (b) in groups; (c) in a combination of the two.
2. I remember best when I've (a) *heard* something; (b) *read* or *seen* something; (c) *done* something active, such as problem solving.
3. I think I'm (a) better with facts, such as names or dates; (b) better with concepts, ideas, or themes; (c) about the same with both.
4. I learn better when I read (a) slowly; (b) quickly; (c) either way.
5. I study more efficiently in (a) one solid study period; (b) small blocks of time.
6. I work (a) well under pressure; (b) poorly under pressure.
7. I work (a) quickly, for short periods of time; (b) at a steady, slower pace for longer periods of time.
8. I (a) do learn best in a structured setting, such as a classroom or laboratory; (b) do not learn best in a structured setting.
9. I think that the greatest strength of my learning style is _____.
10. I think that the greatest weakness of my learning style is _____.

You'll improve your chances of success if you balance this knowledge of your learning style with a willingness to remain flexible. For example, you may be thinking, "It's true. I'm a sprinter who begins working with a burst of energy and then slacks off. That's the way I've always been. How can I possibly change?" Or you may believe that studying all night is an effective way of coping with a tight schedule and that you have no need for a more conventional strategy. These ways of thinking probably feel comfortable, but they may have created blind spots in your view of studying. To get a sense of how blind spots can limit you, try to solve the problem shown in Figure 1. Odds are that a blind spot will prevent you from solving it. Yet once you see the solution, you'll probably say, "How easy! Why didn't I think of that tactic myself?"

FIGURE 1

The Nine-Dot Problem
Connect these dots by drawing four straight lines without taking your pencil from the paper and without retracing any lines. The solution appears on page xxii.

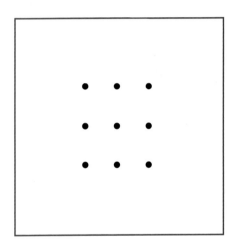

A Second Chance

The Nine-Dot Problem (Figure 1) not only demonstrates a point, but it is also an excellent learning device. For instance, although very few students have solved the puzzle, they nevertheless have learned to break out of the conventional-thinking mold and let their minds rove more freely, which leads to more innovative and imaginative approaches to solving problems.

To prove that you, perhaps, have learned a great deal from this one puzzle, apply your newfound knowledge to the problem shown in Figure 2.

FIGURE 2
The Puzzle of Squares
How many squares are there
in this figure? The solution
appears on page xxii.

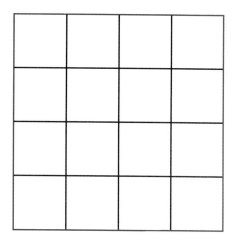

Take Advantage of This Book's Additional Resources

Many of this book's important skills and systems are enriched and brought
to life on our website. You'll have an opportunity to boost your vocabulary
skills with electronic flash cards, to test your knowledge and comprehension
with additional questions, and to customize and print out your own copies of
the time- and task-based schedules discussed in Chapter 2. You can also learn
more academic strategies in online supplementary chapters on studying foreign
languages, studying literature, studying science and mathematics, and using a
computer for school. To visit the *How to Study in College* website, go to http://
collegesurvival.college.hmco.com/students.

Take Advantage of Your School's Resources

College or university website.   It's a rare college these days that doesn't have
a website. What sort of information do these sites contain? That's going to vary
widely depending on the college. Some have simply converted the text of their
college catalog into an online form. Others provide elaborate and interactive
repositories of information that keep you up-to-date on a variety of college
news and often enable you to conduct some transactions that might otherwise
need to be done by mail, over the phone, or in person. Regardless of the scope
of your college's site, it is often a good place to start. Check the site's FAQs (Frequently Asked Questions) to see if your concern has already been addressed.

College catalog.   General information about your college's requirements, policies, programs, and services appears in the college catalog. Even if your college provides this information on its website, it still helps to have a hard copy of the catalog handy during the first weeks of classes to remind yourself of requirements and deadlines to be met.

Student handbook.   The student handbook provides information about your school's procedures, regulations, and code of conduct. It may also describe the school's requirements for good academic standing and graduation. For details or for specific department requirements, consult your department office or your academic adviser.

Admissions or registrar's office.   You can find answers to questions about grades, transcripts, and college requirements in the admissions or registrar's office. Admission to college and registration for courses begin with this office.

FIGURE 3
Answer to the Nine-Dot Problem
Begin at the top left corner and follow the arrows.

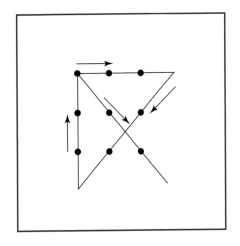

FIGURE 4
Answer to the Puzzle of Squares
30 squares.

1×1 squares 16
2×2 squares 9
3×3 squares 4
4×4 squares 1
Total squares   30

Office of financial affairs. For answers to questions about scholarships, loans, and grants, contact the financial affairs office. You will come here to pay fees and fines and to pick up your checks if you are in a work-study grant or program. If you want a part-time job on campus for which you must qualify on the basis of your financial status, you will fill out application forms in this office.

Career development and placement office. If you want help choosing a major or setting a career goal, contact the career development and placement office. People in this office can administer various interest, personality, and skills assessment tests to help you determine the kind of work for which you are best suited. They can help you find jobs on and off campus. Some career development centers sponsor on-campus recruitment, inviting businesses to interview prospective graduates and aiding them in submitting applications and résumés. After graduation, you can file a résumé in the placement office if you want your school's help with landing a job.

Academic advising office or counseling department. Academic and guidance counselors can help you with everything from choosing the right course to solving personal problems that prevent you from meeting your academic goals. The academic office or counseling department may be part of the admissions office, or it may be a separate department. In many colleges students are assigned to an adviser or a counselor who follows their progress throughout their college careers.

Student health center. If you become ill, you can go to a doctor at the health center. The health center may have a pharmacy and may provide a limited amount of hospital care. Some mental health services may be available through this center, through the office of a school psychologist or psychiatrist, or through a peer-counseling group. The health center may also refer students to an agency outside the college.

Student government association. Working with the dean of students, the student government association sponsors student activities such as intramural events, dances, special-interest organizations and clubs, and other social and academic events. (Joining a club or taking part in campus events is a good way to meet other students who share your interests.) In addition, your student government may publish a weekly bulletin or a student handbook that summarizes college requirements and resources.

Student publications. The college newspaper or literary magazine offers contributors unique opportunities for self-expression and provides readers with information and entertainment. Serving on the editorial staff of one of these publications may also fulfill some journalism or English requirements.

Learning lab or skills center. You may turn to the learning lab or skills center for help in improving your study, reading, writing, math, or computer skills. Whether you are required to spend time in a lab because of your performance on a college skills assessment test or you choose to go on your own, take full advantage of the opportunity to gain the skills you need.

Special student services. Veterans, students with physical or learning disabilities, minority students, international students, and students who are economically disadvantaged may need the special assistance of a trained support group to meet their academic goals. If you think you qualify for these services, ask your counselor or adviser about them. Your college may also offer services such as off-campus residence listings.

Athletics office. A listing of the college's athletic programs and events is available in the athletics office. This is the office to visit if you are interested in participating in sports.

Resident assistant. For on-campus students, resident assistants (RAs) can be a great source of information about campus services. Although RAs are not professional counselors, they have recently been through many of the experiences you're undergoing and can probably direct you to the campus office best suited to your needs.

Final Words

Our ultimate goal in this book is to provide you with tools, skills, and systems that will lead to self-sufficiency. Or, as Ralph Waldo Emerson once expressed it: "The best service one person can render another person is to help him help himself."

Building a Foundation

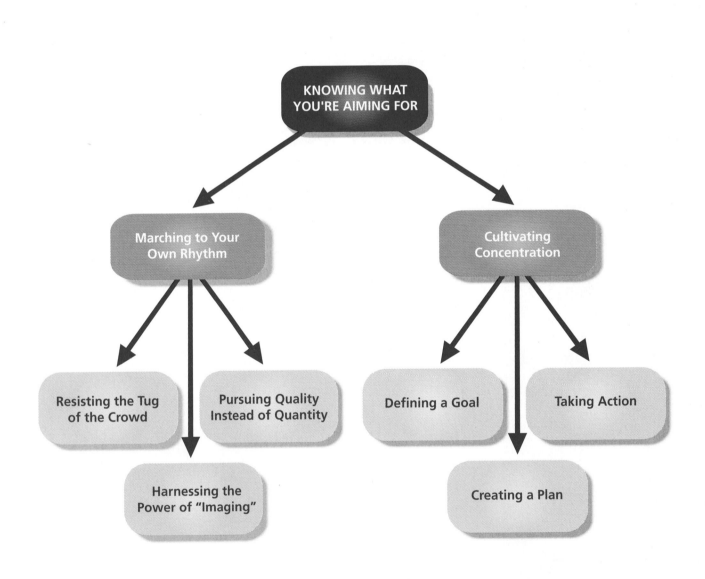

Knowing What You're Aiming For

There's something deep inside each of us that yearns for fulfillment. We were meant for something to which our nature inclines. But what? No one really knows. So, you yourself must dig. Dig—but for what? Start by digging for happiness. Ask, "What kind of work would I be happiest in? Doesn't it make sense that every day's work should be a joy?" In this chapter, you can begin to focus your life as you read and think about:

- **Marching to Your Own Rhythm**
- **Deciding What Would Make You Happy**
- **Redefining GPA**

What are the risks of having no goal?

Goals bring meaning to life; otherwise, life can be aimless. Viktor Frankl's research revealed these stark data:

> When 60 students were asked why they had attempted suicide, 85% said the reason had been that "life was meaningless."[1]

How do goals go beyond simple survival?

Goals have to go beyond earning your "bread and butter," as is shown in the following slice of human life:

> Governments, guided by social scientists, used to say that if you just improve the socio-economic status of the people, everything will be OK, people will become happy. The truth is that as the struggle for survival has subsided, the question has emerged: survival for what? Ever more people today have the means to life, but no meaning to live for.[2]

How do goals relate to purpose?

Goals and purpose breathe meaning into life. Goals and purpose form the psychological underpinnings of our individual lives. There's power in purpose, as is shown in this excerpt:

> We cannot have deep and enduring satisfaction unless we have self-worth. We cannot have self-worth unless our lives are an earnest attempt to express the finest and most enduring qualities that we are aware of. Purpose is an important condition for an enduring satisfaction with life.[3]

Marching to Your Own Rhythm

What was Thoreau's advice?

The nineteenth-century American writer, philosopher, and naturalist Henry David Thoreau famously wrote:

> If a man does not keep pace with his companions, perhaps it is because he hears a different drummer. Let him step to the music which he hears, however measured or far away.[4]

[1] Viktor Frankl, an Austrian psychiatrist and psychotherapist, created the theory of Logotherapy, which states that a person's primary motivation is his or her search for meaning in life.

[2] Richard J. Leider, *The Power of Purpose* (San Francisco: Berrett-Koehler Publishers, 1997), p. 35.

[3] Ibid.

[4] Henry David Thoreau, *Walden and Resistance to Civil Government*, 2nd ed. (W. W. Norton, 1992), p. 217.

CHAPTER 1

How can you bring meaning into your life?

This doesn't mean, as some have suggested, that you need to be an outcast or iconoclast or that you have to live alone in the woods of Walden Pond, as Thoreau once did. Many people who are intricately woven into the fabric of society still manage to adhere to ideals that they have sharpened and defined on their own. To bring meaning into your life, you must decide on your own goal. Avoid the trap of surrendering to the expectations of others instead of pursuing a goal that is personally meaningful.

What role should friends and family play in your goals?

This doesn't mean that you shouldn't discuss your goals with friends and family. It is helpful to ponder their thoughts and advice. But process these through your own brain cells and heart cells, and then make a decision, which must be your very own. Above all, set your own pace instead of marching along with the crowd.

Resisting the Tug of the Crowd

What happens when people think as a crowd instead of individually?

When you become part of the crowd, your individual thinking is replaced by crowd psychology. Here's how Gustave LeBon, a French social scientist, described crowd psychology:

> The most striking peculiarity presented by a psychological crowd is the following: Whoever be the individuals that compose it, however like or unlike be their mode of life, their occupations, their character, or their intelligence, the fact that they have been transformed into a crowd puts them in possession of a sort of collective mind which makes them feel, think, and act in a manner quite different from that in which each individual of them would feel, think, and act were he in a state of isolation.[5]

What did Gould observe about the psychology of a crowd?

LeBon's observations about crowds were adopted and furthered by Edson Gould, one of the most respected names on Wall Street, who used this easily visualized example to illustrate how the individual is almost powerless to resist the powerful magnetism of the crowd:

> You're *alone* in an empty movie theater and hear the cry of "fire." You look around, see no flames, smell no smoke, you *calmly walk* to the nearest exit. But, repeat the same cry of "fire" (again without flames visible or the smell of smoke) in a *crowded* theater and once the *crowd* starts *running* for an exit, you'll find *yourself running*, too. That's crowd psychology.[6]

[5]Quoted in Dan Sullivan, *The Chartist* (December 30, 1997): 4.

[6]Quoted in Edson Gould, *Findings and Forecasts* (New York: Anametrics, 1974).

 *Online Study Center*   www.college.hmco.com/pic/pauk9e

What should you guard against in crowd psychology?

Don't let crowd psychology rob you of your independence or rob you of your freedom to think and decide individually. In sum, preserve yourself as a sovereign individual so that, for better or for worse, you are the ruler of your career and destiny.

Harnessing the Power of "Imaging"

In what way does a goal go beyond a statement?

A goal is much more than just a simple statement. Actually, it's a vivid dream that has been mentally acted and reenacted. What lawyer hasn't first imagined presenting a closing argument to judge and jury? What business executive hasn't imagined outlining an exciting plan to staff members seated around the board of directors' table?

What is Peale's explanation of imaging?

Although *imagined* is generally used to denote imagination, in his landmark book *Positive Imaging* Norman Vincent Peale used the word *imaging* to convey a much deeper concept:

> Imaging consists of vividly picturing, in your conscious mind, a desired goal or objective, and holding that image until it sinks into your unconscious mind, where it releases great, untapped energies.[7]

How does imaging your goal affect it?

So, if we think deeply enough and image vividly enough about what we want to do with our lives, our whole being can be energized. Peale, who is one of the most widely read inspirational writers of all time, goes on to say,

> There is a powerful and mysterious force in human nature that is capable of bringing about dramatic improvement in our lives. It is a kind of mental engineering. . . . In imaging, one does not merely think about a hoped-for goal; one "sees" or visualizes it with tremendous intensity. Imaging is a kind of laser beam of the imagination, a shaft of mental energy in which the desired goal or outcome is pictured so vividly by the conscious mind that the unconscious mind accepts it and is activated by it. This releases powerful internal forces that can bring about astonishing changes in the life of the person who is doing the imaging.[8]

Pursuing Quality Instead of Quantity

How has money affected the way we define goals?

Over time, Peale's pristine image of a goal has been diluted by the dollar sign. Everyone, it seems, is out to make money. Look at the crowds thronging the racetracks, the casinos, the state lotteries, and even the frequently bubbling

[7]Norman Vincent Peale, *Positive Imaging*. Copyright © 1982. Published by Fleming H. Revell, a division of Baker Book House. Reprinted with permission.

[8]Ibid.

stock market. Apparently this "money idea" has steadily seeped into the career goals of students. According to a poll conducted by consulting firm KPMG (Klynveld, Peat, Marwick, Goerdeler), New York, three out of four college students expect to become millionaires.[9]

What advice does John Rau give his students?

The Siren song of money may be difficult to ignore, but is it really the key to happiness or the true mark of success? John Rau, who has been the CEO of three corporations, dean of Indiana University's business school, and no stranger to success himself, offers a straight-shooting sanity check for students who are thinking of sacrificing quality in the pursuit of quantity. "Unless you're doing the stuff you like," he cautions, "you can burn out."[10]

What does Dr. Williams conclude about defining your goals?

In line with Rau's succinct pronouncement, Dr. David Williams pulls no punches. Few people know more about "burnout" than medical doctors. After years of treating people who were experiencing burnout, Dr. Williams wrote this compelling article on choosing a career that will enhance the possibilities of living a healthier life.

What Do You Want to Be When You Grow Up?

If you're like me, the last time someone asked you this question was quite some time ago. Most of us guys probably responded with something like a fireman, forest ranger, cop, race car driver or even the President. I'm not being sexist (I'm not even sure there was such a word when someone last asked me the question), but if you're female you probably answered the above question with occupations like a model, flight attendant, school teacher or movie star. You chose these answers because at the time you thought these endeavors would be enjoyable. You could visualize being happy. Maybe a more appropriate question than "What do you want to be when you grow up?" would have been "What would make you happy?" And since the answer to this question changes throughout your life, it's a question we really need to ask ourselves more often.

When was the last time you actually got away by yourself and seriously thought about what you needed to be happy? Maybe it's time to do so.

As hectic as life has become, we see happiness as a luxury. Surveys have shown that most people really don't believe it's possible to be happy the majority of the time. They think that true happiness is an unobtainable goal. It's an unpredictable, fleeting sensation over which one has little control. But accepting this idea, that you have no or little control over your own happiness, can have serious health consequences. Happiness is just as important, if not more so, to good health as proper nutrition and adequate exercise. Happiness is a powerful healing force. On the

---

[9]Pamela Sebastian, *The Wall Street Journal* (March 25, 1999), p. A1.

[10]Quoted in Hal Lancaster, "Managing Your Career," *The Wall Street Journal* (May 6, 1997), p. B1.

opposite side of the coin we have stress. There seems to be an inverse relationship between stress and happiness. In other words, less happiness leads to more stress. And stress can be an extremely powerful destructive force. Stress is one of the best examples of the power the mind can have over the body.

In animal studies, French researchers at the University of Bordeaux have recently shown that depression and anxiety in adults can be a direct result of placing the mother under stress prior to birth. Stress causes the adrenal glands to produce more of the "stress hormone," corticosterone. Corticosterone easily passes from the mother to the fetus through the placenta. Consistently high levels of corticosterone desensitize brain receptors, altering the feedback system and making it more difficult to shut down the excess corticosterone production. After birth these receptors in the brain remain desensitized, which can lead to suppression of the immune system, depression and anxiety later in life. *(J Neurosi 96;15[1 Pt1]:110-6.)*

In an amazing study recently performed at Columbia University, New York, researchers found that young girls who suffer from undue stress grow up to be 5 cm. (2 in.) shorter than their happier contemporaries. Stress stunts their growth by depressing the levels of growth hormone in the body.

Volumes have been written on the detrimental effects of stress. And while I won't bore you with all the detailed research here, stress has been linked to everything from asthma and cardiovascular disease to cancer and practically every disease in between. The point to be made here is that happiness replaces and counteracts stress. Probably more than any other single factor, discovering and acting on what makes you happy can improve both the quality and length of your life.

Over the next few hours, days and weeks, I urge you to invest some time in seriously deciding what you want out of life. What would make you happy? I am not talking about what would make you happy for a moment or a day, but instead, what you want and need to be happy for the long term. I can assure you it will be one of the most productive things you will ever do.

Discovering what it would take for you to be happy is, without a doubt, one of the most powerful tools you'll ever possess. It defines your basis for living. It gives you a purpose and provides the answers to life's day-to-day problems. It almost miraculously provides direction at each of life's crossroads. It crystallizes and clarifies your day-to-day goals and activities. It allows you to focus your talents and energies toward achieving the rewards that are most important to you.

If you can't honestly verbalize what you *need* to make you happy, you're going to wander aimlessly throughout life. The clock keeps ticking whether you decide to answer "what would make me happy" or not. Instead of participating and reveling in life, you end up simply reacting to situation after situation. You unquestionably embrace the idea that your own happiness is out of your control. You then begin to believe that it will suddenly appear just as soon as someone or something in your life changes. Unfortunately, that's like playing the state lottery. Your chances of getting hit by lightning are far better than finding real happiness and meaning in your life.

Most of us (I'm as guilty as anyone, if not more so) have a tendency to take life much too seriously. When we were younger it was easier to be less serious. It reminds me of a Bob Dylan song, in which he says, "If you ain't got nothing, you ain't got nothing to lose." The older and more responsible we become, the more we feel we have to lose. We begin to perceive changes in our lives as risks rather than opportunities. As such, we try to avoid change. But in reality, change is not something over which we have any control.

I'm sure you've heard the saying that there are only two things you can count on: death and taxes. Well, there are actually a couple more. One is that your surroundings will change. Technology changes. Weather changes. People change. Everything changes. Always has. Always will. Accept it. Accept the fact that people and situations are *always* going to be changing throughout your life. Fighting change is like swimming against the current in a river. You're so busy trying to keep your head above water that you never get a chance to see or enjoy what's on the bank. The quicker you accept the fact that everything will change, the quicker you can get out of the water. You can sit on the bank, relax for a moment and evaluate your surroundings. In a life that's always too short, you can then decide how best to spend your remaining time. This brings up the other thing you can always count on—the God-given, human ability to make choices.

Through changes in your thinking, your actions and your lifestyle, you can choose to live your life in a state of unhappiness or in a state of happiness. It's totally up to you.

Although it was several decades ago, I remember sitting at my desk in Mrs. Benger's first-grade class back in Friona, Texas. Above the chalkboard there were two large handwritten signs. One read, "Act the way you want to be and soon you'll be the way you act." It's probably one of the more lasting lessons I've learned in life thus far. (The other sign said, "One who thinketh by the inch and talketh by the yard should be kicketh by the foot." [I'm still working on that one.])

Before you can "act the way you want to be," and before you can expect to find happiness, you must answer that one simple question. "What would make me happy?" It's a difficult question, probably the most difficult you'll ever have to answer. Getting the answer will require some time and serious thinking. Strangely, there's no right or wrong answer. And even stranger is the fact that only you know the answer. Don't think of this as some kind of test. Nobody is going to give you a grade or set any time limits. The only way you can really fail is aimlessly wandering through life and simply not answering the question at all.

So "What do you want to be when you grow up?" "What would make *you* happy?"

Dr. David G. Williams, "What Do You Want to Be When You Grow Up?" from *Alternatives for the Health Conscious Individual* 6, no. 15 (September 1996): 119–120. Copyright © 1996, Mountain Home Publishing (800-527-3044). Reprinted with permission.

Changing the Meaning of GPA

What is the best way to become a success?

"If you want to make it in college, your GPA is the key." Students who tell you this are talking about your grade point average, your report card, the number of As and Bs you get in relation to the number of Cs, Ds, and Fs. Grades are certainly important, but they aren't as important as another GPA: your goal, your plan, and the action you take. If you really want to make it, *that's* the GPA you should strive for. If you are able to set a specific goal in your life, if you can come up with an efficient plan for that goal, and if you have the discipline to take action, there's an excellent chance that you will be headed down the road to success.

Defining a Goal

What is the purpose of a goal?

Where are you headed? That's the question that your goal is designed to answer. Imagine throwing ingredients into a mixing bowl without any idea of what you are making. Think of running around on the basketball court with no knowledge of the object of the game. The best cooks and the best basketball players know what they are doing and why they are doing it. They have a clear idea of where they are headed. In short, they have a goal in mind.

Although winning a basketball game and baking a cake can both be seen as goals, it can be easier to think of your goal as a kind of destination. A lot of our common expressions use this idea. "Making it to the top," "climbing the corporate ladder," and even "reaching for the stars" portray the goal as a place in the distance that you are trying to reach. Of course, some goals really are destinations. When American pioneers declared that their goal was "Pike's Peak or Bust" and tacked signs saying so to their wagons, they were talking about an actual destination hundreds of miles to the west and more than fourteen thousand feet above sea level. When President Kennedy made the moon the country's goal in 1961, he was aiming for a destination that was about 238,900 miles out into space.

Set Minor Goals

Are smaller goals useful?

Your life should be full of both major and minor goals. Most of us set minor goals all the time. Passing a test can be seen as a minor goal. So can completing a homework assignment or even finishing a chapter before dinnertime. Having minor goals can be a great help. Each time we reach a minor goal, we get a small sense of victory that helps spur us on toward something even bigger.

Notice in a basketball game how the crowd cheers and the scoring team's pace quickens each time a basket is made. Everyone knows that one basket by itself won't win the game, but when the score is added up, each basket can prove to

---

A FAMOUS GOAL, PLAN, AND ACTION

The Goal

First, I believe that this nation should commit itself to achieving the goal, before this decade is out, of landing a man on the moon and returning him safely to earth.

President John F. Kennedy
before a joint session of Congress
May 25, 1961

The Plan

The Mercury Program:	Each rocket would send a single astronaut into space.
The Gemini Program:	Each rocket would send two men into space to orbit the earth, to practice docking with other spacecraft, and to test human beings' ability to withstand prolonged periods in space.
The Apollo Program:	Each rocket would send three men into space in order to leave the earth's orbit, to orbit the moon, and eventually to land on the moon and explore it.

The Action

The United States sent twenty manned flights into space between May 1961 and June 1969. In July 1969, eight years and two months after President Kennedy set the country's original goal, astronauts Neil Armstrong and Edwin "Buzz" Aldrin set foot on the moon and returned safely to earth.

---

be crucial. The same is true in school. Although no one has gained success by virtue of a single test or paper, these little victories will add up and help you move toward your major goal. In the meantime, minor goals provide the encouragement you need to cheer yourself on and quicken your pace.

Set Major Goals

How do you choose your major goal?

Choosing a major goal will come naturally for some, while it may be an agonizing decision for others. For every person who says, "I've always wanted to be a doctor" or "I know that teaching others is what really matters to me," there are those who complain, "There's really nothing I'm interested in" or "I'm interested in practically everything; how am I ever going to choose?" Although goals may vary widely from person to person, they all grow out of the same source: the things we want and need. Therefore, choosing your goal means deciding what you value most in life.

Your major goal should be large and distant. It should be a target that you can aim for, something to inspire you. Don't let short-term minor goals such as finishing an assignment, passing an exam, and simply getting through the day mark the limits of your dreams. Aim high, but at the same time be sure that the goals you set are specific and distinct. Health, happiness, security, love, and money are all ideals that people aim for, but they are far too vague to be considered goals. On the other hand, "discovering a cure for cancer" and "becoming the best possible parent" are both admirable and specific goals that can help you approach the broad ideals we all share.

Make Your Goal Official

What should you do with your goal once you've chosen it?

If the goal you have chosen is a clear one, you should have no trouble writing it down. Goals that stay only in your head have too great a chance of remaining vague. Furthermore, once you write down your goal, that documentation can act as a constant reminder. If you're feeling discouraged, a quick look at your goal can inspire you. (That's what the signs on the covered wagons did.) And if for some reason you forget your goal, a written description can refresh your memory.

Are you stuck with a goal until you reach it?

The purpose of a goal is not to force you on a course that you don't want to follow; it is to give you a target so that your efforts can be more focused than they would be if you had nothing to aim for. Time and fate have a way of shifting our priorities. People change, and so do the things they view as important. If the goal you once wrote down no longer matches your ambition in life, come up with another goal to replace it.

Devising a Plan

How does your plan relate to your goal?

If you think of your goal as your destination, then a plan can be seen as the route that will take you there. Coming up with a plan is like drawing a map. You need to know where you are starting, where you are heading, and where you plan to stop along the way. Most goals will have several possible plans. The challenge comes in choosing the best one.

How can you choose the most efficient plan?

An efficient plan is a balancing act between what you need and want and what you are able to pay. Paying, as far as a plan is concerned, doesn't always mean money. It can mean time and energy as well. For example, a one-week plan for reviewing your notes is "too expensive" if the test is only two days away. In the same way, a plan that forces you to stay up all night will often cost too much because what you gain in knowledge you will lose in sleep. The most efficient plan will meet your goal without being too costly.

Shouldn't it be easy to tell which plan is the most efficient?

The best plans aren't always obvious from the outset. For example, many students approach an exam by answering questions as soon as they receive the test. Given the time limit, that plan may seem to make sense, even though it's actually a bad idea. The most efficient strategy is to read the exam directions, look over all the questions, and even come up with a time plan before answering a single question. The first plan is fast but reckless, whereas the second is steady and dependable. Now you have a more structured and efficient approach to test taking. When you make an effort to devise a systematic plan, you will usually gain more benefits than you would with a hastily drawn up strategy.

What sort of impact should flexible thinking have on your goal?

Devising the best plan can require flexible thinking. For example, when you look at a map, you may conclude—as commercial airline navigators once did—that the best way to get from Amsterdam to Tokyo is to head in an easterly direction along what is known as the Mediterranean route. But look at a globe instead of a map, and your perspective may change. Rather than heading east on the Mediterranean route, commercial planes going from Amsterdam to Tokyo now fly north! That's right. They take what is known as the "polar route," flying over the North Pole to Alaska, and then west to Tokyo—for a savings of roughly fifteen hundred miles! The lesson is this: After you've decided on a goal, work vigorously to accomplish it, but keep looking for ways of achieving the goal more efficiently, perhaps from a different angle.

When is a good plan the wrong plan?

No single plan will work for every goal, and few plans are flexible enough to work for several goals. Using the wrong plan can be inefficient and sometimes even comical. Perhaps you remember the folktale about the lazy son who gets scolded by his mother for losing the money he received as payment from a local farmer. "Next time you get paid," she tells him sternly, "be sure to carry it home in your pocket." But the following day the boy goes to work for a dairy farmer who pays him with a pail of milk instead of money. Anxious not to anger his mother, the boy dutifully pours the milk into his pocket. Although his mother's plan was a good one, it could work only when used in the right circumstance. The same idea applies to your study plans. For example, writing out your notes in full sentences makes sense if the goal is to study a textbook assignment. But if you used the same plan for taking lecture notes, you'd move so slowly that you'd miss most of what the instructor said. The secret is to find a plan that fits the goal you have in mind.

In the same way that good plans may not work for every goal, plans that work for most people may not always work for you. That's why the best way to come up with a plan for success is to balance wise advice with your own experience. This book is full of plans for success and tricks of the trade. All of them have been proven to work, and most should work for you. Use trial and error to determine which plans work best for you, and be prepared to adapt some plans to better fit your needs. Even the best plans can fail if they are used too rigidly. Allow a little breathing room. If things go wrong, don't give up. Adjust and keep on going.

```
┌─────────────────────────────────────────────────────────────────┐
│  ┌───────────────────────────────────────────────────────────┐  │
│  │                   THE GPA OF SUCCESS                       │  │
│  │                                                           │  │
│  │  GOAL—should reflect your wants and needs. Make it large  │  │
│  │     and ambitious without being vague. Write it down!     │  │
│  │                                                           │  │
│  │  PLAN—lists the route you plan to take in order to reach  │  │
│  │     your goal. It should be efficient and specific. Good  │  │
│  │     advice and personal experience combine to create the  │  │
│  │     most effective plans.                                 │  │
│  │                                                           │  │
│  │  ACTION—brings your goal and your plan to life. Requires  │  │
│  │     confidence, self-discipline, and a power over         │  │
│  │     procrastination.                                      │  │
│  └───────────────────────────────────────────────────────────┘  │
└─────────────────────────────────────────────────────────────────┘
```

Taking Action

What is action?

Goals and plans won't do you any good unless you take some action. Action is the spark that brings your goal and plan to life. Without action, goals and plans are moot. You can decide you want to finish a book, and you can even plan the pages that you need to read each day, but until you actually start reading, all your preparations will be pointless. In the same way, the goal to reach the moon and the plans for the spacecraft were impressive, but they didn't come to life until the first rocket left the launch pad and headed into space.

Overcome Your Obstacles

What prevents people from taking action?

Having a goal and a plan is no guarantee that you will take action. Procrastination stops many people from taking action. Procrastination is the tendency to put things off, to write that paper the night before it is due, to cram for a test instead of studying for it right from the start. Although it is just one of many common bad habits, procrastination may be the single greatest obstacle to success. It is also, as we'll see in Chapter 4, a prime source of stress.

How can you prevent procrastination?

The first step in fighting procrastination is to develop a goal and a plan. If you have a goal and a plan but you're still procrastinating, you should take aim at your excuses for not getting your work done. Dream up reasons why you can instead of reasons why you can't. That will often be all it takes to pull yourself out of the vicious circle of inactivity and low self-esteem and put yourself on the road to progress and success.

What does Peale say about taking action?

This chapter would not be complete without more wisdom from Norman Vincent Peale, who expresses the vital importance of *taking action* throughout the entire process of personal goal setting:

> I suggest that you write down what you want to do with your life. Until you write a goal, it is only a wish; written, it becomes a focused objective. Put it down on paper.

When it is on paper, boil it down to a single sentence: what you want to do, exactly when you intend to start (which should be right now), exactly when you plan to achieve your goal. Nothing fuzzy or hazy. Everything sharp and clear and definite. No reservations or qualifications. Just one strong, simple, declarative sentence. . . . I want you to make half a dozen copies of that sentence and put them where you'll see them at least three times a day. I want that pledge to sink down through all the levels of your conscious mind and deep into your unconscious mind, because that is where it will unlock the energies that you will need to achieve your goal.

If setting worthy goals is the first step on the road to success, the second is the belief—the conviction that you are capable of achieving those goals. There has to be in your mind the unshakable image of yourself *succeeding* at the goal you have set yourself. The more vivid this image is, the most obtainable the goal becomes.

Great athletes have always known this. The high jumper "sees" himself skimming over the bar; the place-kicker in football keeps his head down as he kicks, but in his mind's eye he holds the mental picture of what he wants to happen in the next few seconds. . . . The more intensely he images this before it happens, the higher his confidence in himself and the better his chances of making it happen.[11]

Put Theory into Practice

How can you use your understanding of goal, plan, and action?

Now that you have a clearer understanding of the role of a goal and the way in which a plan and action can turn a dream into reality, you are ready to put theory into practice by writing out your goal or goals. The following four steps are designed to help you in this process.

Step 1: Brainstorm. On a clean sheet of paper, do some brainstorming about your goals. Jot down possible goals or words about them that come to mind, and do so quickly and freely. Use brainstorming as an opportunity to explore any aspects of any goals you choose. Don't stop to correct your spelling, polish a phrase, reorganize your notes, or analyze a thought. Just keep going until you've jotted down all that you can think of about your possible goals. Next, look over what you've written, and group similar items. Formulate each group into a goal by writing a sentence that summarizes its main idea.

Step 2: Plan. Focus in on one of the goals you've arrived at, and write it down as a heading on another clean sheet of paper. Beneath your goal, make a chronological list of all the steps you'll need to take in order to achieve it.

Step 3: List your strengths. On another sheet, jot down those academic and personal strengths that will help you achieve your goal. These could

[11]From Norman Vincent Peale, *Positive Imaging.* Copyright © 1982. Published by Fleming H. Revell, a division of Baker Book House. Reprinted with permission.

 **Online Study Center** www.college.hmco.com/pic/pauk9e

include skills you already have or classes you have taken as well as personal qualities such as discipline and perseverance.

Step 4: Assess your weaknesses. Identify any academic weaknesses (such as difficulty writing papers) or personal obstacles (such as financial, family, or health problems) that you will have to overcome to reach this goal, and list them either alongside your strengths or on a separate sheet of paper.

What should you do after you've completed the steps?

Don't be surprised if you feel a great sense of relief once you've completed these steps. Even if you're not certain that your goal and your plan are precisely on target, at last you have something concrete that you can adjust and refine. You also have an excellent starting point for guidance and advice. Talk with your academic adviser or with a counselor in your school's career center. Don't underestimate the value of discussing your goals and your plans for achieving them. Get as much feedback as you can. Then, if necessary, modify your goals and plans into realistic, attainable maps for your future. By getting into the goal-setting mode, you can put yourself in control not only of your academic life but also of your life after college.

FINAL WORDS

What should you do if you're worried that your goals are going to change?

Goals can change. There's no rule that you can't rethink your objectives after you've defined them. One student seemed genuinely irked that she had to check in with an academic adviser before registering for her first semester of classes. She knew without a doubt that she wanted to go into dentistry and didn't feel that she needed advice from anyone. But the adviser pointed out something she had overlooked. She needed to take an English course in order to meet the college's distribution requirement. That course was a revelation. She fell in love with literature and shifted sharply toward a career in publishing, a goal she pursued with the same passion, determination, and planning that she had originally devoted to dentistry. Yes, goals can change. But that's no excuse to settle for murky, ill-defined objectives. The skills you develop and the lessons you learn in defining your goals will serve you well, no matter where they wind up taking you.

HAVE YOU MISSED SOMETHING?

SENTENCE COMPLETION — *Complete the following sentences with one of the three words listed below each sentence.*

1. Based on many of our common expressions, it seems that a goal is considered a _____.

   promise   destination   liability

2. The best way to come up with a plan is to balance wise advice with your own personal _____.

   shortcomings   experience   success

3. Goals and plans won't do you any good without _____.

   action   education   discussion

MATCHING — *In each blank space in the left column, write the letter preceding the phrase in the right column that matches the left item best.*

_____ 1. Frankl

a. Warned that "burnout" may result if you aren't doing "the stuff you like"

_____ 2. Thoreau

b. Defined a clear goal of putting Americans on the moon and returning them safely to earth

_____ 3. LeBon

c. Suggested that we should regularly ask ourselves what would make us happy

_____ 4. Gould

d. Suggested that those who seem out of step may just hear a different drummer

_____ 5. Peale

e. Noticed the collective mindset that emerges when people become part of a crowd

_____ 6. Rau

f. Reported that 85 percent of students who attempted suicide said that "life was meaningless"

_____ 7. Williams

g. Used the shout of "fire" in a theater as an illustration of crowd psychology

_____ 8. Kennedy

h. Advocated vividly picturing a desired goal or objective in your conscious mind

TRUE-FALSE

Circle T *beside the* true *statements and* F *beside the* false *statements.*

1. T   F   It's not a good idea to discuss your goals with close friends and family.

2. T   F   When you join a crowd, your individual thinking is replaced by crowd psychology.

3. T   F   Norman Vincent Peale was a nineteenth-century naturalist and philosopher who lived in the woods near Walden Pond.

4. T   F   The purpose of a goal is to give you an idea of where you are headed.

5. T   F   Health, happiness, and security are all excellent career goals.

MULTIPLE CHOICE

Choose the word or phrase that completes each sentence most accurately, and circle the letter that precedes it.

1. When it comes to setting goals, GPA stands for a goal, a plan, and an
   a. acumen.
   b. article.
   c. average.
   d. action.

2. Passing a test is generally considered to be a
   a. minor goal.
   b. major goal.
   c. common excuse.
   d. scholastic requirement.

3. Once you arrive at a goal, you should
   a. stick with it.
   b. keep it a secret.
   c. write it down as a reminder.
   d. come up with a backup goal.

4. Coming up with a plan is like
    a. running a race.
    b. building a fire.
    c. drawing a map.
    d. none of the above.

5. One of the greatest obstacles to success is
    a. procrastination.
    b. lack of money.
    c. education.
    d. boredom.

SHORT ANSWER   *Supply a brief answer for each of the following items.*

1. Explain Norman Vincent Peale's notion of "imaging."
2. Relate the story of the "polar route" to the discussion of planning.
3. Discuss the role of minor goals.
4. Elaborate on the four recommended steps for arriving at a goal.

IT'S YOUR Q

The Q System uses marginal questions to encourage active reading. You'll notice that most but not all paragraphs in this chapter are accompanied by marginal questions. Now it's your Q. Scan the chapter for any paragraph that is missing a question, reread the paragraph, establish the main idea, and then arrive at a question that elicits it. Use the questions in the surrounding paragraphs as models for your own marginal questions.

WORDS IN CONTEXT

From the three choices beside each numbered item, select the one that most nearly expresses the meaning of the italicized word in the quote. Make a light check mark (✓) next to your choice.

Nothing in the world can take the place of *persistence*. *Talent* will not; nothing is more common than unsuccessful men of talent. *Genius* will not; unrewarded genius is almost a byword. Education will not; the world is full of educated *derelicts*. The slogan "Press on" has solved and always will solve the problems of the human race.

—Calvin Coolidge (1872–1933), thirtieth president of the United States

1. place of *persistence*	perseverance	principles	mottoes
2. *talent* will not	nobility	tradition	natural gift
3. *genius* will not	high aptitude	distinction	status
4. educated *derelicts*	snobs	vagrants	tycoons

Don't be afraid to take a big step. You can't cross a *chasm* in two small jumps.

—David Lloyd George (1863–1945), British statesman and prime minister

5. cross a *chasm*	river	gorge	peak

Call it what you will. *Incentives* are the only way to make people work harder.

—Nikita Khrushchev (1894–1971), Soviet premier

6. *incentives* . . . make people work harder	rewards	praise	punishment

THE WORD HISTORY SYSTEM

Tantalize
to torment with the punishment of Tantalus

tantalize   TAN'-ta-lize' *v.*
To excite (another) by exposing something desirable while keeping it out of reach.

In Greek mythology, King Tantalus offended the gods and was punished in an extraordinary manner. He was placed in the midst of a lake whose waters reached his chin but receded whenever he attempted to allay his thirst. Over his head hung branches laden with choice fruit, which likewise receded whenever he stretched out his hand to satisfy his hunger. Tantalus became the symbol of such teasing, and his name is the root of our verb *tantalize*.

Reprinted by permission. From *Picturesque Word Origins* © 1933 by G. & C. Merriam Co. (now Merriam-Webster, Incorporated).

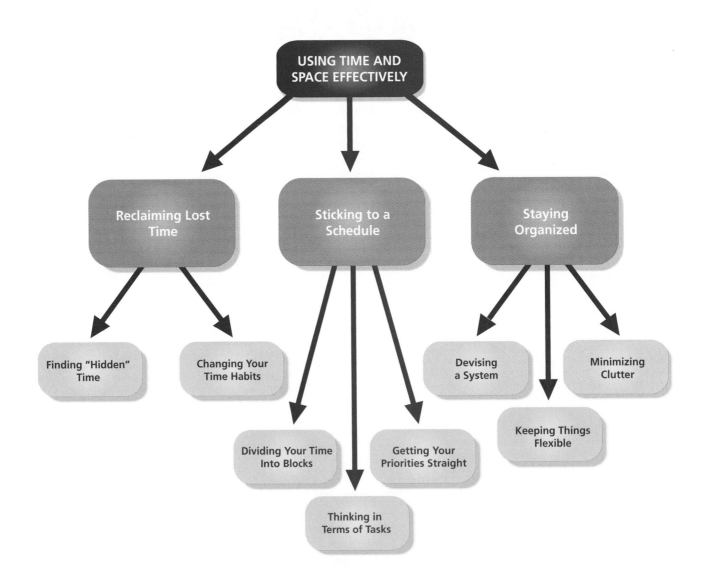

Using Time and Space Effectively

Perhaps the most valuable result of all education is the ability to make yourself do the thing you have to do, when it ought to be done, whether you like it or not.

Thomas Huxley
(1825–1895), English biologist

Time flies, but that's no reason for you to go through each day simply "winging it." Through conscientious use of time and commonsense planning, you can make the most of your day. This chapter ticks off the important elements of effectively managing your time and organizing your space, including:

- **Finding "Hidden" Time**
- **Changing Your Time Habits**
- **Dividing Your Time into Blocks**
- **Thinking in Terms of Tasks**
- **Getting Your Priorities Straight**
- **Staying Organized**

How important is time management to your academic success?

Time is a precious and irreplaceable commodity. As she lay on her deathbed, Queen Elizabeth I of England (1533–1603) reportedly said, "All my possessions for a moment of time." How you use time can determine your success or failure in college. If you use time wisely, you'll prosper. If you use it poorly, you'll fail in the job you came to do. That's why the management of time is the number-one skill to master in college.

How can you gain extra time?

Although many people waste time needlessly and habitually, you needn't put yourself in the same position. You can gain extra time by reclaiming lost time, by sticking to a schedule, and by staying organized, which will help you use your time more efficiently.

Reclaiming Lost Time

How can you put your time to better use?

All of us have claimed that we don't have enough time to accomplish what we need to do. But the fact is that everyone is allotted the same amount of time: twenty-four hours a day. Many of us allow a lot of this time to go to waste by failing to realize it is available in the first place. In addition, it's often our day-to-day habits, activities we no longer notice, that save time or waste it. You can put your time to better use by pinpointing areas of "hidden" time and cultivating time-saving habits.

Finding "Hidden" Time

What is "hidden" time?

There's a lot of valuable time in your day that is being overlooked, simply because you didn't realize it was time you could use. For those who flush tiny slivers of soap down the drain or toss small scraps of cloth into the wastebasket, there are others who combine those slippery bits and pieces into a whole new bar or stitch discarded shreds into a comfortable quilt. Think of all the time you spend standing in line or even waiting for a traffic light to change. If you could find ways to make use of this "hidden" time, you could almost certainly add hours to each week.

How does pocket work use hidden time?

- *Carry Pocket Work* Many situations may leave you with a few moments of unexpected free time—a long line at the bank or supermarket, a delayed bus or train, a wait at the doctor's office, a lunch date who arrives late. If you make a point to bring along a book, a photocopied article, index cards on which you've written key concepts, vocabulary words, or formulas, you'll be able to take advantage of otherwise frustrating experiences.

When is your mind free for studying?

- *Use Your Mind When It's Free* Some activities may afford an overlooked opportunity for studying if you're prepared. For example, if you're shaving, combing your hair, or washing dishes, there's no reason you can't be studying at the same time. Since many of us tend to "zone out" in such situations, they are excellent opportunities to use time that might otherwise be squandered. Attach small metal or plastic clips near mirrors and on walls at eye level. Place a note card in each clip. Do a problem or two in math or master some new vocabulary words as you eat a sandwich at work.

How can recording information use hidden time?

- *Record Study Information*   Another way of using hidden time is by listening to information you've recorded on audiocassettes or MP3 files or burned onto CDs. Recorded information enables you to keep studying in situations where you're moving about or your eyes are otherwise occupied, such as when you're getting dressed or driving. In addition, recorded information can provide a refreshing change from written material.

What is spare-time thinking?

- *Employ Spare-Time Thinking*   You can make the most of the moments immediately before or after class by recalling the main points from the last lecture as you're heading to class or by quickly recalling the points of a just-completed lecture as you're leaving class.

How can you use your subconscious to save time?

- *Use Your Subconscious*   At one point or another, you have awakened during the night with a bright idea or a solution to a problem that you had been thinking about before bedtime. Your subconscious works while your conscious mind is resting. If you want to capture the ideas or solutions produced by your subconscious, write them down as soon as you wake up; otherwise, they'll be lost. Many creative people know this and keep a pad and pencil near their beds. For example, Nobel Prize winner Albert Szent-Györgyi said, "I go to sleep thinking about my problems all the time, and my brain must continue to think about them when I sleep because I wake up, sometimes in the middle of the night, with answers to questions that have been eluding me all day."[1]

Changing Your Time Habits

What's a good way to begin saving time?

Habits, by their very nature, are things we do routinely without even thinking. Most of us are unaware of our habits unless someone or something draws attention to them. A good way to take inventory of your time habits is by keeping a daily activities log. From the time you wake up to the time you go to sleep, note all your major activities, the time you started and finished each, and the time each activity consumed. With your day itemized on paper, you can gain a clearer picture of where your time is being spent and where it's being wasted.

[1]Originally published in *Some Watch While Some Must Sleep*, by William C. Dement, as a volume in the Portable Stanford series published by the Stanford Alumni Association. Copyright © 1972. Reprinted by permission of the Stanford Alumni Association.

Online Study Center   www.college.hmco.com/pic/pauk9e

Figure 2.1
Record of One Day's Activities and Suggestions for Making Better Use of Time

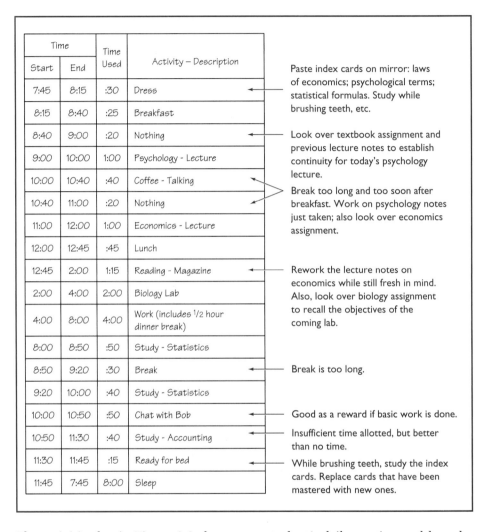

Time		Time Used	Activity – Description	
Start	End			
7:45	8:15	:30	Dress	← Paste index cards on mirror: laws of economics; psychological terms; statistical formulas. Study while brushing teeth, etc.
8:15	8:40	:25	Breakfast	
8:40	9:00	:20	Nothing	← Look over textbook assignment and previous lecture notes to establish continuity for today's psychology lecture.
9:00	10:00	1:00	Psychology - Lecture	
10:00	10:40	:40	Coffee - Talking	← Break too long and too soon after breakfast. Work on psychology notes just taken; also look over economics assignment.
10:40	11:00	:20	Nothing	←
11:00	12:00	1:00	Economics - Lecture	
12:00	12:45	:45	Lunch	
12:45	2:00	1:15	Reading - Magazine	← Rework the lecture notes on economics while still fresh in mind. Also, look over biology assignment to recall the objectives of the coming lab.
2:00	4:00	2:00	Biology Lab	
4:00	8:00	4:00	Work (includes ½ hour dinner break)	
8:00	8:50	:50	Study - Statistics	
8:50	9:20	:30	Break	← Break is too long.
9:20	10:00	:40	Study - Statistics	
10:00	10:50	:50	Chat with Bob	← Good as a reward if basic work is done.
10:50	11:30	:40	Study - Accounting	← Insufficient time allotted, but better than no time.
11:30	11:45	:15	Ready for bed	← While brushing teeth, study the index cards. Replace cards that have been mastered with new ones.
11:45	7:45	8:00	Sleep	

The activities log in Figure 2.1 shows one student's daily routine and how he decided to put his time to better use.

Once you have the concrete evidence of a daily activities log before you, you can begin to eliminate your time-wasting habits and develop or reinforce the time-saving ones.

What can you learn from Parkinson's Law?

Defy Parkinson's Law   Parkinson's Law says that work expands to fit the time allotted.[2] To avoid running out of time, work Parkinson's Law in reverse:

[2]C. Parkinson, *Parkinson, the Law* (Boston: Houghton Mifflin, 1980).

For each task, set a deadline that will be difficult to meet, and strive to meet that deadline. Each time you achieve your goal, reward yourself with some small but pleasant activity. Take a break. Chat with a friend. Stroll around the room. Have a special snack, such as a bag of peanuts (keep it in your desk, to be opened only as a reward). If you fail to meet a deadline, don't punish yourself. Just hold back your reward and set another goal. Positive reinforcement is powerful in effecting a change in behavior.

Why is it so important to obey your alarm?

Obey Your Alarm Clock　　How many times do you hit the snooze button on your alarm clock before you finally get out of bed? Even one time is too many. Set your alarm for the time you want to get up, not for the time you want to start getting up. If you can't obey your alarm, you'll have a hard time sticking to your time schedule. After all, it doesn't even buzz.

Limit E-mail and Internet Time　　As marvelous as they both can be, e-mail in particular and the Internet in general can be tremendous "time sinks," swallowing up hours in a typical day. Rather than checking it constantly, designate specific times during the day when you read and send e-mail. It's true that e-mail has sped up communication, but it's a rare message that can't wait a few hours before being read or sent. The same applies to any Web surfing you may do, whether for schoolwork or pleasure. Time has a tendency to fly by as you click from one link to the next. You can help keep things under control by setting a timer when you surf and returning to your studies when the timer goes off.

What is the value of taking time out?

Take "Time Out"　　Reward yourself with regular short breaks as you work. Learning in several small sessions, rather than in one continuous stretch, increases comprehension. In one study, students who practiced French vocabulary in three discrete sessions did 35 percent better on an exam than those who tried to learn the words in one sitting.[3] So take a breather for ten minutes every hour, or rest for five minutes every half-hour. Whichever method you choose, keep your breaks consistent. This way, you'll study with more energy and look forward to your regular rests. When you return to your desk, you'll find that you feel more refreshed.

How can understanding circadian rhythms affect your scheduling?

Listen to Your Body　　All of us are subject to circadian rhythms. That is, we have periods when we're most wide-awake and alert and other periods when we're sluggish or drowsy. In general, we're sleepiest a few hours before dawn and twelve hours later, in mid-afternoon. In keeping with these natural cycles,

[3]Kristine C. Bloom et al., "Effects of Massed and Distributed Practice on the Learning and Retention of Second-Language Vocabulary," *Journal of Educational Research* 74, no. 4 (March–April 1981): 245–248.

Online Study Center　www.college.hmco.com/pic/pauk9e

we're widest awake about every twelve hours, usually at mid-morning and again in mid-evening. Knowing this can help you plan the day's activities more strategically.

1. *Schedule cerebral tasks for mornings and evenings*. Reading, writing, problem solving, and other "thinking tasks" should be done when you're likely to be most alert.
2. *Save active behavior for mid-afternoon*. Fieldwork, lab work, exercise, and errand running are best done at this time of day, when more sedentary activities may make you feel drowsy. If you're not a heavy coffee drinker, a cup of coffee might get you through the afternoon slump.
3. *Resist the temptation to sleep in on the weekends*. Changing your sleep schedule on the weekends can have a chain reaction effect on the following week. You may find yourself feeling jet-lagged on Monday or Tuesday if you sleep in on Saturday or Sunday.
4. *Read in the morning; review in the afternoon*. Scientists have discovered that short-term memory peaks at about nine o'clock in the morning and that long-term memory is strongest at about three o'clock in the afternoon.

Sticking to a Schedule

What is the function of a time schedule?

A time schedule is a game plan, a written strategy that spells out exactly what you hope to accomplish—during a day, a week, or even the entire term—and how you plan to do it. Committing yourself to planning and keeping to a schedule can seem a bit frightening at first, but following a schedule soon becomes a source of strength and a boon to your life. There are several benefits to a schedule.

How will a schedule provide greater control?

A schedule provides greater control.   A thoughtfully constructed time schedule can increase your sense of control in four ways. First, because your schedule is written down, your plans seem more manageable. You can start working without delay. Second, you know you'll study all your subjects—even those you dislike—because you've allotted time for them in your schedule. There's less of a temptation to skip disliked subjects when study time has already been allotted for them. Third, a schedule discourages laziness. You've got a plan right in front of you, and that plan says, "Let's get down to business!" Fourth, you can schedule review sessions right from the start and avoid last-minute cramming for tests.

How does a schedule encourage relaxation?

A schedule encourages relaxation.   At the same time, because your plan is written down instead of floating around in your head, your mind is freed for other things. There's no time wasted worrying about what to do next. It's all there on paper. There's no guilt either. Both work and play are written into your schedule. This means that when you take a break, you know you deserve it.

Why are some students reluctant to use time schedules?

Despite these benefits, many students are reluctant to start using time schedules. They feel not only that a schedule will do them little good but also that keeping track of time will turn them into nervous wrecks. Neither worry is warranted.

How does a schedule save you time?

A schedule saves time. Yes, it takes time to devise a schedule, but that time is rewarded. You will be able to shift smoothly from one activity to another, without wondering what to do next.

How does a schedule provide freedom?

A schedule provides freedom. Scheduling frees you from time's control. The people you see dashing from class to library to gym, or eating lunch on the run, are slaves to time. The students who schedule time, who decide how time will be used, are the masters of time.

In what way does scheduling increase flexibility?

A schedule increases flexibility. Disorganized people often waste so much time that there's no room for flexibility. People who use schedules free their time for a variety of activities and are therefore more flexible.

Which schedule type is best: time-based or task-based?

If you are a full-time student or have considerable control over the hours in your day, your best bet is to rely on traditional schedules that divide your time into manageable blocks. If, however, you are juggling your academic life with the responsibilities of a job or the demands of raising a family, you're probably better off using schedules that focus on tasks instead of on time. Each approach has advantages, but both provide an opportunity to tackle tasks with a genuine game plan instead of flailing at them haphazardly. Regardless of the approach you take, it's important to use your scheduling system not simply as a tool for efficiently filling up your days but as an instrument to help you get your priorities straight.

Dividing Your Time into Blocks

What does the story of the sticks illustrate about time?

A father once tied a bundle of small, thin sticks together with a strand of twine, handed the bundle to his youngest son, and said, "Son, break these sticks in half." The boy used his hands and knees but could not break the bundle. Sadly, he handed it back to his father. Without a word, the father untied the twine, and using only his fingers, snapped each stick one by one.

What is the advantage of dividing your time into blocks?

When the sum total of your obligations and academic assignments seems overwhelming, it helps immensely to split them up into small, manageable units. By dividing each day into blocks, time schedules break up your responsibilities and allow you to deal with them one by one. Assigning a block of time to each activity ensures that you will work at peak efficiency.

What are the components of the three-part scheduling system?

Using time blocks, you can create a three-part scheduling system consisting of (1) a master schedule, (2) a weekly schedule, and (3) a daily schedule. Each

Online Study Center   www.college.hmco.com/pic/pauk9e

plays an integral role in managing your time. The master schedule serves as a basic structure for organizing your activities; the weekly schedule adds specific details to the master schedule; and the daily schedule puts the weekly schedule into a portable form. Although each schedule performs a different function, all three follow the same basic scheduling guidelines:

What is the best way to use big blocks of time?

1. *Don't waste big blocks.* If you have a big block of time, use it for a big assignment. There's a strong tendency to say, "I'm going to get these smaller assignments out of the way before I tackle the big assignment." This is a poor decision. Instead, use the large block of time for a large and time-intensive assignment, and save your small assignments for the little slivers of time.

When it comes to studying, what is prime time?

2. *Study during prime time.* For most of us, prime time is daytime. In fact, research has shown that each hour used for study during the day is equal to an hour and a half at night. Even so, you may find that you have dead hours during the day when you are less productive than you'd like to be. Schedule less-demanding tasks for these hours.

How does the type of class influence when you should study for it?

3. *Study before recitation classes and after lecture classes.* A study session before a recitation or discussion class (a foreign language course or a psychology seminar, for example) helps warm you up. When you walk into class, the material is fresh in your mind. For lecture classes, use the time immediately after class to fill in any gaps in your notes and to review the information you've just learned.

Why should you shy away from making your schedule too detailed?

4. *Don't let details tie your hands.* Account for all your time, but don't be overly detailed. The time you'd take to make an overly meticulous schedule can be better used in studying a subject directly, and the chances of your following such a strict plan are slim.

What sorts of nonacademic activities belong in your schedule?

5. *Include nonacademic activities.* Always set aside time for food, sleep, and recreation as well as the other activities of your life. Cheating yourself out of a meal, a good night's sleep, a swim, a family get-together, or a meeting with friends won't save you time in the long run. In fact, it may cost you time because all these activities are necessary for your overall mental and physical wellness. Make your plan for living, not just for studying.

Lay a Foundation with a Master Schedule

What is the purpose of the master schedule?

A master schedule provides an agenda of fixed activities around which your varying activities are arranged. Unless changes occur in your basic program, you need to draw up a master schedule only once per term.

What does a master schedule look like?

A master schedule grid lists the days of the week at the top and the hours of the day down the left side. The boxes in the grid are filled in with all your required activities: sleep, meals, job, regular meetings, community activities, sports, and, of course, classes. The empty boxes that remain represent your free time. Figure 2.2 provides an example of a typical master schedule.

Figure 2.2
A Master Schedule with Work

	Mon.	Tues.	Wed.	Thurs.	Fri.	Sat.	Sun.
7-8	← Dress and Breakfast →						
8-9	Bio-Sc		Bio-Sc		Bio-Sc	Dress & Breakfast	
9-10		P.E.		P.E.		P.E.	Dress & Breakfast
10-11	History		History		History		
11-12		Spanish		Spanish		Spanish	
12-1	← Lunch →						
1-2	Math	Computer Lab.	Math	Computer Lab.	Math		
2-3	English		English		English		
3-4		Work-study Prog.		Work-study Prog.			
4-5	Work-study		Work-study		Work-study		
5-6							
6-7	← Dinner →						
7-8							
8-9							
9-10							
10-11							
11-12	← Sleep →						

How does a master schedule help?

A master schedule, on a five-by-eight-inch card taped over your desk or carried in your notebook, unclutters your mind. More important, it enables you to visualize actual blocks of time into which you can fit necessary activities.

Account for Changing Details with a Weekly Schedule

What is the purpose of a weekly schedule?

The weekly schedule is built on the foundation of the master schedule. To construct it, photocopy or print out another copy of your master schedule, and fill in the empty blocks with the activities you have planned for the upcoming week. If you have a math test on Friday, for example, you will need to schedule a little extra study time for math. Next week you may be assigned a research paper. If so, you'll probably want to leave space in your schedule for library or Internet research. The weekly schedule helps you adapt your time to your changing priorities. Keep it posted by your desk or pasted on the inside cover of your notebook.

A sample weekly schedule is shown in Figure 2.3. The lists that follow show how the guidelines for scheduling were used to set it up.

Monday Through Friday/Saturday

7–8 a.m.	Avoid the frantic dash and the gobbled (or skipped) breakfast by getting up on time.
12–1 p.m.	Take a full, leisurely hour for lunch.
5–6	Relax before dinner—your reward for a day of conscientious work.
7–9	Keep up with current notes and assignments through systematic studying.
9–10	To forestall cramming at quiz and examination times, give some time every day to a review of previous assignments and ground covered to date.
10	A cease-study time of 10 p.m. provides an incentive for working hard during the day and early evening.
10–12	Devote some time every day to reading books that truly interest you. Recreational reading and conversation help you unwind for a good night's sleep.

Tuesday/Thursday/Saturday

8–9 a.m.	Because chemistry (10–11) is your hardest subject, build your morning study program around it. An hour's study before class will make the class period more meaningful.
11–12 p.m.	Another hour's study immediately after chemistry class will help you remember the work covered in class and move more readily to the next assignment.

Figure 2.3
A Detailed Weekly Schedule
Based on a Master Schedule

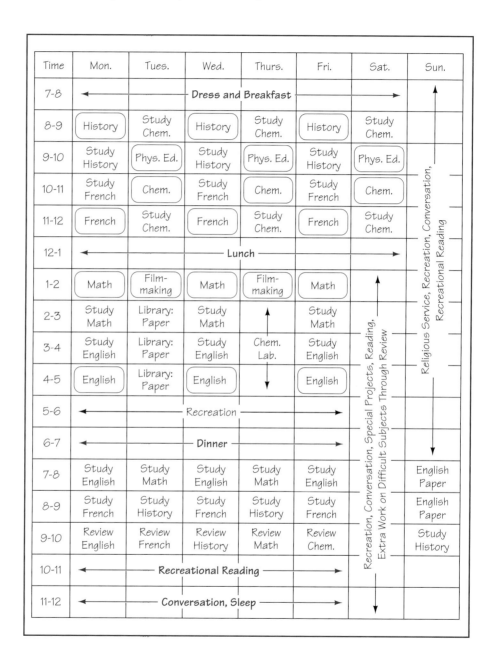

Time	Mon.	Tues.	Wed.	Thurs.	Fri.	Sat.	Sun.
7-8	Dress and Breakfast →						
8-9	History	Study Chem.	History	Study Chem.	History	Study Chem.	
9-10	Study History	Phys. Ed.	Study History	Phys. Ed.	Study History	Phys. Ed.	
10-11	Study French	Chem.	Study French	Chem.	Study French	Chem.	
11-12	French	Study Chem.	French	Study Chem.	French	Study Chem.	
12-1	← Lunch →						
1-2	Math	Film-making	Math	Film-making	Math		
2-3	Study Math	Library: Paper	Study Math		Study Math		
3-4	Study English	Library: Paper	Study English	Chem. Lab.	Study English		
4-5	English	Library: Paper	English		English		
5-6	← Recreation →						
6-7	← Dinner →						
7-8	Study English	Study Math	Study English	Study Math	Study English		English Paper
8-9	Study French	Study History	Study French	Study History	Study French		English Paper
9-10	Review English	Review French	Review History	Review Math	Review Chem.		Study History
10-11	← Recreational Reading →						
11-12	← Conversation, Sleep →						

Sat. column (5-6 through 9-10): Recreation, Conversation, Special Projects, Reading, Extra Work on Difficult Subjects Through Review

Sun. column: Religious Service, Recreation, Conversation, Recreational Reading

Special

Tuesday	2–5 p.m.	Library: paper
Sunday	7–9 p.m.	English paper

	For some assignments you will need to schedule blocks of time to do research or to develop and follow up on ideas.
Saturday	From noon on, Saturday is left unscheduled—for recreation, for special projects to which you must devote a concentrated period of time, for extra work on difficult subjects, for thorough review.
Sunday	This is your day until evening. Study history before you go to bed because it is the first class you'll have on Monday morning.

Provide a Portable Game Plan with a Daily Schedule

What goes into a daily schedule?

A daily schedule is a brief yet specific list of the day's tasks and the time blocks you plan to accomplish them in. You should be able to fit all this information on an index card that you can carry around with you all day. Make up your daily schedule each night before you go to bed. Once you have put your worries and concerns on paper, your mind will be free for sleep. You will also have thought through your day and will be better prepared when the morning comes. Figure 2.4 shows one student's daily schedule and explains why it is effective.

Use Scheduling Tools If You Feel Comfortable with Them

What are the pros and cons of special scheduling tools?

These days, you can choose from a growing variety of tools and utilities, from computer software to personal digital assistants to Internet applications to hefty loose-leaf notebooks, all designed to make scheduling your time both easier and more intelligent. These tools may provide the breakthrough that some students need to finally begin to appreciate the importance of keeping a schedule. For other students, they are an elaborate, costly, time-intensive distraction that does little to control or organize time. Index cards and blank sheets of paper may not be all that sophisticated, but they are extremely inexpensive, refreshingly flexible, and breathtakingly simple, and they can usually provide all you need to get a firm grasp on your available time. If you swear by your PDA or your store-bought appointment book, that's fine. As long as you keep in mind that your goal is managing time, you can make just about any system work. The essential component is not the tool, but rather the person who is using it.

Thinking in Terms of Tasks

When is it preferable to use task-based scheduling?

Because of the way a schedule based on time blocks divides the day into manageable bite-sized segments, it is often preferable for most students. But some of us don't have the luxury of predictably structuring our days from top to bottom.

Figure 2.4
A Daily Schedule

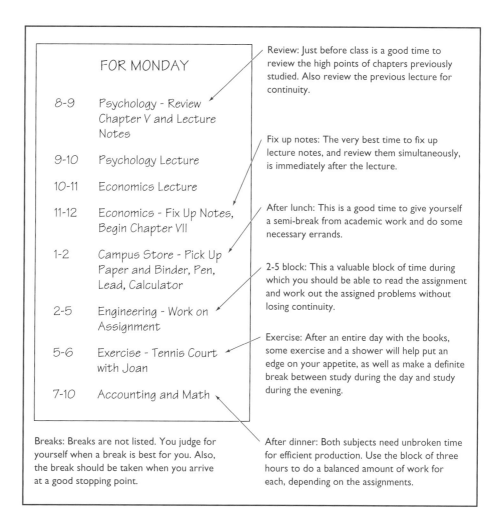

FOR MONDAY

8-9 　Psychology - Review Chapter V and Lecture Notes

9-10 　Psychology Lecture

10-11 　Economics Lecture

11-12 　Economics - Fix Up Notes, Begin Chapter VII

1-2 　Campus Store - Pick Up Paper and Binder, Pen, Lead, Calculator

2-5 　Engineering - Work on Assignment

5-6 　Exercise - Tennis Court with Joan

7-10 　Accounting and Math

Review: Just before class is a good time to review the high points of chapters previously studied. Also review the previous lecture for continuity.

Fix up notes: The very best time to fix up lecture notes, and review them simultaneously, is immediately after the lecture.

After lunch: This is a good time to give yourself a semi-break from academic work and do some necessary errands.

2-5 block: This a valuable block of time during which you should be able to read the assignment and work out the assigned problems without losing continuity.

Exercise: After an entire day with the books, some exercise and a shower will help put an edge on your appetite, as well as make a definite break between study during the day and study during the evening.

After dinner: Both subjects need unbroken time for efficient production. Use the block of three hours to do a balanced amount of work for each, depending on the assignments.

Breaks: Breaks are not listed. You judge for yourself when a break is best for you. Also, the break should be taken when you arrive at a good stopping point.

If your days are largely unpredictable or your free time is fluid, you may need schedules that emphasize tasks instead of blocks of time. In addition, long-term assignments, which can't always be squeezed into time blocks, may require a task-based approach.

How did Ivy Lee demonstrate the value of tasks?

Anyone who's ever had the satisfaction of systematically crossing items off a lengthy to do list has at least an inkling of the effectiveness of a task-based approach. During the first half of the twentieth century, legendary management consultant Ivy Lee demonstrated just how effective—and lucrative—it could be to view things in terms of tasks.

Online Study Center　www.college.hmco.com/pic/pauk9e

Charles Schwab, then chairman of the Bethlehem Steel Company, challenged Lee: "Show me a way to get more things done with my time, and I'll pay you any fee within reason." Lee thought for a while, then said,

- Every *evening* write down the six most important tasks for the next day in order of priority.
- Every *morning* start working on task #1 and continue until you finish it; then start on task #2, and so on. Do this until quitting time and don't be concerned if you have finished only one or two tasks.
- At the end of each day, tear up the list and start over.

When Schwab asked how much he owed for this advice, Ivy Lee told him to use the plan for a few weeks, then send in a check for whatever he thought it was worth.[4] Three weeks later, Lee received a check for $25,000, which is equal to about $250,000 in today's dollars!

Of course, just as a daily schedule would provide only a limited view of your tasks, a single to do list is not sufficient for a task-based approach to help you through the entire semester. Whether it hinges on time blocks or tasks, a three-part scheduling system still makes sense. If you're focusing on tasks, you'll need (1) a task-based master schedule and (2) a weekly assignment-oriented schedule in addition to (3) a daily to do list.

Develop a Task-Based Master Schedule

A task-based master schedule enables you to keep track of one or more assignments or goals over an extended period of time. Figure 2.5 provides an example of a task-based schedule. Across the top of the schedule, instead of the days of the week, list the major goals you hope to accomplish or the assignments you plan to complete. Deadlines for subgoals may be written down the left side, where the hours of the day would normally be written in a standard master schedule.

Now divide each goal or long-term assignment into manageable subgoals. List them in a column beneath the task they refer to. For example, if you've been assigned a research paper, you may arrive at the following subgoals: do preliminary research, choose topic, plan outline, conduct research, complete first draft, and revise first draft. As you reach each milestone on the way to completing your assignment, cross it off your schedule. As you do, you provide yourself with visual evidence of and positive feedback for the progress you've made.

What sort of schedules do you need for a task-based approach?

How does a task-based master schedule differ from a standard master schedule?

How do you divide your goals into subgoals?

[4]T. W. Engstrom and R. A. Mackensie, *Managing Your Time* (Grand Rapids, MI: Zondervan, 1967).

Figure 2.5
A Task-Based Master Schedule

	Psychology Research Paper April 21	Train for Amateur Triathlon May 1	Self-Paced Computer Course
Feb. 7	Select Three Topic Ideas	Up Minimum to 60 Laps	Complete Ch. 1-3
Feb. 10	Do Preliminary Research	Try Ride Up Satyr Hill	
Feb. 14	Make Final Topic Choice	Run 30 Miles Per Week	Complete Ch. 4-6
Feb. 18	Complete Bibliography		
March 15	Finish First Draft		Mid-term Exam
March 18	Begin Rewriting		
April 21	Paper Due		Final

When should you use an
assignment-oriented weekly
schedule?

Make Your Weekly Schedule Assignment-Oriented

If the span of your goal or assignment is a week or less, you can use an assignment-oriented weekly schedule as a supplement to your master schedule. Figure 2.6 shows such a schedule. The format is simple. Draw a horizontal line to divide an 8½ × 11" sheet of paper in half. In the top half, list your subjects, assignments, estimated study times, and due dates. Then, with the due dates and estimated times as control factors, check your master schedule for available

Figure 2.6
A Weekly Schedule Based on Assignments

Subject	Assignment	Estimated Time	Date Due	Time Due
Electronics	Chapter V - 32 pp. - Read	2 hr.	Mon. 13th	8:00
English	Paper to Write	18 hr.	Mon. 20th	9:00
Math	Problems on pp. 110-111	3 hr.	Tues. 14th	10:00
Industrial Safety	Make Shop Layouts	8 hr.	Fri. 17th	11:00
Computer Graphics	Generate Slide Presentation (2-4 slides)	6 hr.	Fri. 17th	1:00
Electronics	Chapter VI - 40pp. - Read	2 1/2 hr.	Weds. 22nd	8:00

Day	Assignment	Morning	Afternoon	Evening
Sun.	Electronics - Read Chap V English - Find a Topic			7:30-9:30 9:30-10:30
Mon.	English - Gather Notes Math - Problems		2:00-6:00	7:00-10:00
Tues.	English - Gather Notes Industrial Safety	8:00-10:00	3:00-6:00	7:00-10:00
Wed.	English - First Draft Computer Graphics		2:00-6:00	7:00-10:00
Thurs.	Industrial Safety English - Paper Computer Graphics	8:00-10:00	3:00-6:00	7:00-10:00
Fri.	English - Final Copy Electronics		2:00-6:00	7:00-9:30
Sat.				

Figure 2.7
A Things-to-Do List

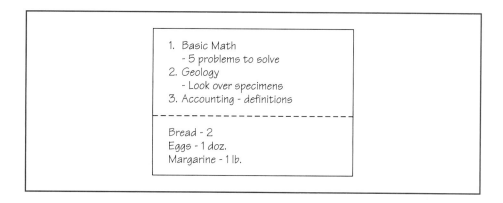

1. Basic Math
   - 5 problems to solve
2. Geology
   - Look over specimens
3. Accounting - definitions
- -
Bread - 2
Eggs - 1 doz.
Margarine - 1 lb.

time. Allocate enough hours to do the job, and write them on the appropriate line on the bottom half of the sheet. Stick to your schedule. As long as you give study hours top priority, your remaining hours will be truly free.

Turn Your Daily Schedule into a To Do List

How should you adjust your daily schedule when your time is unpredictable?

Your daily study schedule should simply be a list of things to do arranged in order of priority on an index card. In this case, assigning specific times is likely to lead to frustration.

Figure 2.7 shows a typical daily list. To be successful, you need to develop a habit of referring to your list continually throughout the day. Cross off the tasks as you complete them.

Getting Your Priorities Straight

When can schedules create a false sense of security?

What's the difference between efficient time management and effective time management?

Even the best schedules can create a false sense of security and accomplishment if they're filled with tasks that may take time but aren't top priorities.

Efficient time management is often mistaken for effective time management. Although it's admirable to work efficiently, that is, to accomplish as much as possible in the time allotted, your efficiency will be wasted if you are focusing on the wrong tasks. As Tom Connellan, an author and consultant, put it, "There's no point in doing well what you should not be doing at all."[5] To manage time effectively, you need to allocate your energy and attention to those tasks that are most important.

What is the purpose of the urgency-importance matrix?

Well-known author, consultant, and time-management expert Dr. Stephen Covey devised a simple, much-imitated matrix to help you to gain a better

[5]Dorothy Lehmkuhl and Dolores Cotter Lamping, *Organizing for the Creative Person* (New York: Crown, 1993), p. 46.

Online Study Center www.college.hmco.com/pic/pauk9e

Why are nonurgent, unimportant tasks considered time wasters?

understanding of the relative values of the tasks you're faced with on a regular basis. The matrix has "urgency" on the vertical axis and "importance" on the horizontal one (see Figure 2.8). Tasks that are urgent demand your immediate attention. Important tasks are tasks that will help you to achieve your goal.[6]

The real time wasters are tasks that are neither urgent nor important. They can be easily ignored and do little or nothing to help you achieve either your short-term or long-term goals. These are the sorts of things we often refer to as busywork. If, for example, you are working on the computer but you still take time out to sharpen all your pencils, you're focusing on a task that isn't urgent or important. This is clearly the sort of thing that can wait.

Where do common interruptions fall in the matrix?

Common interruptions—such as a ringing telephone or a friend who drops by unexpectedly while you're studying— tend to fall into the urgent but unimportant category. These things rarely relate to your goals, but they're hard to ignore. If you need to get work done, it's generally a good idea to put yourself in a position in which you are less susceptible to these sorts of interruptions. (See Chapter 3.)

How should you handle tasks that are both urgent and important?

Urgent and important items are tasks you can't ignore and shouldn't ignore. They include things such as scheduled classes or looming deadlines, as well as more spectacular unscheduled tasks, such as dodging projectiles or escaping burning buildings. If you have a class that starts in five minutes, then that's urgent and important. You need to attend the course, and you can't be late. If your paper is due tomorrow, and you've hardly started, then you've really got

Figure 2.8
An Urgency-Importance Matrix

Source: From *Organizing for the Creative Person* by Dorothy Lehmkuhl and Dolores Cotter Lamping. Copyright © 1993 by Dorothy Lehmkuhl and Dolores Cotter Lamping. Reprinted by permission of Random House, Inc.

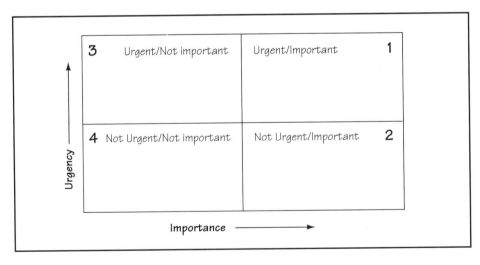

[6]Ibid., pp. 44–45.

no choice but to work until you finish it. All items in this category should get top priority on your task list.

What sorts of tasks are important but not urgent?

The most valuable quadrant in the entire matrix in Figure 2.8 is the one for tasks that are important but aren't yet urgent. This is where your long-range planning occurs. The more you accomplish in this area, the more successful and organized you're likely to be. What are some examples of important but not-yet-urgent tasks? Mastering the notes for a recent textbook reading assignment is one. Beginning research on a paper that isn't due for another month is another. Mastering your notes will put you in a good position the next time a test or quiz is announced (or sprung upon you by surprise). Getting a head start on your paper will prevent you from having to compete with fellow students for limited resources at the library (see Chapter 14) or from having to put in an all-nighter before the paper is due. Some urgent and important tasks (like attending class or leaving the building when a fire alarm sounds) are unavoidable, but, in general, the more time you devote to important but not urgent tasks, the more likely you'll be able to avoid the tasks that increase your stress, force you to cram, or make you skip sleep.

How should the urgency-importance matrix affect the way you plan out your time?

When planning out your time, tackle the tasks in quadrant 1 first, but see if you can keep them to a minimum, and spend the bulk of your time on tasks in quadrant 2. Avoid adding tasks from quadrant 3 or 4 to your task list. The former are typically going to be unexpected interruptions. Try to establish a study environment where you are less likely to encounter these. And as for the items in quadrant 4, they really don't belong on any task list. If you find you're spending time on tasks that are neither urgent nor important, make a point to avoid doing so in the future. Adding such items to your schedule or task list is likely to give you a false sense of accomplishment and distract you from completing truly important tasks.

How can you put the matrix to practical use with task-oriented schedules?

Once you've figured out the urgency and importance of each task you plan to accomplish, you can use this information in a number of ways.

1. Go back to a task list you may have already written and number each item depending on whether it's urgent and important, important but not urgent, and so on.
2. Use the urgency-importance matrix as your actual task list. Looking at which quadrant has more crossed off items will provide a snapshot of how truly productive your day has been.
3. Position your tasks in the matrix first and then create a standard task list, ordering the items by priority based on where you placed them in the matrix.

How can you put the matrix to practical use with a traditional three-part schedule?

If you are using a traditional schedule, the matrix can help you decide how to budget your available time blocks. Begin by using the master schedule as your template, just as you normally would, adding in any tasks or events for the week that already have specific time frames. Then use your matrix to help you decide how to fill in the remaining blocks in your schedule. The weekly view provides excellent reinforcement for those important but not urgent tasks that call for long-term planning.

Staying Organized

What does staying organized have to do with managing time?

Of course, the effort you devote to finding "hidden" time, changing your time habits, and sticking to a schedule will be squandered if the tools you use to tackle your tasks are in a state of disarray. A huge part of being a successful student has to do with being able to find exactly what you need as quickly and efficiently as possible. After all, what good is a carefully planned schedule if you spend the first twenty minutes of the hour you planned to use for mastering your notes, searching for those very notes under a pile of papers or in a maze of nested computer directories? To stay organized and thereby make the best use of that time you've so carefully plotted, you need to devise a system, keep it flexible, and minimize clutter.

Devising a System

What sort of organizational system do you need to devise?

Like so many successful study techniques, organizing your work area depends on a system. To a great extent, the kind of system you use doesn't matter just as long as you have one and it works for you. But in general, it pays to follow the old saying "A place for everything and everything in its place" by designating a logical home base for all the materials you are likely to encounter in your work area. In addition, it makes sense to organize things strategically, so the materials you need most often are easiest to reach and those you need rarely are out of your way. And finally, it helps to logically label items so you can tell at a glance what they contain and where they belong.

Find a Place for Everything

Why is it important to find a place for everything?

There are several reasons why papers, books, and other materials may be obstructing your workspace and even littering your floor, but one of those reasons is so painfully obvious that it's amazing that it doesn't occur to those students who have to wade through a sea of supplies each time they try to do some work: *You never found a place for them.* Although some people may be too tired or lazy to put things away, more people leave things lying about simply because they never figured out where to put them in the first place.

How can you gradually find places for your possessions?

If the prospect of designating a place for everything you own seems complicated and scary, start gradually by designating broad areas for things: bookshelf for your books, drawer for your notebooks, file box for your papers, basket for your mail, jar for your pencils and pens, and so on. Using that as a starting point, start to subdivide your broader areas by, for example, putting this semester's books on the easiest-to-reach shelf and last semester's books on another or by putting science and math books on the first shelf, history and English books on the second. As your refine your system, you'll find it easier to go directly to what you need. But even from the very beginning, you will be in the right ballpark each time you go to look for what you need.

Organize Things Intelligently

How do you organize things intelligently?

Have you ever reached into the refrigerator at breakfast and found that a ketchup bottle, a covered casserole dish, and half an apple are all blocking your access to the carton of milk? Some people have a workspace that is similarly arranged, where the materials they don't need are right there in front of them, and the supplies they do need take some effort to reach. The ketchup, the casserole, and the apple are all things you can use at some point. You just don't need them now. It makes sense to arrange things so they're where you need them when you need them.

How does the CIA system help you arrange your materials?

Just as you arrange your tasks in order of their priority, you should arrange you supplies in a similar fashion. CIA creates a mnemonic to remind you how to arrange things intelligently; that is, they should be arranged according to whether they are current, imminent, or archived.

- *Current.* Current items are the notes and materials you're using right now. They usually belong on your desktop or somewhere close by. They should all be within easy reach. And there's another implied message in this routine: Before you settle down to study, not only should you have the things you need at your fingertips, but also you should get those things you don't need *out of your way.*
- *Imminent.* Imminent items are those you aren't using right now, but plan on using shortly. These are typically the notes and materials from your other classes this semester. In addition, imminent items may include textbooks or materials from previous semesters if they provide background, support, or context for your current semester's work. Imminent items typically sit on a nearby shelf or in a desk drawer.
- *Archived.* Archived items are those you've used in past semesters that may help you this semester or in some future semester but that aren't necessary

for your day-to-day work. This would include your notes from previous classes as well as any textbooks from those classes that you've held onto. Because these items don't have to be easy to reach, you can place them on a less accessible shelf in your bookcase, in a file cabinet, or in banker's boxes. If you do put these items in boxes, be very specific in the way you label them so that you can still find the right book or set of notes if it turns out that you need them.

Choose Logical Labels

What good are labels?

Imagine how difficult it would be to pick out the right book from a shelf if all the books were shelved backward. Although we depend a great deal on labeling, we frequently take it for granted. Labels are designed to make it easier to recognize and find what you need and to organize things systematically, whether by alphabetizing or some other system.

What should you label?

Label notebooks, individual note pages, and computer files. If you're putting things in a file cabinet, label those folders as well. If you're burning files onto CDs, be sure to label the CDs so that you can quickly differentiate one from another. Anything you're likely to sort through, organize, or search for should be labeled. It just takes a second, and it can save you a lot of time. There are lots of good reasons to label your materials and few if any not to do so.

What should the labels say?

How you choose to label your materials is basically up to you as long as you label things consistently. The idea is to be able to find what you need as quickly as possible. That said, here are some suggestions you may want to adopt:

How do you label folders or computer directories for a course?

Label folders or directories according to the course identifier.   Rather than labeling a folder or directories with the title of your course (e.g., "Introduction to Macroeconomics"), it's usually better to start with the course identifier (e.g., "ECON102"), which should be easier to locate when you are rifling through a notebook or cabinet or searching through a computer directory. Also, it will mean that all folders from the same subject when alphabetized will wind up in the same basic location.

How should you organize the different kinds of materials for each course?

Use separate labeled folders or dividers for different parts of a class.   Keep class notes, lab notes, textbook notes, handouts, and any other course materials in separate labeled sections of your notebook or in their own subfolders in your file cabinet or computer directory.

What sorts of labels do your notes need?

Add enough information to each note page or file so that it can stand alone. It's almost inevitable that your notes will get shuffled at some point. In fact, there are some situations in which you may even want to shuffle them. To ensure that your notes don't get easily mixed up, label each note sheet with a course identifier (e.g., "BIO203" or "Biology 203"), the date you took the notes, and the page number. Put the information on an outside corner, so it's easy to flip through and find what you need. With the Cornell System (see Chapter 10), the outside upper corner is probably best because the label is less likely to get in the way of your summary area jottings or marginal cues. To make any notes you've taken on your computer easier to find, name the file after the date (expressed numerically by year, month, and day) and the course identifier. So, for notes you took on February 12, 2008, for a reading in your Biology 203 class, the file name might be 20080212-biology203. If this type of label seems complicated or a little unfriendly to you now, you'll soon get used to it. And you'll discover how much easier it is to quickly find the notes you need.

How can you keep file folders better organized?

Provide an index for any file folders.   If you're keeping materials in a file cabinet, create an alphabetical list of the all the folder names and attach it to the cabinet door. That way you'll be able to search for the right folder before you even open the drawer. Also, it should make it easier to tell if you accidentally have two folders serving the same purpose (such as "Lecture Notes" and "Class Notes").

Keeping Things Flexible

Why should you keep your organization system flexible?

Perhaps somewhere there's a gigantic landfill devoted to obsolete organizers, to partially completed plans, to filing systems gone awry, and to calendars that were abandoned or ignored. Why do so many of these systems wind up on the trash heap? It's true that in many cases people simply lose interest, but it's just as likely that the systems were far too rigid and demanding. Ultimately, a simple, bare-bones system that works is more powerful than a complex, powerful one that fails. You can keep your organization system going for the long haul if you keep things flexible, by doing things like using loose-leaf paper instead of spiral notebooks and by keeping each class in a separate binder instead of combining them all into one.

Use Loose-Leaf Paper

You want any notes you take to be as flexible as possible. Spiral-bound notebooks may seem appealing, but they put your notes into sort of a straitjacket, limiting the things you can readily do with your notes once you've taken them. Of course, you can tear out sheets from a spiral-bound notebook, but that leaves a residual of paper bits that can sometimes have a negative psychological effect on your productivity. Lined-paper tablets are also popular with some students, and although these tablets aren't quite as messy and limiting as spiral notebooks,

they still force you to go through your notes in order. If you do write on lined-paper tablets, buy the three-hole kind and then carefully tear off the pages of notes once you've taken them and store them in a loose-leaf binder. As you'll discover in Chapter 11, being able to separate your notes into individual sheets instead of keeping them as part of a notebook or pad will prove to be a real advantage when it comes time to prepare for a test or quiz. Also, if you keep blank sheets of loose-leaf paper in each notebook, you'll always be prepared, even if you make the mistake of bringing the wrong notebook to class.

Limit Each Notebook to One Class

Why should you have a different notebook for each class?

Standard loose-leaf notebooks can be large and unwieldy, not to mention kind of expensive. Luckily, you don't really require anything so elaborate for your class. All you really need are three rings and a cover. Full-sized, soft-sided notebooks still hold standard-sized paper. But these are thinner and less expensive and enable you to use a different notebook for each class instead of putting the materials from several, often unrelated classes in a single binder. Then you can take only what you need when you head to class. Why do you need your economics notes when you're in class taking notes for sociology? Besides, most of the loose-leaf additions that improve the organization of a large notebook— pockets, dividers, graph paper, and so on— work just as well in a thinner, more flexible notebook. In fact, thinner notebooks often come with a pocket on the inside of the front and back covers. Also, you can buy a notebook of a different color for each class, making it easy to distinguish one from another.

Minimizing Clutter

What causes clutter and how can you reduce it?

Although getting organized involves far more than just minimizing clutter, clutter is generally what most people think of when they imagine disorganization. The cause of clutter is pretty straightforward. It usually results when too many things are out of place. If you reduce you level of "stuff" and make a routine of putting the things that remain back in their place, you should go a long way to reducing clutter.

Use the OHIO Rule for Papers and E-mail

What does the OHIO rule suggest?

The acronym OHIO stands for "Only Handle It Once."[7] When you get a new piece of paper, do something with it right away. Read it and then throw it out, file it, or if it's something that requires your immediate attention, act on it.

---

[7]Edward M. Hallowell, "Overloaded Circuits: Why Smart People Underperform," *Harvard Business Review* (January 2005): 60.

Many people needlessly pick up the same sheets of paper again and again without doing anything decisive. That wastes time and it usually leads to clutter. By the way, the same advice applies to e-mail. If your inbox is filled with e-mail messages, you're creating electronic clutter. Delete the message, file it in a directory, or act on it right away if it's urgent. But don't leave it sitting in your inbox, to be scrolled past day in and day out or repeatedly opened and closed.

Don't Print It Out If You Can Avoid It

Why is it a good idea to avoid printing out materials?

One simple way to reduce the paper-based clutter on your desk or work area is to limit the things you print out. In many colleges, your syllabus, your assignments, and other course materials, sometimes including tests and texts, come to you via e-mail or through a website or a course management system. Some students go through "paper withdrawal" and have a tough time keeping all their materials on the computer instead of in a stack of sheets on their desk. There may still be some materials that you prefer to have on paper, but don't be like the person who salts her food without tasting it first. Try to refrain from automatically printing out your materials. Of course, if your course materials are only available in hard copy, you have no choice.

Allow Time for Cleanup and Setup

What's the last thing you should do at the end of the study day?

When you reach the end of your study day, instead of abruptly getting up from your chair and moving on to something else, take just a few minutes to stow away the things you've been working on in their proper places and to set out the things you plan to be working on the next time you sit down. Organizational experts Dorothy Lehmkuhl and Dolores Lamping have a similar suggestion that encourages you to keep things straight even if you're still working. They call it the Five-Minute Plan.[8] Take five minutes out of every hour to straighten your desk area. Set the timer for five minutes, and you'll be amazed at how much you accomplish in a very short time.

Anything you leave lying around from the previous day is likely to interfere with the work you do the following day. Also, things you leave out have a tendency to pile up. After all, no one plans to have a messy desk or work area. It tends to happen over time. Most cluttered surfaces are covered with items that were left there just "temporarily." Take a few minutes to put books, notebooks, and other supplies back in their places. The few minutes you devote to this end-of-study ritual will ensure that your well-organized work area remains organized. If you feel as though you're too tired, or you're concerned that it will take too much time, try an experiment: Look at your watch or a stopwatch as you go through the process of reshelving books, putting away pens, pencils, and

---

[8]Dorothy Lehmkuhl and Dolores Cotter Lamping, *Organizing for the Creative Person* (New York: Crown, 1993), p. 66.

Online Study Center   www.college.hmco.com/pic/pauk9e

papers, and logging off your computer. You are almost certain to find that the routine doesn't take long at all. And yet it can save you a good deal of time in the long run.

What if your desktop is a computer desktop?

The practice of straightening your desktop is still helpful, even if that desktop is a computer desktop. In fact, it's usually a lot easier to straighten your computer desktop. The process of moving, storing, and deleting files is much faster when those files are computer files.

What's the advantage of setting out your materials in advance?

If you gather together materials that you plan to use the next day, you'll have an important head start. If you have a class the first thing in the morning and there's a risk that you may have to head out the door a little faster than you'd like, the few minutes you spent the night before, calmly getting everything together, should minimize the risk that you will forget something if you're in a hurry. Also, setting out the next day's materials has an important psychological effect. It gets you to think about the following day's activities and helps to put you in the proper mindset. Finally, assembling tomorrow's materials in advance helps to counteract inertia and discourage procrastination. When you wake up the next day and find that everything you need is there waiting for you, you should find it easier to hit the ground running instead of just spinning your wheels.

FINAL WORDS

Why do people who understand the importance of time continue to waste it?

Let's face it. Most people understand the supreme importance of time and the value of sticking to a schedule, yet many of us continue to waste time needlessly. Why? Perhaps it is because we are human beings, not machines. Learning to use time wisely after years of wasting it doesn't happen by simply flipping a switch. Controlling your time is ultimately a matter of developing the right mindset. If the dying words of Queen Elizabeth and the compelling evidence of this chapter haven't been enough to convince you to change your time-wasting ways, perhaps the following tidbits about time will finally make things click.

Seven Valuable Tidbits About Time

1. One of America's greatest composers, jazz giant Duke Ellington, still wasn't ashamed to admit, "Without a deadline, I can't finish nothin'."
2. Be a contrarian. Go to the library when almost nobody is there. Get into the dining-hall line before the crowd. Get the reserved books before the line forms. The time you save will add up quickly.
3. Make decisions wisely by asking, "What are the alternatives?" Make a list of the alternatives, and then put pluses and minuses alongside them. Learn this process. It will save lots of time.

4. Don't spread yourself thin by attempting to become an "information junkie." This scattershot approach takes up a great deal of time and can still leave you feeling stressed and dissatisfied. Just make sure that you gain a firm grip on your own field.

5. When you're really through studying, spend an extra fifteen minutes studying just an extra bit more.

6. If the thought of saving time sounds sensible but uninspiring, ask yourself this simple question: What do I want to save time for? Suddenly, the efficient use of time may take on a significance that it never had before.

7. A Sanskrit proverb puts everything in proper perspective:

Today well lived
Makes every yesterday a dream of happiness
And every tomorrow a vision of hope
Look well therefore to this day.

HAVE YOU MISSED SOMETHING?

SENTENCE COMPLETION   *Complete the following sentences with one of the three words listed below each sentence.*

1. A time schedule functions as a _____.

   reward   game plan   punishment

2. When it comes to studying, "prime time" is usually _____.

   daytime   mid-afternoon   flexible

3. A master schedule should normally be drawn up once a _____.

   day   week   term

MATCHING   *In each blank space in the left column, write the letter preceding the phrase in the right column that matches the left item best.*

_____ 1. Pocket work   a. Work expands to fit the time allotted

_____ 2. E-mail   b. Method for minimizing paper clutter

_____ 3. Master schedule   c. Nobel Prize winner who used sleep time to solve problems

_____ 4. OHIO   d. Provides a basic structure for organizing the term's activities

 *Online Study Center*   www.college.hmco.com/pic/pauk9e

_____ 5. CIA   e. Rhythms that influence your body's cycle of sleeping and waking

_____ 6. Szent-Györgyi   f. Productivity boon that can sometimes be a "time sink"

_____ 7. Parkinson's Law   g. Supplies study material for unexpected free time

_____ 8. Circadian   h. Method for arranging your study materials

TRUE-FALSE

Circle T _beside the_ true _statements and_ F _beside the_ false _statements._

1. T F Taking breaks has a detrimental effect on comprehension.

2. T F Schedules don't have to be effective as long as they're efficient

3. T F Using a time schedule can make you a slave to time.

4. T F Scheduling saves time that might otherwise be wasted.

5. T F An hour of daytime work is usually more productive than an hour at night.

MULTIPLE CHOICE

Choose the word or phrase that completes each sentence most accurately, and circle the letter that precedes it.

1. When your obligations and assignments begin to seem overwhelming, it helps to
   a. take a nap.
   b. divide your time into blocks.
   c. use Parkinson's Law.
   d. all of the above.

2. "Hidden" time is time that you
   a. aren't allowed to use.
   b. managed to overlook.
   c. reserve for recreation.
   d. leave off your schedule.

3. The most *valuable* quadrant of the urgency-importance matrix is
    a. urgent but not important.
    b. important but not urgent.
    c. not urgent and not important.
    d. none of the above.

4. The master schedule provides
    a. an alternative to a weekly schedule.
    b. an excuse for increased recreation.
    c. a basic structure for organizing your activities.
    d. a solution to the problem of hidden time.

5. A task-based schedule may be your best bet if
    a. your days are unpredictable.
    b. your free time is fluid.
    c. you have a full-time job.
    d. all of the above.

SHORT ANSWER   *Supply a brief answer for each of the following items.*

1. What is the purpose of keeping a daily activities log?
2. In what ways does a schedule promote relaxation?
3. Discuss how to prepare a task-oriented master schedule.
4. Explain the urgency-importance matrix.

IT'S YOUR Q

The Q System uses marginal questions to encourage active reading. You'll notice that most but not all paragraphs in this chapter are accompanied by marginal questions. Now it's your Q. Scan the chapter for any paragraph that is missing a question, reread the paragraph, establish the main idea, and then arrive at a question that elicits it. Use the questions in the surrounding paragraphs as models for your own marginal questions.

Online Study Center   www.college.hmco.com/pic/pauk9e

WORDS IN CONTEXT

From the three choices beside each numbered item, select the one that most nearly expresses the meaning of the italicized word in the quote. Make a light check mark (✓) next to your choice.

Mathematics has given economics *rigor*, but *alas*, also *mortis*.

—Robert L. Heilbroner (1919–2005), American economist

1. *rigor*	strength	exactitude	precision
2. *alas*	sorrowfully	interestingly	happily
3. *mortis*	humanity	fear	death

Interest you owe works night and day, in fair weather and foul. Interest gnaws at a man's *substance* with invisible teeth.

—Henry Ward Beecher (1813–1887), newspaper editor and clergyman

4. man's *substance*	brain	worth	body

Of all the mysteries of the stock exchange, there is none so *impenetrable* as why there should be a buyer for everyone who seeks to sell.

—John Kenneth Galbraith (1908–2006), Canadian-born American economist, writer, and diplomat (ambassador to India)

5. *impenetrable*	incredible	inexplicable	important

"Involvement" in this context differs from "commitment" in the same sense as the pig's and the chicken's roles in one's breakfast of ham and eggs. The chicken was *involved*—the pig was *committed*.

—Anonymous

6. chicken was *involved*	primed	rejected	associated
7. pig was *committed*	solicited	included	affiliated

THE WORD HISTORY SYSTEM

Tally
a reminder of the early method of counting

tally   tal'-ly   *n.* 1. A reckoning or score. 2. A mark used in recording a number of acts or objects.

Tally goes back to the time when things were commonly counted by cutting notches in a stick of wood. The word was borrowed in Middle English as *taille,* from Old French *taille,* "a cutting." It was formerly customary for traders to have two sticks and to mark with notches on each the number or quantity of goods delivered, the seller keeping one stick and the purchaser the other. When such records came to be kept on paper, the same word was used for them; and it now means almost any kind of count or score.

Reprinted by permission. From *Picturesque Word Origins* © 1933 by G. & C. Merriam Co. (now Merriam-Webster, Incorporated).

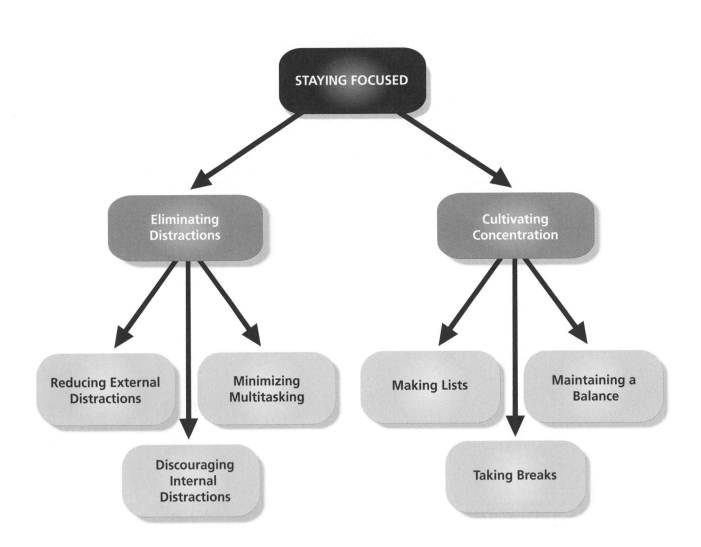

Staying Focused

Consider the postage stamp. It secures success through its ability to stick to one thing until it gets there.

Josh Billings (1818–1885), pen name of Henry Wheeler Shaw, American humorist

Everyone—from astronauts to athletes, from merchants to musicians—appreciates the value of being able to focus on the task at hand. Yet few of us know how to attain and then sustain this kind of concentration. Although concentration does not appear at the snap of the fingers, there are ways you can improve the conditions for concentration. To help you stay focused, no matter what your task may be, this chapter deals with:

- **Reducing External Distractions**
- **Overcoming Internal Distractions**
- **Minimizing Multitasking**
- **Adopting Strategies for Concentration**

What are some examples of concentration?

Concentration can sometimes be difficult to define, but most of us know it when we see it. Watch a good bowler as she takes her position and directs all her thoughts on knocking down the pins at the end of the alley. Watch a quarterback as he focuses on getting a pass to an open receiver, even while linebackers rush in on him from several directions. That's concentration! Imagine becoming so absorbed in your textbook that you find yourself "talking" to the author: "That's not proof enough," or "Other writers explain it differently," or "I never thought about the problem that way before." Imagine studying your notes so intently that when you finally look up, you see that it's been two hours since you last checked the clock. That's concentration!

What makes concentration elusive?

Concentration is focused thinking. Just as light waves can be focused into a single powerful beam—a laser—concentration can focus the power of your thoughts, enabling you to think with greater precision and penetrate difficult ideas. But powerful as it can be, concentration has an elusive quality. In fact, concentration comes only when you don't think about it. Ironically, if you were thinking deeply about a subject and suddenly realized that you were concentrating, at that moment you would have broken your concentration. Such prolonged, undivided attention can be difficult to achieve. After all, in normal circumstances there are dozens of things competing for your attention. Thoughts and ideas constantly bang, rattle, and knock on the door of your consciousness, trying to gain entry.

What does Figure 3.1 tell us about concentration?

Figure 3.1 provides a vivid illustration of the natural tendency to divide attention. As you gaze at this picture, you'll probably discover that your visual focus is shifting every few seconds so that you first see a goblet, then two profiles, and then the goblet again. Once you're aware of both images, it is difficult for your eyes to focus on one and ignore the other. Similarly, it is hard for your mind to focus on one idea at a time. People who can focus exclusively on the

Figure 3.1
A Goblet or Two Profiles?

task before them have a much better chance of completing that task more quickly and accurately than those who divide their attention even when they don't mean to do so.

How can you concentrate if you can't do it directly?

So how do you stay focused? Because you can't strive for concentration directly, you must instead try to improve the conditions that promote concentration. That involves eliminating distractions and adopting strategies to enhance concentration.

Eliminating Distractions

What's the first step in eliminating distractions?

Trouble concentrating may come from external distractions, such as sights or sounds that compete for your attention; from internal distractions, such as worries or daydreams; and from multitasking, which can splinter your concentration into unproductive pieces. Once recognized, these obstacles to concentration can be overcome.

Reducing External Distractions

What is an external distraction?

Anything that stimulates your senses and in the process disrupts your concentration can be considered an external distraction. Study halls and living quarters are overflowing with such distractions, everything from banging doors to baking bread. To work in a way that is compatible with concentration, you need the proper environment as well as the right equipment.

Select the Proper Environment

What elements make up a proper study environment?

Your study environment should be used exclusively for study. In addition, it should be quiet and well lighted. You can take your work to a place that is already designed for study, or you can create your own study environment.

What is the best environment for study?

Find a Workshop   You'd be hard-pressed to find an environment more suitable for high-quality concentration than a library. It offers a minimum of nonacademic distractions, a quiet atmosphere (usually as a matter of policy), and sufficient lighting. Get in the habit of studying at the library right away, on the first day of class. Even the walk to the library can be used productively as a review session or a refreshing break.

Why is it important to use your study area for studying only?

Whether you choose to work in the library or somewhere else, make sure your study area is reserved for studying. Psychologists emphasize that a conditioning effect is created between the desk and you: If you nap or daydream a lot while sitting at the desk, the desk can act as a cue for napping or daydreaming. By the same token, if you read or work in bed, you make it difficult to work

Online Study Center   www.college.hmco.com/pic/pauk9e

energetically and fall asleep easily. To avoid this negative conditioning, use your desk only for studying. When you feel the urge to nap or daydream, leave your desk to nap or daydream elsewhere.

Your study area should be your workshop, a place where you feel secure and comfortable. You can ensure that you have the proper environment for study and concentration if you minimize visual distractions, avoid or eliminate distracting noises, refrain from playing music, beware of e-mail and the Internet, control the impulse to register distractions, and provide the area with plenty of light.

What other steps can you take to ensure a proper study environment?

Minimize Visual Distractions   A sheet of notes or a page from a textbook can seem dull compared with a glimpse of a softball game being played on a nearby diamond or a view of gently falling snow. To improve your chances of concentration, avoid competition for your eyes' attention. Study by a window so you can take advantage of the natural light, but keep your head turned away from the potentially distracting view. Of course, not all visual distractions lie on the other side of the windowpane. If your study area contains photographs you're liable to look at, gadgets you're likely to fiddle with, or books you'll be tempted to pick up and read, remove them until you have completed your work.

What can you do to eliminate noise when you study?

Eliminate Noise   If you need a quiet spot for efficient study, do your utmost to find one. Noise can be one of the most serious obstacles to effective study. Nothing is more wasteful than going over the same paragraph again and again because the noise makes it impossible to absorb what you are reading. If the library is the right place for you, make an effort to study there whenever you can. If you study at home, achieving quiet can sometimes be as simple as closing a door or inserting earplugs.

Is music a distraction?

Turn Down the Loud Music   When studying, loud music, especially vocal music, can break your concentration. To keep your concentration from bouncing between the music and your books, you expend energy that could be put to better use. However, some students can tolerate music better than others. If you find music nonintrusive, then instrumental music—played softly—could form a pleasing background, and such a background can actually muffle some external, intermittent noises.

What can you do to prevent e-mail and the Internet from becoming distractions?

Beware of E-mail and the Internet   E-mail has been a tremendous boon to communication. And the Internet has opened vast avenues of information that were available only to experts just a decade or so ago. But when you're trying to concentrate, both e-mail and the Internet can be gigantic distractions. Unless you're working *on* your computer, you shouldn't be working *at* your computer. Avoid the temptation to surf or constantly check e-mail by keeping your screen out of your line of sight. If you *are* working on your computer, turn off your e-mail application and limit your Web surfing to the work at hand. If you're expecting important e-mail, set a timer for an hour or so, and work without interruption before checking. When the timer goes off, check for mail, then start the timer again.

What does the spider technique involve?

Try the Spider Technique   A vibrating tuning fork held close to a spider's web sets up vibrations in the web. After the spider makes a few hurried investigations and finds no fly in the web, it learns to ignore the vibrations. The next time you are studying in the library and the door opens, don't look up. Controlling your impulse to look up will disturb your concentration the first few times. But very soon, like the spider, you'll learn to ignore these external disturbances.

Use the Right Equipment

What is the most important piece of concentration equipment?

Because proper lighting is an important component of your study environment, the right light should head your list of equipment to promote concentration and reduce external distractions.

What is the best kind of light for studying?

Find the Right Light   Whether it comes from conventional light bulbs, fluorescent tubes, or the newer compact fluorescent bulbs, the best light for study is bright, even, and steady (remember B, E, and ST).

Bright.   The emission of light is measured in lumens. For studying, you need at least 2,500 lumens. Two standard 100-watt bulbs (1,750 lumens each) will meet that requirement. So will a double-tube fluorescent lamp or two compact fluorescent bulbs of approximately 25 to 30 watts each. Fluorescents cost more than standard bulbs, but they can be just as bright and can last up to 100 times longer!

Even.   Shadows in your work area or "hot spots" caused by glare will tire your eyes and make concentration difficult. Get rid of glare by shielding your lamp with a shade and by using a light-colored, nonglossy blotter on your desk. Eliminate shadows by using two lamps, fluorescent light, or diffuse light.

STeady.   A constant flicker will undermine concentration. If you use fluorescent light, try a double- or triple-tube lamp or use compact fluorescent bulbs, which are less likely to strobe than traditional fluorescents. If you are using conventional (incandescent) light, make sure the bulb is screwed in properly.

What are the drawbacks of studying under bad light?

Good lighting makes for good studying. By contrast, poor lighting causes eyestrain, general tension, headaches, and sleepiness—irritations that interfere with concentration. If you study under good light but your eyes still bother you, have them examined by an ophthalmologist or optometrist. Clear and comfortable vision is essential to good studying.

 *Online Study Center*   www.college.hmco.com/pic/pauk9e

What is the pencil technique?

Use a Pencil to Catalyze Concentration   A technique that does not fail is the simple, humble *pencil technique*. The technique is this: *Whenever you are working to learn, study with a pencil in hand.* And use it! For example, if you are reading a textbook chapter, stop after several paragraphs and very briefly, in your own words, write down the key points made by the author. If, after reading several paragraphs, you find that no words come to you, you have no recourse but to go back and read the passage again. This time, read with determination and concentration to make sure you learn the key points. The secret: Activity promotes and almost ensures concentration. The pencil provides the activity!

What is the best kind of chair for promoting concentration?

Find the Right Kind of Chair   More ink and more words have been wasted extolling the virtues of a straight-backed, hard-seated hickory chair than on any other single piece of study equipment. Forget it: Use a comfortable, well-cushioned chair. Staying awake or falling asleep does not depend on your chair; rather, it depends primarily on the method of study, your attitude and self-discipline, the light, and the room temperature. A hard, straight-backed chair can't take the place of these basic requirements.

Use a Bookstand   An extremely practical piece of equipment is a bookstand—not a bookshelf or bookends, an actual stand placed on your desk that holds the book in a tilted position and holds the pages down so that they do not flip over. Older ones are made out of metal. Newer ones come in plastic. A bookstand can work for you in many ways. First, and very important, it can give you a feeling of readiness to study—a feeling of being a scholar in the traditional sense. This alone is worth many times the price of the stand. Second, the stand provides physical freedom. It eliminates the strain of continually holding the book open, pressing down on two sides to keep the pages from flipping over, tilting the book to avoid glare, and trying to find something heavy enough to hold the book open so you can free your hands to make notes. It permits you to sit back with arms folded, to contemplate and reflect on the meaning of what you are reading.

What other equipment can be helpful for concentration?

Keep Other Equipment Nearby   Remember the mnemonic for organizing your workspace with intelligence: CIA (Current, Imminent, and Archived; see Chapter 2). Make sure your current materials include any basic equipment that will help you to study without interruption. Depending on the classes you are taking and your own personal preferences, that may mean an up-to-date dictionary, a calculator, a clock, a calendar, paper, notebooks, paper clips, tape, rubber bands, pencils, pens, erasers, and index cards. If you make it a habit to keep your desk well stocked, you won't derail your concentration with unplanned emergency trips to obtain necessities.

Discouraging Internal Distractions

What are internal distractions?

Internal distractions are distractions that *you* create: daydreams, personal problems, anxiety, indecision, forgetfulness, and unrealistic goals. These distractions are as disruptive as the sights, sounds, and smells that make up the external variety, even though in this case the only one who is aware of them is you. Because internal distractions come from within, you have the power to eliminate or at least control them.

Use a Concentration Scoresheet

What is a concentration scoresheet?

Keep a sheet of paper handy. Whenever you catch your mind wandering, keep score by putting a check mark on the sheet. The mere act of doing this reminds you to get back to work. Students report that when they first tried this system, they accumulated as many as twenty check marks per textbook page, but after one or two weeks, they were down to one or two check marks per page.

How does keeping score help you concentrate?

The concentration scoresheet encourages self-observation. Making note of your breaks in concentration—when they happen, how often they occur, and what triggers them—will help you realize just how intrusive the lapses are and will enable you to gradually eliminate them.

Put Stray Thoughts on a Worry Pad

What is the purpose of a worry pad?

Although pleasant plans and diverting daydreams can be major sources of internal distraction, nagging worries and obligations can also take your mind off your work. The concentration scoresheet will alert you to these breaks in your attention, but it won't address the problems that prompted the distraction. To prevent the same worries from interfering with your concentration again and again, you must address them. A worry pad provides an excellent short-term solution to the problem.

How do you use a worry pad?

When an intrusive thought disrupts your concentration, write it down on your worry pad with the idea that you will attend to it just as soon as you get the chance. Then with your conscience clear and your bothersome thought recorded on paper, you can get back to the business of concentration. After you have finished studying, read over your list and give these concerns your full attention. If you cannot alleviate them yourself, get the help of friends or counselors.

Use the Stop! Technique

What is the Stop! technique?

Of course, not all distractions are worth writing down. Sometimes thoughts will flit into your mind that seem to have no other purpose than to throw you off course. The Stop! technique, suggested by authors Judith Greenbaum and

How do you use the Stop!
technique?

Geraldine Markel in their book *Finding Your Focus*,[1] is a red light for distractions. It's designed to arrest any dark thoughts or daydreams before they have a chance to gain momentum.

The Stop! technique is a simple and powerful tool that relies on what psychologists call self-talk. Whenever you find that you're heading in the wrong direction because of distractions or you feel you've been spinning your wheels, just tell yourself "Stop!" That's right. Say the word. Do it out loud and with authority if you can. Letting yourself know you're aware that your focus has been drifting and that you don't intend to let it go any further is often enough to set you right back on the road to concentration. Try it.

Minimizing Multitasking

As we've seen, distractions are unwanted intrusions that vie for your attention and make concentration difficult if not impossible. Now imagine if you deliberately subjected yourself to several distractions at once. Sounds crazy, eh? That may be so, and yet many of us do it all the time. We call it multitasking. Although we might think of each concern as a task, not a distraction, when you're focusing on one task, all the others are distractions. For example, if you're doing research for a term paper, answering e-mail, listening to the radio, and finishing your lunch all at once or in rapid succession, you're almost certainly multitasking. *Multitasking* means working on several tasks simultaneously or rapidly shifting back and forth between them. The term comes from computer operating systems, which are able to keep several applications running at the same time. The difference, of course, is that people are not machines. Sometimes mistakenly held up as a model of efficiency, multitasking is not only less productive than working on one task at a time, it's also a troubling source of stress.[2] Luckily, there are a handful of simple steps you can take to avoid it.

Multitasking Makes You Less Productive

Why does multitasking make
you less productive?

Dividing your brainpower between several tasks at once has a predictable effect. As a study published in the *Journal of Experimental Psychology* concludes, people

[1]Judith Greenbaum and Geraldine Markel, *Finding Your Focus* (New York: McGraw-Hill, 2006), pp. 36–37.

[2]Christina Tibbits, "Just Throw Multitasking Out Your Window of Work," *Austin Business Journal* (online), (June 10, 2002), available at http://austin.bizjournals.com/austin/stories/2002/06/10/smallb3.html.

who multitask are less efficient than people who don't. According to the study's coauthor, Dr. David Meyer, "There's scientific evidence that multitasking is extremely hard for somebody to do, and sometimes impossible."[3]

What are the costs of multitasking?

Of course, in spite of the evidence, thousands of people continue to multitask and would appear to be doing so successfully. "It doesn't mean you can't do several things at the same time," says Dr. Marcel Just, codirector of Carnegie-Mellon University's Center for Cognitive Brain Imaging. "But we're kidding ourselves if we think we can do so without cost."[4] According to studies by Dr. Just, Dr. Meyer, and others, those costs include forgetfulness and difficulties in concentrating.[5]

How does multitasking result in forgetfulness?

Forgetfulness. Chronic multitaskers often feel that their memories are failing them when in fact the converse is true: They are failing their memories. As we'll see in Chapter 9, you need something called consolidation if you want to be able to remember what you've learned for any length of time. Multitasking monopolizes this valuable consolidation space with additional activities that make forming a permanent memory trace more difficult.[6]

What is it about multitasking that makes concentration difficult?

Difficulty in concentration. With multitasking, regardless of what you're working on, there's a good chance that at least part of your mind will be elsewhere. Nothing is as concentrated as it was initially when it's been diluted, and that includes the power of your thinking. Or, as Dr. Meyer explains, "No matter how hard you try, you will never be as good multitasking as you are concentrating on one [task]."[7]

Multitasking Increases Stress

Why does multitasking increase stress?

Not surprisingly, the drain on productivity results in an increase in the potential for stress.[8] You are compelled to struggle against the inevitable pseudo forgetting that occurs and fight to maintain your concentration in a climate of relentless

[3]Sue Shellenbarger, "Juggling Too Many Tasks Could Make You Stupid," *Wall Street Journal Online* (February 28, 2003), available at http://www.careerjournal.com/columnists/workfamily/20030228-workfamily.html.

[4]Ibid.

[5]John McChesney, "Minds Weren't Made for Multitasking," interview with Dr. Michelle Weil, *Hot Seat* (November 5, 1997), available at http://hotwired.lycos.com/synapse/hotseat/97/44/transcript2a.html.

[6]Shellenbarger, "Juggling Too Many Tasks."

[7]Amanda S. Fox, "Tallying the Cost of Doing Too Much," *CIO Magazine* (March 15, 2000).

[8]Larry Rosen and Michelle Weil, "Multitasking Madnesss," *Context* (Fall 1998), available at http://www.contextmag.com/archives/199809/InnerGameOfWork.asp.

distractions. Moreover, multitasking forms an unhealthy alliance with two major culprits in stress, procrastination and loss of control, and can sometimes start you on a vicious cycle of insomnia as well. And some multitaskers have been exhibiting symptoms that are similar to those of attention deficit disorder.

What is the connection between multitasking and procrastination?

Procrastination.   That other notorious source of self-imposed stress, procrastination, often works hand in hand with multitasking. After all, one technique that procrastinators frequently use to put off assignments is to shift back and forth between several tasks instead of focusing on a single one. Avoid multitasking and you may succeed in discouraging procrastination in the same stroke.

Why does multitasking sometimes lead to a loss of control?

Loss of control.   As we'll learn, your sense of control can have a dramatic effect on your level of stress. Students, even overworked students, feel less stress when they are able to maintain a sense of control over what they are doing. Multitasking robs you of that control. All your activities and obligations are moving targets, and thus maintaining equilibrium becomes difficult for most and impossible for some.

Insomnia.   People who multitask—or attempt to—are often compelled to shift into a kind of mental overdrive that doesn't necessarily downshift when the day's work is done.[9] "Part of what's happening," says Michelle Weil, coauthor of the book *Technostress*, "is that we're overstimulating our physiological capabilities as well as our cognitive capabilities, and this leads to sleep interruption, the waking in the middle of the night, where it feels like your brain's just firing off ideas."[10] As we'll see in Chapter 4, sleep loss not only results from stress, but can in turn be the source of *more* stress.

Multitasking Can Lead to Attention Deficit Trait

How does multitasking lead to attention deficit trait (ADT)?

Multitasking can short-circuit the sophisticated, reasonable area of your brain and hand control over to the ancient "fight or flight" region, an area fueled primarily by fear. As Dr. Edward Hallowell, an expert on attention deficit trait (ADT) explains, "Fear shifts us into survival mode and thus prevents fluid learning and nuanced understanding."[11] The attempt to overload what are known as the brain's executive functions with too many tasks at once sends a distress signal to

[9]McChesney, "Minds Weren't Made for Multitasking."

[10]Ibid.

[11]Edward M. Hallowell, "Overloaded Circuits: Why Smart People Underperform" *Harvard Business Review* (January 2005): 58.

the primitive part of the brain, which abruptly takes over.[12] One minute you're a student, the next you're a cave man or cave woman, fleeing an unwelcome lion—all without even leaving your desk!

What are the symptoms of ADT?

With ADT, your patience grows short, your thinking becomes black and white, your intelligence falters, and you are unable to effectively focus on the tasks at hand.[13] In other words, for a student it spells disaster. According to Dr. Hallowell, "People with ADT have difficulty staying organized, setting priorities, and managing time."[14]

How does ADT differ from attention deficit disorder (ADD)?

Students with ADT sometimes mistake their symptoms as being those of the attention deficit disorder (ADD). Although people with ADT and those with ADD share many of the same symptoms, there is a crucial difference. ADD is a neurological disorder with a genetic component, whereas ADT springs entirely from your surroundings.[15] If you have ADD, you will always have ADD. But with ADT, a change of scene and strategy can make the symptoms disappear. As Dr. Hallowell explains, "ADT can be controlled only by creatively engineering one's environment and one's emotional and physical health."[16] One way to do this is by adopting the strategies for managing stress outlined in Chapter 4, which include eating well, exercising, and getting enough sleep. The other is to minimize multitasking.

Multitasking Can Be Minimized

What can you do to minimize multitasking?

Obviously, some multitasking is arguably beyond your control. If you're in the middle of an assignment and the phone rings or someone comes to your door, it's natural to want to answer. But most factors that lead to multitasking are well within the realm of your control. You can reduce the risk that multitasking will break your concentration by slowing down and planning your day carefully, by making a point to finish one task before beginning another, and by keeping a pad handy to deal with the distractions that may lead to multitasking in the first place.

How does slowing down help if you're feeling overloaded?

Given that many people multitask because they feel pressed for time, it might seem strange to suggest that slowing down can actually help improve both your attention and your productivity. But it can. If you move too quickly, you're apt to grow flustered and confused. If your executive functions get overloaded and succumb to your stone-age side, you're unlikely to get any quality studying

[12]Ibid.

[13]Ibid.

[14]Ibid, p. 56.

[15]Ibid.

[16]Ibid, p. 59.

Online Study Center www.college.hmco.com/pic/pauk9e

done. On the other hand, if you take the time to figure out what's what, to listen carefully, ask questions, and think deeply, your tension should diminish and your attention should increase. You may be moving more deliberately, but you'll also be working more productively.

Why does a plan discourage multitasking?	*Plan your day.* Use the time-based scheduling outlined in Chapter 2 to inoculate yourself against multitasking. For many people multitasking provides a way of getting to work without ever having to decide which task is the most urgent, or the most interesting, or the most important. If each block of time has a specific task associated with it, you're less likely to bounce back and forth between several tasks.[17]
What can you do to make sure you work to completion?	*Work to completion.* Don't start a new task until you've finished the old one.[18] This may be difficult with long-term tasks. But with short-term tasks, it should be achievable. If you do have a task that is stretched out over a longer period of time, try to create subtasks that you can tackle and complete before moving on.
What does a nearby pad do to prevent multitasking?	*Keep a pad handy.* The worry pad is an excellent antidote to multitasking. It is designed to serve as a temporary holding area for pending ideas and concerns and can also be used to arrest early impulses to multitask. It's common to "task-shift" when there's a concern that "if I don't take care of it now, I never will." That's an understandable worry with a simple solution. Write it down, and get back to the task at hand. When you've finished the first job, you'll have the pad to remind you of what to do next.

Cultivating Concentration

What sorts of strategies will encourage concentration?	Although the best way to encourage concentration is usually to discourage distractions and keep multitasking to a minimum, you can also take positive actions to improve your concentration. Get into the habit of making lists, taking regular breaks, and maintaining a balance between the challenge of a particular assignment and your skill level.

[17]Rosen and Weil, "Multitasking Madness."
[18]Ibid.

Making Lists

What is the value of lists?

As we have seen, keeping random thoughts and information in your head instead of writing them down is a primary impediment to concentration. Lists allow you to free up your mind without losing important information. Use lists to remind yourself of day-to-day obligations and to catalog all the study equipment you're likely to need.

How can you prevent goals and appointments from distracting you?

To avoid worrying about the possibility of missing personal appointments and forgetting those things you've set out to do, write them down on your daily schedule (see Figure 2.4, page 35). This should enable you to shift smoothly from one activity to the next without breaking your concentration.

Are hand-held computers good tools for keeping lists?

Some students may prefer to keep their lists on hand-held personal digital assistants (PDAs) that can be easily stowed in a pocket or purse. If you have a PDA and are comfortable using it, fine. But if you don't have a PDA, don't feel that you are somehow at a disadvantage. In general, it's quicker and more convenient to jot your list of items down on an ordinary paper pad. PDAs excel when you've got information you want to keep around for an extended period of time, but they aren't usually as time-efficient for making short-term lists. The tiny typewriter keypads or the handwriting recognition software that some PDAs employ may be ingenious, but they aren't flawless, and they do take some practice to perfect. It's important not to let keeping your list become its own distraction. This can be a danger with a handwritten list, but it's an even greater risk with a PDA.

Taking Breaks

How important is it to take breaks?

Breaks can sometimes be as vital as the work itself. Although some students with short attention spans may be tempted to take a rest after only a brief time of working, others have the exact opposite problem. As tempting as it may be to put your nose to the grindstone and just keep working until all of your assignments are completed, this sort of strategy can often be a recipe for distraction and burnout.

What happens if you don't take breaks?

If you allow physical energy to build up unabated, your mind will race. If you keep repressing concerns that compete for your attention, those concerns will eventually triumph and scuttle your concentration. And if you persist in denying such a basic instinct as hunger, all you'll be able to think of is food.

What are the benefits of taking a break?

If, however, you take a few minutes to defuse these distractions, stand up and stretch, address a problem you've been avoiding, or grab a healthy snack to tide you over, you can return to your work ready to concentrate.

How often should you take breaks?

Breaks are essential. But like almost anything beneficial, they're susceptible to abuse. If you're making progress, it's important not to take an open-ended break that interrupts your momentum. And if you're not making progress, don't let a break serve as an excuse for evasion. Be as precise about allocating your breaks as you are about scheduling your work time. In general, keep a ratio of no less than five to one between work time and break time. In other words, work for fifty minutes and then take a ten-minute break. Or work for twenty-five minutes and take a break of five minutes.

Maintaining a Balance

How do you obtain the most rewarding kind of concentration?

Psychologist Mihaly Csikszentmihalyi believes that the most intense and rewarding kind of concentration (which he calls "flow") comes about when you develop a balance between the challenge of the work you are doing and the level of skills you possess.[19] If the challenge of an assignment overwhelms your skill level, anxiety—not concentration—is likely to result. Conversely, if your skills are at a high level but the assignment isn't challenging, you're apt to become bored and easily distracted. Finally, if both your skill level and the challenge of an assignment are low, you'll probably grow apathetic and have no desire to concentrate (see Table 3.1).

How can you cultivate the balance of challenge and skills that lead to "flow"?

When your challenge and skill levels seem out of balance, there are several solutions to help get them in sync:

- *If your skill level is low*, you may need academic assistance. Your college should have a tutoring service. If not, see if you can get help from a classmate or even the instructor. If you recognize that you're having a problem, it's better to arrange for a tutor now instead of letting the problem fester. Occasionally a perceived low skill level is just a matter of overly high expectations. Don't try to be an overnight success. Work methodically and patiently and there's a good chance that things will click. If after a time you still find you're floundering, then you may need a tutor's help.
- *If your challenge level is low*, you probably need some outside stimulus to boost your interest either in a class or for the text. Studying in groups can be a great way to liven up a course that doesn't seem to challenge or excite you. The enthusiasm of other students can often prove infectious. An alternate solution is an alternate text. It may be that the voice, the style, or the organization of the required text doesn't interest you. Reading another text on the same topic or using related workbooks or programmed materials that encourage active participation may boost your interest and put you in a better frame of mind for giving your course text another try. (For more on group study and alternate texts, see Chapter 8.)

[19]Richard Flaste, "The Power of Concentration," *The New York Times Magazine* (October 8, 1989), p. 26.

Table 3.1
Achieving Concentration by
Balancing Challenge and Skills

Status	Symptom	Solution
Challenge and skill level low	Apathy	Group study; Tutoring
Skill level exceeds challenge	Boredom	Group study; Alternate text
Challenge exceeds skill level	Anxiety	Tutoring; Rethink goals
Challenge and skill level balanced	Concentration	No solution necessary: *Optimal condition for "flow"*

FINAL WORDS

How is learning to concentrate like gardening?

Ultimately, learning to concentrate is like learning to be a good gardener. Anyone who has had experience raising flowers, fruits, or vegetables knows that you can't actually make them grow. The plant takes care of that, not you. All you can do is improve the conditions for growth. That requires skill, planning, and a little bit of luck. It's the same with concentration.

HAVE YOU MISSED SOMETHING?

SENTENCE COMPLETION   *Complete the following sentences with one of the three words or phrases listed below each sentence.*

1. Concentration is focused _____.

   light   thinking   intensity

2. The best light for studying is bright, even, and _____.

   strong   stylish   steady

3. It's important not to let your efforts at keeping a list become their own _____.

   distraction   advantage   list

 **Online Study Center**   www.college.hmco.com/pic/pauk9e

MATCHING

In each blank space in the left column, write the letter preceding the phrase in the right column that matches the left item best.

_____ 1. "Flow"

a. Self-talk technique that discourages distractions

_____ 2. Library

b. Tires the eyes and makes concentration difficult

_____ 3. Stop!

c. Provides physical freedom and promotes readiness

_____ 4. Glare

d. Involves working on several things at once

_____ 5. Bookstand

e. Stopgap measure for dealing with internal distractions

_____ 6. Multitasking

f. Helps you keep track of breaks in your concentration

_____ 7. Worry pad

g. Describes an especially rewarding kind of concentration

_____ 8. Check mark

h. Best environment for high-quality concentration

TRUE-FALSE

Circle T *beside the* true *statements and* F *beside the* false *statements.*

1. T F   Concentration only occurs when you're not thinking about it.

2. T F   Anything that stimulates the senses is a potential external distraction.

3. T F   E-mail and the Internet both have a positive influence on concentration.

4. T F   Whether you stay awake or fall asleep depends on the type of chair you use.

5. T F   Multitasking generally makes you more productive.

MULTIPLE CHOICE

Choose the word or phrase that completes each sentence most accurately, and circle the letter that precedes it.

1. Trouble concentrating is due primarily to
   a. internal and external distractions.
   b. boredom.
   c. anxiety.
   d. poor eyesight.

2. The face-goblet image in Figure 3.1 illustrates our natural tendency to
   a. forget faces.
   b. divide attention.
   c. recognize people.
   d. focus thoughts.

3. Although concentration is powerful, it is often
   a. unnecessary.
   b. elusive.
   c. underestimated.
   d. time consuming.

4. Multitasking can interfere with
   a. sound sleep.
   b. concentration.
   c. consolidation.
   d. all of the above.

5. When the challenge is high but your skill level is low, you will probably experience
   a. concentration.
   b. boredom.
   c. anxiety.
   d. apathy.

Online Study Center   www.college.hmco.com/pic/pauk9e

SHORT ANSWER   *Supply a brief answer for each of the following items.*

1. Explain how smells can act as external distractions.
2. Discuss some methods for minimizing multitasking.
3. Explain how a pencil can be used to promote concentration.
4. Describe strategies you can use to eliminate noise.

IT'S YOUR Q

The Q System uses marginal questions to encourage active reading. You'll notice that most but not all paragraphs in this chapter are accompanied by marginal questions. Now it's your Q. Scan the chapter for any paragraph that is missing a question, reread the paragraph, establish the main idea, and then arrive at a question that elicits it. Use the questions in the surrounding paragraphs as models for your own marginal questions.

WORDS IN CONTEXT

From the three choices beside each numbered item, select the one that most nearly expresses the meaning of the italicized word in the quote. Make a light check mark (✓) next to your choice.

If I were asked to name the deadliest *subversive* force within capitalism, I would without hesitation name advertising.

—Robert L. Heilbroner (1919–2005), American economist

1. *subversive* force   underlying   substantial   corruptive

Marketing is merely a civilized form of warfare in which most battles are won with words, ideas, and *disciplined* thinking.

—Albert W. Emery (1923–), American advertising agency executive

2. *disciplined* thinking   informed   orderly   shrewd

Gentility is what is left over from rich ancestors after the money is gone.

—John Ciardi (1916–1986), American poet and critic

3. *gentility*   refinement   large debts   large family

The ideals which have lighted my way, and time after time have given me new courage to face life cheerfully, have been Kindness, Beauty, and Truth. The *trite* subjects of human efforts—possessions, outward success, luxury—have always seemed to me *contemptible.*

—Albert Einstein (1879–1955), German-born American theoretical physicist

4. *trite* subjects | concise | precise | unappealing

5. seemed . . . *contemptible* | temporary | despicable | probable

THE WORD HISTORY SYSTEM

Acumen
the sharpness of the mind

acumen   a-cu′-men *n.*
Quickness, accuracy, and keen-ness of judgment or insight.

A keen mind may be likened to a sharp knife, which penetrates easily and quickly. For clean-cut action, both the knife and the mind must be sharp. So it is natural that when a word was needed to denote the faculty of keen, penetrating thought, the Latin word for "sharpness" should be borrowed. *Acuere,* in Latin, means "to sharpen," and *acumen* means "sharpness." English borrowed *acumen* and used it figuratively for sharpness of the mind.

Reprinted by permission. From *Picturesque Word Origins* © 1933 by G. & C. Merriam Co. (now Merriam-Webster, Incorporated).

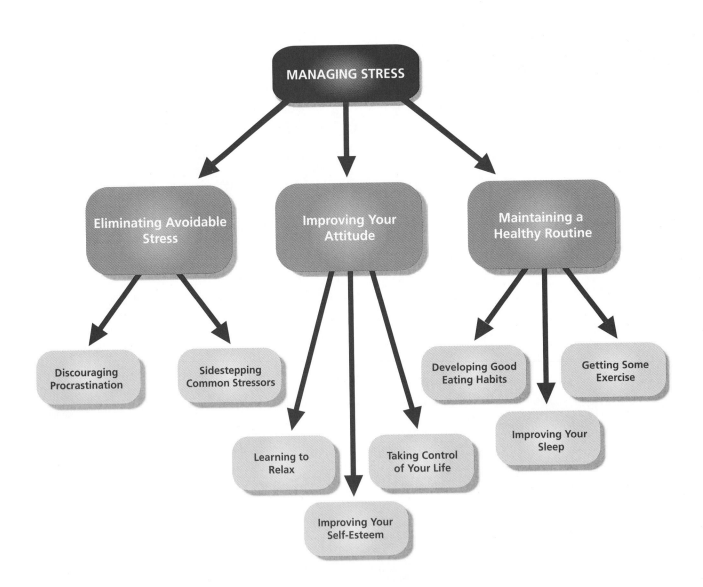

Managing Stress

*Life is a journey,
not a guided tour.*

Anonymous

Stress, writes Dr. Hans Selye, a pioneer in its study, is "the spice of life or the kiss of death—depending on how we cope with it."[1] Unfortunately, most of us cope with it poorly. We worry too much, criticize too much, get angry too often, and become too tense. But if you can learn to deflect the stress that comes your way, you can thrive as a student and as a human being. This chapter helps you manage stress by focusing on:

- **Eliminating Avoidable Stress**
- **Improving Your Attitude**
- **Following a Healthy Routine**

[1]Hans Selye, "How to Master Stress," *Parents* 52 (November 1977): 25.

When can stress be a good thing?

Mere mention of the word *stress* is enough to make most people anxious. It brings to mind images of frayed nerves, shortened tempers, and rising blood pressure. But being under stress isn't always a bad thing. In fact, stress can prompt us to respond effectively to a tough situation, to rise to the occasion when a paper comes due or a test is handed out. According to Marilyn Gist, a professor at the School of Business Administration of the University of Washington, "A certain amount of stress is healthy and beneficial; it stimulates some to perform, makes them excited and enthusiastic."[2]

What is the medical definition of stress?

"Stress," according to Dr. Hans Selye, "is the nonspecific response of the body to any demand made upon it."[3] In other words, it is the body's attempt to adjust to a demand, regardless of what the demand may be. You undergo stress when you run or walk at a brisk pace. Your body responds to the demand for more oxygen by increasing your breathing and causing your heart to beat faster. Yet most people view exercise not as a source of stress, but as a means of stress relief. Likewise, watching a quiz show or doing a crossword puzzle can be considered stressful. In each case, the brain responds with increased mental activity. Yet most people undertake these activities specifically for relaxation.

What makes stress a problem?

The problem is that we don't always respond to the sources of stress (known as *stressors*) in a positive fashion. If instead of running for exercise, you're racing to catch a bus, or instead of solving a crossword puzzle, you're struggling with a math test that you didn't study for, your reaction is apt to be quite different. Rather than experiencing the exhilaration of exercising or the stimulation of solving a puzzle, you may wind up feeling exhausted or intimidated.

How can we better manage stress?

That's the two-sided potential of stress. Instead of compelling us to rise to the occasion, stress can sometimes plunge us into a sea of anxiety, worry, hostility, or despair. The way we respond to stress, whether we use it as a boon or a burden, depends on two major factors: our overall approach to life, and the number of stressors we face at any one time. To better manage the stress in your life, it helps to eliminate the avoidable sources of stress, improve your overall attitude, and maintain a healthy routine.

Eliminating Avoidable Stress

What can you do to eliminate avoidable stress?

Not all stress is unavoidable, of course. But a lot of it is. You can work to eliminate needless stress by discouraging procrastination and by sidestepping some of the other common sources of stress.

[2]Quoted in Pam Miller Withers, "Good Stress/Bad Stress: How to Use One, Lose the Other," *Working Woman* (September 1989): 124.

[3]Hans Selye, *Stress Without Distress* (New York: J. B. Lippincott, 1974), p. 27.

PEANUTS reprinted by permission
of United Features Syndicate, Inc.

Discouraging Procrastination

How can you avoid
procrastination?

"Nothing [is] so fatiguing as the eternal hanging on of an uncompleted task."[4] These words of William James, distinguished American psychologist, strike at the hearts of us all. Everyone has had bouts with procrastination. The best way to avoid future ones is to learn why people procrastinate and what you can do to prevent procrastination.

Learn Why You Procrastinate

What are the common sources
of procrastination?

There's no single explanation for why people procrastinate. Nevertheless, many of the stressors already discussed in this chapter can trigger procrastination. Here's a list of common sources:

How does fear of failure
prompt procrastination?

Fear of failure.   Many students hesitate to begin a task because they're afraid they won't be able to complete it successfully. Have some faith in yourself. Think back to past successes, and realize that if you've achieved success before, you can achieve it again. If you've failed in similar situations in the past, think of times when you've succeeded in other areas and apply the confidence you gained then to the present.

Why would fear of success
make you put things off?

Fear of success.   Some students put tasks off because they are afraid of succeeding. A person might be afraid of success for at least two reasons. First, successful people are a minority. There is a kind of loneliness in success. Some students unconsciously procrastinate because they don't want to be resented by people who aren't as successful. Second, success brings responsibility and choices. When a person succeeds, doors suddenly open. That should be good news, but some students view these opportunities as threats and burdens instead of challenges and choices. The solution involves a shift in attitude—to embrace success instead of fleeing from it.

[4]Criswell Freeman, ed. *Wisdom Made in America* (Nashville, TN: Walnut Grove Press, 1995), p. 97.

Online Study Center   www.college.hmco.com/pic/pauk9e

What's at the heart of the problem of lack of time as a cause of procrastination?

Lack of time. If you used all the time you've been spending worrying about the time you don't have, you'd be well on your way to completing the task you've been putting off. This is a problem of control. Realize that how you budget your time is up to you (see Chapter 2). If you feel in control, you'll find it easier to complete the jobs that need to be done.

Why does poor organization sometimes lead to procrastination?

Poor organization. Perhaps you begin each day determined to get started on that task you've been putting off. But when nighttime comes, you find that despite your best intentions, you didn't get around to it. If that's your trouble, the cause may be a lack of priorities and/or poor organization. Draw up a to do list and use the urgency-importance matrix (explained in Chapter 2) to help you put your priorities in perspective.

Devise Ways to Prevent Procrastination

Although the roots of procrastination are varied, the following methods of preventing procrastination should work regardless of the cause:

With so many sources of procrastination, what's the solution?
How does publicizing your plans discourage procrastination?

Make your plans a part of the public record. When you have a job that has to be completed or a goal that you want to reach, write it down. Or announce your intentions to close friends or family members. For example, "I plan to finish the bibliography for my research paper this weekend." Once you've made your intentions official, you're less likely to put them off. Procrastinators commonly fall into the habit of deceiving themselves, but they are less likely to deceive the people around them.

How do progress checks keep procrastination from getting out of hand?

Step back and check your progress from time to time. One way many people procrastinate is by getting needlessly entangled in the details of their work. If, as you're working, you periodically step back and measure your progress, it will be easier to tell if you've gotten unnecessarily bogged down. If you discover that you have, you should be able to pick up your pace so you can reach your goal in the allotted time.

What is the five-minute plan?

Use the five-minute plan. William J. Knaus, author of *Do It Now: How to Stop Procrastinating*, recommends what he calls the "five-minute plan."[5] Tackle a long-neglected task by agreeing to work on it for only five minutes. When the five minutes are up, decide whether you want to keep going. You usually will. The hardest part of almost any job is getting started. The five-minute plan takes the sting out of that painful first step.

[5]Quoted in Emrika Padus, *The Complete Guide to Your Emotions and Your Health* (Emmaus, PA: Rodale Press, 1986), p. 393.

How can you use momentum to halt the progress of procrastination?

Let your momentum work for you. If you've successfully completed a task that you were eager to finish, let your momentum carry over to an activity that you aren't as enthused about. Your extra energy can help you get started on the dreaded task, and once you've begun (the hardest part), completion will become much easier.

Why is a timer more effective than a watch for beating procrastination?

Use a timer instead of a watch. Clock-watching is a time-honored technique of perpetual procrastinators. If you want to keep to a schedule but avoid disrupting your concentration by constantly checking your watch or clock, use a timer instead. Many watches come with them. If your watch doesn't have one, an ordinary kitchen timer should do.

How can being specific prevent you from putting things off?

Be specific. A task is almost always more intimidating and stressful when it looms large and undefined. Instead of constantly telling yourself, "I've got to start writing that research paper," zero in on a specific aspect of your paper, such as choosing the topic or compiling a working bibliography. Suddenly your goal becomes more concrete, more doable, and thus much easier to complete. Or as James R. Sherman, author of *Stop Procrastinating*, puts it, "A job well defined is a job half done."[6]

What happens when you verbalize your reasons for procrastination?

Verbalize your excuses. You may think you've got perfectly good reasons for putting off what needs to be done. If you let your excuses see the light of day by writing them out or explaining them to a friend, you'll often find that your reasoning isn't nearly as logical as you'd thought.

How does imagining success fight procrastination?

Visualize success or completion. Take a moment to imagine yourself accomplishing a task, passing a test, or achieving a goal. Through visualizing, you chart a course in your mind's eye. That course gives you a tangible game plan. The positive outcome you've imagined provides an incentive to follow that course until you reach the point of completion.

Sidestepping Common Stressors

What are some other tips for sidestepping stress?

Although procrastination may be one of the more avoidable causes of stress, there are several other minor sources that can be sidestepped relatively easily. Here are some suggestions for doing so:

[6]James R. Sherman, *Stop Procrastinating* (Los Altos, CA: Crisp Publications, 1989), p. 38.

Online Study Center www.college.hmco.com/pic/pauk9e

Wake up a half-hour earlier.   If you find yourself skipping breakfast or taking your last bite just as you race out the door, you're starting your day on a stressful note. Although getting an adequate amount of sleep is crucial, waking up a half-hour earlier than usual won't significantly affect your sleeping habits but can do wonders to ease the pace of your morning preparations.

Allow yourself plenty of travel time.   High-strung travelers are easily aggravated by slow drivers or long traffic lights. But slow drivers and long lights are facts of every commute. Factor them into your travel time.

Never wait empty-handed.   The stress that comes from standing in line or waiting in traffic stems from boredom and from irritation about wasting time. Both problems have the same easy solution: Have a book to read or some notes to review the next time you're kept waiting, and the time will fly by. Simply listening to the radio while waiting may be relaxing for some, but in general it won't provide the same sense of accomplishment.

Eat dinner early.   If you eat at a college dining hall, it's usually wise to get there early. The trivial but real stress that comes from waiting in line, searching for a seat, or racing to get a second helping before the kitchen closes can be eliminated if you show up soon after the dining hall opens. Whether you eat your meals at home or at school, an early dinner gives you more time before bed to be productive.

Don't take your work to bed with you.   Your bed is for relaxation. Don't mix your mind's signals by turning it into an auxiliary workspace. If you establish a clear boundary between where you work and where you sleep, your work will become more productive, and your sleep will be more restful. And both activities will tend to improve your approach to life's stressors.

Stay calm, cool, and in queue.   Try this Buddhist "loving kindness" meditation to help maintain a positive attitude while waiting in ticket or baggage lines. Take a few deep breaths and say these words slowly and silently several times: "May I be peaceful. May I be happy. May I be free from harm." Then say this blessing for each person in line one by one: "May you be peaceful," and so on. By the time you've reached the front of the line, you'll likely feel more generous and forgiving.[7]

---

[7]Andrew Weil, "A Healthier Way to Fly," *Self Healing* (August 2000).

Improving Your Attitude

What did James, Lange, and Peale suggest about attitude?

Although you can't turn away disaster simply by keeping a smile on your face, there are now abundant indications that your overall attitude can have a powerful influence on the outcome of potentially upsetting or stressful situations. The first evidence was offered near the end of the nineteenth century, when American philosopher and psychologist William James and Danish psychologist Carl Lange simultaneously developed a remarkable theory of emotion. You don't cry because you're sad, they suggested. You're sad because you cry. This revolutionary reversal of the apparent cause and effect of emotions briefly sent the scientific community into an uproar. As the twentieth century progressed, the controversial proposal, known as the James–Lange theory, was scoffed at by most members of the mainstream scientific community and was advocated instead by "inspirational" writers and speakers such as Dr. Norman Vincent Peale, who championed the virtues of "positive thinking." Now the James–Lange theory has been vindicated, and Peale's ideas, bolstered by recent scientific evidence, have garnered mainstream defenders.

How did one study test the effect of facial expressions?

As part of a study conducted by Paul Ekman, Robert W. Levenson, and Wallace V. Friesen at the department of psychiatry of the University of California, San Francisco, subjects were given specific instructions for contracting various facial muscles to imitate six basic emotions: happiness, sadness, disgust, surprise, anger, and fear.[8] Instead of being told, for example, to "look scared," the subject was instructed to "raise your brows and pull them together, now raise your upper eyelids and stretch your lips horizontally, back toward your ears."[9] Expressions were held for ten seconds, while electronic instruments measured the subjects' physiological responses.

What effect did the facial expressions have on the subjects' bodies?

The results were fascinating. Simply imitating an emotional expression was enough to trigger the physiological changes normally associated with that emotion. The most interesting contrast was between expressions for anger and for happiness. The average subject's heart rate and skin temperature increased more with anger than they did with happiness. Yet the subjects weren't truly angry or happy: They were just imitating the expressions associated with the two emotions.

How can you improve your attitude?

We can conclude from this study that simply putting on a happy face may make you feel happier and that taking a dim or overly pessimistic view can lead to the discouraging outcome you expected. But managing stress shouldn't simply

[8]Paul Ekman, Robert W. Levenson, and Wallace V. Friesen, "Autonomic Nervous System Activity Distinguishes Among Emotions," *Science* 221 (1983): 1208–1210.

[9]Ibid., p. 1208.

Online Study Center www.college.hmco.com/pic/pauk9e

be a fuzzy-headed smile-at-all-your-troubles strategy. Improving your attitude should be done systematically by learning to relax, by improving your self-esteem, and, above all, by *taking control of your life.*

Learning to Relax

What does *relaxation* mean?

The regular use of relaxation techniques, according to studies at the Mind/Body Medical Institute of Harvard Medical School, reduces stress and the prevalence of stress-related illness.[10] But many of us don't consider using such techniques because we misinterpret what the word *relaxation* means. Relaxation doesn't necessarily mean that you're about to fall asleep. In fact, some World War II pilots used relaxation techniques not to prepare themselves for sleep or to "take it easy," but to stay alert and avoid fatigue during bombing missions.[11]

What effect does relaxation have on your muscles?

Nor is relaxation a synonym for lethargy. "Relaxation," wrote psychologists Edward A. Charlesworth and Ronald G. Nathan in *Stress Management*, "simply means doing nothing with your muscles."[12] Relaxation is relief from wasted effort or strain, an absence of tension. Indeed, explains author Emrika Padus, "Tenseness wastes energy; tenseness causes anxiety. . . . The best performances come when the mind and body are *floating,* enjoying the activity just as we did when we were young children, completely absorbed in the experience and unaware of any consequences of the actions. This is true relaxation."[13]

What techniques can you use to encourage relaxation?

There's nothing mystical about relaxation. Two simple techniques—breathing deeply, and using progressive relaxation—can help you get the hang of this life-sustaining practice.

Breathe Deeply

What is the connection between the way you breathe and how you feel?

There is a strong connection between the way you breathe and the way you feel. When you're relaxed, your breaths are long and deep, originating from your abdomen. When you're anxious, your breathing is often short and shallow, originating from high in your chest.

What have experiments shown about the effect of rapid breathing?

The link between breathing and emotion operates in both directions. Just as the way you feel affects the way you breathe, the way you breathe affects the way you feel. A handful of experiments have established this connection. Dr. James Loehr found that when relaxed subjects were asked to take short, rapid, and irregular breaths for two minutes—in other words, to pant—nearly every-

---

[10]Stephanie Wood, "Relax! You've Earned It," *McCall's* 118 (July 1991): 50.

[11]Edward A. Charlesworth and Ronald G. Nathan, *Stress Management* (New York: Atheneum, 1984), p. 41.

[12]Ibid., p. 42.

[13]Padus, *Complete Guide to Your Emotions and Your Health*, p. 490.

one interviewed felt worried, threatened, and panicky.[14] Simply by imitating the response of an anxious person, the subjects had made themselves anxious.

> How can experiments about rapid breathing promote relaxation?

Luckily, this principle can be used to encourage relaxation as well. By breathing slowly, steadily, and deeply and by beginning your breaths in your abdomen instead of up in your chest, you can encourage a feeling of relaxation. So just before an exam, an interview, or a dental appointment, when your palms are sweating, your body is tense, and your breath is short and shallow, try the count-of-three method to induce a more relaxed state. Count slowly and calmly through each step:

> What are the steps in the count-of-three relaxation method?

1. Inhale slowly through your nose while silently counting to three.
2. Hold your breath for the count of three.
3. Exhale slowly through your nose while silently counting to three.
4. With your breath expelled, count to three.
5. Repeat steps 1 to 4 several times. (Once you have the rhythm, you need not continue counting; but maintain the same timing and the same pauses.)

Use Progressive Muscle Relaxation

A big advantage of the count-of-three method is that it can be done inconspicuously almost anywhere, including in an exam room. But if you have some time, a quiet place, and a little privacy, you may want to try progressive muscle relaxation (PMR), a method for systematically tensing and relaxing the major muscles in your body.

> When can you use progressive muscle relaxation?

> What is the history of PMR?

PMR was developed more than seventy-five years ago by Edmund Jacobson, a doctor who saw the connection between tense muscles and a tense mind. PMR works by helping you become aware of the difference between how your muscles feel when they're tensed and how they feel when they're relaxed.

> What are the steps involved in progressive muscle relaxation?

Start PMR by assuming a comfortable position, either sitting or lying down, and by closing your eyes. Make a tight fist with your right hand, and at the same time tense your right forearm. Hold this position for five seconds, feeling the tension in both your hand and arm, and then slowly release that tension, letting it flow out of you as you unclench your fist. Repeat the procedure with your left hand, noting the difference between how this hand feels tensed compared with your right hand and arm, which are now relaxed. Continue by separately tensing your shoulder muscles, your neck, and the muscles in your face. Then start with your feet and toes, moving up each leg; finish by tensing the muscles in your abdomen and chest. Once you've tensed and released every muscle group in your body, take a moment to savor the overall feeling of relaxation. Then open your eyes and end the exercise.

[14]James E. Loehr and Peter J. McLaughlin, with Ed Quillen, *Mentally Tough* (New York: M. Evans and Company, 1986), pp. 141–142.

Online Study Center   www.college.hmco.com/pic/pauk9e

Improving Your Self-Esteem

What is self-esteem?

Self-esteem is your personal assessment of your own value. Unfortunately, many of us are our own toughest critics. We overlook our positive attributes and forget our successes, emphasizing our shortcomings instead and providing ourselves with a silent but constant stream of discouraging dialogue. The stress that results from this inner discouragement is far worse than criticism from a nagging parent, an insulting instructor, or an overly demanding boss.

What can you do to improve your self-esteem?

A healthy level of self-esteem is crucial to keeping stress at bay. If your self-esteem needs improvement, rewrite the potentially destructive inner dialogue that haunts you throughout the day and take some time to dwell on your successes.

Rewrite Your Inner Dialogue

What's the first step in rewriting your inner dialogue?

You can't rewrite your inner dialogue unless you've seen the script. So, the first step in eliminating the destructive thoughts that undermine your self-esteem is to become aware of them.

YOUR Q

Most of us talk silently to ourselves almost continually. Psychologists commonly refer to this inner conversation as *self-talk*. Although you may have learned to ignore the sound of your self-talk, the effect it has on your overall attitude can still be damaging. So when you enter a new situation or are faced with a difficult challenge, take a moment to express your apprehensions to yourself. Then listen to your self-talk. Whenever you have a negative thought, counteract it with a positive one. Remember that the thoughts you have are your own and are under your control. You can open the door of your mind to whatever thoughts you want. Admit only the positive ones, and leave the negative ones out in the cold.

Build on Your Success

How do you build on your past success?

All of us have experienced success at one time or another. When you feel your self-esteem slipping, remember when you did a job you were proud of, when you overcame an obstacle in spite of the odds, or when everything seemed to go smoothly. It helps to congratulate yourself from time to time, to put yourself in an achieving frame of mind so that you can achieve success again.

Taking Control of Your Life

How does self-esteem relate to your sense of control?

One of the results of increased self-esteem is an increased sense of control, a quality that both medical doctors and psychologists are finding can have a measurable effect on your physical well-being and state of mind. According to the *Wellness Letter* from the University of California, Berkeley, "A sense of control may, in fact, be a critical factor in maintaining health."[15] When you're in control, you act; you set your own agenda instead of reacting to the wishes or whims of others or resigning yourself to what we often call "fate."

Appreciate the Significance of Control

How did Norman Cousins use control to change his life?

In the early 1960s writer and magazine editor Norman Cousins was stricken with a painful life-threatening illness. Determined not to let the illness control his life and sentence him to death, Cousins fought back. He watched movie comedies, one after another. The laughter the films elicited made the sleep that had eluded him come more easily and ultimately reversed the crippling illness.[16] In fact, the results so impressed the medical community that Cousins, who had no medical background, was awarded an honorary degree in medicine by the Yale University School of Medicine and was appointed adjunct professor in the School of Medicine at the University of California, Los Angeles.

What quality do many survivors of stress share?

Norman Cousins is not the only person who has demonstrated the importance of a sense of control. Author Richard Logan investigated the lives of people who were able to survive extreme stress—such as imprisonment in a concentration camp—and found that they all had at least one quality in common: a belief that their destiny was in their own hands. In other words, they had a sense of control.[17]

What did one experiment show about the relationship between control and the hormone cortisone?

The importance of control was reinforced in a study that provided a physiological insight into the phenomenon. When your body is under stress, your adrenal glands release *cortisone*, a hormone that in small doses can fight allergies and disease but that in larger amounts can impair the body's ability to fight back. When the two groups of employees who made up the study worked almost to the point of exhaustion, only one group experienced a significant increase in cortisone production. Those employees with high levels of cortisone had jobs that allowed them very little control. Employees who experienced no increase in cortisone held positions with a high level of control.[18]

What are the long-term effects of lack of control?

Lack of control can result in a sense of helplessness almost guaranteed to bring about the frayed nerves, tense muscles, and overall feeling of panic normally associated with short-term stress. If these conditions persist, they can

[15]"Healthy Lives: A New View of Stress," University of California, Berkeley, *Wellness Letter* 6, no. 9 (June 1990): 4.

[16]*Managing Stress—From Morning to Night* (Alexandria, VA: Time-Life Books, 1987), p. 21.

[17]Mihaly Csikszentmihalyi, *Flow: The Psychology of Optimal Experience* (New York: Harper & Row, 1990), p. 203.

[18]Robert M. Bramson, *Coping with the Fast Track Blues* (New York: Doubleday, 1990), p. 217.

How did a button affect the stress level of office workers?

have an adverse effect on your body's immune system, making you more susceptible to illness. Robbed of your sense of control, you not only react instead of acting but also overreact. Turned outward, this overreaction may surface as anger. Turned inward, it can lead to fear, anxiety, and general depression.

In *The Joy of Stress*, Dr. Peter Hanson described an experiment in which two groups of office workers were exposed to a series of loud and distracting background noises. One group had desks equipped with a button that could be pushed at any time to shut out the annoying sounds. The other group had no such button. Not surprisingly, workers with the button were far more productive than those without. But what's remarkable is that no one in the button group actually *pushed* the button. Apparently, the knowledge that they could shut out the noise if they wanted to was enough to enable them to work productively in spite of the distractions. Their sense of control resulted in a reduction in stress and an increase in productivity.[19]

Understand How Attitude Affects Control

As a student, how can you gain a better sense of control?

Dr. Hanson's story of the control button underscores an important element of control: Taking control is primarily a matter of adjusting your attitude. As a student, you can achieve a sense of control by changing the way you view your courses, assignments, and exams.

What can you do to change your attitude about your classes and assignments?

Taking control of your classes and assignments means viewing them as choices instead of obligations. The stressed-out, overwhelmed student looks to the next lecture or reading assignment with dread. The student who feels in control (and feels confident as a result) understands that attending lectures and completing assignments are a matter of choice and that the benefits derived from both are not only practical but also enjoyable. According to psychologist Mihaly Csikszentmihalyi, "Of all the virtues we can learn, no trait is more useful, more essential for survival and more likely to improve the quality of life than the ability to transform adversity into an enjoyable challenge."[20]

Learn to Cope with Out-of-Control Circumstances

What's a good way to cope with out-of-control circumstances?

Clearly, a great many situations in life are out of your control. But even in unavoidable or unpredictable situations, you can still exercise some degree of influence. Psychologists have found that as your coping resources increase (both in number and variety), so does your sense of control. Thus, a person with multiple coping strategies, instead of just one plan, is better able to adapt to the inevitable surprises that can accompany almost any undertaking.

[19]Peter Hanson, *The Joy of Stress* (New York: McMeel & Parker, 1985), pp. 15–16.
[20]Csikszentmihalyi, *Flow*, p. 200.

How can you increase your sense of control over an upcoming exam?

For example, you have no control over whether an upcoming exam will be made up of essay or multiple-choice questions. If the instructor doesn't tell you which type it will be, you can increase your coping resources by preparing for both types of questions. Then, regardless of the type the instructor chooses, you will be ready. You will have a feeling of control.

How can you apply a sense of control to mundane annoyances?

The same strategy can be applied to a number of mundane situations that often generate unwanted stress. An unexpected line at the bank or the grocery store can leave you feeling helpless and anxious. You can't make the line disappear or move more quickly, but you can control the situation by reading a book or reviewing a set of vocabulary cards while you wait. As you can see, even a small degree of control can be used to minimize a large amount of stress.

Following a Healthy Routine

What can you do to your physical self to minimize the effects of stress?

Stress isn't all in your head. It has a noticeable effect on your body and can often be avoided through changes in your physical routine. If you make a concerted effort to improve your sleep, develop good eating habits, and get some exercise, you'll make yourself more stress-resistant and decrease your chances of being subjected to stress in the first place.

Developing Good Eating Habits

How are stress and eating interconnected?

Stress may harm your immune system, and eating well can restore it. But that connection doesn't stop there. There is a destructive, cyclical nature involving stress and eating that you want to work hard to avoid. If you develop poor eating habits, the negative effect on your body may make you more susceptible to stress. And there's ample evidence that a by-product of stress is poor eating habits. Because stress is so demanding, your body needs extra energy to address it. According to Dr. Robert Sapolsky, we expend between 10 and 23 percent of our energy on digestion.[21] It's not surprising, then, that when your body undergoes stress it often robs energy from the digestive process. In response to stress, corticotropin releasing factor (CRF) shuts down your digestion. This accounts not only for the lack of appetite, but also for the dry mouth that many of us experience in a stressful situation. But stress also triggers glucocorticoids, which enter your bloodstream at a slower pace. Whereas CRF depresses your appetite, glucocorticoids actually stimulate it and, according to Sapolsky, serve as the means for recovering from the stress response.[22]

[21]Robert M. Sapolsky, *Why Zebras Don't Get Ulcers* (New York: W. H. Freeman, 1998), p. 64.
[22]Ibid., p. 78.

 **Online Study Center** www.college.hmco.com/pic/pauk9e

How does the length of the stress affect your appetite? How can you break the cycle of stress and bad eating habits?

"Thus, lots of short stressful events should lead to overeating," Dr. Sapolsky explains, "while one long, continuous stressor should lead to appetite loss."[23]

If you're overfed or undernourished, you may be putting an extra strain on your body that could be resulting in stress. And with that, the cycle continues. The way to break this vicious cycle is by taking time out for meals, rather than letting stress dictate whether you eat, and by eating in a way that counteracts stress instead of contributing to it.

Take Time Out for Meals

How do erratic meal schedules affect stress?

Stress can diminish or deplete certain vitamin and mineral supplies. An erratic meal schedule can aggravate this problem. According to nutritionist Jane Brody:

> Millions of Americans have fallen into a pattern of too-late-for-breakfast, grab-something-for-lunch, eat-a-big-dinner, and nibble-nonstop-until-bedtime. They starve their bodies when they most need fuel and stuff them when they'll be doing nothing more strenuous than channel-surfing or flipping through pages of a magazine. When you think about it, the pattern makes no biological sense.[24]

What's the best way to restore a sensible eating routine?

The simplest way to put some sense back into your eating routine is by beginning each day with breakfast. Breakfast stokes your body's furnace so you have energy to burn for the rest of the day. Lunch and dinner simply throw a few coals on the fire; breakfast gets that fire burning.

What are some other nonnutritional benefits of meals?

Meals not only provide needed nutrients; they also supply you with a necessary break from the stresses of school or work. Here are some stress-relieving suggestions for mealtime:

Why is it a bad idea to work while you eat?

Don't work as you eat.   Time will have been wasted, and you won't have gained the break you deserved when you sat down to eat. As a result, you'll probably feel more stressed than you were before you ate.

What is the difference between eating quickly and rushing your meal?

Eat quickly, but don't rush.   There's a difference. If you have a lot of work to do, you won't have time for a leisurely lunch. But if you keep one eye on your sandwich and the other on the clock, you'll increase your chances of getting indigestion and stress without significantly speeding up your meal.

Eat the Right Foods

What are the drawbacks of the USDA's food pyramids?

More than a decade ago, the U.S. Department of Agriculture (USDA) unveiled the Food Guide Pyramid, which was designed to provide consumers with easy-to-follow nutritional guidelines. Unfortunately, in an effort to keep things sim-

---

[23]Ibid., p. 79.

[24]Jane E. Brody, *Jane Brody's Good Food Book* (New York: W. W. Norton, 1985), p. 187.

ple, the USDA created considerable confusion. For example, people who saw the pyramid or read the recommendations were likely to conclude that fat is bad and that complex carbohydrates are good. That's only partially true. Not all fats are bad, and not all complex carbohydrates are good. In 2005, the USDA replaced its Food Guide Pyramid with a multicolored diagram called MyPyramid. Although the new pyramid looks good and has corrected some of the flaws of its predecessor, it lacks the kind of specifics that many consumers require to make sensible food choices. Between the demise of the Food Guide Pyramid and the arrival of MyPyramid, two professors at the prestigious Harvard Medical School, Walter C. Willett and Meir J. Stampfer, set out to clarify and refine the USDA recommendations.[25]

What is the simple math behind calorie consumption?	**Curb Your Consumption of Calories** Strictly speaking, fat doesn't make you fat. Calories do. The confusion lies in the fact that there are more calories in a gram of fat than in the same amount of protein or carbohydrate. Thus, some people overcompensate by avoiding fats and piling up calories from proteins and carbohydrates instead. Ultimately, it's a matter of simple math. If you consume more calories than you use up, you will gain weight. If you burn up more than you consume, you will have a "caloric deficit" and will lose weight as a result. Over the past few decades there has been an alarming rise in the incidence of obesity in the United States. Not everyone is destined to be as skinny as a rail. Nor should they be. But if you're above or below your natural weight, you may be putting extra stress on your body. The way to control that weight is by watching your calories.[26]

What are the drawbacks of butter, red meat, and refined carbohydrates?

Avoid Butter, Red Meat, and Refined Carbohydrates   Just because fats can't be entirely blamed for obesity doesn't mean that some of them don't have faults. The old pyramid treated all fats as bad in order to discourage people from eating those that are bad. The "bad fats" are saturated fats, most commonly found in butter and red meat. It's their content, not their calories, that causes trouble. Saturated fats are high in low-density lipoprotein (LDL), also known as "bad cholesterol" and associated with an increased risk of heart disease. Refined carbohydrates, such as white rice, white bread, sugar, and even potatoes, have an indirect link to cholesterol that is potentially troubling. Because these carbohydrates break down so quickly, they can spark a rapid rise in both glucose (blood sugar) and insulin, the hormone designed to keep glucose in check.[27] According to Willett and Stampfer, "High levels of glucose and insulin can have

[25]Walter C. Willett and Meir J. Stampfer, "Rebuilding the Food Pyramid," *Scientific American* (January 2003).

[26]Ibid.

[27]Ibid.

negative effects on cardiovascular health."[28] In addition, there's evidence that the sudden drop in glucose that results when insulin washes it away can make you feel hungrier faster, thus prompting you to eat more than you need.[29]

Emphasize Healthy Fats and Whole-Grain Foods   The big losers in the previous pyramid were probably unsaturated fats, which got unfairly swept up in the "fat is bad" barrage. As it turns out, polyunsaturated fats (found in fish and flax seeds) and monounsaturated fats (found in nuts, olive oil, and other vegetable oils) are actually quite good for you. Unlike eating their saturated siblings, consuming these fats can result in a reduced risk of heart disease.[30] Similarly, the whole grains you find in brown rice, whole-wheat flours, and a handful of other whole foods are far superior to the stripped-down, fast-acting refined version of these same foods. For one, they take longer to metabolize and thus do not trigger potentially damaging glucose and insulin spikes. In addition, they hold on to the valuable vitamins and nutrients that are normally removed when carbohydrates are refined.

What are the advantages of fruits and vegetables?

Eat Lots of Fruits and Vegetables   Despite the heated disagreements between nutritionists on a wide variety of topics, very few have anything bad to say about fruits and vegetables. High in fiber, high in vitamins, and low in the sort of "gotchas" that seem to dog almost every other type of food, fruits and vegetables may well be the most beneficial foods to eat in abundance.

What is so important about water?

Drink Plenty of Water   Our world and our bodies are primarily made up of water. Second only to air as the source of our survival, water is the medium for every bodily process and the primary means by which toxins are expelled. It is absolutely essential to remain properly hydrated. Depending on your size, age, and body weight, doctors generally recommend consuming at least six to eight 8-ounce glasses of water per day.[31]

Why can't other beverages be used as a substitute for water

Don't mistakenly assume that you are meeting your body's need for fluids by consuming liquids other than water, such as coffee, tea, alcohol, or soft drinks. Many of these beverages contain harmful ingredients that offset or undermine plain water's beneficial effect. Among these, the worst offenders are soft drinks, which have become the drink of choice in the United States. In 2001 Americans consumed more than fifty gallons of soft drinks per person per year and

[28]Ibid.

[29]Ibid.

[30]Ibid.

[31]Dr. Fereydoon Batmanghelidj, *Global Health Discoveries* 5, no. 1: 4.

only forty gallons of water.[32] What's more, a typical 12-ounce can or bottle of soda is sweetened by a whopping ten teaspoonfuls of sugar,[33] empty calories that are almost certainly contributing to the epidemic of obesity in this country. Making matters worse, tests done in 2006 on soft drinks in Britain and France found that they contained dangerous levels of benzene, a compound known to cause cancer.[34] If you're congratulating yourself for drinking diet soda instead, not so fast. Common artificial sweeteners can actually increase your appetite for sugar and carbohydrates and may be metabolizing into dangerous carcinogens![35] All these ominous findings reaffirm that clean, cool, fresh water is best.

Improving Your Sleep

Are most of us getting enough sleep?

If your morning starts with the sound of an alarm clock, you're probably not getting the sleep you need. According to Dr. Wilse Webb, a psychologist at the University of Florida, Gainesville, "If that's how you wake up every day, you're shortening your natural sleep pattern."[36] And yet an alarm clock is a part of most people's lives. Does that mean all of us are cheating ourselves on sleep? Perhaps not all, but most Americans are getting less sleep than they need. In fact, according to an article in the *New York Times*, "Sleep scientists insist that there is virtually an epidemic of sleepiness in the nation."[37]

What are the dangers of sleep loss?

The image of a nation filled with semiconscious citizens may seem comical, but in reality the effects of widespread sleep deprivation are seldom humorous and sometimes deadly. The U.S. Department of Transportation estimates that up to 200,000 traffic accidents each year are sleep related.[38] Furthermore, the worst nuclear power emergency in this country's history, at Three Mile Island, occurred at night, when workers were most susceptible to the effects of insufficient sleep.[39]

[32]Wine Institute, *Wine and Other Beverage Consumption in America*, available at http://www.beekmenwine.com/prevtopat.htm.

[33]Donald S. McAlvany, *The McAlvany Health Alert*, 2, Issue 4 (April 2002).

[34]Rajeev Syal, "Soft Drinks Found to Have High Levels of Cancer Chemical," *London Times* (March 2, 2006), available at http://www.timesonline.co.uk/article/0,,8122-2065539,00.html.

[35]Dr. William Campbell Douglass, "NutraSweet Is Not So Sweet," *Second Opinion* VI, no. 3: 1–4.

[36]Quoted in Natalie Angier, "Cheating on Sleep: Modern Life Turns America into the Land of the Drowsy," *New York Times* (May 15, 1990), pp. C1, C8.

[37]Ibid., p. C1.

[38]Anastasia Toulexis, "Drowsy America," *Time* (December 17, 1990): 80.

[39]Angier, "Cheating on Sleep," p. C8.

Online Study Center   www.college.hmco.com/pic/pauk9e

How does sleep loss affect learning?

Of course, sleep loss isn't usually deadly for students, but it can be damaging. Dr. Charles Czeisler, director of circadian (the daily rhythmic sleep/wake cycle) and sleep disorders medicine at Brigham and Women's Hospital in Boston, outlined some of the penalties that people pay when they get too little sleep: "Short term memory is impaired, the ability to make decisions is impaired, the ability to concentrate is impaired."[40] Clearly, a student who can't remember, can't make decisions, and has trouble concentrating will have a tough time surviving in an academic setting. Furthermore, the struggle to overcome the disabilities that sleep loss creates frequently leads to an even more pervasive problem: stress.

What is the connection between weariness and stress?

"Weariness corrodes civility and erases humor," reads an article in *Time* magazine. "Without sufficient sleep, tempers flare faster and hotter at the slightest offense."[41] The day-to-day challenges and inconveniences of going to school and of living in the modern world are potentially stress inducing. Add habitual sleep loss, and you turn a chronic problem into an acute one. Dr. Ernest Hartmann's study of "variable sleepers" (patients whose sleep and wake-up times are not consistent) revealed that people under stress tend to need more sleep than do those who lead lives relatively free of anxiety and change. Yet stress often triggers insomnia, which leads to less sleep and the possibility of even more stress.[42] The results can be a vicious circle of stress and sleeplessness.

How do you break the circle of stress and sleeplessness?

You can work to break this circle by getting the right amount of sleep, by following a regular sleep schedule, by avoiding naps, and by taking steps to improve the quality of your sleep.

Get the Right Amount of Sleep

Are you getting enough sleep? In general, your overall alertness provides a pretty good indicator. If you are getting the right amount of sleep, you should be able to stay awake through twenty minutes of darkness at midday. Students in art history and film courses, where slides or movies are commonly shown, often complain that a darkened auditorium or classroom makes them sleepy. These situations don't create sleepiness. They simply reveal a problem of insufficient sleep and should serve as a warning to get more rest. Sleep behavior experts tell us that, on average, most people fall short of their needed amount of sleep by sixty to ninety minutes each night.[43] Aggravating this daily deficit is

---

[40]Quoted in ibid.

[41]Toulexis, "Drowsy America," p. 80.

[42]Lynne Lamberg, *The American Medical Association (Straight-Talk, No-Nonsense) Guide to Better Sleep*, rev. ed. (New York: Random House, 1984), p. 35.

[43]Angier, "Cheating on Sleep," p. C1.

Can you make up for lost sleep on the weekends?

the fact that sleep loss is cumulative; it adds up. If you feel tired on Monday morning, you're apt to feel even more so when Friday rolls around.[44]

Although sleep loss adds up, sleep does not. You can't stash away extra hours of sleep like money in the bank. You need to get sufficient sleep seven nights a week. Just as so-called weekend athletes engage in strenuous exercise only on Saturday and Sunday and thereby jeopardize their hearts and their overall health in their effort to "stay fit," people who "sleep in" on weekends don't eliminate the effects of a week of sleep deprivation. In fact, they complicate the problem by disturbing their rhythm of sleeping and waking.

Keep to a Schedule

What effect do circadian rhythms have on sleep?

Achieving full alertness isn't simply a matter of getting enough sleep. It's equally important to do your sleeping at the right time of day. Thanks to *circadian rhythms*, the body's natural pattern of wakefulness and sleep, when morning arrives you instinctively become more alert in anticipation of the day that lies ahead. With the advent of evening, signals in your brain begin preparing you for needed sleep. You go to sleep, and when you wake up the process is repeated.

How can you take advantage of circadian rhythms?

The way to make the most of these circadian rhythms is to maintain a regular sleep/wake schedule. Sleeping late on the weekends or going to bed at widely varying times throws your circadian rhythms out of whack. You find yourself feeling drowsy when you should be alert and wide-awake when you should be fast asleep.[45] If you consistently rise at the same time regardless of when you went to bed, you'll keep your circadian rhythms in tempo.[46] Furthermore, an unwavering wake-up time should help discourage you from staying up too late.

Recognize the Truth About Naps

What are the drawbacks of taking naps?

Students and others who have flexible schedules often see naps as the solution to sleep deprivation. Unfortunately, naps fall far short of their reputation and actually create a number of problems: They're impractical; they adversely affect learning; they harm both sound sleep and the sleep cycle; and they act as a convenient excuse for chronic procrastinators.

What do you lose by taking a nap?

In addition, naps generally deprive you of two of sleep's more important components: dream, or rapid eye movement (REM), sleep, the period in which all our dreaming occurs; and deep sleep (also called *delta sleep*), which many sleep experts believe recharges our batteries and increases our overall alertness.[47]

---

[44]Ibid., p. C8.

[45]Richard M. Coleman, *Wide Awake at 3:00 a.m.* (New York: W. H. Freeman, 1986), p. 149.

[46]Robert K. Cooper, *The Performance Edge* (Boston: Houghton Mifflin, 1991), p. 222.

[47]Dianne Hales, *The Complete Book of Sleep* (Menlo Park, CA: Addison-Wesley, 1981), p. 18.

Therefore, if you take a nap, you may be adding to the quantity of your sleep but you will probably be lacking the dream and deep sleep your body requires. According to Dr. William Douglass, "There is no doubt that this deep sleep is essential to health. Muramyl peptides, which are vital to tissue renewal and immune enhancement, are only released during deep, slow-wave sleep."[48]

How do naps interfere with your sleep/wake cycle?

As you might expect, naps also interfere with your sleep/wake cycle. Unless you take a nap every day at the same time and for the same duration, you will probably wind up with stay-at-home jet lag and have difficulty falling asleep at night.

What is the connection between naps and procrastination?

Finally, the temptation to misuse naps can be great. Many students give in to the urge to sleep, rationalizing that when they awaken they will feel refreshed and perform more productively. Unfortunately, few students report this happy result. The harsh reality is that if you try to escape a mountain of work by taking a nap, you will wake up to face the same amount of work, and you'll have less time in which to do it. It is far better to combat the desire to sleep, get the work done, and go to bed at your usual time with a clear conscience. You'll get the sleep you need; you'll minimize disruptions to your body's circadian rhythms; you'll feel healthier and more alert; and you'll be less susceptible to the potentially corrosive effects of stress.

Take Solid Steps for Better Sleeping

What are the advantages of optimal sleep?

Optimal sleep promotes not only a more alert, energetic, zestful life but also, according to some studies, a longer life. If you're not concentrating, if you're dozing off in class and at your desk, or if you're feeling dragged out, take steps to put yourself on the right track.

Why is sleeping in a dark room so important?

The right track means deep sleep in a dark room, which activates secretion of melatonin by the pineal gland. According to Dr. Alexander Grant's *Health Gazette*, "Melatonin not only helps us to sleep, but also may help to prevent tumors since it stimulates our tissues to destroy oxidants, chemical pollutants that produce cancer."[49] Also, under these favorable conditions, the pituitary gland releases large quantities of growth hormone into the blood. The hormone travels throughout the body to restore and rebuild body tissue. When you don't give the rebuilding process enough time, you upset the body's processes. For example, in a sleep-deprived state, the rate that the brain metabolizes glucose slows down; thus thinking slows down. Researchers calculate that a sleep-deprived person takes about one hour to do the work that could be done in forty-five minutes during the feeling-good stage.

[48]William Campbell Douglass, M.D., *Second Opinion* 4, no. 12 (December 1994): 7.

[49]*Dr. Alexander Grant's Health Gazette* 18, no. 2 (February 1995).

What other steps can you take to improve sleep?

You can incorporate a few simple practices into your daily life to optimize the quality of your sleep:

Don't use caffeine after 4 p.m.   Caffeine can often result in insomnia and thus throw your sleep/wake schedule off.[50] In addition, laboratory studies show that from 200 to 500 milligrams of caffeine per day may produce headaches, nervousness, and gastrointestinal disturbances, symptoms that can trigger or exacerbate stress. Keep in mind that coffee is not the only substance that contains caffeine. There's also caffeine in tea, some soft drinks, chocolate, and some nonprescription drugs.

Don't drink alcohol after 8 p.m.   Although it has a reputation for making you drowsy, alcohol actually upsets your body's sleep pattern, first by reducing your REM sleep and then by triggering a "REM rebound," which can result in excessive dreaming and/or nightmares.[51]

Reserve your bed for sleeping.   Eating, doing coursework, and even worrying in bed can scramble your body's contextual cues. If your bed becomes a multipurpose area, you may find it more difficult to fall asleep when the time comes.

Exercise!   In addition to the benefits it provides to your heart, muscles, and self-esteem, exercise also enhances both the waking and sleeping phases of your circadian rhythms. Twenty minutes or more of vigorous aerobic exercise will boost your alertness in the daytime and improve the quality of your sleep at night. People who exercise regularly have been found to enjoy more deep sleep than people who don't.[52]

Getting Some Exercise

What does research show about the relationship between exercise and stress?

According to respected American cardiologist Dr. Paul Dudley White, "Vigorous . . . exercise is the best antidote for nervous and emotional stress that we possess."[53] In study after study, experts are corroborating the finding that exercise decreases stress and anxiety. Many other researchers report that regular exercise raises self-esteem and well-being and decreases depression. A study of forty-eight students who had been suffering from test anxiety found that their

[50]Milton K. Erman and Merrill M. Mitler, *How to Get a Good Night's Sleep* (Phillips Publishing, 1990).

[51]Coleman, *Wide Awake at 3:00 a.m.*, p. 124.

[52]Ibid., p. 146.

[53]Quoted in Robert K. Cooper, *Health and Fitness Excellence* (Boston: Houghton Mifflin, 1989), p. 100.

 *Online Study Center*   www.college.hmco.com/pic/pauk9e

Caffeine: A Poor Substitute for Sleep

Caffeine is the most widely used drug in the United States. Many people drink a cup of coffee or a can of caffeinated soda to produce the feeling of alertness normally associated with sound sleep. Ironically, though, caffeine can actually lead to sleepiness.

- Although morning coffee can mean morning alertness, afternoon coffee may cause afternoon blahs.
- Regular use of caffeine reduces its ability to stimulate alertness.
- Large quantities of caffeine can induce behavioral depression, which results in sleepiness and decreased performance.
- Caffeine burns calories (energy) as it stimulates insulin production, leading to a sudden drop in blood sugar and feeling of lethargy.
- Drinking only 250 mg of caffeine can produce symptoms associated with clinical anxiety.

Sources: Richard M. Coleman, *Wide Awake at 3 a.m.* (New York: W. H. Freeman & Co., 1986); Susan Perry and Jim Dawson, *The Secret Our Body Clocks Reveal* (New York: Rawson Associates, 1988); Jere E. Yates, *Managing Stress* (New York: AMACOM, 1979).

anxiety was reduced after meditative relaxation and exercise.[54] In another study, both prisoners and prison guards took part in a carefully monitored exercise program. After a regimen of aerobic exercise, participants on both sides of the law found that they were able to sleep better, that their sense of well-being and self-esteem often improved, and that they experienced less tension and depression.[55]

What effect does exercise have on depression?

The relationship between exercise and depression, one of the most damaging emotional outgrowths of prolonged stress, led psychologist William Morgan, past president of the American Psychological Association's Division of Exercise

[54]Kenneth H. Cooper, *The Aerobics Program for Total Well-Being* (New York: Bantam Books, 1982), p. 186.

[55]Ibid.

and Sport Psychology, to suggest "that running should be viewed as a wonder drug, analogous to penicillin, morphine and the tricyclics [drugs used to treat depression]. It has a profound potential in preventing mental and physical disease and in rehabilitation after various diseases have occurred."[56] And the most effective exercise is that done regularly and aerobically.

Exercise Regularly

What are the advantages of exercising regularly?

You don't have to be an Olympic athlete to reap the benefits of exercise. Exercising three or more times per week is usually enough to improve your overall conditioning, although many students who follow an exercise routine look forward to the time away from their desks and exercise between five and seven times per week. Aside from its well-documented benefits, one of the reasons that exercise is so effective in reducing stress is a simple one. Like eating, sleeping, or any other type of recreation, it provides a welcome break from studying and recharges your mental and physical batteries.

Exercise Aerobically

Why is aerobic exercise especially important?

Although all exercise can provide relief from stress, only aerobic exercise can actually prevent the harmful effects of negative stress. Aerobic exercise is any activity that causes a steady, prolonged increase in your breathing and heart rate. A quick sprint across a football field or a dash from home plate to first base is certainly exercise, but it isn't aerobic exercise. You are inhaling lots of oxygen and speeding up your heart, but you are doing so for only a few seconds, probably not at a steady rate, and definitely not for a prolonged period of time. If, however, you swim twenty-five laps or so, pedal your bike steadily for several miles, or take a brisk thirty-minute walk, you are getting aerobic exercise.

Perhaps the greatest benefit of aerobic exercise is that it lowers your heart rate. Once your heart muscle has been strengthened through exercise, it acts more efficiently, beating fewer times to circulate the same amount of blood. And if anxiety should strike, the increase in the heart rate of an aerobically fit person is not as drastic as it is in someone who gets little or no aerobic exercise. Furthermore, if your heart rate remains comparatively low when subjected to stress, you are less likely to overreact emotionally. The result not only discourages overreaction to stress but also may save your life. A person in poor health who is subjected to unexpected stress can die from the sudden strain the excitement puts on his or her heart.[57]

What are the effects of the hormones that exercise releases?

Exercise provides a perfect example of good stress. It works as a stimulant to release the hormone *norepinephrine*, which promotes enhanced awareness, and

---

[56]Quoted in Keith W. Johnsgård, "Peace of Mind," *Runner's World* 25, no. 4 (April 1990): 81.

[57]Cooper, *The Aerobics Program for Total Well-Being*, p. 189.

endorphins, morphinelike hormones that provide the euphoric feeling commonly referred to as "runner's high." According to Dr. Kenneth Cooper, if you exercise at the end of the day when stress levels are traditionally highest, "you can continue to work or play much later into the evening than might be possible otherwise."[58] Exercise leaves you feeling simultaneously alert and relaxed, a nearly ideal state for efficient, prolonged, and stress-free study.

FINAL WORDS

Why are the stress habits you develop in college so important?

Many students are tempted to write off their college days as a time when anything goes. They eat too much (or too little), drink too much, rob themselves of sleep, and subject their bodies to an extraordinary amount of stress. As removed as college may seem to be from the "real world," the habits you develop in school may well set the tone for the rest of your life. Health doesn't take a holiday simply because you're at school. By all means, work hard and enjoy yourself. But do so in a healthy and sensible way. Keep in mind that you are gaining more than academic expertise while you're in school. You're also learning how to live your life. And in the grand scheme of things, that is the grade that truly matters.

HAVE YOU MISSED SOMETHING?

SENTENCE COMPLETION   *Complete the following sentences with one of the three words listed below each sentence.*

1. Sources of stress are called _____.

   lesions   endorphins   stressors

2. Self-esteem is your personal assessment of your own _____.

   intelligence   value   finances

3. The "bad fats" are _____.

   polyunsaturated   saturated   monounsaturated

MATCHING   *In each blank space in the left column, write the letter preceding the phrase in the right column that matches the left item best.*

_____ 1. Timer   a. Has a silent effect on self-esteem

_____ 2. Panting   b. Developed progressive muscle relaxation

[58]Ibid., p. 191.

_____ 3. Jacobson   c. Illustrates the U.S. government's nutritional guidelines

_____ 4. Cortisone   d. Defined as "doing nothing with your muscles"

_____ 5. Self-talk   e. Released when body undergoes stress

_____ 6. Caloric deficit   f. Tool to counteract clock-watching

_____ 7. Relaxation   g. Has been shown to cause feelings of panic

_____ 8. MyPyramid   h. Necessary for weight loss

TRUE-FALSE

Circle T _beside the_ true _statements and_ F _beside the_ false _statements._

1. T F You can undergo stress when you run or walk at a brisk pace.
2. T F Caffeine is the most widely used drug in the United States.
3. T F Fear of success is one cause of procrastination.
4. T F Some artificial sweeteners may actually increase your appetite for sugar.
5. T F "Sleeping in" should eliminate the effects of sleep deprivation.

MULTIPLE CHOICE

Choose the word or phrase that completes each sentence most accurately, and circle the letter that precedes it.

1. Stress is the body's attempt to adjust to a
   a. crisis.
   b. test.
   c. demand.
   d. situation.

2. One way to counteract procrastination is by
   a. taking a cat nap.
   b. eating complex carbohydrates.
   c. using the five-minute plan.
   d. all of the above.

3. The simplest way to put some sense back into your eating routine is by
   a. avoiding fats.
   b. eating breakfast.
   c. drinking water.
   d. taking vitamins.

Online Study Center   www.college.hmco.com/pic/pauk9e

4. A typical 12-ounce can of soda contains
   a. a generous supply of nutrients.
   b. five grams of fat.
   c. ten teaspoons of sugar.
   d. all of the above.

5. Exercise has been shown to
   a. improve self-esteem.
   b. increase well-being.
   c. reduce depression.
   d. all of the above.

SHORT ANSWER   *Supply a brief answer for each of the following items.*

1. Explain the "two-sided potential of stress."
2. What is the James–Lange theory?
3. Discuss some of the drawbacks of taking a nap.
4. What makes an exercise aerobic?

IT'S YOUR Q

The Q System uses marginal questions to encourage active reading. You'll notice that most but not all paragraphs in this chapter are accompanied by marginal questions. Now it's your Q. Scan the chapter for any paragraph that is missing a question, reread the paragraph, establish the main idea, and then arrive at a question that elicits it. Use the questions in the surrounding paragraphs as models for your own marginal questions.

WORDS IN CONTEXT

From the three choices beside each numbered item, select the one that most nearly expresses the meaning of the italicized word in the quote. Make a light check mark (✓) next to your choice.

In a political speech, we catch the phrases that are *emphasized*, and the rest becomes a *mumbo-jumbo* of political *innuendoes.*

—Louis E. Boone, author of *Quotable Business*

1. phrases . . . *emphasized*   quoted   stressed   repeated

2. *mumbo-jumbo*   recital   routine   gibberish

3. political *innuendoes*   promises   campaigns   insinuations

Perhaps no other president preferred listening over speaking more than the *taciturn* thirtieth president of the United States, Calvin Coolidge.

—Louis E. Boone, author of *Quotable Business*

4. *taciturn* . . . president   untalkative   calculating   diplomatic

Only *mediocrities* rise to the top in a system that won't tolerate wave-making.

—Laurence J. Peter (1919–1990), American author

5. *mediocrities* rise   intelligent   average   reliable
                                people   people   people

Advertising has *annihilated* the power of the most powerful adjectives.

—Paul Valéry (1871–1943), French poet and philosopher

6. *annihilated* the power   exploited   enhanced   nullified

THE WORD HISTORY SYSTEM

Bedlam
really, a madhouse

bedlam   bed'-lam *n.* A place
or situation of noisy uproar
and confusion.

In 1247 the priory of St. Mary of Bethlehem was founded in London. In
the early fifteenth century it came to be used as a hospital for lunatics.
Familiarly known as *Bethlehem*, the name of the asylum was contracted in
popular usage to *Bethlem, Bedlem,* or *Bedlam*. The name came to be applied
to any lunatic asylum, and consequently, in our own day, *bedlam* is used to
signify any scene of uproar or confusion that is suggestive of a madhouse.

Reprinted by permission. From *Picturesque Word Origins* © 1933 by G. & C. Merriam Co. (now
Merriam-Webster, Incorporated).

Gaining Information

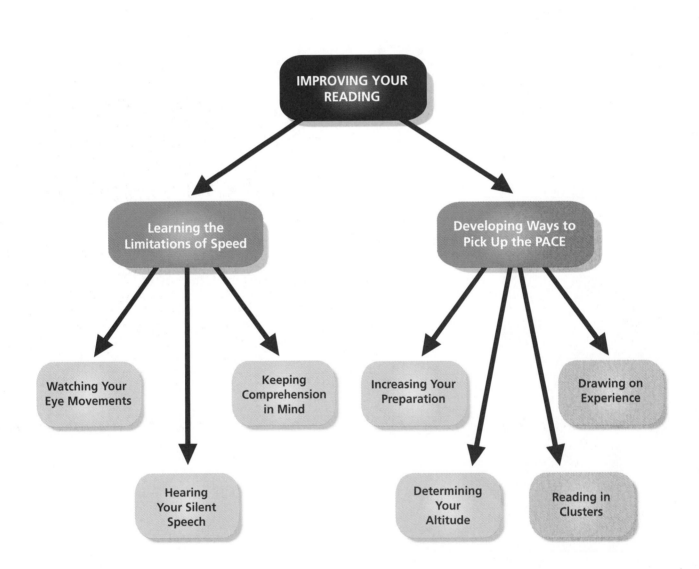

Improving Your Reading

When we read too fast or too slowly, we understand nothing.

Blaise Pascal (1623–1662), French philosopher, mathematician, and scientist

Almost anyone who reads can read faster. The way to do so, however, is to strengthen your natural way of reading and thinking—not to use some artificial method. This chapter uses solid research and sound learning principles to explain:

- **The Limitations of Speed**
- **Ways to Pick Up the PACE**

How can you improve your reading?

The simple question "How can I improve my reading?" does not have a simple answer. There are many different purposes in reading, many different reading techniques that can be used, and many ways in which reading can be "improved." However, when this question is asked by a student, it usually means "How can I speed up my reading so I can finish my homework in half the time with high comprehension and almost complete retention?" There is no easy way to do so, despite the numerous brochures, newspaper and magazine articles, and television programs that extol the marvels of "speed-reading." To truly improve your reading, you need to learn the limitations of speed and then, given those limitations, develop ways that you can sensibly, naturally pick up your pace.

Learning the Limitations of Speed

Why can't you read at the rates that the speed-reading advocates promise?

Many students, as well as the general public, are convinced that speed-reading is an easy-to-learn technique that can be used with any page of print. Unfortunately, speed-reading is virtually useless to anyone who desires to learn from the printed page. It's certainly possible for you to read faster. But slowed down by your eyes, by your vocal cords, and by the necessity to both comprehend and consolidate what you've read, you'll never be able to come close to some of the spectacular claims that the speed-readers make.

Watching Your Eye Movements

What do recent experiments tell us about how we read?

State-of-the-art computerized measurement of eye movements during reading confirm what reading researchers have long suggested. Your eyes don't glide along the words in a fluid motion. They jerk their way across the page, alternating fast, forward movements with momentary pauses. The pauses (called fixations) are absolutely necessary, for they allow the eyes to focus on the type, to get a clear image of it. When the eyes are in motion (known as saccades), they record nothing but a blur on the retinas.

What sort of speeds do speed-readers claim?

Keep this in mind as you consider the claims of speed-reading courses, some of which boast graduates who read thousands of words per minute, always making the point, "with nearly 100 percent comprehension."

What is the basic premise of speed-reading?

The basic premise of speed-reading advocates is this: The eye is able to see a vast number of words in one fixation. Some advocates say the eye can see phrases at a glance; others say entire lines; still others say paragraphs at a time; and a few say the eye can see an entire page at a glance. Get out your calculator and let's look at the facts.

How fast can a better-than-average reader read?

Eye-movement photography shows that the average college student makes about four eye fixations per second. Good readers take in an average of about six to eight usable letters per fixation: four letters to the left of the center of fixation and five or six letters to the right of the center of fixation.[1] There is no evidence, by the way, that anyone's eyes can see a whole line of type "at a glance." So any advice to run your eyes down the middle of a page or column in order to speed-read the page is nonsense. All you'll get is a word or two from each line—a handful of scrambled words. (Figure 6.1 shows the fixations of a typical reader.)

These facts indicate that only a most unusual person can see 10 words per second (2.5 words per fixation at four fixations per second). So, in sixty seconds it is arithmetically possible for the eye to take in 600 words. This calculation does not include the time needed to return the eyes to the beginning of each line and to turn pages. It also doesn't include *regressions*, the regular, imperceptible backtracks the eyes make (10 to 15 percent of the time) to reread a word or phrase. Nor does it allow time for comprehension and consolidation. These factors make some speed-reading claims sound even more absurd, if not outright unethical. In fact, in 1998, the United States Federal Trade Commission charged a well-known, heavily advertised speed-reading system with making claims for their products that were false or unsubstantiated.[2]

Figure 5.1

Typical Eye Fixations Through a Reading Passage

The eyes move in fits and starts—both backward and forward—through a textbook page.

Source: Kevin Larson, "The Science of Word Recognition," *Microsoft typography*, available at http://www.microsoft.com/typography/ctfonts/WordRecognition.aspx.

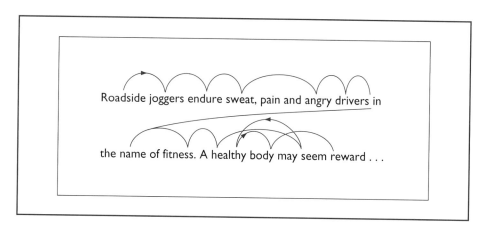

[1]John M. Henderson and Fernanada Ferreira, "Effects of Foveal Processing Difficulty on the Perceptual Span in Reading: Implications for Attention and Eye Movement Control," *Journal of Experimental Psychology: Learning, Memory and Cognition* 16, no. 3 (1990): 417–429.

[2]http://www.quackwatch.org/02ConsumerProtection/FTCActions/trudeau.html.

What is Cunningham's attitude toward speed-reading rates?

Anne Cunningham, a professor of education at the University of California at Berkeley, is not quite as optimistic. She points to tests that put the speed-reading ceiling at closer to 300 words per minute.[3] Then what of the claims of speed-reading entrepreneurs, who trumpet per-minute totals in the thousands or tens of thousands of words? "People who purport to read 10,000 words a minute," Cunningham explains, "are doing what we call skimming."[4]

Hearing Your Silent Speech

What is vocalization?

Another notorious impediment to faster reading is "vocalization," which is best embodied by people who move their lips as they read. Here's a case where the speed-reading advocates appear to be right. Vocalization probably *does* decrease your reading speed. No, we don't all move our lips as we read. Some of us actually whisper our words, while others move only our vocal cords or simply think the sound of each word as we read it. No matter what form our vocalization takes, it appears to be an important part of the reading process. Speed-reading courses that try to train you to resist vocalizing may actually be interfering with your ability to understand and remember what you're reading. Recent reading research suggests that as you're silently reading a word, you're simultaneously sounding it out. This provides a kind of double-check for each word as you identify it visually. Your eyes attempt to identify the word while the sounds you process confirm that you've identified that word correctly. And if for some reason you aren't able to recognize the word visually, the sounds may jump in and identify it for you instead.[5]

What is Hall's opinion on vocalization?

Robert A. Hall Jr., an internationally known linguist, has this to say about vocalization, or silent speech:

It is commonly thought that we can read and write in complete silence, without any speech taking place. True, many people learn to suppress the movements of their organs of speech when they read, so that no sound comes forth; but nevertheless, inside the brain, the impulses for speech are still being sent forth through the nerves, and only the actualization of these impulses is being inhibited on the muscular level, as has been shown by numerous experiments. No act of reading takes place without a certain amount of subvocalization, as this kind of "silent speech" is called, and we normally subvocalize, when we write, also.[6]

[3]Quoted in Blair Anthony Robertson. "Speed-reading Between the Lines," *Sacramento Bee* (October 21, 1999), p. A1.

[4]Ibid.

[5]Carol Fraser, "Reading Fluency in a Second Language," *UTP Journals* 56 (1999).

[6]Robert A. Hall Jr., *New Ways to Learn a Foreign Language* (New York: Bantam Books, 1966), pp. 28–29.

What did Edfeldt's research conclude about "silent speech"?

Åke Edfeldt, of the University of Stockholm Institute of Reading Research, has studied vocalization with a team of medical doctors who used electrodes to detect movement in the lips, tongues, and vocal cords of volunteer readers. After exhaustive medical tests, Edfeldt concluded:

> On the basis of the present experimental results, earlier theories concerning silent speech in reading may be judged. These theories often appear to have been constructed afterwards, in order to justify some already adopted form of remedial reading. In opposition to most of these theories, we wish to claim that silent speech occurs in the reading of all persons.
>
> In any case, it seems quite clear that all kinds of training aimed at removing silent speech should be discarded.[7]

What does more recent research say about Edfeldt's conclusions?

Edfeldt's conclusions, now almost a half a century old, have been borne out repeatedly since then. In fact, engineers at NASA have recently embraced silent speech as a potential communications breakthrough. By attaching sensors under a subject's chin, they are able to do more than just measure the presence of silent speech; they are able to understand it. According to Chuck Jorgensen, a member of the NASA team, "A person using the subvocal system thinks of phrases and talks to himself so quietly, it cannot be heard, but the tongue and vocal chords do receive speech signals from the brain."[8]

Keeping Comprehension in Mind

What does recent research tells us about how the mind handles words?

Even if you could take in words at a phenomenal rate, would it do any good? Probably not. Remember the processing part of the reading equation. Just because you see doesn't mean you understand. Research at the Massachusetts Institute of Technology, using MIT undergraduates, gives scientific evidence that the mind can attend to only one word at a time. The researchers concluded that "even the skilled reader has considerable difficulty forming a perception of more than one word at a time."[9] What's more, as researchers Carpenter and Just found, your eyes continue to fixate on a word not simply until you *recognize* that word but until you *understand* it.[10]

[7]Åke W. Edfeldt, *Silent Speech and Silent Reading* (Chicago: University of Chicago Press, 1960), p. 154.

[8]"NASA Develops System to Computerize Silent, 'Subvocal Speech,'" available at http://www.nasa.gov/home/hqnews/2004/mar/HQ_04093_subvocal_speech.html.

[9]Paul A. Kolers, "Experiments in Reading," *Scientific American* 227, no. 1 (July 1972): 84–91.

[10]M. A. Just and P. A. Carpenter, "A Theory of Reading: From Eye Fixations to Comprehension," *Psychological Review* 87, no. 4: 329–354.

 **Online Study Center** www.college.hmco.com/pic/pauk9e

Why does it seem that we read words in rapid succession?

You often have the impression that you are seeing more than one word at a fixation because your eyes are moving rapidly from left to right, taking in words in rapid sequence. This process is almost like watching a movie. Although each film frame is a still picture, you "see" motion and action when the film is projected at a rate of twenty-four frames per second. Similarly, words projected on the brain at the rate of seven or eight words per second give the impression of living, moving ideas. Nevertheless, the brain is "viewing" only one word at a time.

Developing Ways to Pick Up the PACE

Given the wealth of evidence that seems to put a huge barrier between you and well-advertised, but insufficiently substantiated, supersonic reading speeds, what can you realistically do to improve your reading? Your hope lies not in lengthening your saccades, shortening your fixations, or even lessening vocalization. Your best chance of success depends on the all-important processing step. If you can reduce the time it takes to extract meaning from what you're reading, you'll boost your comprehension and increase your speed, the very essence in almost everybody's book of improving your reading. You can do this—you can pick up your PACE—by increasing your preparation, determining your altitude, reading by clustering, and drawing on your experience.

P: Increasing Your Preparation

Why is it risky to begin reading when you aren't well prepared?

Although it might seem to save time in the short run, it's unwise in the long term to begin reading without investing some effort to warm up first. Beginning to read unprepared will often mean that you have to stop and reread a portion that was unclear, or, worse, that you will overlook or misunderstand crucial information because you weren't properly prepared for it. What does preparing for your reading entail? The bare-bones approach is a quick overview of the assignment. If you want to increase your preparation, you might consider adopting the distinctive regimens of two of history's great thinkers, Edward Gibbon and Daniel Webster.

Overview Your Assignment

What does overviewing an assignment involve?

At minimum, you should prepare for a reading assignment by conducting a quick overview. (Chapter 9 discusses this approach in greater detail.) In most cases, it involves understanding captions, headings, subheadings, and portions of paragraphs well enough to locate key concepts in the chapter. This kind of overview enables you to see the relative importance of each part to the whole

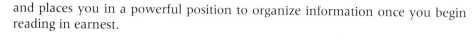
and places you in a powerful position to organize information once you begin reading in earnest.

Use Edward Gibbon's "Great Recall"

Think of the classic operating room scene that you've witnessed in countless movies and TV shows. The surgeon, face covered by a mask, eyes concentrating on the task at hand, has a nearby tray of tools, a carefully arranged array of shiny medical instruments, ready in case she should need them. The great English historian Edward Gibbon (1737–1794), author of *Decline and Fall of the Roman Empire*, took a similar approach that he called "the great recall." Before reading a new book, and before beginning to write on any subject, Gibbon would spend hours alone in his study, or he would take a long walk alone to recall everything that he knew about the subject. In a sense, like a surgeon, he was assembling his mental tools, preparing them for his intellectual operation. Gibbon's system was highly successful. His old ideas were brought to the forefront of his mind, like a tray of shiny tools that could be used to understand new ideas and new information. Nearly two centuries later, reading research provides scientific support for Gibbon's method. His activation of prior relevant knowledge has been found to enhance comprehension.[11]

Try Daniel Webster's Way

What was Daniel Webster's approach to reading preparation?

Daniel Webster (1782–1852), American statesman and orator, also placed a premium on preparation. After scanning the book's table of contents, reading the preface, and flipping through some of its pages, Webster would make lists of (1) questions that he expected to be answered in the book, (2) the knowledge he expected to gain from his reading, and (3) where the knowledge would take him. The three lists provided a strong prescription for preparation. They guided him through the book and ensured that his attention and concentration were intense.

A: Determining Your Altitude

What does *altitude* refer to when it comes to reading?

It's a waste of time to read everything with the same attention to detail. Different texts and different situations require different types of reading. There are some situations in which simply scanning will do, in which you're content to take the 35,000-foot view of a reading assignment, just enough to spot a name, date, word, or phrase, without paying any real attention to its meaning. There are others in which you'll want to fly in a little closer, to clip the treetops, to go beyond the faint outline of letters and skim the text to glean the meanings that the letters hold. Skimming at this level comes in handy if you're searching for

---

[11]P. Carrell, J. Devine, and D. Eskey (Eds.), *Interactive Approaches to Second Language Reading* (Cambridge: Cambridge University Press, 1988).

clues in your text or trying to gain the gist of an article or book. And, finally, there are occasions when you want to be right there at ground level, grasping the meaning of every word and combining them to comprehend each sentence, paragraph, and page. Of course, the closer you get to the ground, the more information you glean. But the closer you get, the slower you go.[12] In other words, it's a tradeoff. That's why it's important to establish your purpose in reading a particular passage and then choose your altitude accordingly.

Scan at 35,000 Feet to Look for Specific Words

When does scanning at 35,000 feet come in handy?

If you want to find a specific name, date, word, or phrase in a textbook or an article, you need to focus on individual words. Searching may be used because it is recognition, not comprehension, that will give you the answer. To ensure that your eyes do not overlook the word or fact you seek, concentrate on it, keeping it in mind as your eyes run over the pages. Concentration will trigger your mind to pick it out of the sea of words. Once you have located the specific word or fact, pause and read the sentence or paragraph surrounding it at a normal rate to make sure, through context, that you have found what you were looking for.

Skim at the Treetops to Search for Clues or Get the Gist

What is the purpose of skimming at the treetops?

When you are seeking specific information but do not know in what words the information may appear or when you are looking over a passage or chapter to glean its basic idea, you must use a slower reading method. In this case, you're looking for more than just characters; you're searching for meaning.

How do you use this kind of skimming to search for clues?

In this kind of searching, you must infer the answer. For example, after reading an article about Paul Bunyan, a legendary giant lumberjack and folk hero, a student was asked a question about Paul Bunyan's birthplace. The answer was Canada, yet nowhere in the article did the word *Canada* appear. The answer had to be inferred from a sentence that stated that Paul Bunyan was born at the headwaters of the St. Lawrence River. Because the student discovered on a map that the headwaters are in Canada, she could answer the question.

How do you use treetop skimming to get the gist of an article or book?

To get the gist of an article, read both introduction and summary rapidly. Then skim any paragraphs that have topic sentences indicating that they contain important data. To get the gist of a book, look at its table of contents, or select a chapter with a title related to your topic, and skim it for its outstanding ideas. This skimming method can help when you have a term paper to write. After you've arrived at a list of books that seem related to your topic, skim through each to eliminate those that are not pertinent and to keep those that are. Obviously, you would waste time and energy if you attempted to read all

---

[12]R. P. Carver, *Reading Rate: A Review of Research and Theory* (San Diego, CA: Academic Press, 1990).

the books on your list. But if you skim them instead, you should glean just enough meaning to determine which of the books will require closer reading.

Read at Ground Level with the Goal of Comprehension

When should you raud instead of scan or skim?

With scanning you look only for a letter combination, whether it is a particular word or a name. With skimming, you seek out meaning, either to ferret out clues from a chapter or passage or to gain the gist of an article or book. The majority of the reading you'll do, however, will be what most of us associate with normal, ordinary reading. You'll be gleaning the meaning of individual words and then piecing them together into complete thoughts. Your goal will be complete comprehension. The influential educational psychologist and reading researcher Ronald Carver called this ground-level reading *rauding* in order to distinguish it from scanning and skimming, both of which he considered types of reading as well. How fast does a typical college student raud? Carver measured the rate at roughly 300 standard words per minute, where a standard word is considered to be six letters long.[13] As you'll see, reading in clusters (see below) and drawing from experience (see page 116) may help you to pick up the pace of your normal reading, but in general, if you're reading for the purpose of comprehension, you're going to be reading relatively slowly. That's why it helps to be selective about when you settle down to read, scanning or skimming instead when you can.

C: Reading in Clusters

How does clustering relate to the way in which we learn to read?

We group our letters into words without even thinking about it. Remember back to when you were first learning to read, how you sounded out a word one letter at a time until you ultimately came to recognize a growing number of words without having to break them down into their component parts? Given the size of the textbook assignments you probably face today, trying to understand what you're reading a letter at a time would be almost unimaginable. But is reading an assignment a word at a time all that much better? If you consider a ten-page assignment with an average of 300 words per page, that's thirty thousand words to keep track of and comprehend.

How can clustering be used to help improve your comprehension?

Although, as we've learned, you can't really transcend the eye's limitations of one or two words per fixation, you can make it easier to grasp what you've read by clustering those words into larger and thus fewer groups. If instead of moving word by word, you work on understanding your assignments a phrase at a time, a paragraph at a time, and even a page at a time, you'll find that your level of comprehension improves considerably.

[13]Ibid.

Online Study Center   www.college.hmco.com/pic/pauk9e

Use the Intonation Way

What role can intonation play in helping you read better?

Research has shown that some level of vocalization is inevitable. So, rather than denying it, why not embrace it? Why not use it to improve your reading instead of interfering with it? The most efficient use of vocalization, to read faster with a high degree of comprehension, is through *intonation*, which is the rise and fall of the voice in speaking. Intonation provides a natural means for combining individual words into meaningful mental "bites" that are a little larger than the word-sized ones we're used to taking. To use this system, read silently, but with expression. In doing so, you will be replacing the important *rhythm, stress, emphasis,* and *pauses* that were taken out when the words were put into written form. This allows groups of words to hold together in clusters in a way they couldn't when the expression was removed. To make silent intonation a regular habit, start by reading aloud in the privacy of your room. Spend ten or fifteen minutes on one chapter from a novel. Read it with exaggerated expression, as if you were reading a part in a dramatic play. This will establish your own speech patterns in your mind, so that you will "hear" them more readily when you read silently. Using the intonation way encourages what is known as "reading fluency." By naturally arranging the words in meaningful bites, it enables you to decode passages more quickly and automatically, allowing your brain to focus on all-important comprehension instead.[14]

Think in Terms of Paragraphs

How do you read when you approach an assignment in terms of paragraphs?

Intonation helps you cluster words into meaningful phrases. You can expand those clusters to paragraph size by stopping at the end of each textbook paragraph to summarize and condense it down to a single sentence. To do this, you must understand the functions of the three main types of sentences: the topic or controlling-idea sentence, the supporting sentences, and the concluding sentence. Figure 5.2 shows these three types of sentences in an actual paragraph.

What is the purpose of the topic sentence?

The *topic* sentence announces the topic (or the portion of the topic) to be dealt with in the paragraph. Although the topic sentence may appear anywhere in the paragraph, it is usually first—and for a very good reason. This sentence provides the focus for the writer while writing and for the reader while reading.

What role do the supporting sentences play?

The bulk of an expository paragraph is made up of *supporting* sentences, which help explain or prove the main topic. These sentences present facts, reasons, examples, definitions, comparisons, contrasts, and other pertinent details. They are most important, because they sell the ideas.

What is the function of the concluding sentence?

The last sentence of a textbook paragraph is likely to be a *concluding* sentence. It is used to sum up a discussion, to emphasize a point, or to restate all or part of the topic sentence so as to bring the paragraph to a close.

---

[14]Carol Fraser, "Reading Fluency in a Second Language," *UTP Journals* 56 (1999).

Figure 5.2
The Three Elements of an Expository Paragraph

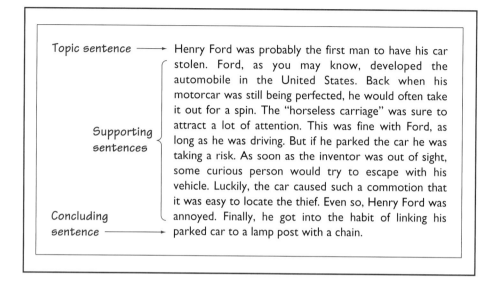

Topic sentence → Henry Ford was probably the first man to have his car stolen. Ford, as you may know, developed the automobile in the United States. Back when his motorcar was still being perfected, he would often take it out for a spin. The "horseless carriage" was sure to attract a lot of attention. This was fine with Ford, as long as he was driving. But if he parked the car he was taking a risk. As soon as the inventor was out of sight, some curious person would try to escape with his vehicle. Luckily, the car caused such a commotion that it was easy to locate the thief. Even so, Henry Ford was annoyed. Finally, he got into the habit of linking his parked car to a lamp post with a chain.

Supporting sentences

Concluding sentence →

How does it help to understand the three basic sentence types?

An understanding of these three sentence types leads in turn to an understanding of each paragraph as a whole. Suddenly, instead of viewing things in terms of words, phrases, or sentences, you're clustering by paragraph, improving your comprehension and even your speed as a result.

Process Your Reading a Page at a Time

What was Macaulay's weakness when it came to reading?

Thomas Babington Macaulay (1800–1859) took the clustering process to the next logical level. He sought out meaning and comprehension by the page. Macaulay was an English statesman, historian, essayist, and poet. When it was published, his greatest work, *The History of England,* outsold all other books except the Bible. Macaulay was also a prodigious reader, who began reading adult books at the age of three. But after consuming shelf after shelf of books, he suddenly came to a discouraging realization: Although he understood every word of what he read and seemed to comprehend what the writer was saying, he was often unable to summarize the ideas presented or even describe, in general terms, what the writer had written. He described his solution to this problem as follows:

> At the foot of every page I read I stopped and obliged myself to give an account of what I had read on that page. At first I had to read it three or four times before I got my mind firmly fixed. But I compelled myself to comply with the plan, until now, after I have read a book through once, I can almost recite it from the beginning to the end.

Online Study Center   www.college.hmco.com/pic/pauk9e

There's something very basic, honest, and refreshing in the Macaulay way. His simple solution was to make the page his fundamental unit of meaning. There are no complicated formulas to follow. You simply stop at the bottom of a page and ask yourself, "In brief, what did the writer say on this page?" And as you'll see in Chapter 11, clustering by page is also a bedrock technique in reviewing your textbook assignments.

E: Drawing on Experience

How would lack of experience affect your reading rate?

Think how long it would take to read a chapter if you had to look up every word in the dictionary. Not just multisyllabic fifty-cent words. Every single word. Or what if a casual reference to "freedom of speech" or "Pearl Harbor" or "1984" or "Judas" sent you rushing off to the library in search of an explanation? A single assignment might take days to read and complete.

How does your experience come into play as you read?

Luckily, even difficult assignments don't normally take days to read. That's because you can count on a certain level of experience each time you begin reading. The definitions of words you might have struggled with in elementary school have long since become hard-wired in your brain. You added more in high school, and continue to add words as you go through college. You read them, unconsciously look them up in your mind's internal dictionary, and keep moving. A maneuver that might have taken minutes if you actually had to flip through the pages of a hard-copy dictionary or surf through the screens of an online one takes a fraction of a second instead.

What do authors assume about their readers' experience?

The same applies to historical or cultural references. Many of them have become part of your personal body of knowledge. Authors know this and can use these references as a kind of shorthand to efficiently express complicated ideas in just a word or two.

How can you increase your experience?

It follows that you can improve both comprehension and speed by minimizing your "lookup time" when you read. The way to do that is by drawing on experience. And the way to increase your experience is to build on your background and to boost your vocabulary.

Bolster Your Background

Why will reading good books improve your reading?

You can improve your reading tremendously by reading good books. The first reason for this is that you'll be getting a lot of practice. Even more important, you'll be storing up a stock of concepts, ideas, events, and names that will lend meaning to your later reading. This kind of information is used surprisingly often. The more good books you read, the easier reading becomes, because with an expanded background, you can more easily and quickly understand the ideas and facts in other books.

What does Ausubel point to as the most important prerequisite for learning?

Psychologist David Ausubel says that the most crucial prerequisite for learning is your already established background of knowledge.[15] Ausubel means that to understand what you read, you must interpret it in the light of knowledge (background) you already have. A background is not something you are born with. You accumulate one through both direct and vicarious experiences. The vicarious experiences, of course, are those you acquire by listening, seeing films, and reading books.

How do you begin to read the great books?

Read the great books, for it is in these books that the wisdom of the ages is passed on to posterity. Begin with the books and subjects that interest you, and don't worry about having only narrow interests. Once you begin reading, your interests will widen naturally. But remember, you are fully responsible for initiating the process and habit of reading. Always keep in mind what Mark Twain once said: "The man who doesn't read good books has no advantage over the man who can't read them."

Beef Up Your Vocabulary

What is the relationship between vocabulary and reading speed?

The fastest readers, according to Berkeley's Cunningham, have excellent "recognition vocabularies." They not only see words faster; they understand them more quickly.[16] In a precise vocabulary, every word is learned as a concept. You know its ancestry, its principal definition as well as several secondary definitions, its synonyms and the subtle differences among them, and its antonyms. Then, when you encounter the word in your reading, this vast store of knowledge flashes before you, illuminating the sentence, the paragraph, and the idea the author is trying to convey. This transfer from word to concept to understanding is quick, automatic, and powerful. Maryanne Wolf, the director of Tufts University's Center for Reading and Language Research, put it simply: "The more you know about a word, the faster you can read it."[17] For more on vocabulary building, refer to the next chapter.

FINAL WORDS

What constitutes victory for readers?

If you're frustrated by the slow pace of your reading, that's understandable. Keep working, and you should steadily improve. We live in a world where everyone wants to get there first. Even so, it pays to remember the famous

---

[15]D. R. Ausubel, J. D. Novak, and H. Hanesian, *Educational Psychology: A Cognitive View*, 2nd ed. (New York: Holt, Rinehart & Winston, 1978).

[16]Robertson, "Speed-reading Between the Lines," p. A1.

[17]"Best Practices: Teaching Fluency with Maryanne Wolf," available at http://teacher.scholastic.com/reading/bestpractices/fluency/understand.htm.

 **Online Study Center** www.college.hmco.com/pic/pauk9e

fable about the tortoise and hare. Slow and steady will often win the race. Fast readers may move through the assignment at a faster pace, but victory comes with comprehension and true understanding, not speed.

HAVE YOU MISSED SOMETHING?

SENTENCE COMPLETION

Complete the following sentences with one of the three words listed below each sentence.

1. In a precise vocabulary, every word is learned as a _____.

   concept   synonym   noun

2. The pauses your eyes make as they read are known as _____.

   saccades   fixations   stops

3. Intonation helps you cluster words in terms of meaningful _____.

   phrases   pages   paragraphs

MATCHING

In each blank space in the left column, write the letter preceding the phrase in the right column that matches the left item best.

_____ 1. Lookup time	a.	Encouraged by the Intonation Way
_____ 2. Fixation	b.	Helps you cluster words into meaningful phrases
_____ 3. Rauding	c.	Slows down your overall reading speed
_____ 4. Fluency	d.	Geared up for a topic by recalling all he knew about it
_____ 5. Gibbon	e.	Allows the eyes to focus
_____ 6. Background	f.	Imperceptible backtracks your eyes make as you read
_____ 7. Regressions	g.	Most crucial prerequisite for learning
_____ 8. Intonation	h.	Carver's term for "normal" reading

TRUE-FALSE

Circle T beside the true statements and F beside the false statements.

1. T   F   There's only one method of skimming.
2. T   F   Daniel Webster prepared for reading by drawing up lists.
3. T   F   Macaulay's technique is a mainstay of textbook reviewing.

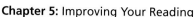

4. T   F   Research suggests that as you recognize each word, you sound it out as well.

5. T   F   One sign of a speedy reader is a good "recognition vocabulary."

MULTIPLE CHOICE   *Choose the word or phrase that completes each sentence most accurately, and circle the letter that precedes it.*

1. When your eyes are in motion, the words on the page
    a. are clearer.
    b. seem larger.
    c. are a blur.
    d. seem smaller.

2. Moving your lips as you read is a form of
    a. fixation.
    b. vocalization.
    c. saccade.
    d. preparation.

3. The goal when you cluster by paragraphs is to come up with a single, summarizing
    a. word.
    b. sentence.
    c. paragraph.
    d. idea.

4. Subvocalization is sometimes called
    a. silent speech
    b. skimming.
    c. saccades.
    d. undertone.

5. The bulk of an expository paragraph is made up of
    a. topic sentences.
    b. supporting sentences.
    c. concluding sentences.
    d. prepositional phrases.

Online Study Center   www.college.hmco.com/pic/pauk9e

SHORT ANSWER   *Supply a brief answer for each of the following questions.*

1. Why is vocalization a necessary part of reading for comprehension?
2. Why do you think the use of intonation helps improve both speed and comprehension in reading?
3. Contrast the different altitudes for reading an assignment.
4. Explain how the process of clustering relates to the way we read.

IT'S YOUR Q

The Q System uses marginal questions to encourage active reading. You'll notice that most but not all paragraphs in this chapter are accompanied by marginal questions. Now it's your Q. Scan the chapter for any paragraph that is missing a question, reread the paragraph, establish the main idea, and then arrive at a question that elicits it. Use the questions in the surrounding paragraphs as models for your own marginal questions.

WORDS IN CONTEXT

From the three choices beside each numbered item, select the one that most nearly expresses the meaning of the italicized word in the quote. Make a light check mark (✓) next to your choice.

Insult: a *callous* or *contemptuous* statement or action; a verbal attack upon another person.
—dictionary definition

1. *callous* . . . statement	thoughtless	unfeeling	careless
2. *contemptuous* statement	disdainful	inconsiderate	impolite

The most important single *ingredient* in the formula of success is knowing how to get along with people.
—Theodore Roosevelt (1858–1919), twenty-sixth president of the United States

3. important . . . *ingredient*	guideline	requirement	component

Too often it's not the most creative guys or the smartest. Instead, it's the ones who are best at playing politics and soft-soaping their bosses. Boards don't like tough, *abrasive* guys.
—Carl Icahn (1936–), CEO, Trans World Airlines

4. *abrasive* guys	strict	irritating	rugged

THE WORD HISTORY SYSTEM

Bonfire
a fire of bones

bonfire   bon'-fire *n.* A large
outdoor fire.

In the Middle Ages, funeral pyres for human bodies were a necessity in emergencies of war or pestilence. *Bonefires* (fires of bone), they were called. Later, when the custom of burning heretics at the stake became common, *bonefires* was the name applied to the pyres of these victims. The same term was used to designate the burning of symbols of heresy or other proscribed articles. Later, its meaning was extended to open-air fires for public celebrations or sports—but by this time in the less gruesome spelling *bonfire*, which today is a comparatively harmless word despite its grim history.

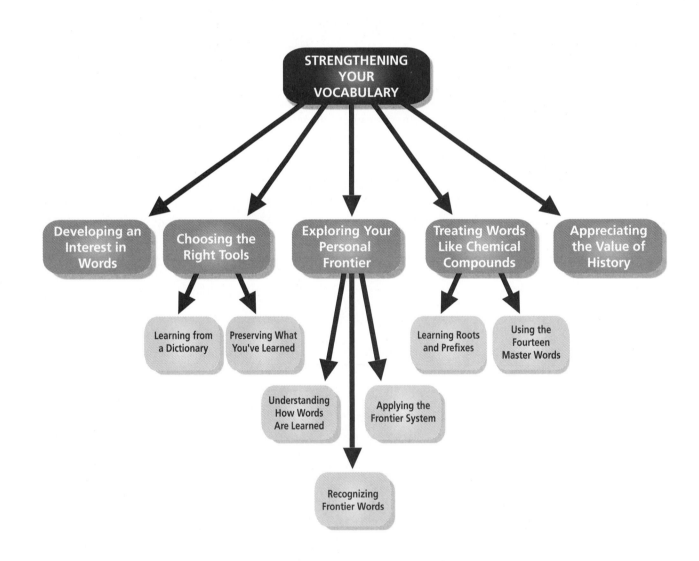

Strengthening Your Vocabulary

> *The difference between the almost right word and the right word is really a large matter— it's the difference between the lightning bug and the lightning.*
>
> **Mark Twain** (1835–1910), pen name of Samuel Clemens, American novelist

Accumulating a large and precise vocabulary can be an adventure. If you're equipped with the right tools and a sense of curiosity, you'll have an exciting journey. And as on most adventures, you'll experience the joy of serendipitous discoveries. When you discover a word you like, increase the pleasure by learning all you can about its ancestry. The territory may seem strange at first, but in time you'll be living in a community of interrelated words where you'll always be genuinely at home. This chapter discusses the value of:

- **Harnessing the Power of Interest**
- **Having the Right Tools Handy**
- **Learning from a Dictionary**
- **Preserving Your Words on Index Cards**
- **Exploring Your Personal Frontier**
- **Treating Words Like Chemical Compounds**
- **Using the Fourteen Master Words**
- **Learning the History of Words**

What is the relationship between thinking and vocabulary?

The quality of our vocabulary can have a direct effect on the quality of our thought. True, some of our thoughts come in images, but we do much of our thinking in words. If we come across a person who is muttering, we're inclined to say, "He's talking to himself," when what we really should be saying is, "He's thinking out loud." Whether spoken or silent, words are the impulses sent over the electrical pathways of the mind. When you're thinking, you're probably talking. It logically follows that the more powerful and precise your vocabulary, the more powerful and precise your thoughts will be.

How can you improve the quality of your vocabulary?

To improve the quality of your vocabulary and with it the quality of your thoughts, you need to harness the power of interest, choose the right vocabulary-building tools, explore the boundaries of your existing vocabulary, learn the components for constructing a variety of words, and learn the stories that lie behind so many words in our language.

Harnessing the Power of Interest

What is the connection between interest and vocabulary?

Interest can be a powerful motivator when it comes to strengthening your vocabulary. Without interest, you'll be average. With it, there is no limit. People with an interest in and even a passion for words have been able to improve their vocabularies as well as their lives, while in some cases their inspiration can be something as commonplace as a newspaper.

What do stories of Malcolm X and the golf caddy illustrate?

The accounts of how words dramatically changed the life of Malcolm X and improved the lot of a Depression-era caddy both can inspire anyone weighing the value of words.

Malcolm X

While in a penitentiary, Malcolm X was unable to answer letters from his brother and sister because he could not write a sentence or spell a word. He felt helpless. In his spare time, he listened to lectures by Bimbi, a self-educated black man.

> What fascinated me with him most of all was that he was the first man I had ever seen command total respect with his words.[1]

Other men commanded respect because of their strength or cunning, the number of robberies they had committed, and so forth. But Bimbi was different. Malcolm X developed a strong desire to be like Bimbi—to learn and use

[1]Alex Haley and Malcolm X, *The Autobiography of Malcolm X* (New York: Ballantine Books, 1964), p. 428.

words. He reasoned that the best way to learn words was by studying a dictionary. So he borrowed one from the prison school and took it to his cell. He described his first encounter:

> In my slow, painstaking, ragged handwriting, I copied into my tablet everything printed on that first page. I believe it took me a day. Then, aloud, I read back to myself, everything I'd written. Over and over, aloud, to myself, I read my own handwriting. I woke up the next morning thinking about those words.[2]

Either Malcolm X shaped his life around words, or the words took over and shaped his life. Either way, he was a winner—he became a "thinking man." He had words with which to think.

Malcolm X went on to become an outstanding leader, preacher, and public speaker. He even lectured to law students at Harvard University. With a wide and exact vocabulary, he was able to express his thoughts and ideas forcefully and intelligently. He earned and commanded respect.

A Caddy's Tale

During the Great Depression of the 1930s, jobs were hard to find. Caddying at the nearby golf course provided some income for high school boys growing up in Branford, Connecticut. Among the caddies, one fellow always got bigger tips than the others. When asked by a friend, he reluctantly divulged his secret.

On the golf course as well as on the street, one common topic of conversation is the weather. It often begins like this: The golfer would say, "Do you think it will rain this morning?" Almost all the caddies would answer "Yep!" or "Nope!" That would be the end of the conversation. But this one fellow had a better scenario. He'd say, "I'm optimistic; there's a bit of blue in the sky. It won't rain." If he were to predict rain, he'd say, "I'm pessimistic today. The clouds are gathering. It'll rain." The magic, of course, was in the words *optimistic* and *pessimistic*. These are college-type words, and they made the caddy the mental equal of the golfer. Psychologically, the golfer wouldn't degrade himself in the eyes of the caddy by tipping him the mere minimum. When his friend learned his secret, he tried it out, and it worked. The story sounds mercenary, but there's a more important dimension; that is, using college-type words creates within you a healthy self-concept—yes, self-esteem.

The Newspaper Way

How can newspapers boost your interest in words?

In print or online, newspapers are a prime source for the clever use of words. Newspaper copy editors, who spend much of their time adding punctuation and correcting grammar, have a real flair for words and a genuine love of language.

[2]Ibid.

 **Online Study Center**   www.college.hmco.com/pic/pauk9e

It is in writing headlines that they get a chance to exhibit their superior skills and even have a little fun in the process. When you catch on to what these copy editors are up to, your interest in words is likely to increase, and with it a desire to strengthen your own vocabulary. To illustrate, the following came from a paper in Springfield, Illinois:

Woman Who Wouldn't Wear Pants Wins Suit

A headline in an Atlanta paper dismissed the notion that children pay attention to height when choosing their friends:

Short-Kid Stereotypes Found to Be Tall Tales

There is nothing earthshaking in these headlines—only the personal delight that comes when you see and appreciate what the writer is doing, using words such as "suit" and "tall" that we'd expect to find in an article about clothes and height but then turning our expectations on their heads. Pick up a paper or go online and find some examples for yourself. Once you become aware of these headlines, it's like discovering treasure that's been hidden in plain sight.

Even the writers at the stately *New York Times* seem to enjoy using mind-catching headlines. An article on the growing popularity of digital cameras was topped off with this ingenious entreaty:

You Ought to Be in Pixels

Here the writer took the old song about Hollywood called "You Ought to Be in Pictures" and puckishly replaced "pictures" with "pixels," which are the tiny dots that make up a digital photograph.

How do you acquire an interest in words?

The question now is how to acquire an interest in words. The creative use of words in newspaper headlines may work for you. Then again, they may not. There is no neat formula. You just need to keep your eyes and ears open. Different people acquire interest in different ways. Within all of us, there is a desire to lift our self-esteem; that is, we want to feel good about ourselves. And a good vocabulary is one excellent way to achieve this.

Choosing the Right Tools

What tools are needed to build your vocabulary?

Regardless of how you choose to build your vocabulary, you're going to need the right tools. One of the great things about building a lasting vocabulary is that it takes so little to do so. You don't need to take a class, use computer software, or purchase some other special book or device. All you really need is a decent dictionary and a generous stack of index cards.

Learning from a Dictionary

What's the best way to learn new words?

The best way to learn new words is to keep a good dictionary close to your elbow and use it. Gliding over a word that you don't quite know can be costly. Consider this sentence: "The mayor gave *fulsome* praise to the budget committee." What does *fulsome* mean? If you think it means "full of praise," you're mistaken. Look it up.

What are the limitations of learning words from context?

Sometimes, you can get some idea of the meaning of a new word from its context, but sometimes you can't. Lee C. Deighton of Columbia University points out three limitations to context: (1) It provides only the meaning that fits that particular situation. (2) You often end up with a synonym, which is not quite the same as a definition. (3) When you have to infer the meaning of a word, you can be slightly (or greatly) in error.[3] Your safest bet is to avoid all the guesswork and go straight to your dictionary.

What should you do when you come across a word you don't understand?

As you study, consult your dictionary whenever you come to a word that you don't know precisely. Find the exact meaning you need; then go back to your textbook and reread the paragraph, with the meaning substituted for the word. If you become interested in a particular word, write it along with the sentence it occurred in on an index card. Later, go back to the dictionary and investigate the word. But don't break into your studying for a long session with the dictionary; save that for later.

Carry a Pocket Dictionary

When does a pocket dictionary come in handy?

Follow the example of thousands of successful people. Get yourself a pocket dictionary such as *Webster's II New Riverside Pocket Dictionary*, and always carry it with you. Instead of reading the print on cereal boxes, or looking at advertising placards on buses and subways, or staring into space, take out your dictionary and *read* it. Its definitions will be terse, consisting mainly of synonyms, but its value lies in its ability to spark a lifelong interest in words as well as increase your vocabulary. Of course, a pocket dictionary is no substitute for a larger desk dictionary, but as a portable learning tool, the pocket dictionary is worth its weight in gold.

How do you read a dictionary?

If the idea of simply reading a dictionary sounds boring or difficult, it's neither. To illustrate how a dictionary is read, let's study Figure 6.1, which is a page from a pocket dictionary.[4] When you open to page 1 and your eyes drift down

[3]Lee C. Deighton, *Vocabulary Development in the Classroom* (New York: Teachers College Press, 1959), pp. 2–3.

[4]*Webster's II New Riverside Pocket Dictionary* (Boston: Houghton Mifflin, 1991), p. 1.

 **Online Study Center** www.college.hmco.com/pic/pauk9e

Figure 6.1
How to Read a Dictionary

Source: Copyright © 1991 by Houghton Mifflin Company. Reproduced by permission from *Webster's II New Riverside Pocket Dictionary*, Revised Edition.

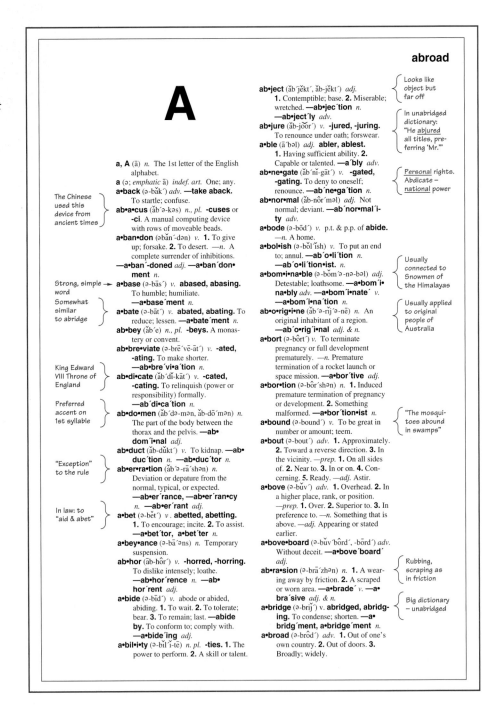

the column of words, an internal conversation takes place: You think about what you already know about the word and you think about the other aspects of the word, such as the syllable that must be accented, the precise definition, and how you could use the word in your writing and speaking.

A number of dictionaries are available for personal digital assistants (PDAs), such as the Palm Pilot or the PocketPC. If you're already carrying one of these electronic devices, adding a dictionary may make sense. But don't buy a hand-held computer just for the dictionary. Also, be aware that some electronic dictionaries do not include all the regular elements that you find in a standard pocket dictionary, such as detailed information on pronunciation. The convenience you gain from storing your dictionary on a hand-held computer can be offset if the information is incomplete or inadequate. Also, depending on the sophistication of the application and the resolution of your screen, you may lose some of the helpful elements—such as boldface, italics, type size, and color—that can make a printed pocket dictionary so easy to consult.

What are the pros and cons of pocket electronic dictionaries?

Keep an Abridged Dictionary at Your Desk

Unless you're really strapped for cash, don't settle for one of those paperback abridged dictionaries, as they are only slightly better than most pocket dictionaries and are too bulky to easily carry around. If you know you're going to stay put, a full-sized abridged dictionary is your best bet. Rather than simply providing pronunciation and bare-bones definitions, good abridged dictionaries tell you far more about the words you are investigating. With an abridged dictionary you usually get more definitions, more information on a word's derivation, and in some instances information about a word's synonyms, usage, and history. Buy and use the best abridged dictionary that you can afford, but be aware that no word is ever fully defined, even by a good abridged dictionary. Words have multiple shades of meaning that add richness to our language. These various shades will become apparent to you as you keep reading, listening, and trying to use words in a variety of contexts.

What advantages does an abridged dictionary provide over a pocket dictionary?

Good abridged desk dictionaries include the following:

The American Heritage Dictionary (Houghton Mifflin Company)
Webster's New Collegiate Dictionary (Merriam-Webster, Inc.)
Webster's New World College Dictionary, 4th ed. (Webster's New World)

Of these three, the *American Heritage Dictionary* has some distinct advantages. Unlike most abridged dictionaries, it offers many of the special features—such as synonyms, usage notes, and word histories—that you normally would expect to find only in unabridged dictionaries. (See Figure 6.2.)

What are some of the features of the American Heritage Dictionary?

Figure 6.2

A Page from The American Heritage Dictionary

Source: Copyright © 2000 by Houghton Mifflin Company. Reproduced by permission from *The American Heritage Dictionary of the English Language, Fourth Edition.*

politician | polonium

pol•i•ti•cian (pŏl′ĭ-tĭsh′ən) *n.* **1a.** One who is actively involved in politics, especially party politics. **b.** One who holds or seeks a political office. **2.** One who seeks personal or partisan gain, often by scheming and maneuvering: *"Mothers may still want their favorite sons to grow up to be President, but . . . they do not want them to become politicians in the process"* (John F. Kennedy). **3.** One who is skilled or experienced in the science or administration of government.

po•lit•i•cize (pə-lĭt′ĭ-sīz′) *v.* **-cized, -ciz•ing, -ciz•es** *—intr.* To engage in or discuss politics. *—tr.* To make political: *"The mayor was given authority to appoint police commissioners and by virtue of that power was able to politicize the department"* (Connie Paige). **—po•lit′i•ci•za′tion** (-sĭ-zā′shən) *n.*

pol•i•tick (pŏl′ĭ-tĭk) *intr.v.* **-ticked, -tick•ing, -ticks** To engage in or discuss politics. [Back-formation from *politicking*, engaging in partisan political activity, from POLITIC.] **—pol′i•tick′er** *n.*

po•lit•i•co (pə-lĭt′ĭ-kō′) *n., pl.* **-cos** A politician. [From Italian or from Spanish *politico*, both from Latin *polīticus*, political. See POLITIC.]

pol•i•tics (pŏl′ĭ-tĭks) *n.* **1.** *(used with a sing. verb)* **a.** The art or science of government or governing, especially the governing of a political entity, such as a nation, and the administration and control of its internal and external affairs. **b.** Political science. **2.** *(used with a sing. or pl. verb)* **a.** The activities or affairs engaged in by a government, politician, or political party: *"All politics is local"* (Thomas P. O'Neill, Jr.). *"Politics have appealed to me since I was at Oxford because they are exciting morning, noon, and night"* (Jeffrey Archer). **b.** The methods or tactics involved in managing a state or government: *The politics of the former regime were rejected by the new government leadership. If the politics of the conservative government now borders on the repressive, what can be expected when the economy falters?* **3.** *(used with a sing. or pl. verb)* Political life: *studied law with a view to going into politics; felt that politics was a worthwhile career.* **4.** *(used with a sing. or pl. verb)* Intrigue or maneuvering within a political unit or group in order to gain control or power: *Partisan politics is often an obstruction to good government. Office politics are often debilitating and counterproductive.* **5.** *(used with a sing. or pl. verb)* Political attitudes and positions: *His politics on that issue is his own business. Your politics are clearly more liberal than mine.* **6.** *(used with a sing. or pl. verb)* The often internally conflicting interrelationships among people in a society.

Usage Note *Politics,* although plural in form, takes a singular verb when used to refer to the art or science of governing or to political science: *Politics has been a concern of philosophers since Plato.* But in its other senses *politics* can take either a singular or plural verb. Many other nouns that end in *–ics* behave similarly, and the user is advised to consult specific entries for precise information.

pol•i•ty (pŏl′ĭ-tē) *n., pl.* **-ties 1.** The form of government of a nation, state, church, or organization. **2.** An organized society, such as a nation, having a specific form of government: *"His alien philosophy found no roots in the American polity"* (New York Times). [Obsolete French *politie*, from Old French, from Late Latin *polītīa*, the Roman government. See POLICE.]

Polk (pōk), **James Knox** 1795–1849. The 11th President of the United States (1845–1849), whose term was marked by the establishment of the 49th parallel as the country's northern border (1846).

pol•ka (pōl′kə, pō′kə) *n.* **1.** A lively dance originating in Bohemia and performed by couples. **2.** Music for this dance, having duple meter. *—intr.* **-kaed, -ka•ing, -kas** To dance the polka. [Czech, probably from Polish, from *Polka*, Polish woman, feminine of *Polak*, Pole. See **pelə-²** in Appendix I.]

polka dot *n.* **1.** One of a number of dots or round spots forming a pattern, as on cloth. **2.** A pattern or fabric with such dots.

poll (pōl) *n.* **1.** The casting and registering of votes in an election. **2.** The number of votes cast or recorded. **3.** The place where votes are cast and registered. Often used in the plural with *the.* **4.** A survey of the public or of a sample of public opinion to acquire information. **5.** The head, especially the top of the head where hair grows. **6.** The blunt or broad end of a tool such as a hammer or ax. ❖ *v.* **polled, poll•ing, polls** *—tr.* **1.** To receive (a given number of votes). **2.** To receive or record the votes of: *polling a jury.* **3.** To cast (a vote or ballot). **4.** To question in a survey; canvass. **5.** To cut off or trim (hair, horns, or wool, for example); clip. **6.** To trim or cut off the hair, wool, branches, or horns of: *polled the sheep; polled the trees.* *—intr.* To vote at the polls in an election. [Middle English *pol*, head, from Middle Low German or Middle Dutch.] **—poll′er** *n.*

pol•lack also **pol•lock** (pŏl′ək) *n., pl.* **pollack** or **-lacks** also **pollock** or **-locks** A marine food fish *(Pollachius virens)* of northern Atlantic waters, related to the cod. [Alteration of Scots *podlok.*]

pol•lard (pŏl′ərd) *n.* **1.** A tree whose top branches have been cut back to the trunk so that it may produce a dense growth of new shoots. **2.** An animal, such as an ox, goat, or sheep, that no longer has its horns. ❖ *tr.v.* **-lard•ed, -lard•ing, -lards** To convert or make into a pollard. [From POLL.]

polled (pōld) *adj.* Having no horns; hornless.

pol•len (pŏl′ən) *n.* The fine powderlike material consisting of pollen grains that is produced by the anthers of seed plants. [Latin, fine flour.]

pol•len•ate (pŏl′ə-nāt′) *v.* Variant of **pollinate.**

pollen count *n.* The average number of pollen grains, usually of ragweed, in a cubic yard or other standard volume of air over a 24-hour period at a specified time and place.

pollen grain *n.* A microspore of seed plants, containing a male gametophyte.

pol•len•if•er•ous (pŏl′ə-nĭf′ər-əs) *adj.* Variant of **polliniferous.**

pollen mother cell *n.* The microsporocyte of a seed plant.

pol•len•o•sis (pŏl′ə-nō′sĭs) *n.* Variant of **pollinosis.**

pollen sac *n.* The microsporangium of a seed plant in which pollen is produced.

pollen tube *n.* The slender tube formed by the pollen grain that penetrates an ovule and releases the male gametes.

pol•lex (pŏl′ĕks′) *n., pl.* **pol•li•ces** (pŏl′ĭ-sēz′) See **thumb** (sense 1). [Latin, thumb, big toe.]

pollin– *pref.* Variant of **pollini–.**

pol•li•nate also **pol•len•ate** (pŏl′ə-nāt′) *tr.v.* **-li•nat•ed, -li•nat•ing, -li•nates** also **-len•at•ed, -len•at•ing, -len•ates** To transfer pollen from an anther to the stigma of (a flower). [New Latin *pollen, pollin-*, pollen (from Latin, fine flour) + –ATE¹.] **—pol′li•na′tion** *n.* **—pol′li•na′tor** *n.*

pollini– or **pollin–** *pref.* Pollen: *polliniferous.* [From New Latin *pollen, pollin-*, pollen. See POLLINATE.]

pol•li•nif•er•ous also **pol•len•if•er•ous** (pŏl′ə-nĭf′ər-əs) *adj.* **1.** Producing or yielding pollen. **2.** Adapted for carrying pollen.

pol•lin•i•um (pŏ-lĭn′ē-əm) *n., pl.* **-i•a** (-ē-ə) A mass of coherent pollen grains, found in the flowers of orchids and milkweeds. [New Latin, from *pollen, pollin-*, pollen. See POLLINATE.]

pol•li•nize (pŏl′ə-nīz′) *tr.v.* **-nized, -niz•ing, -niz•es** To pollinate. **—pol′li•ni•za′tion** (-nĭ-zā′shən) *n.* **—pol′li•niz′er** *n.*

pol•li•no•sis also **pol•len•o•sis** (pŏl′ə-nō′sĭs) *n.* See **hay fever.**

pol•li•wog also **pol•ly•wog** (pŏl′ē-wŏg′, -wôg′) *n.* See **tadpole.** [Variant of *polliwig*, from Middle English *polwigle* : *pol*, head; see POLL + *wiglen*, to wiggle; see WIGGLE.]

pol•lock (pŏl′ək) *n.* Variant of **pollack.**

Pol•lock (pŏl′ək), **Jackson** 1912–1956. American artist. Using his drip technique of painting, he became a leader of abstract expressionism.

poll•ster (pōl′stər) *n.* One that takes public-opinion surveys. Also called *polltaker.*

Word History The suffix *–ster* is nowadays most familiar in words like *pollster, jokester, huckster,* where it forms agent nouns that typically denote males. Originally in Old English, however, the suffix (then spelled *–estre*) was used to form feminine agent nouns. *Hoppestre*, for example, meant "female dancer." It was occasionally applied to men, but mostly to translate Latin masculine nouns denoting occupations that were usually held by women in Anglo-Saxon society. An example is *bæcester*, "baker," glossing Latin *pistor*; it survives as the Modern English name *Baxter.* In Middle English its use as a masculine suffix became more common in northern England, while in the south it remained limited to feminines. In time the masculine usage became dominant throughout the country, and old feminines in *–ster* were refashioned by adding the newer feminine suffix *–ess* (borrowed from French) to them, such as *seamstress* remade from *seamster.* In Modern English, the only noun ending in *–ster* with a feminine referent is *spinster*, which originally meant "a woman who spins thread."

poll•tak•er (pōl′tā′kər) *n.* See **pollster.**

poll tax *n.* A tax levied on people rather than on property, often as a requirement for voting.

pol•lut•ant (pə-lo͞ot′nt) *n.* Something that pollutes, especially a waste material that contaminates air, soil, or water.

pol•lute (pə-lo͞ot′) *tr.v.* **-lut•ed, -lut•ing, -lutes 1.** To make unfit for or harmful to living things, especially by the addition of waste matter. See synonyms at **contaminate. 2.** To make less suitable for an activity, especially by the introduction of unwanted factors: *The stadium lights polluted the sky around the observatory.* **3.** To render impure or morally harmful; corrupt. **4.** To make ceremonially impure; profane: *"Churches and altars were polluted by atrocious murders"* (Edward Gibbon). [Middle English *polluten*, from Latin *polluere, poll t-.*] **—pol•lut′er** *n.*

pol•lu•tion (pə-lo͞o′shən) *n.* **1.** The act or process of polluting or the state of being polluted, especially the contamination of soil, water, or the atmosphere by the discharge of harmful substances. **2.** Something that pollutes; a pollutant or a group of pollutants: *Pollution in the air reduced the visibility near the airport.*

Pol•lux (pŏl′əks) *n. Greek Mythology* **1.** One of the Dioscuri. **2.** A bright star in the constellation Gemini. [Latin *Poll x*, from Greek *Poludeukēs.*]

Pol•ly•an•na (pŏl′ē-ăn′ə) *n.* A person regarded as being foolishly or blindly optimistic. [After the heroine of the novel *Pollyanna*, by Eleanor Hodgman Porter (1868–1920), American writer.]

pol•ly•wog (pŏl′ē-wŏg′, -wôg′) *n.* Variant of **polliwog.**

po•lo (pō′lō) *n.* **1.** A game played by two teams of three or four players on horseback who are equipped with long-handled mallets for driving a small wooden ball through the opponents' goal. **2.** Water polo. [Balti (Tibeto-Burman language of Pakistan), ball.] **—po′lo•ist** *n.*

Po•lo (pō′lō), **Marco** 1254–1324. Venetian traveler who explored Asia from 1271 to 1295. His *Travels of Marco Polo* was the only account of the Far East available to Europeans until the 17th century.

polo coat *n.* A loose-fitting, tailored overcoat made from camel's hair or a similar material.

pol•o•naise (pŏl′ə-nāz′, pō′lə-) *n.* **1.** A stately, marchlike Polish dance, primarily a promenade by couples. **2.** Music for or based on the traditional rhythm of this dance, having triple meter. **3.** A woman's dress of the 18th century, having a fitted bodice and draped cutaway skirt, worn over an elaborate underskirt. [French, from feminine of *polonais*, Polish, from Medieval Latin *Polōnia*, Poland.]

po•lo•ni•um (pə-lō′nē-əm) *n. Symbol* **Po** A naturally radioactive metallic element, occurring in minute quantities as a product of radium

ă pat	oi boy
ā pay	ou out
âr care	o͝o took
ä father	o͞o boot
ĕ pet	ŭ cut
ē be	ûr urge
ĭ pit	th thin
ī pie	*th* this
îr pier	hw which
ŏ pot	zh vision
ō toe	ə about, item
ô paw	♦ regionalism

Stress marks: ′ (primary); ′ (secondary), as in **dictionary** (dĭk′shə-nĕr′ē)

1359

Synonyms   Synonyms not only help clarify the meaning and usage of the word you initially looked up, but also provide an opportunity to weave more strands into your background. Finding a cluster of synonyms is like finding a cache of gold nuggets. But watch out. Not all words in a cluster are interchangeable. Each word has a color, flavor, and niche of its own. It fits perfectly in a specific context where its meaning, feeling, and tone are just right.

Take, for example, this cluster of common synonyms: *eat, consume, devour, ingest*. The central meaning shared by these verbs is "to take food into the body by mouth." Now, notice the appropriate contexts:

> ate a hearty dinner; greedily consumed the sandwiches; hyenas devouring their prey; whales ingesting krill[5]

Nothing can give greater precision to your words than knowing the fine differences among synonyms.

What is the purpose of usage notes?

Usage Notes   It's possible to learn a word's definition and still use it incorrectly. For example, a student who learned that the word *incite* means "to stir up" wrote: "The cook incited the soup." Usage notes provide clarification that goes beyond standard definitions. A form of this category is found in almost all unabridged dictionaries, but rarely in abridged dictionaries. Such notes are interesting and instructive. Here is an example:

> USAGE NOTE: In nautical usage knot is a unit of speed, not of distance, and has a built-in meaning of "per hour." Therefore, a ship would strictly be said to travel at ten knots (not ten knots per hour).[6]

Usage notes impart information in an easy-to-read, nontechnical, nonobfuscating manner.

What is the value of knowing a word's history?

Word History   The story of a word's origin adds dimension and life to something we might otherwise view as flat and inert. The end of each chapter in this book contains an excerpt from *Picturesque Word Origins*, which describes the background and evolution of some commonly used words. *Picturesque Word Origins* was published more than seventy years ago and may not be readily available, but the word history items you can find in the *American Heritage Dictionary* as well as in most unabridged dictionaries can serve as very good substitutes. A

---

[5]*The American Heritage Dictionary of the English Language*, 4th ed. (Boston: Houghton Mifflin, 2000), p. 564.

[6]Ibid., p. 970.

plus factor is that these histories are written in an easy-to-read narrative manner. Here's a sample:

> The identity of the Pueblo peoples is undeniably connected to the stone and adobe dwellings they have occupied for more than 700 years—especially from an etymological point of view. Originally coming from the Latin word populus, "people, nation," the Spanish word pueblo, meaning "town, village," as well as "nation, people," was naturally applied by 16th-century Spanish explorers to villages they discovered or founded in the Southwest.[7]

What are the pros and cons of electronic dictionaries?

Electronic Dictionaries   Many dictionaries, including the *American Heritage Dictionary*, may be available in an electronic form. Electronic dictionaries—the ones you get on CD or find online—have become increasingly sophisticated in their presentation, navigation, resolution, and design. For example, instead of having to flip through paper pages, you can often go directly to the word you're looking for and jump to the definition of a synonym just by clicking on a link. Some of the dictionaries allow you not only to read a word's pronunciation, but also to hear it pronounced correctly. If you spend a lot of your study time on the computer, these dictionaries can be very convenient. On the other hand, each electronic dictionary may have a slightly different (and often copyrighted) system for navigating its words. And, of course, you lose some of the tactile experience of turning pages and the serendipity of stumbling upon one fascinating word while looking up another. Ultimately, it's a question of personal taste.

YOUR
Q

Dig Deeper with an Unabridged Dictionary   Although abridged dictionaries occasionally provide interesting and important details about words, for intensive word study, there is no substitute for an unabridged dictionary. Locate the unabridged dictionaries in your library—usually they are in the reference room—and use them to supplement your abridged desk dictionary. An unabridged dictionary provides more definitions, more about the derivations of words, and more on usage. Good one-volume unabridged dictionaries include *Webster's Third New International Dictionary of the English Language* and the *Random House Dictionary of the English Language*. The *Oxford English Dictionary*, in twenty volumes plus supplements, is indispensable for the historical study of words but is more detailed than you will need for most purposes.

How do the definitions in an unabridged dictionary differ from those in an abridged dictionary?

Whereas synonyms, usage notes, and word histories are considered extras in abridged dictionaries, they are standard in most unabridged dictionaries. In addition, for words that have multiple meanings, an unabridged dictionary will include all the definitions instead of just the most common ones.

---

[7]Ibid., p. 1417.

That fact came in handy when a friend wrote a letter about attending a seminar on Vladimir Nabokov, the Russian-born American writer who was best known for the satirical novel *Lolita*. "All the experts were there," he explained in his letter. "Lots of discussion, but it was too precious for me." Too precious? The sentence was startling. After all, *precious* is commonly used to refer to something valuable. But a quick look at the word's definitions helped clear up the mystery. Here they are:

1. Of high cost or worth; valuable
2. Highly esteemed; cherished
3. Dear; beloved
4. Affectedly dainty or overrefined: *precious mannerisms*[8]

The fourth definition was the one that slid into the context of the letter perfectly. "Overrefined" was the answer. By reading all the definitions of a word, we weave more strands into the background of each word we look up. This will enable us to later use and understand such words with greater correctness and precision.

What makes the Oxford English Dictionary special?

The *Oxford English Dictionary*   When it comes to unabridged dictionaries, the *Oxford English Dictionary* (popularly known as the *OED*) is in a class by itself. It presents the words that have formed the English vocabulary from the time of the earliest records to the present day. Five million excerpts from English literature were amassed during preparation of the work; about 1,800,000 quotations were actually printed.

Work began on the *OED* in 1878, and the last page was delivered to the press on April 19, 1928. It took fifty years to produce all the volumes. On its completion in 1928, it was presented to King George V, and a copy was also officially provided to Calvin Coolidge, the president of the United States.

Here is a brief sample of information gleaned from the *Oxford English Dictionary*. The word is *acre*.

    a. The historical spellings of *acre* are: acer, aker, & akre.
    b. The historical meanings of *acre*, in order of time, are:
       (1) a piece of tilled land.
       (2) as much as a yoke of oxen could plow in a day.
       (3) consists of 32 furrows of the plow, a furlong in length.
          [A furlong is about 220 yards.][9]

[8]Ibid, p. 1381.
[9]*Oxford English Dictionary*, vol. 1, 2nd ed. (Oxford: Clarendon Press, 1989), pp. 117–118.

Online Study Center   **www.college.hmco.com/pic/pauk9e**

The ruling king had the power to stipulate weights and measures. For example, under Henry VIII, an acre was forty poles long and four poles wide. The measures, though varied, were somewhat similar throughout history.

Over the years, with each printing, the *OED* has increased in size. The latest edition, printed in 1989, consists of twenty volumes, made up of 22,000 pages. Use this prodigious dictionary with gratitude and respect.

Preserving Your Words on Index Cards

How do you make new words a permanent part of your vocabulary?

Once you find the words you need or that interest you, you'll want to hold onto them. Using the word in a sentence is a common suggestion, and it's good as far as it goes. But if you want to make sure that each new word becomes a permanent part of your vocabulary, you have to go a little further. The only sure way to master words is to *overlearn* them by using the undisputedly best memory-enhancing technique of *recitation*.

Write One Word per Card

What should you write on each vocabulary card?

To get started, all you need is a dictionary and a stack of index cards (see Figure 6.3). On the cards, write the difficult words that you find in your textbooks and hear in the classroom. These are words you need to know to understand your coursework. Here are the steps to make the system work for you:

1. *Consider its context.* When you select a word, write it on the front of an index card. But don't just write it in isolation. To provide a meaningful context, write the complete sentence in which the word occurs and underline the word so that it stands out.
2. *Sound it out.* Look the word up in a dictionary and, on the front of the card, write the word out in syllables, including accent and diacritical marks, so that you can pronounce it correctly. If you can't pronounce it and spell it correctly, you won't use it later.
3. *Break it down.* On the back of the card, write the prefix and root that make up your word. The prefix and root will help you remember the word by showing you its logical linguistic structure.
4. *Find its meaning.* Still on the back of the card, write the several pertinent definitions of the word. You might as well extract the maximum in meanings while you're at it! Then put an asterisk beside the definition that best fits the meaning of your word in its specific context.

How should you handle vocabulary cards for technical terms?

Technical terms can be handled in almost the same way. However, for these words you may want to rely on the definitions in your textbook. Special terms are usually defined in a glossary or when they are first introduced. Even for a special term, on the reverse side record any information you find about its derivation. Often, you'll have to consult an unabridged dictionary.

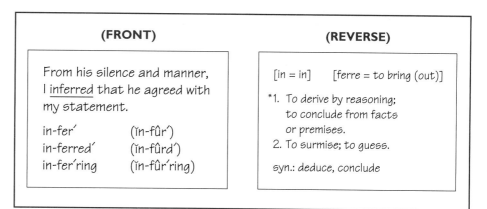

(FRONT)	(REVERSE)

(FRONT)

From his silence and manner, I <u>inferred</u> that he agreed with my statement.

in-fer′　　　　　(ĭn-fûr′)
in-ferred′　　　(ĭn-fûrd′)
in-fer′ring　　　(ĭn-fûr′ring)

(REVERSE)

[in = in]　　　[ferre = to bring (out)]

*1. To derive by reasoning; to conclude from facts or premises.
2. To surmise; to guess.

syn.: deduce, conclude

Figure 6.3
Index Card System
The front and back of this vocabulary card for the word *inferred* demonstrates the format of the index card system. Notice that the front of the card shows the new word underlined in a complete sentence. It also shows how to pronounce the word. The reverse of the card defines prefixes and roots and gives important dictionary definitions of the word. An asterisk is placed beside the definition that most nearly matches the use of the word on the front of the card. Synonyms are also given.

Master Each Word

How do you master the words you've collected on index cards?

In the above four steps we've covered how to construct cards for the index system. Now, we'll present the steps for using the cards efficiently and effectively. You've put in a lot of work. Get the maximum learning from it. To master the words on the cards, do the following:

1. *Start with the front.* Always look first at the front of the card. First, pronounce the word aloud and correctly. Then read the sentence aloud and think about it momentarily. Next, define the word—not necessarily in a dictionary's language, but in your own words. Read the sentence aloud. All this should be done before you look at the definition on the back. Reading and speaking aloud forces you to think alertly, and hearing the word brings your auditory memory into play. Thus, seeing, saying, hearing, and thinking are all working for you.

2. *Check your work.* After you have defined the word to the best of your ability, turn the card over to check the accuracy of your definition.

3. *Say it again.* If you are not satisfied with your definition, keep reciting until your definition is correct. For memory's sake, you must, in order to extract it

later, enter into your mind a correct, crisp, concise meaning for the word. This is pure logic.

4. *Mark the difficult ones.* When you fail to define the word correctly on your first try, place a dot in the upper-right-hand corner of the front of the card. The next time you go through your cards, the dot will remind you that you missed the word on a previous try. When a card has three dots, it is time to give that word extra attention by determining why you keep getting it wrong.

5. *Try another stack.* After you have mastered a small stack of cards, place them in a shoebox and put together another small stack for studying.

6. *Conduct a review.* From time to time, review the words that you have mastered. Reviewing mastered words will take much less time than learning un-mastered ones. The erosive power of forgetting is working day and night. A quick periodic review will foil this relentless force.

Although you might be tempted to type your new vocabulary words into a computer instead of writing them on index cards, here is a case where the "old-fashioned" method is still superior. The advantage of index cards is that they are convenient to carry around for study at odd moments. At all times, carry a few blank cards on which to record interesting words. Learning words that intrigue you will be immeasurably more valuable than memorizing a list made up by someone else. Finally, as you master the precise meaning of each word, there will be a corresponding advance in your reading, writing, speaking, and thinking. The index card system doesn't exhaust its usefulness when your college education ends. Successful people, including company presidents, frequently carry around a small stack of vocabulary cards.

Exploring Your Personal Frontier

How can you increase your vocabulary systematically?

Consulting the dictionary whenever you encounter a word you don't know can help increase your vocabulary a word at a time. But it can be an inconsistent and unpredictable process. One highly effective way to increase your vocabulary more systematically is by using the Frontier Vocabulary System developed by Johnson O'Connor.

What did Johnson O'Connor conclude about how we learn words?

From his analytical research, O'Connor concluded that learning new words is much like learning any other skill. We progress from simple words to more difficult ones in an orderly sequence. The difficulty or ease of learning a word does not depend on the length of the word, its frequency of use, its geographic origin, or its pronunciation—or on teachers, books, or parents. Instead, difficulty in learning a word depends on the complexity of the *idea* that the word stands for. Defining words with simple synonyms does not provide the learner with a background sufficient to think with the words. Because words stand for ideas, the ideas behind them must also be learned.

What was Hayakawa's view on vocabulary building?

S. I. Hayakawa, the noted semanticist, shared this view. He questioned the old-fashioned notion that the way to study words is to concentrate exclusively on words. Hayakawa suggested that words should be understood in relationship to other words—not only other words on the same level but also words at a higher (more abstract) level and words at a lower (more concrete) level.

Understanding How Words Are Learned

What principles underlie the Frontier Vocabulary System?

The following findings by O'Connor form the basis of the Frontier Vocabulary System:

1. The easiest words are learned first; then the harder ones are learned.
2. At the forward edge of the mass of all the words that have been mastered is the individual's *frontier*. Only a very few words *beyond the frontier* have already been mastered.
3. The greatest learning takes place in the frontier area, which lies between the zone of known words and the zone of totally unknown words (see Figure 6.4).
4. The most significant characteristic of the words in the frontier area is that they are, to some extent, familiar. The maximum advancement in a person's mastery of words takes place in the frontier area, where hundreds of almost known words need only a slight straightening out to make them familiar.
5. Learning becomes extremely inefficient and may actually break down when a person skips the frontier area and tries to learn totally unknown words.

What is the value of being familiar with words in the frontier area?

Familiarity with a word in the frontier area means that you already know something about the word or its definition. You may, for example, know its general meaning and how to pronounce it. Or you may know one of its several meanings. The important point is this: By singling out a frontier word and learning its specific meaning, or its several definitions, you can master the word with minimal time and effort. By working continually in the frontier area, you can rapidly master words. At the same time, you will continually be discovering new frontier words to conquer. As the process continues, the frontier area will push further into the zone of what were once totally unknown words.

Recognizing Frontier Words

How can you find your own frontier words?

To find your own frontier words, first become aware of your daily speech, and make a list of the unusual words you use. Next, be on the lookout for words that you recognize in reading but do not use in speaking and writing. From this source choose *only* the words that appeal to you. Listen attentively while other

Online Study Center www.college.hmco.com/pic/pauk9e

Figure 6.4
The Concept of Frontier Words

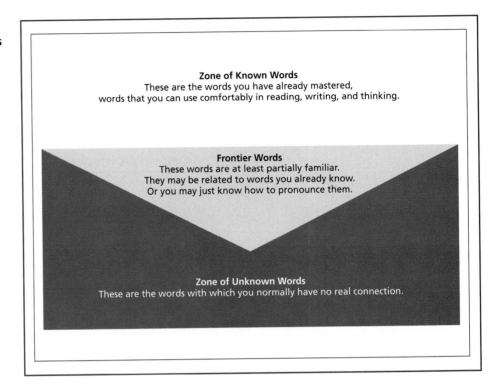

Zone of Known Words
These are the words you have already mastered,
words that you can use comfortably in reading, writing, and thinking.

Frontier Words
These words are at least partially familiar.
They may be related to words you already know.
Or you may just know how to pronounce them.

Zone of Unknown Words
These are the words with which you normally have no real connection.

people speak. The chances are great that you will recognize and know the general meaning of all the words you hear. From this stream of speech, choose the words that appeal to you—words that you would like to incorporate into your own speech.

What is the value of learning a word's antonym?

Later, after writing out the definition for each of your frontier words, look for its antonym (opposite). If it interests you, learn that word, too. Learning pairs of contrasting words creates the strong force of spontaneous suggestion—either word suggests the other.

Applying the Frontier System

How do you master your frontier words?

After you have selected words from your own frontier, you must have a system for memorizing them. Luckily, you already have one. There is no better system than the one already explained in detail: the index card system (see Figure 6.3 on page 135). As you master the precise meaning of each frontier word, there will be a corresponding advance in your reading, writing, speaking, and thinking.

Treating Words Like Chemical Compounds

The Frontier System paints a picture of realms or regions of words. But what about the individual words themselves? It's not unusual to think of a word as being indivisible, like an atom, the smallest part of a sentence. In some cases this is true. In English, words such as *who, what, where, when,* and *why* can't be broken down any further. But many other words in our language—most of them in fact—are products of smaller components that, when pieced together in different combinations, can provide a variety of different words. In that sense, a word can be compared to a chemical compound: Although a word may hold together as a single unit, in reality it is made up of individual atoms or elements. With words, these elements are known as roots, prefixes, and suffixes.

Learning Roots and Prefixes

How can you learn whole clusters of words?

It has been estimated that 60 percent of the English words in common use are made up partly or entirely of prefixes or roots derived from Latin and Greek. If you would like to learn whole clusters of words in one stroke, you should get to know the most common roots, prefixes, and suffixes. A word *root* is the core of a word, the part that holds the basic meaning. A *prefix* is a word beginning that modifies the root. A suffix is an element tacked on to the end of a word that alters or refines its meaning. Table 6.1 lists some common word roots, and Table 6.2 lists some common prefixes.

What is the value of learning prefixes and roots?

The value of learning prefixes and roots is that they illustrate the way much of our language is constructed. Once learned, they can help you recognize and understand many words without resorting to a dictionary. With one well-understood root word as the center, an entire "constellation" of words can be built up. Figure 6.5 shows such a constellation, based on the root *duct,* from the Latin *ducere* ("to lead"). Notice that it makes use of some of the most common prefixes and of other prefixes and combining words as well as various word endings. This does not exhaust all the possibilities either; you should be able to think of several other words growing out of "duct."

Should you memorize prefixes and roots instead of consulting the dictionary?

Although knowing the meanings of prefixes and roots can unlock the meanings of unfamiliar words, this knowledge should supplement, not replace, dictionary use. Over the centuries many prefixes have changed in both meaning and spelling. According to Lee Deighton, "Of the 68 prominent and commonly used prefixes there are only 11 which have a single and fairly invariant meaning."[10] The remaining 57 common prefixes have more than one meaning each.

[10]Deighton, *Vocabulary Development in the Classroom,* p. 26.

Table 6.1
Common Word Roots

Root	Meaning	Example	Definition
agri	field	agronomy	*Field*—crop production and soil management
anthropo	man	anthropology	The study of *humans*
astro	star	astronaut	One who travels in interplanetary space (*stars*)
bio	life	biology	The study of *life*
cardio	heart	cardiac	Pertaining to the *heart*
chromo	color	chromatology	The science of *colors*
demos	people	democracy	Government by the *people*
derma	skin	epidermis	The outer layer of *skin*
dyna	power	dynamic	Characterized by *power* and energy
geo	earth	geology	The study of the *earth*
helio	sun	heliotrope	Any plant that turns toward the *sun*
hydro	water	hydroponics	Growing of plants in *water* reinforced with nutrients
hypno	sleep	hypnosis	A state of *sleep* induced by suggestion
magni	great, big	magnify	To enlarge, to make *bigger*
man(u)	hand	manuscript	Written by *hand*
mono	one	monoplane	Airplane with *one* wing
ortho	straight	orthodox	Right, true, *straight* opinion
pod	foot	pseudopod	False *foot*
psycho	mind	psychology	Study of the *mind* in any of its aspects
pyro	fire	pyrometer	An instrument for measuring high temperatures
terra	earth	terrace	A raised platform of *earth*
thermo	heat	thermometer	Instrument for measuring *heat*
zoo	animal	zoology	The study of *animals*

For example, the prefix *de-* means "of" or "from"; yet the dictionary lists four different meanings for it:

1. It means "down" as in *descend*, which means to pass from a higher to a lower place.
2. It indicates separation as in *dehumidify*, which means to separate moisture from air, or in decapitate, which means to behead—that is, to separate the head from the rest of the body.
3. It indicates reversal as in *decode*, which means to convert from code into ordinary language, or in *depreciate*, which means to lessen in value.
4. It may be used to intensify as in *demonstrate*, which means to show or prove publicly, or in declare, which means to announce.

Where do suffixes come in?

In some ways, suffixes can be more helpful than prefixes in understanding words. And—the best part—learning and remembering a handful of suffixes is relatively easy.

For example, we come across many medical words, such as *laryngitis* and *tonsillitis*. Once we know that the suffix *-itis* means "inflammation or disease of,"

Table 6.2
Common Prefixes

Prefix	Meaning	Example	Definition
ante-	before	antebellum	*Before* the war; especially in the U.S., before the Civil War
anti-	against	antifreeze	Liquid used to guard *against* freezing
auto-	self	automatic	*Self*-acting or *self*-regulating
bene-	good	benefit	An act of *kindness*; a gift
circum-	around	circumscribe	To draw a line *around;* to encircle
contra-	against	contradict	To speak *against*
de-	reverse, remove	defoliate	*Remove* the leaves from a tree
ecto-	outside	ectoparasite	Parasite living on the *exterior* of animals
endo-	within	endogamy	Marriage *within* the tribe
hyper-	over	hypertension	*High* blood pressure
hypo-	under	hypotension	*Low* blood pressure
inter-	between	intervene	Come *between*
intra-	within	intramural	*Within* bounds of a school
intro-	in, into	introspect	To look *within,* as one's own mind
macro-	large	macroscopic	*Large* enough to be observed by the naked eye
mal-	bad	maladjusted	*Badly* adjusted
micro-	small	microscopic	So *small* that one needs a microscope to observe
multi-	many	multimillionaire	One having *two* or *more* million dollars
neo-	new	neolithic	*New* stone age
non-	not	nonconformist	One who does *not* conform
pan-	all	pantheon	A temple dedicated to *all* gods
poly-	many	polygonal	Having *many* sides
post-	after	postgraduate	*After* graduating
pre-	before	precede	To go *before*
proto-	first	prototype	*First* or original model
pseudo-	false	pseudonym	*False* name; esp., an author's pen-name
retro-	backward	retrospect	A looking *back* on things
semi-	half	semicircle	*Half* a circle
sub-	under	submerge	To put *under* water
super-	above	superfine	*Extra* fine
tele-	far	telescope	Seeing or viewing *afar*
trans-	across	transalpine	*Across* the Alps

we see how logically the words were put together, and their meanings become obvious—with hardly any work at all.

Once we know that the suffix *-ectomy* means "surgical removal," the words *laryngectomy* and *tonsillectomy* and *appendectomy* are no longer the sole possession of doctors. We, too, know and can use them.

Take the suffix *-cide,* which means "killer." Now the words *insecticide* and *germicide* become fully understandable.

What is the key benefit of learning prefixes, roots, and suffixes?

Learn as many of the common prefixes, roots, and suffixes as you can, but learn them for better and more precise understanding of words you already

**Figure 6.5
A Constellation of Words
from One Root**

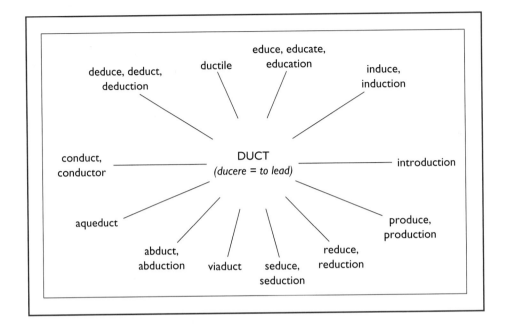

know and words that you have yet to look up in the dictionary. The key benefit of learning these components comes from the precision they provide. When you go to the dictionary, make sure to spend some time on the prefixes and roots that make up each word. You will soon become convinced that a word is not an assemblage of letters put together like an anagram, but the true and natural outcome of evolution.

Using the Fourteen Master Words

What are the Fourteen Master Words?

Recognizing our reliance on Latin and Greek for the components of many English words, Professor James I. Brown of the University of Minnesota decided to find out which prefixes appear most frequently in English. To do so, he recorded the number of times certain word-elements appeared in an unabridged dictionary. He found that twenty prefixes and fourteen roots were part of 14,000 relatively common English words and of an estimated 100,000 words in that dictionary. He then compiled a list of common English words that contained the twenty prefixes and fourteen roots. These words he called the *Fourteen Master Words* (see Table 6.3).[11] The value of this list is that it illustrates the

[11]Professor Brown's findings are described in detail in "Reading and Vocabulary: 14 Master Words," which appeared in the May 1949 issue of *Word Study*, published by G. & C. Merriam Co., Springfield, MA.

Table 6.3
Fourteen Master Words:
Key to Meanings of More
Than 14,000 Words

Words	Prefix	Common Meaning	Root	Common Meaning
precept	pre-	(before)	*capere*	(take, seize)
detain	de-	(away, from)	*tenere*	(hold, have)
intermittent	inter-	(between)	*mittere*	(send)
offer	ob-	(against)	*ferre*	(bear, carry)
insist	in-	(into)	*stare*	(stand)
monograph	mono-	(alone, one)	*graphein*	(write)
epilogue	epi-	(after)	*logos*	(say, word)
aspect	ad-	(to, toward)	*specere*	(see)
uncomplicated	un-	(not)	*plicare*	(fold)
	com-	(together with)		
nonextended	non-	(not)	*tendere*	(stretch)
	ex-	(out of)		
reproduction	re-	(back, again)	*ducere*	(lead)
	pro-	(forward)		
indisposed	in-	(not)	*ponere*	(put, place)
	dis-	(apart from)		
oversufficient	over-	(above)	*facere*	(make, do)
	sub-	(under)		
mistranscribe	mis-	(wrong)	*scribere*	(write)
	trans-	(across, beyond)		

James I. Brown "A Master-Word Approach to Vocabulary" by James I. Brown. Reprinted by permission from the May 1949 issue of *Word Study* © 1949 by Merriam-Webster, Inc. Publishers of the Merriam-Webster ® Dictionaries.

way much of our language is constructed. If learned, it can help you recognize and understand many words without resorting to a dictionary. With one well-understood root word as the center, an entire "constellation" of words can be built up, as was shown in Figure 6.5.

Appreciating the Value of History

What does learning words through their components overlook?

What are some of the benefits of learning a word's history?

Breaking down words into their component parts and reassembling them in different combinations can be an extremely efficient way to learn huge numbers of words. But this process, as helpful as it can be, tends to overlook one important aspect of words: their history.

Many of the words we use didn't simply materialize when someone mixed a prefix, a root, and a suffix together like chemicals in a laboratory. Words are vibrant, dynamic things, each with a history, a story of its own. Learn the story, and you'll remember the word. Better yet, if you learn the life history of a word, the chances are great that you'll grow to *like* the word, not simply *learn*

Online Study Center www.college.hmco.com/pic/pauk9e

it. Learning words in this fashion may not be as efficient as finding them with the Frontier System or arriving at long lists based on commonly used prefixes and roots. But if you learn a word by learning its history, the connection you establish is almost certain to make that learning last. To help you in this endeavor, at the end of each chapter are both a picture and the story of a word, taken from *Picturesque Word Origins*, one of the best books of its kind. Each story not only provides a definition of the word; it also establishes a bond.

The stories behind two common words in a college context—*scholar* and *sophomore*—are entertaining examples of how histories can strengthen your understanding and appreciation of the words around you.

What is the connection between the word scholar and leisure?

Scholar.   Although we generally think of a scholar as a hard-working, serious student, the word has a surprisingly different history. *Scholar* comes from the ancient Greek word for leisure. That's because the only people who had the luxury of learning were the children of the privileged classes. Everyone else was expected to work. In time the connection with leisure was lost, and most scholars would bristle at any suggestion that they are simply taking it easy.

How does the origin of sophomore convey the status of a second-year student?

Sophomore.   The word *sophomore* may be viewed as a rather harmless label for a second-year student, but its derivation provides a fascinating insight into how students partway through their education are viewed. The word originates from the Greek word *sophos* for "wise," but also from *moros*, which means stupid! So, although sophomores may feel as though they know it all, the people who coined the word *sophomore* must have felt these students still needed a little humility.

Finding Books That Tell the Stories of Words

How can you locate books that discuss the histories of words?

There are dozens of books that relate the often-fascinating histories of words. Of these, *Picturesque Word Origins* is one of the best, but because it has been out of print for quite some time you may have difficulty locating a copy. Ask your librarian or visit any of a number of Web sites, such as http://www.alibris.com, devoted to rare or used books. In the meantime, here's a list of books both in and out of print that tell the stories behind some well-known words. You should be able to find many of the books in library catalogs. The books still in print should also be available for purchase in bookstores or online.

Books still in print

Almond, Jordan. *Dictionary of Word Origins: A History of the Words, Expressions and Clichés We Use*. Citadel Press, 1995.

American Heritage Dictionary Editors. *Word Mysteries and Histories: From Abracadabra to Zeus*. Houghton Mifflin, 2004.

American Heritage Dictionary Editors and Barry Moser. *Word Mysteries and Histories: From Quiche to Humble Pie.* Houghton Mifflin, 1987.

Ayto, John. *Dictionary of Word Origins.* Arcade, 1993.

Funk, Charles Earle. *Thereby Hangs a Tale: Stories of Curious Word Origins.* Collins, 2002.

Hendrickson, Robert. *The Facts on File Encyclopedia of Word and Phrase Origins.* Checkmark, 2000.

Isil, Olivia A. *When a Loose Cannon Flogs a Dead Horse There's the Devil to Pay: Seafaring Words in Everyday Speech.* International Marine/Ragged Mountain Press, 1996.

Liberman, Anatoly. *Word Origins . . . and How We Know Them: Etymology for Everyone.* Oxford University Press, 2005.

Morris, Evan. *The Word Detective: Solving the Mysteries Behind Those Pesky Words and Phrases.* Algonquin, 2000.

Quinion, Michael. *Ballyhoo, Buckaroo, and Spuds: Ingenious Tales of Words and Their Origins.* Smithsonian Books, 2004.

Rees, Nigel. *Cassell's Dictionary of Word and Phrase Origins.* Cassell Academic, 2002.

Out-of-print books

Ernst, Margaret S. *In a Word.* Alfred A. Knopf, 1939.

Picturesque Word Origins. G. & C. Merriam, 1933.

FINAL WORDS

How does strengthening your vocabulary relate to learning career skills?

Thus far in this book, you've seen how words shaped the life of Malcolm X and improved the lot of a golf caddy. Words can shape your life and career as well. It's natural to focus most of your academic energy on preparing for your future career and employment. But let the success stories at the beginning of this chapter be a constant reminder of the importance of a lasting vocabulary. Once you are established in your career, professional progress will depend, of course, on your work skills; but your ability to use words—to express yourself clearly and convincingly—may be the real propellant in climbing the ladder. So, let strengthening your vocabulary go hand in hand with building your career skills.

HAVE YOU MISSED SOMETHING?

SENTENCE COMPLETION   *Complete the following sentences with one of the three words listed below each sentence.*

1. Building your vocabulary can increase your _____.

    self-esteem   self-consciousness   self-promotion

2. A chief advantage of vocabulary cards is their _____.

    completeness   convenience   complexity

3. The most significant characteristic of a frontier word is its _____.

    difficulty   familiarity   pronunciation

MATCHING   *In each blank space in the left column, write the letter preceding the phrase in the right column that matches the left item best.*

_____ 1. Interest   a. Has limitations as a means of learning new words

_____ 2. 60   b. Provides clarification that goes beyond a word's definition

_____ 3. Constellation   c. Percentage of English words derived from Latin or Greek

_____ 4. 20   d. Can be a powerful motivator for strengthening vocabulary

_____ 5. Context   e. Greatest learning takes place here

_____ 6. Usage   f. Number of volumes in the current *Oxford English Dictionary*

_____ 7. Serendipity   g. A group of words with a common root

_____ 8. Frontier area   h. Can be lost when you use an electronic dictionary

TRUE-FALSE   *Circle* T *beside the* true *statements and* F *beside the* false *statements.*

1. T F   Quality of vocabulary can have a direct effect on quality of thought.
2. T F   The creative use of words can generate interest in an audience.
3. T F   Not all electronic dictionaries contain the features that you find in a pocket dictionary.

4. T F No word is ever fully defined in an abridged dictionary.
5. T F Unabridged dictionaries normally include only the most common definition for each word.

MULTIPLE CHOICE

Choose the word or phrase that completes each sentence most accurately, and circle the letter that precedes it.

1. After he left prison, Malcolm X went on to become an outstanding
    a. leader.
    b. preacher.
    c. public speaker.
    d. all of the above.

2. Frontier words are
    a. inexhaustible in their supply.
    b. the easiest words to master.
    c. familiar in one way or another.
    d. all of the above.

3. From his analytical research, Johnson O'Connor determined that learning new words
    a. requires an above-average memory.
    b. is much like learning any other skill.
    c. interferes with your ability to concentrate.
    d. enables you to clarify your career goals.

4. With some electronic dictionaries, a word's pronunciation can actually be
    a. incorrect.
    b. heard.
    c. abridged.
    d. none of the above.

5. Three dots on a vocabulary card indicate that the word
    a. has three different definitions.
    b. may require extra attention.
    c. has been properly mastered.
    d. consists of a common prefix and root.

SHORT ANSWER

Supply a brief answer for each of the following questions.

1. Suggest at least two reasons why index cards are an effective tool for building your vocabulary.
2. Contrast learning words in context with the vocabulary-building method that Hayakawa advocated.
3. Compare and contrast strengthening your vocabulary by learning word histories and by memorizing prefixes and roots.
4. Discuss places and situations in which you would be likely to encounter frontier words.

IT'S YOUR Q

The Q System uses marginal questions to encourage active reading. You'll notice that most but not all paragraphs in this chapter are accompanied by marginal questions. Now it's your Q. Scan the chapter for any paragraph that is missing a question, reread the paragraph, establish the main idea, and then arrive at a question that elicits it. Use the questions in the surrounding paragraphs as models for your own marginal questions.

WORDS IN CONTEXT

From the three choices beside each numbered item, select the one that most nearly expresses the meaning of the italicized word in the quote. Make a light check mark (✓) next to your choice.

When strangers start acting like neighbors, communities are *reinvigorated*.

—Ralph Nader (1934–), American lawyer, consumer advocate, and presidential candidate

1. are *reinvigorated*   given new leaders   given old standards   given new life

If you help others, you will be helped, perhaps tomorrow, perhaps in one hundred years, but you will be helped. Nature must pay off the debt. It is a *mathematical* law and all life is mathematics.

—George Ivanovitch Gurdjieff (1872–1949), Armenian mystic and philosopher

2. a *mathematical* law   probable   improbable   absolute

It is one of the most beautiful *compensations* of life that no man can sincerely try to help another without helping himself.

—Ralph Waldo Emerson (1803–1882), American writer and philosopher

3. *compensations* of life   thoughts   acts   rewards

THE WORD HISTORY SYSTEM

Neighbor
once a nearby farmer

neighbor neigh'-bor *n.*
1. One who lives near or next to another. 2. A person, place, or thing adjacent to or located near another. 3. A fellow human being.

Neighbor is one of those interesting words that carry us back to Anglo-Saxon days. In Anglo-Saxon, néah meant "nigh," and gebūr meant "dweller," "farmer." These two words were combined into néahgebūr, meaning, literally, "a nearby farmer." Its meaning, changing with the evolution of civilization, no longer applies particularly to neighboring farmers, but refers to persons living near each other. Even nations in the modern world are called "neighbors"—an interesting development of a word that means, literally, "nearby farmers."

Reprinted by permission. From *Picturesque Word Origins* © 1933 by G. & C. Merriam Co. (now Merriam-Webster, Incorporated).

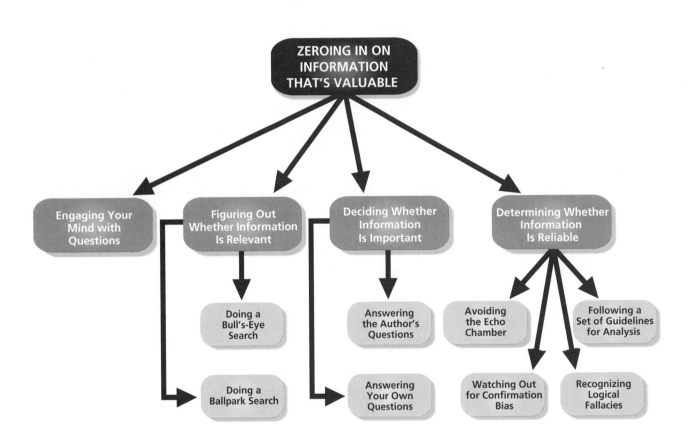

Zeroing In on Information That's Valuable

You don't have all day. You've got textbooks to plow through, articles to read, research to do, and lectures to attend. In addition, you might take time to watch the news, read the paper, or get the latest from the Internet. How in the world are you going to retain all this information?

You're not.

The simple fact is that you can't possibly hold on to all the information you're bombarded with on a given day. You have to make some choices. That's why it's essential to be able to zero in on the most valuable information by

- **Engaging Your Mind with Questions**
- **Figuring Out Whether Information Is Relevant**
- **Deciding Whether Information Is Important**
- **Determining Whether Information Is Reliable**

Why is so much information so readily available?

There has never been a time when more information has been more readily available than right now. Thanks primarily to the Internet but also to a wealth of electronic documents and databases, many of us have at our fingertips what students in the past had to walk or drive miles to gain access to. But all this information has its drawbacks. Author David Shenk calls this glut of information "data smog." As Shenk explains, "We thrive on the information, and yet we can also choke on it."[1]

How can we take advantage of all this information instead of being overwhelmed by it?

So, how can we benefit from all this information without being asphyxiated by it? Start by being specific and selective about what you're searching for, by using questions to activate your learning and help you zero in on information that is relevant, important, and reliable.

Engaging Your Mind with Questions

How do questions engage your mind?

You shouldn't simply *ingest* what you read or hear. You should *digest* it. The words on the page or the screen or coming from the mouth of a speaker are lifeless until you interact with them, converting information into knowledge and integrating ideas into your own web of understanding. One of the best ways to set this process in motion is by asking questions.

What powers do questions provide?

Questions are the engine that drives the whole understanding process. They are what give you the power to make choices between what's relevant and what's irrelevant, what's important and what's unimportant, what's reliable and what's unreliable. In short, questions enable you to zero in on the information that is valuable and leave the rest behind.

How does Eddie Ricken-backer's story illustrate the effect of questions on understanding?

The story of Eddie Rickenbacker provides a dramatic illustration of the effect that questions can have on understanding. Rickenbacker was a highly decorated World War I flying ace who went on to become chairman of Eastern Airlines. Brought up in humble circumstances, he was forced to leave school at the age of twelve so he could find work and support his widowed mother.

Although Eddie couldn't attend school regularly, he still appreciated the value of an education and later decided to take a correspondence course in mechanical engineering. Here's part of his story:

> The first lesson, I do not mind admitting, nearly finished my correspondence-school education before it began. It was tough. . . . As there was no teacher of whom I could ask a question, I had to work out the answers myself. Once I reached

[1]David Shenk, *Data Smog: Surviving the Information Glut* (New York: HarperCollins, 1997), p. 22.

the answer through my own individual reasoning, my understanding was permanent and unforgettable.[2]

Perhaps you can picture young Eddie Rickenbacker with paper and book spread out on a kitchen table, struggling to gain meaning from a paragraph. Doubts began to mount. Plain grit wasn't enough. He felt overwhelmed. Then, in desperation, he probably said to himself, "All right, Eddie, try it once more: What's this fellow trying to tell me?"

Why did questions provide such a breakthrough in Rickenbacker's learning?

Right then, he created a miniature miracle. How? He asked a question! Armed with this questioning technique, he became his own teacher. Previously, his eyes touched the words on the page and, in touching, expected that meaning would somehow, like a jack-in-the-box, pop up. Unfortunately, it didn't (and it doesn't). But with a question ringing in his ears, Rickenbacker was able to focus on hearing an answer. He heard it and understood it. You can too.

How did Socrates use questions?

We shouldn't be surprised that questions are packed with so much power. Human beings have known this for more than 2400 years. Socrates (469–399 BC), the greatest of the Greek philosophers, developed what is known as the Socratic method, *the questioning method.* By employing a series of carefully directed questions, Socrates would lead another person, through his own step-by-step answers, to arrive at the understanding or conclusion himself.

Why are questions so powerful?

What is it that makes a question so powerful? Maybe, as the psychologists say, questions promote concentration. Using questions as your laser beam, you can focus all your energy on the relevant, important, and reliable information—in other words, on the stuff that's worth retaining.

Figuring Out Whether Information Is Relevant

How can you tell if information is relevant?

Relevant information has a connection to your focus. If you're living in Los Angeles, today's weather in New York probably isn't relevant. That's because it has no obvious connection to your life in Los Angeles. On the other hand, the temperature in Los Angeles and the traffic conditions there will probably be relevant, particularly if you're venturing outside.

What's wrong with irrelevant information?

Irrelevant information is a little like the distractions described in Chapter 3. It can gum up the works of understanding, making it difficult to concentrate properly, to think clearly, or to make decisions quickly and effectively. Math instructors frequently assign word problems that deliberately contain some irrelevant information. For example, a problem designed to see if you can calculate

[2]Edward V. Rickenbacker, *Rickenbacker* (Englewood Cliffs, NJ: Prentice-Hall, 1967), pp. 31–32.

the distance that a person will be able to travel at a particular rate of speed in a set amount of time may describe the color of the person's shoes or running shorts. Neither of these details is relevant, because they have nothing to do with the focus of the problem, namely, how far someone can travel at a given speed in a given amount of time.

The sharper your focus the more readily you'll be able to discard irrelevant information. If you want to learn everything you can about the Empire State Building, then the height of the building (1,472 feet) is relevant. But if your purpose is to find what you need to know to visit the Empire State Building, your focus is sharper and the height is no longer relevant. What *is* relevant is the location of the building and how to get there, its hours, and how much it will cost to visit. That's because all of this information has a connection to your purpose: visiting the Empire State Building.

You can't tell whether information is connected unless you know what it's connecting to. That normally requires a clearly articulated focus. The best way to obtain such a focus is with a question. The more specific your question, the sharper your focus is likely to be. Asking a question is like pointing a camera at a field of facts. All those facts you can see in the viewfinder are relevant. All those that you can't see are not.

There are lots of books and websites devoted to search engine tips. Most of them devote a fair amount of time to the individual idiosyncrasies of particular search engines, the symbols and keywords that certain engines recognize that will help you focus your search. These details are helpful, although most of them are typically explained in the particular search engine's "advanced search" area. What's more important and more fundamental is to know what you're searching for before you begin searching. Back before the Web was commonplace, it was often possible to do computer-based searches of online databases with the help of a librarian or other trained researcher. The searches took time and in some cases they cost money. Both factors tended to discourage the casual, hit-or-miss approach that has gradually become more common.

In general, there are two types of searches: bull's-eye and ballpark. With a bull's-eye search, you are looking for a specific document or fact. With a ballpark search, you are seeking information on a particular topic, but you don't have a specific fact or document in mind.

Doing a Bull's-Eye Search

With a bull's-eye search, your best approach is to be as specific as possible. After all, if you know exactly what you're looking for, there's no real value in being vague about it.

How can you reduce irrelevant information?

How do you find relevant information?

How do you find relevant information using a search engine?

What are the differences between a bull's-eye search and a ballpark search?

What approach should you use for a bull's-eye search?

How do you do a bull's-eye search in a book?

Searching in a book.   If you're doing a bull's-eye search in a book, begin with the index. If the index is detailed and your search is sufficiently specific, you should be able to find an entry that takes you straight to the page or pages you're looking for. If the index is sparse or doesn't list what you're searching for, try the table of contents. Based on the chapter titles, find the chapter most likely to contain the information you're looking for, turn to that chapter, and then use the 35,000-foot scanning technique (see Chapter 5) to locate it.

How do you do a bull's-eye search in a magazine or journal?

Searching in a magazine or journal.   Individual magazine or journal articles are rarely indexed. To do a bull's-eye search in these articles, your only real option is the 35,000-foot scanning technique (see Chapter 5). If the article uses subheadings, they can help to narrow your search. Skim the subheadings first and find the one that seems most likely to contain the information you're searching for. Then focus your attention on that section with your bull's-eye search.

Searching online or other electronic text.   Doing a bull's-eye search in a specific online or other electronic text is comparatively easy. Most applications that read electronic documents (web browsers, word processors, portable document readers) have a Find command that should enable you to type in the name, word, or phrase you're seeking and then go straight to it. By the way, these tools don't care if you've typed in the entire word or phrase; they just take the characters you've typed and find a match within the document. So, for example, if you're not sure how to spell the name of German composer Ludwig van Beethoven, you'd be safer searching for a part of his name—such as "hoven"—rather than run the risk of spelling it wrong. (A search for "Ludvig von Baythoven," for example, would turn up nothing.) On the other hand, if you've spelled your search words correctly and there are several occurrences within the text of them, most tools will normally take you to the first instance of their occurrence and enable you to search again for others.

Doing a Ballpark Search

What approach should you use for a ballpark search?

A ballpark search differs from a bull's-eye search in that you don't know exactly what you're looking for. You just have a general idea. Perhaps you're searching for information on Beethoven, but for some reason you don't remember his name. However, you know the person you are thinking of was German and a composer. The more clues you can assemble for a ballpark search, the more focused your search will be. But you have to be careful. If you include a clue that turns out to be incorrect, you may leave the ballpark entirely.

How do you do a ballpark search in a book?

Searching in a book.   If your ballpark search is in a book in hard-copy format, you'll eventually be doing the treetop skimming described in Chapter 5. Once

again, you can start with the index to see if you can find any clues, although it's less likely this time that you'll be able to find something this way. Then move on to the table of contents to see if there's a chapter title that will put you in the ballpark. For example, if you were skimming a book called either "Famous Germans" or "Famous Musicians" you might find a chapter that would help to refine your search further (perhaps "Germans in Music" in the former and "German Composers" in the latter). If you're lucky enough to be searching a particular chapter, you may be able to zero in even further by reading the chapter subheadings for additional clues. Beyond that point, the treetop skimming begins in earnest as you try to grasp the context that might be likely to surround the information you're seeking.

How do you do a ballpark search in a magazine or journal?

Searching in a magazine or journal.   Because a magazine or journal probably won't have an index, your only real hope of further narrowing a ballpark search in a magazine or journal article would be in its subheadings. Beyond that, you'll have to do your search using treetop skimming.

How can you do a ballpark search for an online document or in an electronic text?

Searching a single online or other electronic text.   It's unlikely that a ballpark search of a specific online or other electronic text document will take you exactly where you want to go. But it may get you in the vicinity. The Find tool in a browser, word processor, or other document reader is not as sophisticated as an Internet search engine. If you're searching for the name of a German composer, it's best to search for either "German" or "composer" in the hopes of finding who you're looking for. (If you were to search for "German composer," you would be successful only if the two words occurred consecutively in the text.) Once the Find tool has you in the right ballpark (and it may take several attempts), you can do treetop skimming to find precisely what you're looking for.

How do you do a ballpark search through multiple documents on the Internet?

Doing a ballpark search on the Internet.   Although the Find tools you can use to search the pages in a single electronic document are limited, if you're searching several documents and they are all available on the Internet, then you should be able to do more sophisticated searches. Search engines allow you to refine your search by combining several searches into one. This approach, known as Boolean searching, allows you to establish a relationship between two or more search terms (see Figure 7.1). The rules for particular search engines may vary slightly, but in general, if you search using the words "German" and "composer," the search engine will return all the documents that contain "German," all the documents that contain "composer," and, most important (and normally at the top of the list), all the documents that contain "German" *and* "composer."

Figure 7.1
How Boolean Searching Works

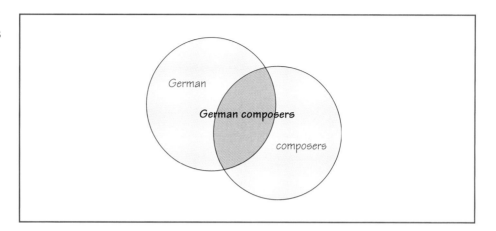

Deciding Whether Information Is Important

How does important information differ from relevant
information?

Of course, just because information is relevant doesn't necessarily mean it's something you want to hold on to. Valuable information is normally both relevant *and* important. Even if you've managed to discard irrelevant information, you may still be left with information of different weights competing for your time and attention. For example, if you had a to do list that listed "Empty garbage" and "Complete research paper," both tasks would be relevant but they clearly wouldn't have the same weight or importance.

The most important information is the information that responds most directly to a particular question. If you ask, "How do I get to the Statue of Liberty from midtown Manhattan?" the most important information is "To get to the Statue of Liberty from midtown Manhattan, take the subway to the South Ferry station and then catch the Liberty Ferry at Battery Park." But if you asked instead, "Where did the Statue of Liberty come from?" information of the subway and ferry routes would no longer be important. In fact, it wouldn't even be relevant. The most important information would be that "The Statue of Liberty was created by Frederic Auguste Bartholdi and was presented to the United States in 1865 as a gift from France."

What happens when you find
an answer to the question?

Few answers mark an automatic end point. Every answer has the potential to generate new questions. An answer such as "The Statue of Liberty was created by Frederic Auguste Bartholdi and was presented to the United States in 1865 as a gift from France" might prompt you to ask "Who was Bartholdi?" and "Why did France give the United States a statue?" If the authors have anticipated your questions, the sentences or paragraphs that follow may answer

Online Study Center   www.college.hmco.com/pic/pauk9e

them. Or it may turn out that you and the authors hit a fork in the road and move in different directions.

How do you determine what's important?

To find what's important, ask questions and then seek to answer them. You can be driven by the engine of the author's questions or by questions of your own.

Answering the Author's Questions

Where do you find the author's questions?

A book can be thought of as the answers to a series of invisible questions. Granted, you can't usually see these questions, but they're there. If this sounds like some sort of fairy tale, think again. Questions are actually built in to the unit that organizes almost everything we read. What unit is that? The paragraph. According to its definition, a paragraph "typically deals with a single thought or topic."[3] Everything in a paragraph points to that thought or topic. All the other sentences in that paragraph are there to support it. If you read a paragraph and ask, "What's important here?" your answer will be the controlling idea and that should lead you to the invisible question.

> The Empire State Building is an impressive symbol of early twentieth century industrial achievement. At 1,454 feet, this massive two-acre office building is the tallest in New York City and the ninth tallest in the world. Started in 1930, it took a total of 7,000,000 work-hours and a little more than a year of almost nonstop work to complete. It weighs 365,000 tons, has 6,500 windows, and boasts a total of 1,860 steps leading from the street level to the 102nd floor.

How are the controlling ideas arranged?

Most information is organized hierarchically. A chapter or an article has a single controlling idea or "thesis" and then all other ideas grow out of that idea. On a smaller scale, each individual paragraph has its own controlling idea, with the rest of the paragraph acting to support it. The maps that open each of the chapters in this book (including this one) provide a good example of how this arrangement works. Each idea is supported by the ideas beneath it.

How do you find the most important information in an article or chapter?

To find the most important information in an article or chapter, look for the controlling ideas in each paragraph. These ideas in turn are likely to cluster around a controlling idea for a particular section. And those ideas should all support the chapter or article's controlling idea. Often, the first paragraph of each section provides the controlling idea for that section and the introductory paragraph for the chapter provides the controlling idea for the entire chapter. Some articles or chapters are better organized than others, but in many cases

---

[3]*The American Heritage Dictionary of the English Language,* 4th ed. (Boston: Houghton Mifflin, 2000), p. 1274.

you should be able to create a framework of controlling ideas that resembles the maps that begin each chapter in this book.

Answering Your Own Questions

What if what I think is important differs from what the author thinks is important?

Of course, your view of what's important may differ from the author's view. Just as the Empire State Building was built around a steel framework, an article or chapter is constructed by the author around a framework of controlling ideas. But these important ideas don't necessarily have to be your important ideas.

How do I find what's important to me?

The way to find the information that is important to you is by asking a focused question and then zeroing in on the area that provides the answer. Depending on the scope of your question, that area might be a sentence, a paragraph, a section, a chapter or article, or even an entire book. The next most important information will be the information that directly supports your original answer.

How can I be sure what I've found is the most important?

Unlike relevance, which has to do with whether a connection exists or doesn't, importance is a relative thing. It has to do with the scope of your topic or question. If relevance can be seen as where the camera lens is pointed, importance is influenced by how far you zoom in or zoom out. The larger something is relative to the other facts around it, the more important it's likely to be. So, if your question asks, "How tall is the Empire State Building?" then its height is likely to be the most important piece of information in your answer. If, on the other hand, your question asks, "How big is the Empire State Building?" then its height would presumably compete with its other dimensions for importance.

What happens to information that is interesting but not important?

Keep in mind that what is important is not the same as what is interesting. A lot of information (such as the number of steps in the Empire State Building) falls under the general heading of trivia. Trivia fascinates some students and bores others. Regardless, it's rarely important. At best it provides support for a controlling idea. If you think trivia is interesting you may find this motivates you to remember it. It's still better to focus your attention on the important ideas though. When you do, the details that interest you will often remain in the picture. If, on the other hand, you focus on trivia instead, the controlling ideas may be pushed out of frame.

Determining Whether Information Is Reliable

How can you tell whether information is reliable?

Questions activate your learning and help you to determine which information is relevant and which information is important. But they play one more especially vital role. They help you put the reliability of information to the test. Compared to finding information that's relevant or deciding which information is important, determining whether information is reliable can be a real challenge.

 **Online Study Center**   **www.college.hmco.com/pic/pauk9e**

It helps to beware of things that can make information unreliable, such as the echo chamber, confirmation bias, and logical fallacies, and then arrive at some guidelines you can use consistently to analyze information for reliability.

Avoiding the Echo Chamber

What is the echo chamber?

The echo chamber describes a situation in which information is amplified by constant repetition. If the information is false, it may be mistaken as true. If the information is true, it may appear to be more relevant or important than it actually is. The satirist H. L. Mencken's "bathtub hoax" offers an interesting insight into the echo chamber run amok, whereas urban legends provide more commonplace examples. And because the echo chamber isn't just for false information, it helps sometimes to take a good look at the "news" that everyone is buzzing about.

The Bathtub Hoax

What was the bathtub hoax?

In 1917, the reporter and satirist Henry Louis Mencken wrote a whimsical, entirely fictional piece for the *New York Evening Mail* called "A Neglected Anniversary," a meticulously fabricated history of the evolution of the bathtub in America and its introduction in the White House during the Millard Fillmore administration in 1850. Unfortunately, many of the people who read the piece must not have been active learners because the joke was lost on them. Soon, Mencken's fictional account of the first White House bathtub made its way into respectable history and reference books. Once the "fact" was available in other sources, the echo chamber effect took hold and the story of the first White House bathtub started popping up in numerous books as though it were the truth. Mencken, who had a distinctly mischievous side, claimed to be astonished by the longevity of his hoax, but given his temperament, he was probably amused by the impact of his stunt, which was an especially colorful illustration of the echo chamber effect.

Urban Legends

Urban legends are modern myths that used to depend almost entirely on word of mouth for their dissemination but have gotten an extra boost with the advent of e-mail. Either method of communication provides the echo chamber. Classic urban legends include the fancy sports car that gets sold for $50, the unsuspecting tourist in Mexico who buys what he or she thinks is a Chihuahua but once home discovers that the little dog is actually a rat, the well-meaning but absentminded woman who tragically tries to dry off her wet poodle in a microwave, and the passing motorist who picks up a hitchhiker in a prom dress but learns later that the girl he drove home died several years before on that very night. None of these stories is true, and yet you're likely to hear many of them told again and again as true, albeit with some variations that either bring them up to date or associate them with local landmarks.

What makes urban legends convincing?

What makes urban legends convincing, among other things, is that they are usually told by someone you know who insists that he or she knows someone who knows the person the incident actually happened to. For this reason, urban legends are sometimes called FOAF or "friend of a friend" stories. Ironically, the same thing that initially makes urban legends seem convincing is what ultimately gives them away as false.

How can you detect an urban legend?

If you hear a story from someone who knows someone who has a friend the story "really happened to," that's usually a dead giveaway. Urban legends almost never hold up to scrutiny if you try to trace them back to the source. Even in those situations in which the legend is based on truth, it inevitably gets distorted or exaggerated. Although e-mail has done a lot to increase the spread of urban legends, the Internet has made it easier to debunk them. Several websites, including snopes.com, track urban legends and provide regularly updated listings of legends and in most cases—although not always—proof that they aren't true. This can be valuable because people who unwittingly pass on an urban legend can often get quite irritable if the reliability of their story is questioned. Actual evidence instead of unsubstantiated disbelief is usually enough to convince most people.

The Dangers of Summer

How does the echo chamber affect information that is true?

Not all information that gets amplified in the echo chamber is false. Sometimes stories are true but they get blown out of proportion. A good example was the widespread fear of shark attacks and the spread of the West Nile virus in the summer of 2003. From the nervous reactions of some vacationers, you might've gotten the impression that if "Jaws" didn't get them, then the West Nile would. Were the fears of ferocious sharks and a mosquito-borne virus justified? Not according to an article and graphic in the *New York Times* that compared the relative dangers of what it called "The Real Dangers of Summer."[4] The greatest risks, according to the piece, were skin cancer and food poisoning. The former would strike one in 200 people, the latter one in 800. But what of the West Nile virus and sharks? The *Times* statistics showed that these were actually the lowest risks of all summertime hazards, affecting one in 68,500 and one in six million, respectively. So why the hysteria? Additional statistics in the same graphic provided a clue. Whereas only 359 newspaper articles had been written the previous summer about the dangers of skin cancer and food poisoning, during the same period a whopping 2,516 articles had dealt with either the West Nile virus or the hungry sharks.

[4]David Ropeik and Nigel Holmes, "Never Bitten, Twice Shy: The Real Dangers of Summer," *New York Times* (August 9, 2003).

 **Online Study Center**   www.college.hmco.com/pic/pauk9e

Watching Out for Confirmation Bias

What happens with
confirmation bias?
What influences whether
we tune in or tune out
information?

Some information that's unreliable may be embraced while other information that's reliable may be overlooked. Why? It's called confirmation bias.

Have you ever had the experience of learning the meaning of a word, only to find that suddenly everyone around you seems to be using that same word? Of course, if the word you learned actually *is* a new word (also known as a *neologism*), then it may well be that the number of people using that word is increasing. But if it's a word that's only new for you, it's unlikely that others have suddenly decided to use it more often on your account. What's more plausible is that you've just become more attuned to that word. As we move through our daily lives, the sheer magnitude of information we confront means it's almost inevitable that we will tune in some information and tune out some other. When the information relates to something you already know or believe, you're more likely to tune it in. And if the information doesn't relate to something you already know or believe, you're more likely to tune it out.

When is selectivity harmful?

In the case of learning a new word, this tendency is relatively harmless. But the same phenomenon can act to reinforce your particular viewpoint or bias at the expense of other information that may actually contradict or modify your beliefs. This is known as confirmation bias. In the journal *Review of General Psychology*, psychologist Raymond S. Nickerson defines confirmation bias as "the unwitting selectivity in the acquisition and use of evidence."[5] So, although selectivity is an essential tool in reducing the glut of information you're exposed to, it can also have a negative effect by shielding you from vital information or depriving you from the complete picture.

What did Forer's experiment
show?

One of the most famous demonstrations of confirmation bias was an experiment conducted by a psychology professor named Forer, who administered a personality profile test to his students. When Forer received the completed tests, he promptly threw them all out and instead, unbeknownst to the students, returned the identical personality profile to each member of his class, asking each student to read his or her profile and then rate its accuracy on a scale of 0 to 5, with five meaning "excellent" and four meaning "good." Incredibly, the personality profile, even though it was written without any of the students in mind, still received a cumulative average of 4.26 for accuracy. What the students didn't realize—until he told them—is that Forer had clipped the profile out of a newspaper horoscope column. The profile was ambiguous but vaguely complimentary. The criticisms were mild. Thanks to confirmation bias, most of the students who read the profile related to its positive elements, ig-

[5]Raymond S. Nickerson, "Confirmation Bias: A Ubiquitous Phenomenon in Many Guises," *Review of General Psychology* 2, no. 2 (1998): 175–220.

nored those elements that were too negative or didn't relate specifically to them, and then concluded that it was an accurate assessment of their particular personality traits![6]

What can you do to avoid confirmation bias?

All of us are susceptible to confirmation bias. It's important to be aware of this tendency and keep your mind open for differing evidence and information that might change your viewpoint. Also, it doesn't hurt to have a set of consistent guidelines that you use to gauge the validity of information.

Why is it risky to make decisions based on your "gut"?

Many people make a decision whether or not to trust information based on their "gut." And it's true that our hunches and instincts do seem to provide us with clues, although there is very little scientific data to support this. Unfortunately, emotional appeals have a way of short-circuiting common sense. It happens to nearly all of us at times. Articulate, charismatic liars can sometimes trigger a positive response while honest but awkward writing or speaking can sometimes put us on guard.

Recognizing Logical Fallacies

What are logical fallacies?

Although your own biases can affect the way you select and interpret information, there are also elements embedded in some arguments that can lead you to unknowingly accept a false conclusion as fact. Usually there is a flaw in an otherwise reasonable argument that renders it invalid. These are commonly known as logical fallacies and are used by writers and speakers sometimes accidentally but often on purpose to lead you to a desired conclusion.

What is an example of a logical fallacy?

One of the best-known logical fallacies has to do with ice cream sales. It suggests that because an increase in ice cream sales seems to correspond with an increase in crime, ice cream must cause crime. What's tricky about a fallacy is that it's usually made up of a true premise or premises that reach a false conclusion. Therefore, a person who isn't listening or reading critically may notice the true statements but overlook the logical leap that leads to a false outcome. It's true that ice cream sales and crime often increase at the same time. But it's not true that one causes the other. (It's more likely that hot weather is the cause for the increase in both.)

Another common fallacy is known as the straw man. That's a situation in which the writer or speaker uses an opposing example that is either weak or imaginary in order to make his argument appear to gain legitimacy or strength. The straw man is often called "some" or "some people" to present the appearance of a real opposition without ever naming it. So, if the authors of a study skills textbook wanted to appear more courageous and defiant than they actually are, they might write: "Although there are some who may want to do away

[6]Robert Todd Carroll, "Forer Effect," *The Skeptics Dictionary,* available at http://www .skepDic.com/forer/html.

Online Study Center   www.college.hmco.com/pic/pauk9e

with study skills textbooks altogether, we were determined to make sure that our book was published." A person who read this might feel increased respect and admiration for these brave authors and might even be tempted to purchase an additional book or two just to spite those who want to do away with study skills textbooks altogether. But there's only one problem. The enemy is never specified. It's a phantom. And that is how the straw man fallacy works.

There are several books and websites devoted to fallacies. All of them are informative, and many are quite entertaining.

Books

Capaldi, Nicholas. *The Art of Deception: An Introduction to Critical Thinking: How to Win an Argument, Defend a Case, Recognize a Fallacy, See Through a Deception.* Prometheus Books, 1987.

Damer, T. Edward. *Attacking Faulty Reasoning: Practical Guide to Fallacy-Free Arguments,* 5th ed. Wadsworth, 2004.

Engel, S. Morris. *With Good Reason: An Introduction to Informal Fallacies,* 6th ed. St. Martins, 1999.

Gula, Robert J. *Nonsense: A Handbook of Logical Fallacies.* Axios, 2002.

Whyte, Jamie. *Crimes Against Logic.* McGraw-Hill, 2004.

Websites

Bruce Thompson's Fallacy Page. http://www.cuyamaca.edu/bruce.thompson/Fallacies/intro_fallacies.asp.

Fallacies: The Internet Encyclopedia of Philosophy. http://www.iep.utm.edu/f/fallacies.htm.

Logical Fallacies: The Fallacy Files. http://www.fallacyfiles.org/.

Logical Fallacies and the Art of Debate. http://www.csun.edu/~dgw61315/fallacies.html.

The Logical Fallacies. http://www.intrepidsoftware.com/fallacy/toc.php.

Following a Set of Guidelines for Analysis

Given all the potential ways in which information can be misleading, how do you consistently establish what's reliable and what isn't?

Critical thinking authority Vincent Ruggiero suggests a four-step "comprehensive thinking strategy."[7]

1. *Identify facts and opinions.* If the information is common knowledge or easily verifiable, it's likely to be factual. If not, treat it as opinion.

---

[7]Vincent Ryan Ruggiero, *Becoming a Critical Thinker,* 5th ed. (Boston: Houghton Mifflin, 1999), pp. 26–27.

Where can you learn more about fallacies?

What guidelines can you follow to test information for reliability?

2. *Check the facts and test the opinions.* If the information is factual, can you verify it? Did the author or speaker seem to leave out anything important? If it's opinion, do the speaker's views stand up to scrutiny or are they easily refuted?
3. *Evaluate the evidence.* If the author or speaker has offered support for any opinions, is this support reasonable and sufficient?
4. *Make your judgment.* Based on the facts and the evidence, rather than your gut feelings or preferences, decide whether you consider the information reliable.

What special challenge does Internet information create?

The proliferation of online news, opinion, and reference sites has led some to question the reliability of Internet information. One of the Internet's greatest strengths—its wide-open, inclusive nature—is also a potential weakness. With a few days' work and a little bit of money, a talented person can put together a website that superficially resembles one of the top professional news and information sites and yet ignores the standards for quality and accuracy that traditional news organizations live by. Although the following questions may be especially important to ask about Internet sites, they can also apply to traditional TV, radio, magazines, and newspapers.

1. *Who owns them?* More and more news and information operations are owned by companies whose emphasis is on something other than news. This may affect their tone or approach. Others aren't news organizations at all but lobbies or think tanks organized to promote a particular product or viewpoint but whose publications are designed to look like news. With newspapers, magazines, and websites, you can usually find information about the ownership in the paper or magazine or on the site. With television or radio stations, it can take a little more digging. Most news operations try to maintain a wall (see #3) between their business and editorial operations, but it isn't always possible.
2. *How do they make their money?* A key rule of investigative journalism is to "follow the money," and to some degree these special journalists are professional critical thinkers. Almost no publication or website relies solely on money from subscribers to exist. As disillusioning as it is to realize, financial obligations to owners or advertisers can sometimes influence what a publication or broadcaster does and doesn't cover. For example, a newspaper that relies heavily on automobile ads may be reluctant to cover a scandal at a car dealership, whereas a magazine that runs ads for a local restaurant may feel pressure to give that restaurant a good review. Advertisements are usually pretty easy to notice and the nature of the advertising can sometimes be illuminating. It can tell you something about the viewers, readers, or listening audience and may give you an idea of what topics could test the organization's editorial independence.

 **Online Study Center**   www.college.hmco.com/pic/pauk9e

3. *Can you tell the difference between news, opinion, and advertising?* In the past, publications and broadcasters have gone to great lengths to distinguish between news and paid advertising, feeling that it serves the public better to make sure that this distinction is clear. In newspapers, this is commonly known as "the wall." Journalists are normally well aware of this wall and are proud of its existence. The wall between news and opinion isn't always as clear, and that can be a problem when one is mistaken for the other.

4. *Where do they get their information?* Some seat-of-the-pants news operations rely on national and international news wires for most or even all of their information. Larger operations have their own staffs of reporters and columnists. Over time, if you pay attention, you should be able to get a sense of a particular news service or journalist's track record for reliability.

5. *How well presented is the information?* Crudely written or clumsily delivered words can occasionally pack a wallop, but, in general, sloppy writing or speaking should set off alarm bells in your head.

6. *What other information is presented?* You can sometimes learn about the reliability of an article from the company it keeps. This is especially true on the Internet. If someone sends you a link to an Internet news story, see if you can navigate back to the homepage of the site where the story came from. The "mix" of a site's stories can be a tip-off. For example, a White House exclusive may not look very reliable if you discover that it's running alongside a story about a dog with two heads and an article about a miracle weight-loss product.

Is there a simpler way to determine if something is reliable?

A simpler way to determine whether information is reliable or not is basically no different than the strategy for zeroing in on all valuable information: Stay alert, think about your thinking, and above all, ask questions!

FINAL WORDS

What surprising result can zeroing in on valuable ideas sometimes produce?

Not only will zeroing in on what's valuable enable you to extract the most relevant, important, and reliable information from what you read and hear and make it a part of your personal web of knowledge, but it will also produce a result that may surprise you: It will help you to derive real pleasure out of thinking!

HAVE YOU MISSED SOMETHING?

SENTENCE COMPLETION

Complete the following sentences with one of the three words listed below each sentence.

1. The story of Eddie Rickenbacker illustrates the importance of _____.

   airlines   questions   reading

2. Information in an article or chapter is usually organized _____.

   hierarchically   collectively   repeatedly

3. In newspapers, the distinction between news and advertising is commonly known as _____.

   "the gap"   "the tower"   "the wall"

MATCHING

In each blank space in the left column, write the letter preceding the phrase in the right column that matches the left item best.

_____ 1. Ballpark

_____ 2. Socratic

_____ 3. Fallacy

_____ 4. Mencken

_____ 5. Forer

_____ 6. Boolean

_____ 7. Bull's-eye

_____ 8. Questions

a. Ancient method of using questions and answers to promote understanding

b. Wrote a fictional story that was adopted as historical fact

c. The engine that drives the whole understanding process

d. Method of searching for information when you're not exactly sure what you're looking for

e. Method of searching when you know exactly what you're looking for

f. Conducted an experiment with his class that demonstrated confirmation bias

g. Method that lets you define a logical relationship between two or more search terms

h. A flaw in an otherwise logical argument

TRUE-FALSE

Circle T *beside the* true *statements and* F *beside the* false *statements.*

1. T   F   Words are lifeless until you interact with them.
2. T   F   Rather than simply *ingesting* what you read or hear, you should *digest* it.
3. T   F   Sharks and West Nile virus are the greatest summertime hazards.
4. T   F   Math instructors are careful to keep irrelevant information out of the word problems they assign.
5. T   F   Most programs that read electronic documents have a Find command.

MULTIPLE CHOICE

Choose the word or phrase that completes each sentence most accurately, and circle the letter that precedes it.

1. Valuable information should be
   a. relevant.
   b. important.
   c. reliable.
   d. all of the above.

2. Many books can be thought of as a series of
   a. answers to invisible questions.
   b. clues to unsolvable mysteries.
   c. episodes from timeless stories.
   d. conclusions to unspoken introductions.

3. The most important information in a paragraph is
   a. the controlling idea.
   b. a question.
   c. the last sentence.
   d. a detail.

4. The story of the Chihuahua that turned out to be a rat is an example of
   a. confirmation bias.
   b. an urban legend.
   c. a logical fallacy.
   d. a controlling idea.

5. A key rule of investigative journalism is
   a. know thyself.
   b. trust but verify.
   c. follow the money.
   d. none of the above.

SHORT ANSWER

Supply a brief answer for each of the following questions.

1. Contrast relevance and importance.
2. Compare the functions of ballpark and bull's-eye searching.
3. "Almost all books come with questions." Discuss this statement.
4. What is confirmation bias?

IT'S YOUR Q

The Q System uses marginal questions to encourage active reading. You'll notice that most but not all paragraphs in this chapter are accompanied by marginal questions. Now it's your Q. Scan the chapter for any paragraph that is missing a question, reread the paragraph, establish the main idea, and then arrive at a question that elicits it. Use the questions in the surrounding paragraphs as models for your own marginal questions.

WORDS IN CONTEXT

From the three choices beside each numbered item, select the one that most nearly expresses the meaning of the italicized word in the quote. Make a light check mark (✓) next to your choice.

Nations are not ruined by one act of *violence*, but gradually and in an almost *imperceptible* manner by the *depreciation* of their circulating currency, through its *excessive* quantity.

—Nicolaus Copernicus (1473–1543), Polish astronomer

1. act of *violence*	damaging force	enormous effect	gigantic power
2. almost *imperceptible*	unknown	controlled	unseen
3. the *depreciation*	stable value	decreased value	increased value
4. *excessive* quantity	commercial	inordinate	required

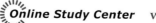 **Online Study Center** www.college.hmco.com/pic/pauk9e

Another advantage of being rich is that all your faults are called *eccentricities*.
—Anonymous

5. called *eccentricities*   creative   peculiarities   inventive

No man can be *conservative* until he has something to lose.
—James P. Warburg (1896–1969), American publicist

6. *conservative*   objective   cautious   judicious

When a subject becomes totally *obsolete* we make it a required course.
—Peter Drucker (1909–2005), American business philosopher and author

7. totally *obsolete*   indispensable   outdated   necessary

THE WORD HISTORY SYSTEM

Enthrall
literally, to enslave

enthrall en-thrall' *v.* 1. To hold spellbound; captivate. 2. To enslave.

Enthrall presents another case of a word the original and literal sense of which is cruel, but the modern, figurative use of which is much more pleasant. When we say that we are *enthralled* by a song, or a book, or something else with captivating charm, it is interesting to remember that the original meaning of the word was "to enslave." *Thrall* is Anglo-Saxon for "slave." To *enthrall* meant, therefore, "to enslave," "to reduce to the condition of a thrall." The literal sense of "enslave," "make captive," easily yields a figurative sense, "captivate the senses," "hold spellbound," "charm," as with a song or a story.

Reprinted by permission. From *Picturesque Word Origins* © 1933 by G. & C. Merriam Co. (now Merriam-Webster, Incorporated).

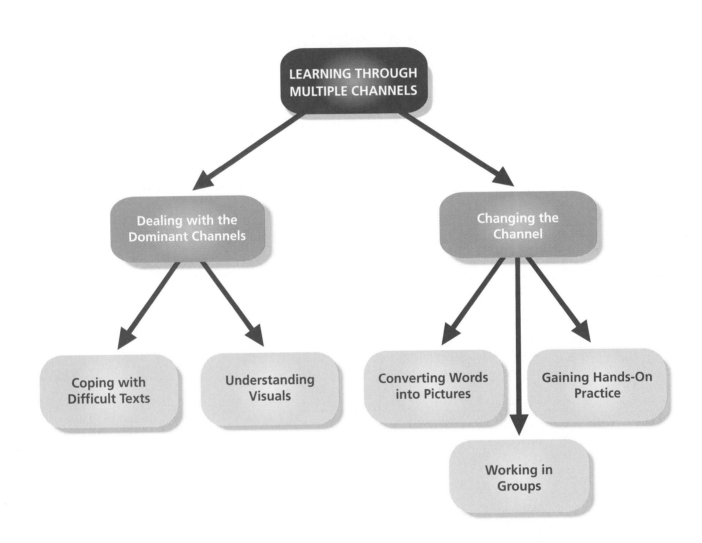

Learning Through Multiple Channels

Instructors don't all teach in the same manner, and students don't all learn in the same way. There are numerous channels for teaching and learning. Some, like words and images, are widespread and unavoidable, whereas others, like group work and hands-on learning, provide alternatives when traditional routes turn out to be tough going. This chapter explains how to tune in to the dominant channels of teaching, how to change the channel to enhance your understanding, and how to make the most of your personal learning style.

- **Coping with Difficult Texts**
- **Understanding Visuals**
- **Turning Words into Pictures**
- **Gaining Hands-On Practice**
- **Working in Groups**

If you wish to advance into the infinite, explore the finite in all directions.

Johann Wolfgang von Goethe (1749–1832), German author, painter, philosopher, scientist, and politician

How will an understanding of learning styles affect your success in college?

Although we may sit in the same classrooms or log on to the same websites, we don't all learn in the same way. Instructors are well aware of this and most students have at least a vague sense that this is true. Unfortunately, despite the diversity of learning styles, course information is still primarily conveyed on two basic channels: as symbols and as shapes. The symbols are the words and numbers we read and hear. The shapes are the graphs, charts, maps, and other illustrations that often accompany those words. First, it helps to have a good sense of what kind of learner you are. (If you haven't done so already, take the ten-question Learning Styles Self-Assessment in the "To the Student" section, page xix.) Then, in order to learn and succeed, you must develop strategies to deal with the dominant channels of symbols and shapes and use your preferred learning styles to provide additional support.

Dealing with the Dominant Channels

What are the dominant learning channels?

It's rare that you'll take a college course that doesn't have text you need to read and images you're expected to understand and interpret. With few exceptions, to succeed in college you will need to learn to operate on these dominant channels, to understand your assigned texts to the best of your ability, and to make sense out of any accompanying charts, graphs, and illustrations.

Coping with Difficult Texts

Why are some textbooks so difficult to understand?

Sometimes you and the required text for your course may not "hit it off." There are several factors that can make a textbook seem difficult. Here are three of them:

Writing style or tone. As we'll see in Chapter 10, most books have a distinctive style or tone, one that usually reflects the voice of the author or authors. Some books are chatty and informal. Others are staid and scholarly. You may not feel as though you are in sync with the way the authors choose to express their ideas. If so, that can make reading the assignments more challenging and even aggravating. Try to stick it out, though. The style may seem jarring at first but there's a good chance you'll grow accustomed to it over time.

Vocabulary. If a book seems to be "over your head," a primary reason for this will often be its vocabulary level. If you're having trouble with a textbook because you don't understand what the words mean, then you probably should be reading two books at once—your text and your dictionary—until you've finally grown accustomed enough to the vocabulary that you can keep reading without stopping to look something up. With some books, the new and challenging words never end, but more often it's just a matter of getting up to speed. Once you learn the lingo, you'll be fine.

Organization.   Trouble with the way a book is organized may indicate a conflict between the author's writing style and your personal learning style. As Felder and Soloman explain,[1] *sequential learners* tend to process things methodically, step by step, relating each new piece of information to the facts that came before it as though following a recipe. *Global learners* tend to learn in bursts and insights, grabbing huge handfuls of seemingly unrelated information and then suddenly (and often unexpectedly) establishing connections between ideas in one great big "Aha!" If you're a sequential learner and you run into that rare textbook that's written globally, your best defense is to search first for some sort of summary at the end of the chapter that will pull things together and provide you with a road map for your wild ride. If the author writes sequentially and you learn globally, you might as well get used to it. The vast majority of courses and texts are delivered in a sequential fashion. Global learners can adjust to a sequential text and add some unaccustomed structure to their way of looking at things by taking a few moments to systematically survey a reading assignment (see Chapter 10) before diving in.

   Keep in mind that most relationships, even those between a student and a textbook, take work and take time. But if there truly seems to be a disconnect between you and your book, you may want to find a supplementary text or "read" the original book in a different form.

Use a Supplementary Text

How will a supplementary text help?

If for whatever reason you're having difficulties understanding the course's primary textbook and you've already sought help from the instructor or a tutor, then a supplementary textbook can sometimes help you gain a better grasp of the subject. In some instances you may be able to find another textbook that covers the same topic that your course textbook does, but it's more likely that you will have to use different supplementary texts for different parts of your course text. It's important to stress that this is a supplementary textbook, not an alternate one. Your instructor still has every right and reason to expect you to be studying from the required text. Therefore, any reading you do in a second text will be in addition to your regular text, not instead of it. Once you have a better grasp of the subject or ideas you were struggling with, return to the regular text and see if it is easier to understand.

[1]Richard A. Felder and Barbara M. Soloman, "Learning Styles and Strategies," available at http://www.ncsu.edu/felder-public/ILSdir/styles.htm.

 **Online Study Center**   www.college.hmco.com/pic/pauk9e

Listen Instead of Reading

What is the value of listening instead of reading?

Auditory learners comprehend better when they hear information instead of reading it on a page or screen. This means that although lectures are helpful, reading assignments can sometimes be a struggle. The organization Recording for the Blind and Dyslexic (RFB&D) provides audio versions of a large number of textbooks (http://www.rfbd.org). In addition, many popular books—both fiction and nonfiction—are released in audio form by commercial publishers and are often available from your college or public library for free. It's important to stick with the unabridged versions, however, or you may miss a part of the book that is stressed in class and on your tests but is absent from the copy you listened to.

Understanding Visuals

All of us are taught to read words at an early age. But when are we taught to read pictures? When you read words, you're cracking a code. That code is the English language, and its message is the meaning you extract from words, sentences, and paragraphs. Although we spend a great deal of time decoding language, most of the codes around us are visual. We can decode a smile, for example, and know how its meaning differs from that of a frown. Visual materials in textbooks use codes as well to supply messages that are often as important as the meanings contained in sentences and paragraphs. For that reason, they must be read every bit as carefully. Like reading a paragraph, reading a picture simply means extracting its message.

Use the OPTIC System

What is the purpose of the OPTIC system?

Many students mistakenly give visuals only a quick glance or even skip over them entirely. But these graphic materials should be scrutinized as carefully and as systematically as paragraphs. The OPTIC system will help you take an organized approach to this task.

What do the five letters in OPTIC stand for?

The five letters in the word *OPTIC* (which means "pertaining to the eye") provide you with a simple system for remembering the five elements of analyzing a visual:

O is for *overview*.
P is for *parts*.
T is for *title*.
I is for *interrelationships*.
C is for *conclusion*.

What are the five steps of the OPTIC system?

Using these five elements as cues, you can conduct a meaningful analysis of almost any diagram, graph, or illustration by following these steps:

1. Begin by conducting a brief *overview* of the visual.
2. Then zero in on the *parts* of the visual. Read all labels, and note any elements or details that seem important.
3. Now read the *title* of the visual so that you're clear on the subject it is covering.
4. Next use the title as your theory and the parts of the visual as clues to detect and specify the *interrelationships* in the graphic.
5. Finally, try to reach a *conclusion* about the visual as a whole. What does it mean? Why was it included in the text? Sum up the message of the visual in just a sentence or two.

Learn the Language of Graphs

What are the most common types of graphs?

You are most likely to encounter three general types of graphs: circle graphs, bar graphs, and line graphs. The purpose of a circle graph is unique, whereas bar and line graphs perform the same basic function.

What is the purpose of the circle graph?

Decode Circle Graphs   The purpose of a circle graph, also known as a pie chart, is to proportionally show the relationship of parts (slices) to a whole (the pie). Although these graphs are relatively rare in highly technical books, they regularly appear in newspapers as well as in textbooks on topics other than mathematics and science. The popularity of the circle graph is mainly due to its simplicity. In most cases, you can tell at a glance the proportions the graph illustrates—that is, the various-sized slices of the pie. For example, in Figure 8.1, the circle graph gives you a clear picture of the population distribution of the United States.

Decode Bar and Line Graphs   The purpose of a bar or line graph is to illustrate the relationship of a set of dependent variables to a set of independent variables. Variables are numbers that can change. For example, the number we use to refer to the year is a variable. It increases by one every twelve months. Population is another variable. It changes when someone is born or dies, when someone becomes a citizen, or when someone leaves the country. Years and dates in general are called independent variables because they change on their own. The population of the United States does not influence the fact that a new year begins every 365 or 366 days. Quantities such as population are called dependent variables because their change occurs in relation to another variable, such as the year. For example, we measure the changes of the U.S. population every ten years when the census is taken.

How do bar and line graphs differ?

Although bar and line graphs both show how a dependent variable such as population increases or decreases in relation to an independent variable such as the year, each takes a slightly different approach. Bar graphs (see Figure 8.2) focus on specific changes; line graphs (see Figure 8.3) illustrate long-term trends.

Online Study Center   www.college.hmco.com/pic/pauk9e

Figure 8.1

U.S. Population by Region
Circle graphs (pie charts) show the relationship of several parts to a whole.

Source: U.S. Census Bureau, Census 2004.

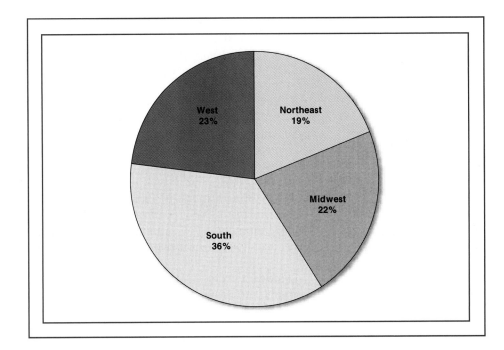

Figure 8.2

Population Growth in the United States and Canada, 1950–2000
Bar graphs show sizes of individual items and illustrate comparisons.

Sources: U.S. Census Bureau; Statistics Canada.

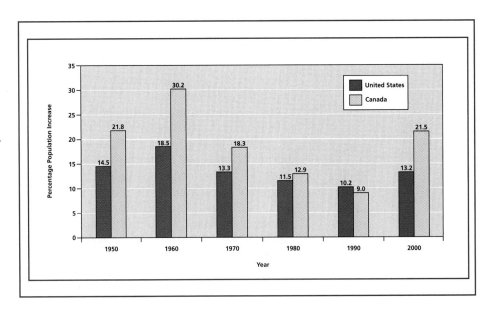

Figure 8.3
Percentage Increase in U.S. Population, 1800–2000
Line graphs show long-term trends in data.
Source: U.S. Census Bureau.

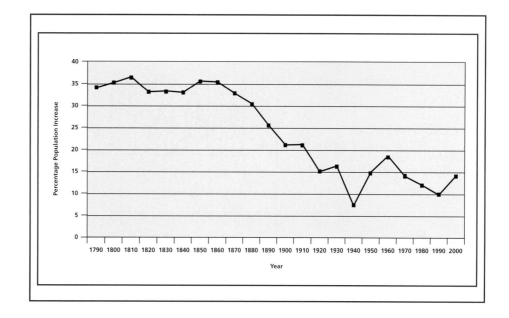

One way to visualize this distinction is to think of bar graphs as snapshots and line graphs as movies. If you were to take successive snapshots of a long jumper, you would have a series of photographs showing successive stages of the jump. If you were to film the same jump with a movie camera, you'd have a continuous record of the entire jump. Figure 8.4 illustrates this idea.

What are the relative strengths and weaknesses of bar and line graphs?

Like snapshots and movies, each type of graph has strengths. Bar graphs are good for comparing the individual sizes or amounts of items, and they provide clear comparisons of several sets of data at once. Line graphs are useful for showing changes in data over long periods of time. For instance, if you wanted to examine the country's population increase over a brief period of time or if you wanted to compare it with the population of another country, you would probably use a bar graph. Figure 8.2 shows that the growth in U.S. population was relatively steady from 1950 through 2000, whereas Canada's population growth surged during the 1950s and 1960s and then again at the end of the twentieth century. But if you wanted to show the percentage increase in U.S. population since the eighteenth century, a line graph would be a better visual. Figure 8.3 shows that the growth in U.S. population has generally slowed since 1850.

What should you do once you understand the language of graphs?

Regardless of whether the graphic is a circle, bar, or line graph, once you understand the language of the particular graph, you can methodically extract its meaning in the same way you would with a picture or diagram—by using the OPTIC system. Figure 8.5 analyzes a graph using this system.

Figure 8.4
Snapshots Versus Movies: Bar Graphs and Line Graphs
A bar graph can be compared to a set of snapshots, whereas a line graph is more like a movie.

Source: Track and Field Omnibook, Fourth Ed., 1985, by Ken Doherty, Tafnews Press (Track and Field News), Mountain View, Calif. Reprinted with permission.

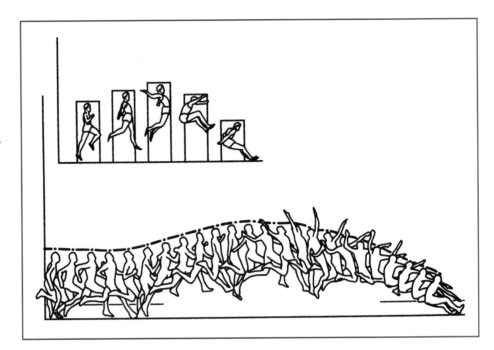

Figure 8.5
Using the OPTIC System to Analyze a Graph
Source: ThinkEquity Partners.

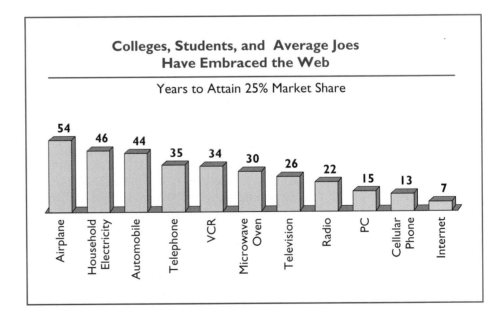

Colleges, Students, and Average Joes Have Embraced the Web

Years to Attain 25% Market Share

Airplane	Household Electricity	Automobile	Telephone	VCR	Microwave Oven	Television	Radio	PC	Cellular Phone	Internet
54	46	44	35	34	30	26	22	15	13	7

Figure 8.5
continued

> **OVERVIEW**
> A graph with a series of bars that gets steadily shorter moving left to right.
>
> **PARTS**
> • The 11 bars represent new technologies or innovations.
> • The names of the technologies run along the bottom of the graph.
> • The height of each bar represents how many years it took each technology to be adopted by 25 percent of the market.
>
> **TITLE**
> * "Colleges, Students, and 'Average Joes' Have Embraced the Web"
> The phrase "Average Joes" seems to suggest in an informal way that Web use is common among all types of people. The subheading "Years to Attain 25% Market Share" says more about what the graph actually shows.
>
> **INTERRELATIONSHIPS**
> • Almost every technology on the graph took at least twice as long to be adopted as the Internet. (Cell phones took almost twice as long.)
> • Three of the most recent innovations—PCs, cell phones, and the Internet—have been adopted much faster than the other eight technologies listed on the graph.
> • Airplanes took the longest (54 years) to be adopted by 25 percent of the market.
> • Although the VCR and microwave oven are more recent innovations than TV and radio, both took longer to be adopted.
>
> **CONCLUSION**
> As the graph's title suggests, at least one-quarter of the market has "embraced the Web." And compared to all the other technologies listed on the graph, it did so in a very short time. The graph doesn't show or explain whether people are simply adopting new technologies faster than they once did or whether the Internet is exceptional.

Watch Out for Distorted Data

How can you avoid being misled by pictures?

Pictures, like words, can occasionally be misleading. Whereas many readers have learned to detect deceptive phrases or sentences, not everyone is quite as sophisticated about detecting distortions in pictures or other kinds of graphic materials. When you consider a graph, illustration, or chart, it helps to do so with a critical eye, paying particular attention to the format, the scale, and the overall context.

How does the way that data are formatted affect their meaning?

Format   Factual data—especially statistics—can be placed in graphic formats that distort the information. The book *How to Lie with Statistics* exposes some of

the devious tricks that are used and is also fun to read.[2] For example, you should be wary of the word *average*, and you should try to find the highest and lowest figures that went into each average. Two companies may have an average salary of $29,000. But if the range of salaries in one company is from $6,000 to $90,000, and the range in the other company is from $20,000 to $35,000, the salary policies of the two companies are quite different.

What effect does scale have on a graphic?

Scale   Don't be overly impressed by the steepness of the lines in graphs. Look at the side of every graph to find the scale—the value of each increment. Units of $100 can make a line much steeper than units of $1,000. Always convert what you see into words; otherwise you'll remember the steepness or flatness but not the real information that is being presented.

How does context affect the meaning of a graphic?

Context   Remember that visual relationships can be tricky. The frame around a diagram can actually change the way you see the diagram. For example, this is a diamond-shaped figure:

But notice that when the same figure is placed in a frame,

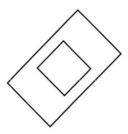

it looks like a square. The size and shape of a chart or graph can also affect what you see. Data that may be quite neutral or ordinary can be made to appear startling by the form and scale of the graphic. If you read graphics carefully, you'll see them properly, rather than as someone else may expect—or want—you to see them.

[2]Darrell Huff, *How to Lie with Statistics* (New York: W. W. Norton, 1993).

Changing the Channel

What can you do to supplement difficult courses with more comfortable learning approaches?

If you're fortunate, your course textbook will be easy to follow and any graphs, charts, or illustrations will make sense to you. However, if you're struggling with the standard way your class is being taught, you can try these other approaches to learning to help the course make sense. If you don't have difficulties with the instructor's approach, you can still use additional learning styles to add extra dimensions to your understanding.

Converting words into pictures.   Even though visual communication is one of the predominant channels for information, visually oriented students can use their graphical way of thinking to actually rethink information that may not have been conveyed visually in the first place.

Working in groups.   Nearly all students, but especially those who demonstrate an interpersonal intelligence, should find it helpful to work in groups.

Gaining hands-on practice.   Active, practical, hands-on learners, who may be impatient with abstractions, can reinforce concepts that might have been difficult to grasp in lectures or readings by trying out examples and drills that should make ideas clearer.

Converting Words into Pictures

How do visual learners incorporate pictures into normally nonvisual areas?

Whereas some students find it difficult to extract meaning from images, many others are predominantly visual and actually prefer the picture perspective. They not only find it easy to analyze graphs and illustrations, but often incorporate visual thinking into other normally nonvisual areas. For example, a visual learner who is listening to a lecture may simultaneously be creating a mental picture of what the speaker is saying. Students who think visually may even find it important to be able to see the speakers during the lecture while listening to them speak.[3] If you are predominantly visually oriented (and even if you're not), you may find it helpful to add an extra dimension to your learning by writing in pictures.

How do you write in pictures?

We now know that reading a visual means studying a diagram or a graph and turning its message into a sentence or two. When you write in pictures, you simply reverse the process. You convert the sentences you've read or heard into a diagram or graph.

[3]Available at http://www.learnativity.com/learningstyles.html.

Online Study Center   www.college.hmco.com/pic/pauk9e

If the information you encounter is concrete, your task is fairly simple. The objects you sketch in your diagram represent real, tangible things. If, however, the ideas you read or hear are more abstract, such as information about the characteristics of amphibians, your approach needs to be a bit more involved. Instead of drawing sketches of the animals, which doesn't tell you much about their characteristics, you need to create a concept map. Although your approach to abstract ideas is different from your approach to concrete ones, your goal is the same: to turn something you can read into something you can see (see Figure 8.6).

Add Illustrations to Your Notes

When should you add illustrations to your notes?

As you read your textbook or go over your lecture notes, don't just jot down the key ideas in words; sketch some of them as well. In some subjects this sketching will come naturally. Science courses, for example, are full of information that can be drawn. The parts of a one-celled organism or the connections in a computer network are much easier to understand if you put little diagrams of them in your notes. Sometimes the drawing is done for you. If the instructor puts a sketch on the board or screen or if the textbook author includes diagrams in the chapter, add these pictures to your notes in the same way that you would jot down important examples. When a drawing doesn't exist, make one of your own.

What should you do in subjects where elements aren't easily drawn?

A history course may not feature easily drawn elements, but it does include plenty of concrete data that can be translated into picture form. A series of important dates, for example, can be turned into a timeline, and individual historical facts can be visualized almost as easily.

Here is an example of how words can be converted into a picture. The following paragraph describes an experiment conducted by the English physicist and chemist Michael Faraday (1791–1867):

> In 1831, Michael Faraday, one of Britain's greatest scientists, did the experiments which completely demonstrated the close relationship between electricity and magnetism. One of his famous experiments was to take a coil of wire and connect the ends across an instrument capable of measuring tiny currents. By quickly pushing a bar magnet through the coil he was able to produce a small current in the coil and to measure that current. What he was really doing was to change the strength of the magnetic field in the coil by inserting and removing the magnet. The more rapidly he changed the field the more current he could generate.[4]

Figure 8.7 is an example of how one student converted this descriptive paragraph into a diagram, which helped the student not only to understand the described process but to visualize and remember it as well. If a question about

[4]J. D. Jukes, *Man-Made Sun* (New York: Abelard-Schuman, 1959), p. 33.

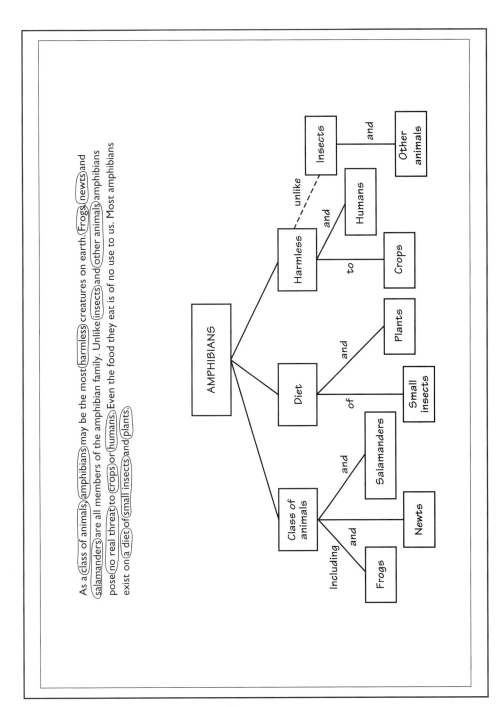

As a (class of animals) (amphibians) may be the most (harmless) creatures on earth. (Frogs) (newts) and (salamanders) are all members of the amphibian family. Unlike (insects) and (other animals) amphibians pose (no real threat) to (crops) or (humans). Even the food they eat is of no use to us. Most amphibians exist on (a diet) of (small insects) and (plants.)

Figure 8.6
A Concept Map of Text Information

Figure 8.7
A Descriptive Paragraph Made Visual

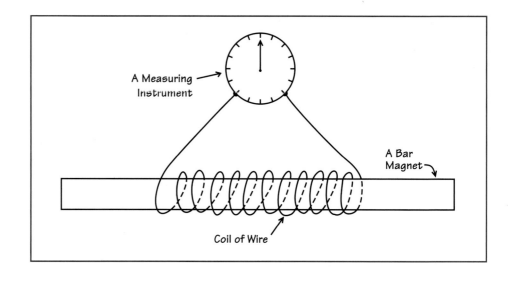

Faraday's experiment appeared on a test, it is not hard to imagine how well a student with this picture in mind would do.

You don't have to be Michelangelo or Leonardo da Vinci to draw diagrams in your notes. The important point is to tap into the right side of your brain, where most of our visual thinking is done. In his influential "dual coding" theory, Allan Paivio from the University of Western Ontario concluded that information is more readily recalled when it is learned as both pictures and words.[5] Thus, if you make both a verbal and a visual effort to recall something you've learned, your memory will have two places in which to search for the information instead of just one. With your full mind at work, you will increase your brain power, regardless of whether your drawing looks like doodling or a priceless work of art.

Why is it helpful to add diagrams to your notes?

Turn Abstract Ideas into Maps

Abstract ideas don't lend themselves quite as easily to diagrams as do concrete ideas. For example, you can draw a rough sketch of farmland, a field worker, and a tractor, but how would you diagram economic production, a procedure that involves all three? That's where a concept map comes in. Concept maps are used to diagram abstract processes and relationships. Drawing a concept map based on a set of abstract ideas is similar to drawing a road map based on a set of hard-to-follow directions. In both cases, the map will make the idea easier to visualize, understand, and remember.

[5]Allan Paivio, Mary Walsh, and Trudy Bons, "Concreteness Effects or Memory: When and Why?" *Journal of Experimental Psychology: Learning, Memory and Cognition* 20, no. 5 (1994): 1196–1204.

Here are the steps for mapping a textbook passage:

1. Determine the topic of the passage you are planning to map. Put the topic at the top of a sheet of paper, and circle it.
2. Go back to the passage and circle or list the concepts involved.
3. Find the two to five most important concepts on your list. These are the key concepts. List them on your map in a row beneath the circled topic. Circle these key concepts as well.
4. Cluster the remaining concepts under the key concepts to which they relate. After adding them to your map beneath the key concepts they support, circle these new concepts.
5. Draw lines connecting related concepts. Along each line, you may want to specify the relationship that connects the concepts.

What is the simplest way to master a map?

Master the Map   Drawing a concept map, like taking notes, does a great deal to help cement important ideas and concepts in your memory. And like your notes, your maps can be mastered. Although there are several systems for mastering your map, the simplest and most effective is to look it over carefully and then, without peeking at the original passage, write a short summarizing paragraph explaining the key concepts and how they relate. The result is like writing your own textbook. You start out with the same concepts the textbook uses, but the words are your own instead of the author's. Figure 8.8 shows a map and its summary paragraph.

What are some other ways to use a concept map?

Concept maps are flexible study aids. They don't lock you into a single method or approach. Here are some additional ways you can use a concept map to improve your studying:

Use the concepts for recitation.   Take one circled concept from your map and explain out loud and without looking at the rest of the map how it relates to the map as a whole.

Add to your map.   New ideas frequently connect with old information. Take a moment to think about how the concepts in your map relate to ideas you already know. Add the appropriate old ideas to your map, and connect them to what you've just learned.

Redraw your map.   There's no right or wrong way to draw a concept map. The same information can be mapped in a number of ways. Look over your original map, and see if you can organize the concepts a little differently. Looking at the information from a different angle often makes some of the concepts clearer. Also, creating a second map of the same information means that the concepts will be stored in your memory an additional time.

 **Online Study Center**   **www.college.hmco.com/pic/pauk9e**

Figure 8.8
Mastering a Concept Map

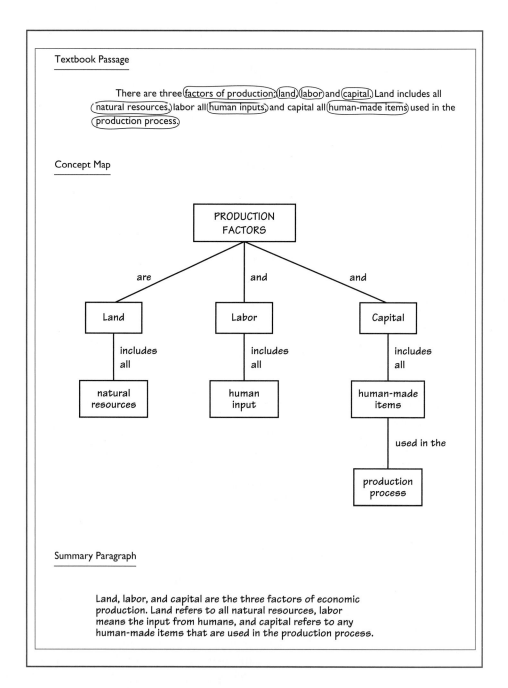

How can you use a concept map to summarize key concepts?

Use Maps for Summaries   Although a map of every concept in a chapter would be huge, and a concept map for even a small book would likely be about the size of a billboard, you can use mapping to summarize the key concepts from chapters, articles, and books. The procedure for summarizing information with a concept map is identical to the one you just followed for mapping a single paragraph from your textbook or section from your notes, except that you cover more ground. Instead of containing information from one paragraph, a summary map may draw from dozens of paragraphs. For this reason, summary maps do not include as much detail as maps created for more specific sections. The maps at the beginning of each chapter in this book are good examples of summary maps. Notice how they include the most important concepts from the chapters they illustrate.

How can you use concept maps to help plan a paper or report?

Use Maps as Planning Strategies   Concept maps can be used to plan a paper or an oral report. First, write the topic you've chosen at the top of a blank sheet of paper. Then, after you have done a bit of preliminary research and have come up with several main concepts, add these to your map, and connect them to your topic with lines. Finally, fill out your map with any supporting ideas you've acquired, making sure to cluster them under the main concepts to which they refer. Once again, draw connecting lines to show how each piece fits into the puzzle. Here is the step-by-step procedure for mapping a paper or an oral report:

1. Do some preliminary research on your subject.
2. Write your topic at the top of a blank sheet of paper.
3. Add two to five main ideas that you plan to cover, and link them to the topic on your map.
4. Cluster subideas under the main ideas that they support. Link them with lines.
5. Survey your map in order to decide whether its branches are evenly developed.
6. If your map seems lopsided, rearrange it or add information so that all its branches are balanced.
7. Use your map as a guide to do in-depth research on the concepts you plan to cover. Add to your map if necessary.

At the very least, your finished concept map can function as an outline, supplying you with all the main ideas and subideas you plan to include in your paper or oral report. In addition, the map can be used as a guide to help you do your more detailed research as systematically as possible.

How do concept maps differ from conventional outlines?

Unlike a conventional outline, a map enables you to see your structure instead of just reading it. In general, a well-organized report looks fairly symmetrical when you map it. If your map has a lopsided appearance, your report may need to be more evenly balanced. Adding some concepts or clustering your existing topics in a different arrangement should do the trick. Once you're happy with the look of your map, it can serve as a plan for further research.

Online Study Center   www.college.hmco.com/pic/pauk9e

Working In Groups

What has research shown
about working in groups?

Concepts that make you wrack your brain and tear your hair out when you listen to lectures or study alone may seem more manageable and understandable when they're handled in a group context. Research has shown that students learn more, retain more, and are generally more satisfied with a course if they are given an opportunity to learn actively, rather than just taking notes in lectures or readings.[6] Group work is an excellent example of this sort of active learning.

What does MIT's Howard
Gardner say about the ability
to work well with others?

MIT's Howard Gardner arrived at a groundbreaking theory to suggest that instead of possessing one single type of intelligence, we have the potential for seven distinct intelligences. Gardner argues that one of these "frames of mind" is interpersonal intelligence, which is essentially the ability to work well with others.[7]

What should you do if your
class doesn't incorporate
group work?

Thanks to Gardner's research and to their own eyewitness observations, many instructors are well aware of the value of groups. As a result, some of your classes may already include group work as part of the curriculum. If they don't and you find that you learn better with group interaction, it is important to take the initiative yourself and see if you can encourage several of your classmates to join you. Try to limit your group to four or five members, though, to assure that everyone participates actively. One of the advantages (and challenges) of working in a small group is that it's not as easy to just "fade into the woodwork" as it can be in some larger classes.

What are some benefits to
working in a group?

Group work offers several benefits that you're unlikely to gain from working on your own:

Explanations from your peers.   Although instructors are experts and often trained "explainers," you may find there are concepts you struggle with from lectures or readings that become clearer and easier to understand when a classmate explains them.

Encouragement and support.   Study groups are also support groups. If you work on assignments on your own, you have only yourself and any grades you might get to encourage you. In a group, the other members have faced the same challenges you have and should be able to share in your success. This is an aspect of collaborative study that transforms group work into teamwork.

Structure for your study.   If you have an assignment to read or some notes to master, it's much easier to simply let things slide when you are working alone. But if you are part of a group, your sense of obligation is extended to several other people. Groups don't work unless everyone pulls his or her own weight.

[6]Available at http://teaching.berkeley.edu/bgd/collaborative.html.

[7]Howard Gardner, *Frames of Mind: The Theory of Multiple Intelligences* (10th anniversary ed.), (New York: Basic Books, 1993).

The sense of obligation to a group can provide a powerful motivation to study and keep up for students who might otherwise fall behind.[8]

Multiple perspectives. Unless your group consists entirely of students who think the same way you do, you will probably find that someone in the group will tackle a topic with a fresh approach that hadn't occurred to you. Almost any time that you can examine an idea or issue from multiple angles you have a greater chance of understanding and retaining it.

Of course, one common type of group activity is a class discussion. In class or online, these discussions not only provide the benefits of group work but may also be a component of your grade. Chapter 13, "Getting the Most Out of Discussions," deals with these in more detail.

Gaining Hands-On Practice

How can you gain hands-on practice from a class made up mainly of abstractions?

Many students are bored, dissatisfied, or intimidated by courses that deal primarily with abstractions and concepts. They seek hands-on, real-world relevance with details and concrete examples. In fact, some research suggests that the majority of high school seniors are so-called "concrete active" students who fit this description.[9] If you're that kind of student and you find yourself in a class that doesn't seem to play to your strengths, you can often supplement your class's core materials by completing the end-of-chapter exercises, by using any ancillary materials associated with your text, by looking for related workbooks or programmed software, and by physically manipulating those abstract ideas and concepts.

Do the Chapter Exercises

Why is it helpful to do the end-of-chapter exercises?

Depending on the nature of your class and the preferences of your instructor, you may or may not be assigned the questions and exercises that often come at the end of a textbook chapter. If you haven't already been assigned these end-of-chapter materials, it still helps to try them, especially if you're finding the course or the text to be a struggle. Once again, it will take you out of the realm of the theoretical and into the realm of the practical.

Use Your Text's Ancillary Materials

What is the value of ancillary materials?

Many textbooks (including this one) come with an array of additional materials known as ancillaries that are sometimes bundled along with the book as a CD or more commonly posted on a website, the address of which is usually provided along with the book, either as part of the purchase price or for a nominal

---

[8]A. Kohn, *No Contest: The Case Against Competition* (Boston: Houghton Mifflin, 1986).

[9]Charles C. Schroeder, "New Students—New Learning Styles," *Change* 25, no. 5 (September/October 1993): 21–26.

 **Online Study Center** www.college.hmco.com/pic/pauk9e

fee. Tests, drills, and exercises included in such materials are usually interactive, which means that you are provided an almost instantaneous assessment of how well you understand what you've read. Using these materials can encourage active learning and can provide an early heads up if you've got textbook troubles that require the help of a tutor.

Look for Programmed Materials and Workbooks

If your skills don't seem to match the requirements of a course, you may need some extra practice. Programmed materials furnish questions and problems closely followed by their answers, thereby enabling you to teach yourself each incremental step of a lesson. These days, the most common programmed materials are found on websites or in specialized software, although some books operate using the programmed format as well. Workbooks provide exercises that apply the ideas explained in your textbooks. These study aids can help minimize the anxiety that arises from feeling uncertain about putting newly learned ideas to use. They can also stimulate your interest by helping you take what you've learned a step further. Unless your text comes with its own programmed materials or workbook, the difference between these and the ancillary materials is that the content may not match your textbook exactly. As a result, you may find yourself spending time on information that won't be covered in your course and perhaps, more important, the programmed or workbook materials may skip over information that will be covered in your text and might even wind up on a test or quiz. So be careful!

Work with Your Hands

What sort of approach do tactile or kinesthetic learners prefer?

Some students are kinesthetic or tactile learners. They understand better when they are able to move things or touch them. This sort of approach can be a natural with some courses in engineering or the sciences, where you are often able to pick up and examine specimens, construct or disassemble apparatuses, or pour things from one container to another. But there's not normally a lot of hands-on opportunities in courses such as history or English, where the emphasis is on the conceptual instead of the concrete.

How can you use kinesthetic or tactile learning with abstract concepts?

Luckily, there's a relatively simple way that you can add an active hands-on element to abstract courses. That's by jotting key dates, themes, or concepts on sticky notes and then arranging and rearranging them in different ways. This is basically a low-tech version of creating a concept map, but if you are a kinesthetic learner, being able to physically arrange and rearrange these concepts with your hands instead of on a screen, on a page, or in your head may make them easier to understand and retain. Another variation on this theme is to transfer some of the key ideas from your notes or text to index cards, putting the term or concept on one side of the card and its definition or explanation on the other. (This is similar to the procedure for creating Frontier Vocabulary cards, explained in Chapter 6.) And while shuffling a pack of index cards may not be quite as active or engaging as looking under the hood of a car or examining the integrated circuits inside a computer, it should help to involve you more fully with a subject.

FINAL WORDS

Why are nondominant learning channels worth pursuing?

The notion that we use only 10 percent of our brains has been repeated so often and attributed to so many experts that despite the absence of actual data, it's readily accepted as fact. There's still something about it that rings true. If you think about it, reading and writing words have been a mandatory element of your education. But other than art, music, and physical education classes, which are often underemphasized and in some schools optional or even nonexistent, there are very few nonverbal equivalents to the elementary school reading group or to those early lessons in penmanship. It's true that we've had a head start with words, but that doesn't mean we shouldn't build up our other learning channels. Like boosting your vocabulary, sharpening your other learning skills will strengthen your thinking. And as someone who approaches learning from a variety of different directions, you're bound to be a better-balanced, more successful student.

HAVE YOU MISSED SOMETHING?

SENTENCE COMPLETION

Complete the following sentences with one of the three words listed below each sentence.

1. Most textbooks are organized _____.

   globally   sequentially   kinesthetically

2. MIT's Howard Gardner suggests that there are seven distinct types of _____.

   intelligence   memory   textbooks

3. When presented as a map, a well-organized report is usually _____.

   detailed   unbalanced   symmetrical

MATCHING

In each blank space in the left column, write the letter preceding the phrase in the right column that matches the left item best.

_____ 1. Circle graphs	a.	Type of learning that favors "hands-on" approach
_____ 2. Global	b.	Used to diagram abstract relationships and processes
_____ 3. Peers	c.	Illustrate the relationship of parts to a whole

 **Online Study Center**   www.college.hmco.com/pic/pauk9e

_____ 4. OPTIC   d. One way to think of the function of line graphs

_____ 5. Kinesthetic   e. Sometimes provide more meaningful explanations than experts

_____ 6. Snapshots   f. Learning style that often comes in bursts and insights

_____ 7. Movies   g. One way to think of the function of bar graphs

_____ 8. Concept maps   h. Method for systematically analyzing graphic materials

TRUE-FALSE

Circle T _beside the_ true _statements and_ F _beside the_ false _statements._

1. T   F   Tactile learning is encouraged in English and history classes.
2. T   F   Line graphs can provide an effective illustration of long-term trends.
3. T   F   The OPTIC system can be used for analyzing both pictures and graphs.
4. T   F   Artistic ability isn't necessary for drawing pictures to help you study.
5. T   F   Group study can provide encouragement and support.

MULTIPLE CHOICE

Choose the word or phrase that completes each sentence most accurately, and circle the letter that precedes it.

1. Research has shown that students learn more, retain more, and are generally more satisfied in a course where they are
   a. required to take notes.
   b. allowed to learn actively.
   c. permitted to use textbooks in tests.
   d. encouraged to work independently.

2. A circle graph is also known as a
   a. Venn diagram.
   b. color wheel.
   c. pie chart.
   d. lookup table.

3. The simplest way to master a concept map is by
   a. erasing it.
   b. summarizing it.
   c. highlighting it.
   d. redrawing it.

4. Summary maps should be drawn with
   a. less detail than standard maps.
   b. black marking pen.
   c. independent variables.
   d. concrete concepts.

5. When used with a paper or an oral report, a map can function as
   a. a guide for research.
   b. a visual outline.
   c. a taking-off point.
   d. all of the above.

SHORT ANSWER   *Supply a brief answer for each of the following items.*

1. Discuss some of the advantages of studying in groups.
2. Outline the steps involved in the OPTIC system.
3. Explain the effect that scale can have on a line graph.
4. Discuss methods for mastering a concept map.

IT'S YOUR Q

The Q System uses marginal questions to encourage active reading. You'll notice that most but not all paragraphs in this chapter are accompanied by marginal questions. Now it's your Q. Scan the chapter for any paragraph that is missing a question, reread the paragraph, establish the main idea, and then arrive at a question that elicits it. Use the questions in the surrounding paragraphs as models for your own marginal questions.

WORDS IN CONTEXT

From the three choices beside each numbered item, select the one that most nearly expresses the meaning of the italicized word in the quote. Make a light check mark (✓) next to your choice.

We have lived through the age of big industry and the age of the giant corporation. But I believe that this is the age of the *entrepreneur*.

—Ronald Reagan (1911–2004), fortieth president of the United States

1. *entrepreneur*   entertainer   computer whiz   impresario

Online Study Center   www.college.hmco.com/pic/pauk9e

The executive's chief business is to organize, *deputize*, and supervise.

—George Ripley (1802–1880), American literary critic

2. *deputize*   enforce   delegate   regulate

Those who make the worst use of their time are the first to complain of its *brevity*.

—Jean de La Bruyère (1645–1696), French writer and moralist

3. *brevity*   briefness   dullness   wastefulness

Nothing is given so *profusely* as advice.

—François, Duc de La Rochefoucauld (1613–1680), French writer

4. *profusely*   expertly   belatedly   abundantly

THE WORD HISTORY SYSTEM

Congregation
a flock

congregation con'-gre-ga'-tion *n.* 1. A body of assembled people or things; a gathering. 2. Those who regularly worship at a specific church or synagogue.

The symbolism so beautifully expressed in David's twenty-third Psalm is fully justified by the origins of our words *congregation* and *pastor*. Latin *grex, gregis,* means "flock" or "herd" and is the basis for the word *congregare,* meaning "to gather into a flock." Derived from this is the Latin *congregatio,* which is taken into English as *congregation*. The word *pastor* carries out the same symbolism. Latin *pascere* means "to pasture," "to feed." The past participle *pastum* gives Latin *pastor,* "a shepherd" or "one who has the care of flocks." Later, the figurative meaning developed, "a keeper of souls" or "minister of the church." The two words, therefore, preserve the symbolism of the shepherd and his flock as applied to the *pastor* and his *congregation*.

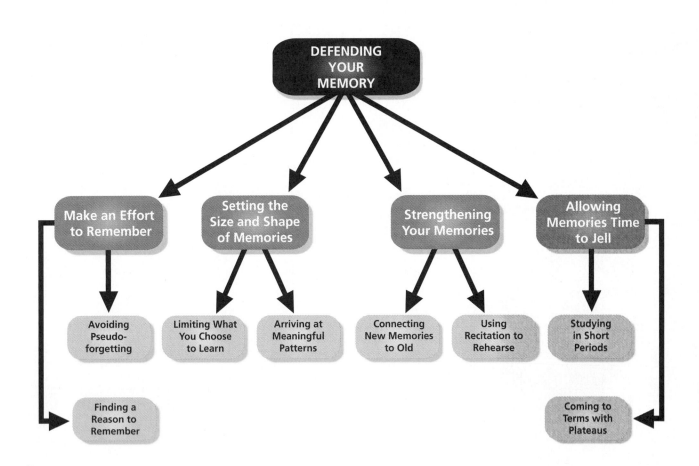

Defending Your Memory

Those who cannot remember the past are condemned to repeat it!

George Santayana
(1863–1952), Spanish-born
American philosopher

Forgetting is like an ocean wave, steadily washing away what you've learned. You can't stop forgetting anymore than you can stop a wave. But you can reinforce what you've learned and strengthen your memories in the face of the incoming tide. To aid you in doing so, this chapter focuses on:

- **Making an Effort to Remember**
- **Setting the Size and Shape of Your Memories**
- **Strengthening Your Memories**
- **Allowing Memories Time to Jell**

Why is forgetting the biggest enemy of academic success?

There's a battle going on in your brain. You may not always be aware of it, but your memory is under constant assault from forgetfulness, the biggest single enemy of your academic success. Forgetting works both massively and rapidly to undo learning. In fact, research has shown again and again that when you learn something new you are likely to forget most of it in a matter of days.

What have experiments shown about forgetting?

In one experiment, people who read a textbook chapter forgot 46 percent of their reading after one day, 79 percent after fourteen days, and 81 percent after twenty-eight days. In other words, subjects could remember slightly more than half of what they'd read the previous day; after less than a month, the information they were able to retain from their reading had dwindled to 19 percent.

Why is it harder to remember what you've heard than what you've read?

Although reading is forgotten quickly, the rate of forgetting for things you hear occurs even faster. This has to do with the way the short-term or *working memory* is designed. The working memory is a way station. All new information passes through there before some of it is sent on to more permanent storage in your long-term memory. Your working memory essentially has two front doors. There's an entrance for the things you see and another for the things you say or hear. Solid evidence suggests that when you read words in a book, you are both seeing and hearing them at once. Images of the words combine with the sounds of those words that you hear in your "inner ear" to make the memories stronger.[1] Contrast that with listening, where there's normally nothing to see, and you can understand why the key points from speech may be easier to forget than the main ideas in a chapter. Besides, when you read, you have an opportunity to set your own pace. You can slow down, pause, reflect, and, if necessary, reread. Listeners have no such luxury; they usually have just one chance to catch spoken words and ideas.

What determines whether information in working memory will be saved to long-term memory?

Almost nothing is a shoo-in for your long-term memory. Anyone who has forgotten a name just moments after hearing it or had to look up a phone number a second time just a few minutes after reading it knows from experience that forgetting can be instantaneous and complete. The way to make memories stick, the way to move them from your working memory to your long-term memory is through rehearsal. The word *rehearse* comes from an old French word that means "to plow again." Each time you repeat or rewrite what you've read or heard, you're rehearsing it; you are deepening and strengthening its memory trace, just like a tractor plow that deepens the furrow in a farmer's field. If you make sure the path is deep, it should last. But if you only plow a shallow path, it can vanish in the first heavy wind or driving rain. It's the same with unrehearsed information.

[1] Alan Baddeley, *Your Memory: A User's Guide* (Garden City Park, NY: Prion, 1993), p. 41.

Experiments have shown that unrehearsed information is sometimes forgotten in as little as twenty seconds.[2] In a classical experiment, Hermann Ebbinghaus (1850–1909), a Germany psychologist and pioneer in the modern study of memory, found that almost half of what is learned is forgotten within an hour.[3] More than a century after Ebbinghaus conducted his original experiment, psychologists continue to affirm his findings.

The following true story further confirms the rapidity and scope of forgetting. Three professors eating lunch in the faculty lounge had this conversation:

Clyde: Did you hear last night's lecture?
Walter: No, I was busy.
Clyde: Well, you missed one of the best lectures in recent years.
Leon: I agree. The four points that he developed were gems.
Clyde: I never heard anyone make his points so clearly.
Walter: I don't want you to repeat the lecture, but what were those four points?
Leon: (Long silence) Clyde? (Passage of two or three minutes; seems like an hour.)
Leon: Well, I'd better get back to the office.
Clyde: Me, too!
Walter: Me, too!

What can we learn from the Leon-Clyde story?

Both Leon and Clyde were brilliant men, yet neither was able to recall even a fragment of any point made in the previous night's lecture. Each had forgotten the four points because neither had transferred those points from working memory to long-term memory by silently reciting them. Instead, both had recited that the speaker was clear, forceful, and wise and that he had made four points—and they remembered only what they had recited.

What did the Cambridge Psychological Society experiment conclude about forgetfulness?

These two learned men were by no means exceptions. Their story has been borne out time and again in traditional research. For instance, in a classic experiment researchers secretly recorded a seminar held by the Cambridge Psychological Society.[4] Two weeks later, the society members who had attended the seminar were asked to write down all they could recall of it. The results were shocking. More than 90 percent of the points from the lecture had been forgotten or confused with the passage of time. The average proportion of specific points each member correctly recalled was 8.4 percent! Much of what

[2]Douglas A. Bernstein, Edward J. Roy, Thomas K. Srull, and Christopher D. Wickens, *Psychology* (Boston: Houghton Mifflin, 1988), p. 293.

[3]Alan J. Parkin, *Memory: Phenomena, Experiment and Theory* (Cambridge, MA: Blackwell, 1993); Hermann Ebbinghaus, *Memory* (New York: Dover, 1964), p. 76.

[4]Ian M. L. Hunter, *Memory: Facts and Fallacies* (Baltimore: Penguin, 1957), p. 83.

members recalled was at odds with what had actually been said. Events were mentioned that never took place; casual remarks were embellished; points were reported that had only been hinted at. This eminent group of psychologists forgot 91.6 percent of the specific points made in the seminar.

How can you defend your memories from forgetting?

When you consider how much resistance your memories face, it's folly to assume that something you've learned will still be there when you need it. You need to put up a fight. You can defend your memories by making an effort to remember, by setting the size and shape of your memories, by working to strengthen your memories, and by giving them time to jell.

Making an Effort to Remember

How does effort affect your memory?

To remember something, you have to make a conscious effort to learn it. If you don't learn new information in the first place, it isn't really yours to forget. And even if you *do* learn new information, it won't stay with you very long unless you're convinced that it's worth hanging on to. The effort you initially make determines whether you'll remember what you've heard or read for a lifetime or forget it in a matter of seconds.

Avoiding Pseudo-Forgetting

What is pseudo-forgetting?

Whenever you cannot remember a name, a telephone number, a fact, an idea, or even a joke, it's quite natural to say, "I forgot." Yet forgetting may not have anything to do with your problem. You may never have learned the information in the first place. This phenomenon is known as pseudo-forgetting. The word *pseudo* means "false" or "phony." Thousands of instances we blame on forgetting are actually a result of this "phony forgetting." As the poet Oliver Wendell Holmes succinctly put it, "A man must get a thing before he can *forget* it."

How can you guard against pseudo-forgetting?

If an idea or a fact is to be retained in your memory, it must be impressed on your mind clearly and crisply at least once. A record of that idea or fact must be laid down in your brain before you can truly recall or forget what you've learned.

Finding a Reason to Remember

What effect does intention have on memory?

If you can find a reason for holding on to information you've learned, you have a much better chance of remembering it. In a carefully designed study, researchers showed how intention can influence the life span of a memory. Two groups of students were asked to master identical material. The only difference was that those in the first group were told to remember the material for only a single day, while those in the second group were instructed to master it for re-call after two weeks.[5] The difference in intention had a noticeable effect. Al-though the two groups studied the same material in a similar fashion, after two weeks the students who had intended to remember over the long term retained more than the students who had intended to hang on to what they had learned for only a day.

What is the strongest source of motivation for remembering?

Of all the sources of motivation, interest is the strongest. If you could study all subjects with motivated interest, you would not have to worry about your final grades. When you are naturally interested in a subject, you have no prob-lem. If you are not naturally interested, try to combat boredom by artificially creating interest. Once you begin to learn something about a new subject, the chances are great that you will find it genuinely interesting. Use the power of interest to work *for* you, not against you.

What are some ways to strengthen your intention to remember?

Whether genuine interest or simple academic survival serves as your motiva-tion, when you hear or read information you want to hold on to, there are ways to strengthen your intention to remember, so that what you've learned will be recalled:

Pay attention. If you're distracted while you're trying to learn, it's unlikely you'll remember anything. Therefore, make a point of minimizing distractions as you read your assignments or listen to lectures.

Get it right the first time. False ideas and misunderstood facts can hang on as tena-ciously as information you learn correctly. Therefore, it pays to be attentive when you learn something new. For example, many people incorrectly pronounce the word *nuclear* (NEW-clee-er) as "NEW-cue-ler." One look at the word shows you that this pronunciation is incorrect. But if you learn a word incorrectly, you'll have difficulty replacing the old memory with the correct pronunciation.

Make sure you understand. Ideas that aren't clear to you when you read or hear them won't miraculously jell and become clearer in your memory. You cannot fashion a lucid, correct memory from a fuzzy, poorly understood concept. There-fore, don't hesitate to ask the instructor to explain any point that you are not clear on. And don't be reluctant to read and reread a passage in your textbook until you're sure you fully grasp its meaning.

How can you use forgetting in a positive way?

Interestingly, the same motivation that enables you to remember can also help you forget. It can be used in a positive way to clear your mind of informa-tion you no longer need to retain.

[5]H. H. Remmers and M. N. Thisted, "The Effect of Temporal Set on Learning," *Journal of Applied Psychology* 16 (June 1932): 257–268.

What are some examples of
intention to forget?

This conscious intention to forget is well demonstrated by servers in restaurants. They exhibit a remarkably good memory for what their customers have ordered up to the moment the bill is paid. Then experienced servers jettison the entire transaction from their minds and give their full attention to the next customer. Just as they intend to remember, so they intend to forget.

This idea of intending to forget explains why Albert Einstein, unquestionably one of the great minds of the twentieth century, was nonetheless unable to provide his home telephone number from memory. He saw no point in clogging his mind with simple numbers that could easily be stored in an address book, so he purposely forgot them.

Setting the Size and Shape of Your Memories

The forgetting that many of us practice instinctively seems to imply that there is a limit to how much we can remember at once. In 1956 psychologist G. A. Miller produced scientific support for this notion. In his article "The Magical Number Seven, Plus or Minus Two," Miller points out that most people are able to hold only seven items in short-term memory at one time. The size of each item, however, can be virtually unlimited as long as the information in it is meaningfully organized. For example, you couldn't expect to remember the following thirty-one items:

aabceeeeeeeilmmmnnnoorrrssttuvy

How does organization help
memory?

But if you organized these items in a meaningful way—as words—you could reduce the number of items to seven and increase your odds of remembering them:

you	can	learn	to	remember	seven	items
1	2	3	4	5	6	7

As Miller explains, "Our language is tremendously useful for repackaging material into a few chunks rich in information."[6]

How important was Miller's
article in the study of learning
and memory?

Although its profound importance wasn't immediately recognized by all, Miller's article has had a dramatic influence on the study of learning and memory. Looking back, Jerome Bruner, a prominent psychologist and former direc-

[6]G. A. Miller, "The Magical Number Seven, Plus or Minus Two: Some Limits on Our Capacity for Processing Information," *Psychological Review* 63 (March 1956): 81–97.

tor of Harvard University's Center for Cognitive Studies, paid tribute to Miller and his groundbreaking work.

> I think if there were a retrospective Nobel Prize in Psychology for the mid-1950s, George Miller would win it hands down—and on the basis of one article, "The Magic Number Seven, Plus or Minus Two."[7]

What has recent research revealed about memory spans?

Since Miller's breakthrough in establishing the limits of memory, other psychologists have gone on to refine our understanding of what has come to be known as *memory span*. Although complex information can be retained in short-term memory if it is "chunked" into roughly seven items, research indicates that it can actually be harder to recall long words than it is to remember shorter ones. It seems that even when we are reading words on a printed page, "silent speech" still plays a role in how we retain them. Because longer words take longer to say, they increase the likelihood that a memory trace will fade. As a rule of thumb, we can hold on to as many words at once as we can say in two seconds.[8] Or, as British psychologist Alan Baddeley explains it, "short words or fast talking gives rise to long spans."[9]

What lesson we can learn from Miller and his successors?

The lesson from research on memory span is this: Improve your chances of remembering by being selective about what you learn and by making sure that what you do choose to remember is meaningfully organized.

Limiting What You Choose to Learn

What were the conclusions from Ebbinghaus's most famous experiment?

Long before Miller's discussion of the "magical number seven," Hermann Ebbinghaus conducted perhaps the most famous experiment in the history of memory research. He counted the number of trials required to learn a series of six nonsense syllables (such as *bik, luf, tur, pem, nif,* and *wox*). He then counted the number of trials required to learn a series of twelve such syllables. Ebbinghaus's tabulations yielded surprising results: The number of trials required to memorize twelve syllables was fifteen times greater than the number required to learn six syllables.[10] So, for example, if it took four minutes to memorize six syllables, it would take an hour to memorize twelve.

[7]Jerome Bruner, *In Search of Mind* (New York: Harper & Row, 1983), p. 97.

[8]Alan Baddeley "The Fractionation of Working Memory," *Proceedings of the National Academy of Sciences of the United States of America* 93, no. 24 (November 26, 1996): 13468–13472.

[9]Ibid.

[10]Matthew High Erdelyl, "Commentary: Integrating Dissociations Prone Psychology," *Journal of Personality* 62, no. 4 (1994): 669–680.

 **Online Study Center** www.college.hmco.com/pic/pauk9e

What does Ebbinghaus's research tell us about mastering textbook and lecture material?

Granted, Ebbinghaus dealt only with nonsense syllables, but his careful research still teaches a valuable lesson that can be applied to both textbook and lecture material: To improve your chances of remembering what you've learned, you must condense and summarize. In practical terms, this means picking out the main ideas from your lecture and textbook notes and leaving the supporting materials and examples aside. Once you have selected the important points from what you've read, you should be able to memorize them in a manageable amount of time.

Another beneficial by-product that comes from limiting what you learn is that in making the choice of what to keep and what to forget you'll be strengthening your overall understanding of the material. In other words, you can't really tell what idea is worth saving and what is worth deleting without having a basic understanding of both. As you'll see in Chapter 11, a method called the Silver Dollar System that is specifically designed to condense your notes provides an opportunity to make what you've learned a permanent part of your knowledge.

Arriving at Meaningful Patterns

How does organizing affect retrieval?

The papers on your desk are easier to keep track of if you organize them into groups and put them into file folders. A textbook is easier to understand because the information in it has been divided into chapters. A single item is easier to find in a supermarket because the products have been grouped together and arranged in different aisles. If you had to look for a jar of peanut butter in a supermarket where the items were randomly placed, you might give up the search.

How should you organize a list of items you need to remember?

The same idea applies to memories. When you have a large list of items to remember, try to cluster similar items around a natural heading or category. Once clustered and categorized, the items will resist the decaying power of forgetting. Just as the stem holds together the individual grapes, so categories and clusters hold together individual facts and ideas. This hanging together is especially useful during an exam: Remembering one item from a cluster is usually the key to remembering all the items. For example, it would take a long time to memorize by rote the following words, which you might encounter in a geology course:

slate	diamond	sapphire
bronze	lead	aluminum
iron	marble	silver
emerald	steel	brass
gold	limestone	ruby
granite	platinum	copper

But when these words are organized into categories and are clustered as shown in Figure 9.1, memorization is relatively easy and remembering is strong.

Figure 9.1
The Category and Cluster System of Organizing Items

Source: Figure from *Psychology: An Introduction*, Sixth Edition, by Jerome Kagan. Copyright © 1988. Reprinted with permission of Wadsworth, a division of Thomson Learning: www.thomsonrights.com. Fax 800-730-2215.

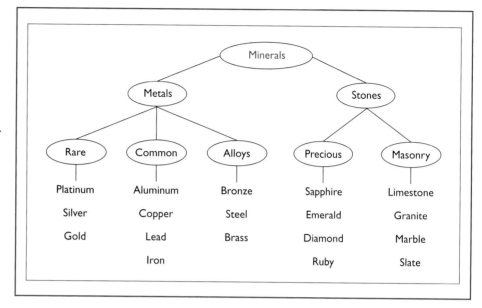

Strengthening Memories

What can you do to help strengthen your memories?

The stronger a memory is, the longer it lasts. If you reinforce new ideas by connecting them to ideas already in your memory, and if you conscientiously use recitation to rehearse what you've learned, that result should be strong enough to stand up to forgetting.

Connecting New Memories to Old

What is the role of association in memory?

The famous line "No man is an island" applies to memories as well. An idea that stands alone is not likely to be recalled. The ideas you remember are woven into a network that connects a single memory with hundreds and often thousands of other memories. The more connections there are in the network and the stronger those connections are, the better the chance for recall.

When are connections made automatically?

Sometimes connections are made automatically, as in the case of traumatic events. Most people easily recall, for example, where they were and what they were doing when they learned of the attack on the World Trade Center in 2001. Previous generations have a similar reaction when recalling the assassination of

President John F. Kennedy or Martin Luther King. In these cases, you instantly connect the memory of the event with the memory of where you were.

But in normal circumstances, relying on your memory to automatically make these connections is risky. If you want to improve your chances of remembering something, you must make a real effort to link what you've learned to your memory network. You can strengthen the staying power of information when you add it to your memory by consciously making either logical or artificial connections.

What can you do to deliberately create associations?

Make Logical Connections

How do you establish logical connections for memories?

Consider how you can recall the written directions to a friend's house by keeping in mind a map you once saw or how you can strengthen your memory of the bones of the body by recalling a diagram of a human skeleton. These are examples of logical connections you make to improve your recall. The best ways of strengthening your memory network through logical connections are by building on your basic background and by using images to support what you're trying to remember.

How does background help strengthen memory?

Build on Your Basic Background   The principle behind basic background is simple but powerful. Your understanding and memory of what you hear, read, see, feel, or taste depend entirely on what you know, on what you already have in your background. Some of this information has been with you for years, whereas other parts of it may be just seconds old. When listening to a speaker, you understand his or her points as long as you can interpret them in light of something you've already learned. When you make connections this way, you increase the power of your memory.

What are ways of building a solid background?
Why are basic courses so important?

Here are some concrete steps to help you build a solid background:

Give basic courses the attention they deserve.   Many students make the mistake of thinking that the basic courses they take in their first year of college are a waste of time. Yet these introductory courses create the background essential for all the courses that follow. Indeed, each student's professional life often begins with first-year courses.

How can you consciously link new information to old?

Make a conscious attempt to link what you learn to what you already know.   When you learn something new, ask yourself questions such as "How does this relate to what I already know?" and "How does this change what I already know?"

How can your instructor help your background?

Ask an instructor to explain what you don't understand.   At times an entire class can hinge on a single point. Miss that and you miss the purpose of the class. Don't feel hesitant or shy about asking an instructor to go back over a point you can't quite get a fix on. After all, the instructor is there to help you learn.

How do pictures strengthen memories?

Strengthen Memories with Pictures   Another way of logically reinforcing what you've learned is by creating a picture of it. Whether you draw the new information on paper or simply visualize it in your mind, you add an extra dimension to your memory. After all, one part of your brain thinks in words and another part thinks in pictures. When you convert words into pictures, you are using more of your brain.

A student who attended a lecture on amoebas included a sketch of this one-celled organism in her notes (see Figure 9.2). The combination of words and picture gave her a clearer understanding of the subject than she would have gained from relying exclusively on written information. When a question about amoebas appeared on a test, the student handled it easily by recalling the picture she had drawn.

What do you do with material that doesn't seem to lend itself to drawing?

Even when material doesn't lend itself to drawing, you can still devise a mental image. According to Dr. Joseph E. Shorr of the Institute of Psycho-Imagination Therapy in Beverly Hills, California, "The human memory would be worthless without the capacity to make mental pictures." Almost any memory can be turned into a mental image. If you need to remember, for example, that Abraham Lincoln was born in 1809, you can picture a log cabin with "1809" inscribed over the doorway. The image you recall doesn't have to be especially detailed; it only has to be strong enough to jog your memory.

Figure 9.2
Structure of the Amoeba

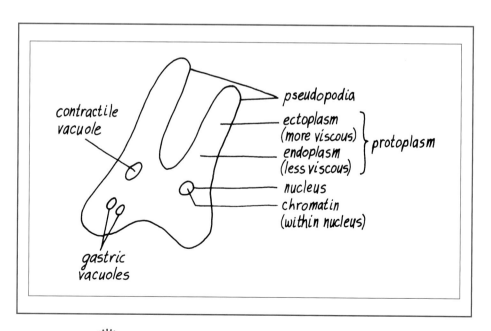

Make Artificial Connections

What is an example of an artificial memory connection?

The connections you make don't always have to be logical. They just need to be memorable. The time-honored practice of tying a string around a finger as a reminder is a classic example of an artificial connection. Perhaps you needed to remember to take out the garbage, to pick up your dry cleaning, or to bring your textbook to class. None of these things has anything logically to do with a piece of string and yet when you look at your finger and say to yourself, "What's this string for?" there's a good chance that you'll recall the task you were trying to remember. You can make equally effective connections to words, to images, and even to locations.

How are words used to make artificial memory connections?

Because words are portable, readable, and usually recognizable, they can be used to store more complicated or difficult-to-remember information. But just as a string has nothing inherently to do with remembering something, the connection between a word and the thing it's designed to remind you of can be artificial. After all, what natural link is there between the word *face* and a group of musical notes? Yet many beginning music students rely on this word to help them recall the notes written in the spaces of the treble clef (F, A, C, E).

Why can made-up words be used to make artificial memory connections?

The words you use don't even have to be real words. They just need to *sound* like words. They differ from many acronyms in that respect because they can be pronounced as though they were words. We find words easy to remember because we don't say their individual letters. We pronounce their *sounds*. For years, computer scientists have used GIGO (pronounced GUY-go) to remind themselves that the value of the data you get out of a computer depends on the value of the data you put into it. GIGO is a mnemonic for the phrase "garbage in, garbage out." (Interestingly enough, although GIGO started out as a nonsense word, it is now listed in the dictionary!)

How do images aid memory?

Our amazing human ability to generate vivid and often nonsensical images also comes in handy when you're trying to remember something. Suppose you have just been introduced to a man named Mr. Perkins. To remember his name, you immediately associate it with a coffeepot *perking*. You even visualize the perking pot and smell the aroma of freshly brewed coffee. And if you really want to make the picture memorable, you imagine the pot where Mr. Perkins's nose normally is. What you have done is tie *new* information (Mr. Perkins) to *old* information (perking coffeepot) that is already well established in your memory. When you meet Mr. Perkins at some future time, you will recall the perking coffeepot (try not to stare at his nose though!), which will prepare you to say, "Hello, Mr. Perkins. Nice to see you again."

What is the loci method?

Another system, known as the loci method, also relies heavily on our ability to conjure up images. The loci method was developed in ancient Greek and Roman times and is still widely used today. The word *loci* is the plural for the root of the word "location," and that is the key to this system. With loci, you remember items by associating them with locations in a familiar physical space, such as your house, apartment, or dorm room. By creating mental pictures of the names or items you want to remember and then associating them with objects in your chosen location, you can then take a tour of the space in your mind's eye and recall each name or item as you encounter it. For example, to remember key physicists who were involved in the top-secret atomic bomb initiative known as the Manhattan Project, you might step into your room and mistakenly trip over J. Robert Oppenheimer, sit down on your couch and disturb Edward Teller, who is napping there, and go over to your dresser, open the top drawer, and be startled when Enrico Fermi pops out. The layout of your room becomes the organizing principle that makes it easier to retain these names.

What are some less ridiculous uses of the loci method?

Loci connections don't always have to be outrageous or comical. An instructor who assigns seats in her class may be using a variation of the loci method. Granted, she may have a seating chart with all the names of her students listed, but it is the position of the students in the classroom that makes it easier to recall their names without consulting the list. That's why it has been a time-honored prank of some students to switch seats in the class of a brand-new instructor.

What do most memory tricks rely upon?

Although we make a lot of logical connections to remember things, the majority of so-called "memory tricks" (also known as *mnemonic devices*) rely on artificial connections, like the ones just mentioned.

How prevalent are mnemonic devices?

Use Classic Mnemonic Devices   Nearly everyone employs at least one or two mnemonic devices to recall specific hard-to-remember facts and information. Probably the most widely used mnemonic device is the old jingle by which many of us keep track of the irregularities in the calendar:

> Thirty days hath September,
> April, June, and November.
> All the rest have thirty-one,
> Except February alone.

Rivaling this days-in-the-month mnemonic is one for spelling:

> *i* before *e* except after *c*
> or when sounding like *a*
> as in *neighbor* and *weigh*

Many people have their own personal mnemonics, such as "Surround the *r* with *a* for the word *separate*."

Why do mnemonics work?

As we've already learned, the cardinal rule for dealing with masses of information is to make sure the information is organized in a meaningful way. A mnemonic device is an organizational system, pure and simple. It is an ordinary means to an important end. Gerald R. Miller conducted a study to evaluate the

Is there a risk to using mnemonics?

effectiveness of mnemonic devices as aids to study.[11] He found that students who used mnemonics raised their test scores by as much as 77 percent!

Miller recognizes that the use of too many mnemonics can overload the memory. Nevertheless, he argues that learning a large number of mnemonics well creates no greater hazard than learning a large amount of material in the traditional way. Here's a sampling of some classic mnemonics you may have encountered:

Spelling. The greatest number of mnemonic devices are aids to spelling. Here's how to remember the correct way to spell two words that confuse many students:

A principal is a pal.
A principle is a rule.

Why is it especially important to memorize mnemonics thoroughly?

If you use classic mnemonic devices to help recall information, make certain you memorize the sentence, word, or jingle thoroughly. The slightest error can throw you off completely. For example, some algebra students use the FOIL method to remember the order for multiplying a binomial: First, Outer, Inner, Last. But if you recall the wrong word instead, say, FILE, you wind up hopelessly confused.

Biology. The first letters of the words in the following sentence stand for the major categories and subdivisions of the animal world—kingdom, phylum, class, order, family, genus, species, and variety:

Kings Play Cards On Fairly Good Soft Velvet.

Geometry. Here's a clever way of remembering the first six decimal places of pi. Just count the number of letters in each word of this rhyme.

How I wish I
could calculate Pi!
(3.141592)

Astronomy. Most people, when pressed, can name the eight planets. But how about listing them in order? (Mercury, Venus, Earth, Mars, Jupiter, Saturn, Uranus, Neptune.)

My Very Economical Mother Just Serves Us Noodles.

[11]Gerald R. Miller, *An Evaluation of the Effectiveness of Mnemonic Devices as Aids to Study*, Co-operative Research Project no. 5-8438 (El Paso: University of Texas Press, 1967).

And here's one for the twelve signs of the zodiac (Aries, Taurus, Gemini, Cancer, Leo, Virgo, Libra, Scorpio, Sagittarius, Capricorn, Aquarius, Pisces)

<u>A</u> <u>T</u>ense <u>G</u>ray <u>C</u>at <u>L</u>ay <u>V</u>ery <u>L</u>ow, <u>S</u>neaking <u>S</u>lowly, <u>C</u>ontemplating <u>A</u> <u>P</u>ounce

Zoology.   Naturalists may automatically know the difference, but many of us get the African and Indian elephants confused.

India's big, but Africa's bigger,
The same as their elephants—easy to figure!

History.   The royal houses of England (Norman, Plantagenet, Lancaster, York, Tudor, Stuart, Hanover, Windsor) are difficult to remember without the help of a mnemonic device:

<u>N</u>o <u>P</u>lan <u>L</u>ike <u>Y</u>ours <u>T</u>o <u>S</u>tudy <u>H</u>istory <u>W</u>isely.

Medicine.   Even doctors and pharmacists use memory systems to help keep certain chemicals straight. To distinguish between cyanates, which are harmless, and cyanides, which are extremely poisonous, they use this device:

-ate, I ate; *-ide*, I died.

What can you do to remember information that doesn't have a common mnemonic device?	**Devise Your Own Mnemonics** Associating new information logically is generally better than doing so artificially, and truly knowing something is always better than using a system to remember it. But if you're required to learn facts that you can't connect with your memory network and that have no classic mnemonic, you may want to invent your own mnemonic device to help yourself remember.
What are the two steps for creating a keyword mnemonic?	*Keyword mnemonic.*[12] Connecting a man named Perkins with a perking coffeepot provides a good example of a *keyword mnemonic* in action. The procedure for devising a keyword mnemonic has two steps, a verbal step and a visual step.
What is involved in the verbal step? What do you do in the visual step?	1. *The verbal step.* Find a familiar word or phrase that sounds like the word you are trying to remember. This is your keyword. For the name *Perkins* the keyword is *perking*. 2. *The visual step.* Connect your keyword with what you want to remember. For example, form a mental image of Mr. Perkins's face on a perking coffeepot.

[12]The keyword mnemonics section is based on a discussion in K. L. Higbee, *Your Memory: How It Works and How to Improve It*, 2nd ed. (New York: Prentice-Hall, 1988).

 **Online Study Center**   www.college.hmco.com/pic/pauk9e

Then when you see him again, you'll recall that image, which will remind you of his name.

What are some common uses for keyword mnemonics?

The keyword system isn't limited to helping you remember the names of people you meet. It also comes in handy for remembering vocabulary from a foreign language. For example, if you want to recall the French word for "butter," *beurre*, connect it with a keyword like *burr*, or *brrr*, and then link the two with a visual image, a pat of butter covered with burrs or a stick of butter wearing a parka and shivering (brrr!).

What is a create-a-word mnemonic?

Create-a-word mnemonic.   The letters of a "created" word can be used to help you remember important information. What if you needed to remember the Great Lakes, for example: Lake Superior, Lake Erie, Lake Michigan, Lake Huron, and Lake Ontario?

What are the steps in creating a mnemonic word?

To devise a *create-a-word mnemonic*, proceed as follows:

1. Underline the keyword in each item. (Superior, Erie, Michigan, Huron, Ontario.)
2. Write down the first letter of each keyword. (S, E, M, H, O.)
3. Create a word or several words from the first letters of the keywords. If the order of the elements isn't important, try rearranging the letters until they spell a word or words. (HOMES.)
4. If possible, make a link between your keyword and the idea for which it acts as a mnemonic. ("The HOMES along the Great Lakes must have a beautiful view.")

Your mnemonic may be a real word or a word you just made up. If you use a made-up word, be sure you have some means of remembering it.

In what cases is a create-a-sentence mnemonic preferable to a create-a-word one?

Create-a-sentence mnemonic.   If the order of the items you want to remember is important, the create-a-sentence mnemonic is often more flexible than the create-a-word mnemonic. For example, if you need to remember the Great Lakes from west to east (Lake Superior, Lake Michigan, Lake Huron, Lake Erie, Lake Ontario), HOMES won't help you. But a create-a-sentence mnemonic will.

What are the steps for a create-a-sentence mnemonic?

Here are the steps for devising a create-a-sentence mnemonic:

1. Underline the keyword for each item. (Superior, Michigan, Huron, Erie, Ontario.)
2. Write down the first letter of each keyword. (S, M, H, E, O.)
3. Construct an easy-to-remember sentence using words whose first letters are the same as the first letters of the keywords. (Super Machine Heaved Earth Out.)

4. Devise a sentence that relates to the information you want to remember. ("Five large lakes in the middle of the country almost make it seem as though a super machine heaved earth out.")

Why is creating a sentence mnemonic sometimes easier than creating a word or two?

In general, creating a simple sentence is easier than taking the first letters from your keywords and turning them into a word or two, especially if the order of the points has to be maintained. Of course, if the initial letters are mainly consonants, both methods can be difficult. To circumvent the problem of having too many consonants, try to choose some keywords (or synonyms of the keywords) that begin with vowels.

Using Recitation to Rehearse

Why is recitation so vital to strengthening your memory?

No single activity is more important in strengthening your memory than recitation. That's because recitation forces you to think seriously about what you've read or heard. This deep thinking (experts call it *deep cognitive processing*) is the key to making memories last. To reap the benefits of recitation, you need to know what reciting involves. It also helps to learn why reciting works.

What Recitation Involves

Reciting simply involves reading a passage in a book or a line of your notes and then repeating it from memory, either out loud or by writing or typing it. Whether you recite out loud or in writing, your goal should be to use your own words rather than parroting what you've just read. Recitation isn't about memorizing words. It's about comprehending ideas. Chapter 11 explains in detail how you can use recitation to master the notes you've taken from lectures or textbook assignments.

Why Recitation Works

What is the secret behind recitation?

Whether you recite by speaking or by writing, the effect on your memory is basically the same. Recitation strengthens the original memory trace by prompting you to think actively about the new material, thus keeping it in your working memory. It gets both your body and your mind involved in the process of learning. It supplies immediate feedback so you can test yourself and check your progress. And it motivates you to continue reading.

How does reciting encourage participation?

Reciting Encourages Participation   Reading is not the same as comprehending. It's possible, for example, to read a book aloud to a child without paying attention to the story. Likewise, if you're having a tough time concentrating, you can read every word on a page and still not understand or even recall what you've read. To truly comprehend what you've read, you need to know both what the words say and what they mean. When you recite, you make yourself

Online Study Center   www.college.hmco.com/pic/pauk9e

stop and wonder, "What did this just say?" You're transformed from a detached observer into an active participant. The physical activity of thinking, pronouncing, and hearing your own words involves your body as well as your mind in the process of learning. The more physical senses you use in learning, the stronger the memory will be.

How does recitation provide feedback?

Reciting Provides Feedback   Reciting not only gets you involved in your reading; it also demonstrates how involved you are. Rereading can give you a false and dangerous sense of confidence. It takes a lot of time and leaves you with the feeling that you've been hard at work, yet it provides no concrete indication of what you're learning. When test time comes, you may blame your mental blanks on test anxiety or on unfair questions when the real culprit is ineffective studying. Unlike rereading, reciting lets you know right away where your weaknesses lie. As you finish each paragraph you find out whether you understand what you've just read. This gives you a chance to clarify and solidify information on the spot, long before you're tested on it.

How does recitation supply motivation?

Reciting Supplies Motivation   Because it gets you involved and checks your progress regularly, recitation provides motivation for studying. And motivated interest promotes a stronger memory. If you struggled to extract the information from a paragraph you just read, you may be motivated to grasp the point of the next paragraph more easily. If you had no trouble finding the meaning in that paragraph, the momentum of your reading may serve as motivation.

Allowing Memories Time to Jell

Why don't new ideas instantly become part of your memory?

How did a mountain climber's injury demonstrate consolidation?

The fact that recitation helps new information jell hints at another aspect of memory: New ideas don't instantly become part of your memory. Your memory needs time to consolidate what you've learned.

A dramatic illustration of memory's need to consolidate comes in a story of a mountain climber who fell and hit his head. Although the man was not permanently injured, he couldn't remember falling. In fact, he couldn't recall anything that had happened to him in the fifteen minutes *before* the accident. Why not? According to the principle of consolidation, the climber's memories before the accident had not had a chance to consolidate. As a result, when the climber hit his head, those unfinished memories were lost.[13]

[13]R. S. Woodworth and H. Schlosberg, *Experimental Psychology*, rev. ed. (New York: Holt, Rinehart & Winston, 1954), p. 773.

What are the similarities between human memory and a computer's memory?

Although analogies between humans and machines can only be taken so far, your working memory shares some interesting similarities with DRAM, the dynamic random access memory (often just referred to as RAM) of a personal computer. If your computer crashes a few minutes after you started typing a paper or letter, there's a good chance that all your work up to that point will be lost. That's because it existed only in dynamic memory and had yet to be transferred to a disk where it could be stored permanently. This explains the advice of many experienced computer users to "save often and always." When you save a file, you move the information from the short-term temporary storage of DRAM to the long-term storage of a disk. Similarly, when you allow time to consolidate your memories, you move them from the limbo of your short-term working memory to the stability of your long-term memory.

What does consolidation tell us about study strategies?

This principle helps explain why in most cases the most effective way to study is in short blocks of time instead of in one long stretch. An understanding of consolidation will help you live through those frustrating times when you don't seem to retain what you're studying.

Studying in Short Periods

What is distributed practice?

In *distributed practice*, you engage in relatively short study periods broken up by rest intervals. In *massed practice*, you study continuously until the task is completed. A number of studies have demonstrated that several short "learning sprints" are more productive than one grueling, long-distance study session. This is sometimes known as the "spacing effect."

What effect did distributed practice have on learning French vocabulary?

For example, Kristine Bloom and Thomas Shuell gave two groups of high school French students twenty new vocabulary words to learn. The first group used massed practice, studying all the words in a single thirty-minute session. The second group spent the same amount of time on the words but spread the sessions over three consecutive days, studying ten minutes per day. When tested immediately after they had completed their practice, both groups remembered roughly the same number of words (sixteen). But when the test was readministered four days later, the massed group had forgotten nearly half of the words, while the distributed group was able to recall all but five.[14]

What effect did distributed practice have on reading comprehension?

In an extensive experiment, researchers D. Krug, T. B. Davis, and J. A. Glover examined the effects of massed and distributed practice on a reading comprehension task and found that distributed practice led to better performance.[15]

[14]Kristine C. Bloom and Thomas J. Shuell, "Effects of Massed and Distributed Practice on the Learning and Retention of Second-Language Vocabulary." *Journal of Educational Research* 74, no. 4 (1981): 245–248.

[15]D. Krug, T. B. Davis, and J. A. Glover, "Massed Versus Distributed Repeated Reading: A Case of Forgetting Helping Recall?" *Journal of Educational Psychology* 82 (1990): 366–371.

 **Online Study Center**   www.college.hmco.com/pic/pauk9e

What are some other advantages of using bite-sized study sessions?

The memory's need to consolidate information seems to play a key role in explaining why distributed practice is superior to massed practice. Other advantages also support these bite-sized study sessions:

Periodic "breathers" discourage fatigue. They refresh you both physically and emotionally.

Motivation is stronger when you work in short blocks of time. The end of each session marks a minivictory that provides momentum and a sense of accomplishment.

Distributed practice wards off boredom. Uninteresting subjects are easier to take in small doses.

In what situations is massed practice superior to distributed practice?

In spite of all the advantages of distributed practice, massed practice is superior in a few cases. For instance, when you are writing the first draft of a paper, massed practice is often essential. You have organized your notes in stacks; discrete bits of information are waiting in your mind like jigsaw-puzzle pieces to be fitted together; and the organizational pattern of your paper, though dimly perceived, is beginning to take shape. To stop working at this point would be disastrous. The entire effort would collapse. So in such a circumstance, it is far more efficient to overextend yourself—to complete that stage of the process—than to take a break or otherwise apply the principle of distributed practice.

Coming to Terms with Plateaus

YOUR
Q

No two people learn at exactly the same rate, yet the learning patterns of most people are similar. We all experience lulls in our learning. Progress is usually slow and steady at first; then for a period of time there might be no perceptible progress even though we are making a genuine effort. This "no-progress" period is called a *learning plateau*. After days, weeks, or even a month of effort, a surprising spurt in learning suddenly occurs and continues until another plateau is reached.

What is the best way to deal with a learning plateau?

When you reach a plateau, do not lose heart. Plateaus are a normal part of learning. You may not see any progress, but learning is still occurring. Once everything is in place, you'll be rewarded for your effort.

FINAL WORDS

How has Alzheimer's disease affected our attitude toward memory?

Alzheimer's disease has recently shifted a great deal of attention to human memory. People—especially older people—worry even more than they once did when a name or a piece of information slips their minds. Some make changes in their diet or lifestyle in the hope of forestalling or turning back the dreaded disease. The fear is understandable, and the attention to health and good habits is commendable. But the preciousness and precariousness of memory is nothing new. Memory has always been a vital component of our humanity, and it deserved our care, our respect, and our attention long before the emphasis turned to Alzheimer's. That is something we should never forget.

HAVE YOU MISSED SOMETHING?

SENTENCE COMPLETION

Complete the following sentences with one of the three words listed below each sentence.

1. G. A. Miller's Magical Number Seven theory teaches the importance of
_____.

   numbers   selectivity   reciting

2. Your brain's short-term working memory can be compared to a computer's
_____.

   mouse   monitor   DRAM

3. No single activity is more important in strengthening your memory than
_____.

   reviewing   reciting   reflection

MATCHING

In each blank space in the left column, write the letter preceding the phrase in the right column that matches the left item best.

_____ 1. Listening

_____ 2. GIGO

_____ 3. Interest

a. Enables large amounts of information to be more readily remembered

b. Illustrated by the story of the injured mountain climber

c. Even more susceptible to forgetting than reading is

Online Study Center   www.college.hmco.com/pic/pauk9e

_____ 4. Einstein

d. Measured the time it took to remember a series of nonsense syllables

_____ 5. Clustering

e. Reminds us that the data we get out is only as good as the data we put in

_____ 6. Ebbinghaus

f. Provided when you recite information either out loud or on paper

_____ 7. Feedback

g. Strongest form of motivation for remembering information

_____ 8. Consolidation

h. Used motivated forgetting to free his mind of unnecessary information

TRUE-FALSE

Circle T _beside the_ true _statements and_ F _beside the_ false _statements._

1. T F   When you learn something new, you are likely to forget most of it in a matter of days.
2. T F   To remember something, you have to make a conscious effort to learn it.
3. T F   Incorrect information can last as long in memory as correct information.
4. T F   Strong, memorable connections between ideas always have to be logical.
5. T F   The loci method uses geometrical figures as memory aids.

MULTIPLE CHOICE

Choose the word or phrase that completes each sentence most accurately, and circle the letter that precedes it.

1. Restaurant servers frequently use
   a. working memory.
   b. motivated forgetting.
   c. pseudo-forgetting.
   d. mnemonic devices.

2. The "basic background" memory principle reinforces the importance of
   a. getting it right the first time.
   b. introductory classes.
   c. pseudo-forgetting.
   d. condensing and summarizing.

3. Memory acquires an extra dimension when information is
   a. written on note cards.
   b. drawn or visualized.
   c. reread or recited.
   d. condensed or reduced.

4. Mnemonic devices are
   a. computer programs.
   b. memory aids.
   c. research instruments.
   d. learning theories.

5. Reciting should always be done
   a. out loud.
   b. silently.
   c. from memory.
   d. on paper.

SHORT ANSWER   *Supply a brief answer for each of the following items.*

1. Explain how reciting provides motivation.
2. Compare the merits of massed and distributed practice.
3. Discuss the types of artificial memory connections.
4. Provide illustrations of G. A. Miller's Magical Number Seven theory.

IT'S YOUR Q

The Q System uses marginal questions to encourage active reading. You'll notice that most but not all paragraphs in this chapter are accompanied by marginal questions. Now it's your Q. Scan the chapter for any paragraph that is missing a question, reread the paragraph, establish the main idea, and then arrive at a question that elicits it. Use the questions in the surrounding paragraphs as models for your own marginal questions.

WORDS IN CONTEXT

From the three choices beside each numbered item, select the one that most nearly expresses the meaning of the italicized word in the quote. Make a light check mark (✓) next to your choice.

Business has two basic functions: marketing and *innovation*. Marketing and innovation produce results: All the rest are "costs."

—Peter Drucker (1909–2005), American business philosopher and author

1. *innovation*   improvements   research   new ideas

Customers deserve the very best. It would be helpful if everyone in business could, to *paraphrase* the American Indian expression, walk a mile in their customer's moccasins.

—Norman R. Augustine (1935–), American author and chairman, Martin Marietta Corporation

2. *paraphrase* the expression   quote   reword   relate

I want this team to win. I'm *obsessed* with winning.

—George Steinbrenner (1930–), American executive, owner, New York Yankees baseball team

3. *obsessed* with winning   concerned   possessed   neutral

War is a series of *catastrophes* that results in a victory.

—Georges Clemenceau (1841–1929), French statesman

4. series of *catastrophes*   battles   tactics   disasters

THE WORD HISTORY SYSTEM

Broker
originally, a retail vendor of
wine

broker bro'-ker *n.* 1. One
that acts as an agent for others,
as in negotiating contracts,
purchases, or sales, in return
for a fee or commission. 2. A
stockbroker.

The modern *broker* who engages in large-scale financial operations takes his
name from a humble origin. *Broker* (spelled in Middle English *brocour*)
appears to be derived from Old French *broquier* or *brokier,* dialect for *brochier,*
"a broacher," "one who broaches or taps" a cask to draw off the liquor. The
modern verb *broach,* besides meaning "to tap" a cask, is used in a figurative
sense of "to open," as in "the subject was *broached."* So the original *broker*
was a retail vendor of wine, and later, any small retailer, middleman,
peddler, or agent in general, as a pawn*broker.* More dignified commodities,
such as stocks and bonds, have in modern times dignified the *broker* and
his occupation.

Reprinted by permission. From *Picturesque Word Origins* © 1933 by G. & C. Merriam Co. (now
Merriam-Webster, Incorporated).

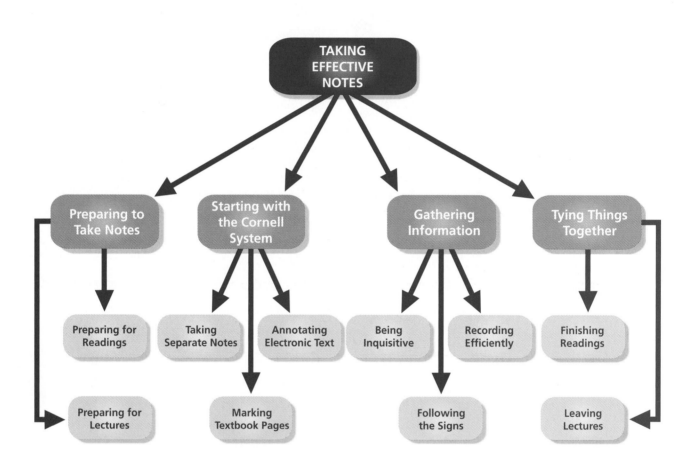

TAKING EFFECTIVE NOTES

Preparing to Take Notes
- Preparing for Readings
- Preparing for Lectures

Starting with the Cornell System
- Taking Separate Notes
- Annotating Electronic Text
- Marking Textbook Pages

Gathering Information
- Being Inquisitive
- Recording Efficiently
- Following the Signs

Tying Things Together
- Finishing Readings
- Leaving Lectures

Taking Effective Notes

Learn, compare, collect the facts!

Ivan Petrovich Pavlov
(1849–1936), Russian physiologist

The lectures you hear and the assignments you read are a potential gold mine. Both include valuable nuggets of knowledge. Because you spend so much of your academic life accumulating information, it's unwise to do so haphazardly. After all, anybody can take notes, just as anyone can doodle. But it's crucial for your notes to go beyond mere busywork. The key is to take notes effectively. This chapter maps out a strategy for effective note taking:

- **Being Prepared**
- **Starting with the Cornell System**
- **Gathering Information**
- **Tying Things Together**

What are the elements of successful note taking?

Taking notes doesn't simply mean scribbling down or marking up the things that strike your fancy. It means preparing properly for text or lecture notes, starting with some sort of system and then gathering information quickly and efficiently before pulling things together.

Preparing to Take Notes

What sort of preparation is required before I start taking notes?

If you don't speak the language of your textbook or have a "big picture" sense of the path of the semester's lectures, it's unlikely that you'll be in a position to take meaningful notes. And even if you do, you still need to take your preparations one step further by previewing each textbook assignment before you begin reading or by setting the table for an upcoming lecture. The time you invest at the beginning will strengthen your memories throughout and make you a much better student in the end.

Preparing for Readings

What's the best way to prepare for readings?

Because you and your textbooks are going to spend a quarter or a semester together, you'd better become friends. How? By getting acquainted with each textbook as a whole and by surveying specific assignments as they arise.

Get Acquainted with Your Textbook

What steps can you take to become acquainted with a textbook?

Give yourself enough time to understand how each of your textbooks works by buying them as soon as you've registered for your classes. This is a wise policy even if your school allows a period in which you can attend many courses before deciding on a final few. Don't wait until the first day of class. Get a head start by reading the tables of contents, prefaces, introductions, and other up-front material in all your books. Underline important words and sentences, and make notes in the margins. Look at the pictures, tables, and diagrams; read the captions. Read chapter titles, headings, and subheadings that interest you. This will give you a good idea of what the book is like and where you will be going during the semester. Later, you'll be glad you did, for you'll be able to see how the various parts of the course fit together.

How does a book's prefatory material differ from the rest of its pages?

Read the Prefatory Material   Although most textbooks are written in a serious, scholarly tone, in the prefatory material—which may be called "Preface," "To the Student," or something similar—the authors often take a more personal approach to their subjects and their readers than they do in the body of the text. This gives you a chance to meet the authors as people and to get comfortable with them. Once you do, you'll find that you can converse and even argue

What sort of valuable information does a preface typically contain?

with them as you read the text. Now and then, you'll find yourself saying, "No, I don't agree with that statement," or "What do you mean by that?"

In the prefatory material you can also find valuable information about the concepts and content of the book. For instance, if you began this book by reading the "To the Student" section, you know the purpose and use of the questions that appear in the margins of every chapter. If, on the other hand, you skipped over this part, you may have squandered a valuable component of the book. In prefaces you can find valuable information such as (1) what the author's objective is and is not, (2) the organizational plan of the book, (3) how and why the book is different from other books about the same subject, (4) the author's qualifications for writing the book, and often (5) an explanation of any supplementary learning aids. As a practical exercise, you might find it interesting to read the preface of this book, if you have not already done so. See how much you can gain toward understanding not only the book but also the authors.

How does learning the author's objective help?

The Author's Objective   Learning the author's objective—the purpose or goal he or she meant to achieve—enables you to read and interpret the text appropriately. For instance, the authors of *American Government* state their objective succinctly:

> In preparing every edition of *American Government*, including this new sixth edition, we have committed ourselves to two major goals: (1) to write a concise yet comprehensive textbook that (2) helps students think critically about the U.S. political system.[1]

In a single sentence, they tell you straight off what to expect and what particular philosophy they will be following.

Why is it helpful to know a book's organizational plan?

The Organizational Plan of the Book   Knowing the book's organizational plan is like having a road map. You know not only what the authors are doing but also where they are going. In the following example, you learn of the carefully organized introduction of topics as well as the self-contained, flexible nature of the individual chapters:

> The contents have been arranged so that as each new topic is introduced, it is fully explained and its fundamentals are thoroughly examined before commencing further study. For example, Chapter 13, Investment Fundamentals and Portfolio Management, precedes chapters on specific types of investments. In addition, not only does each chapter follow an overall logical sequence, but each is also a complete

[1]Alan R. Gitelson, Robert L. Dudley, and Melvin J. Dubnick, *American Government*, 6th ed. (Boston: Houghton Mifflin, 2001), p. xv.

 *Online Study Center*   www.college.hmco.com/pic/pauk9e

entity. The chapters can therefore be rearranged to follow any instructor's developmental sequence without losing students' comprehension.[2]

How and Why the Book Is Different   Recognizing what makes the textbook unique enables you to read with greater awareness and comprehension and to avoid the trap of thinking the book is "more of the same old stuff." In this case, the author chooses to reinforce the unique nature of his textbook by placing this paragraph in boldface:

> The text you are holding in your hands is literally the product of the research program undertaken in our laboratory. I have had opportunities to present these data at professional conferences and am encouraged by the responses I have received from course instructors. As one reviewer of the book put it, "Finally there is a text that uses psychology to teach psychology."[3]

Why do writers want you to know they are experts?

The Author's Qualifications   Writers usually try in some subtle way to let the reader know that their book is written by an expert on the subject and that therefore the information is trustworthy and credible. Note in the following example how the authors allude to their "considerable experience" while explaining their book's philosophy:

> It is our conviction, based on considerable experience in introducing large numbers of students to the broad sweep of civilization, that a book reflecting current trends can excite readers and inspire a renewed interest in history and the human experience.[4]

What does the prefatory material tell you about learning aids?

Supplementary Learning Aids   Today's textbook is often one component of a larger package of learning aids. The prefatory material generally names these aids and tells how they'll benefit you. In addition to in-text features, supplementary materials such as workbooks, study guides, software, websites, and videos are often available. Reading the introductory material will alert you to the presence of these features and ancillary materials, as you can see from the following example:

[2]E. Thomas Garman and Raymond E. Forgue, *Personal Finance*, 7th ed. (Boston: Houghton Mifflin, 2003), p. xxviii.

[3]Jeffrey S. Nevid, *Psychology: Concepts and Applications* (Boston: Houghton Mifflin, 2003), p. xviii.

[4]John P. McKay, Bennett D. Hill, John Buckler, and Patricia Buckley Ebrey, *A History of World Societies*, 5th ed. (Boston: Houghton Mifflin, 2000), p. xxvii.

The teaching package for the fifth edition includes the *Instructor's Resource Manual with Test Questions, Case Teaching Guide*, a computerized test bank, a videotape with instructor's guide, PowerPoint slides, and student and instructor web sites, which are new to this edition.[5]

Read the Introduction

What is the role of a book's introduction?

While the prefatory material often supplies a glimpse of the author's personality, the introduction provides a preview of the book itself. The introduction is the book's showcase. It is designed not only to introduce a book, but also to sell it. Authors and publishers both know that this is the place prospective customers often go to decide whether a book is worth reading and worth buying. As a result, the introduction is often especially well written and inviting.

Figure 10.1 is a densely packed introduction containing information of great and immediate value for the sharper reading of textbooks. It is from a book titled *Six-Way Paragraphs*.[6] The book's sole purpose is to teach students how to spot main ideas. One hundred paragraphs are provided for practice. To prepare students for such practice, the introduction strives to explain the ins and outs of the paragraphs found in textbooks. As you read it, be aware not only of *what* the writer says but also of *how* he says it and his *purpose* for saying it.

Preview from Front to Back

What can you learn from a book's table of contents?

After you've read the introductory material, survey the rest of the book. Begin by scanning the table of contents (TOC). It lists the parts, the chapters, and sometimes the major headings within each chapter. Some books, such as this one, actually have two TOCs, an abbreviated one that supplies the part and chapter names and a more detailed table of contents that lists the names and page references of sections and subsections in addition to those for the chapters and parts. General or detailed, the TOC is designed to show the overall organization of the book and how the chapter topics relate to one another. It also indicates whether the book contains extra material: appendixes, glossaries, bibliographies or references, and indexes.

What sort of valuable information can you glean from a book's extra sections?

Now turn to the back of the book and look at these extra sections. Appendixes contain additional information such as tables and graphs, documents, or details about specific aspects of a subject. Glossaries are specialized dictionaries of terms common to the subject the book discusses. Bibliographies and references list the

---

[5]Jean-Pierre Jeannet and H. David Hennessey, *Global Marketing Strategies*, 5th ed. (Boston: Houghton Mifflin, 2001), p. xviii.

[6]Walter Pauk, *Six-Way Paragraphs* (Providence, RI: Jamestown Publishers, 1974).

Figure 10.1
The Content of an Introduction

Source: Walter Pauk, *Six-Way Paragraphs* (Providence, RI: Jamestown Publishers, 1974), pp. 7–8. Reprinted by permission.

what: wants you to focus on
         the paragraph – unit

how: brings you and the
         writer together

purpose: wants you to look at the
         paragraph through the
         eyes of the writer

The paragraph! That's the working-unit of both writer and reader. The writer works hard to put meaning into the paragraph; the reader works hard to take meaning out of it. Though they work at opposite tasks, the work of each is closely related. Actually, to understand better the job of the reader, one must first understand better the job of the writer. So, let us look briefly at the writer's job.

what: each paragraph has
         but one main idea

how: shows you how a
         writer thinks

purpose: to convince you to look
         for only one idea per
         paragraph because
         writers follow this rule

To make his meaning clear, a writer knows that he must follow certain basic principles. First, he knows that he must develop only one main idea per paragraph. This principle is so important that he knows it backward, too. He knows that he must not try to develop two main ideas in the same, single paragraph.

what: the topic of the main
         idea is in the topic
         sentence, which is
         usually the first one

how: the writer needs to
         state a topic sentence
         to keep his own writing
         clear and under control

purpose: to instill confidence in
         you that the topic sentence
         is an important tool in a
         writer's kit and convince you
         it is there, so, look for it!

The next important principle he knows is that the topic of each main idea must be stated in a topic sentence and that such a sentence best serves its function by coming at or near the beginning of its paragraph. He knows, too, that the more clearly he can state the topic of his paragraph in an opening sentence, the more effective he will be in developing a meaningful, well-organized paragraph.

what: developing main ideas
         through supporting material

how: "more to a writer's job,"
         still keeps you in the
         writer's shoes

purpose: to announce and advance
         the new step of supporting
         materials

Now, there is more to a writer's job than just writing paragraphs consisting of only bare topic sentences and main ideas. The balance of his job deals with *developing* each main idea through the use of supporting material that amplifies and clarifies the main idea and many times makes it more vivid and memorable.

Figure 10.1
continued

what: (a) main ideas are often supported by examples, (b) other supporting devices listed

how: still through the writer's eyes

purpose: to develop the new idea of supporting materials

To support his main ideas, a writer may use a variety of forms. One of the most common forms to support a main idea is the *example*. Examples help to illustrate the main idea more vividly. Other supporting materials are anecdotes, incidents, jokes, allusions, comparisons, contrasts, analogies, definitions, exceptions, logic, and so forth.

what: paragraph contains (a) topic sentence, (b) main idea, and (c) supporting material

how: transfer the knowledge from the writer to you, the reader

purpose: to summarize all the three steps

To summarize, the reader should have learned from the writer that a textbook-type paragraph usually contains these three elements: a topic sentence, a main idea, and supporting material. Knowing this, the reader should use the topic sentence to lead him to the main idea. Once he grasps the main idea, then everything else is supporting material used to illustrate, amplify, and qualify the main idea. So, in the final analysis, the reader must be able to separate the main idea from the supporting material yet see the relationship between them.

sources the authors consulted in writing the book and can point you in the direction of further reading. Indexes—alphabetical listings of significant topics, ideas, and names along with page references that appear at the end of texts—give you a sense of the scope of the book and help you locate specific material quickly.

What is the general advantage of getting to know your textbook?

By familiarizing yourself with your textbook, you not only bolster your background knowledge about the subject; you also become aware of the features of the book you can use throughout the term. As a result, future assignments will be easier and less time consuming, and you'll have a greater chance to master the material.

 **Online Study Center**   www.college.hmco.com/pic/pauk9e

Survey Specific Assignments

What is the value of surveying a reading assignment?

Moving systematically through your textbook at the beginning of the semester will give you a strong context and a solid foundation that you can strengthen and further build on by briefly surveying your assignment before you begin reading it.

How does surveying make a difference in your reading?

Why Surveying Is Important   There are three practical ways that surveying can make a real and immediate difference in your reading: by creating a background, by limbering your mind, and by overcoming inertia.

How does surveying create a background?

1. Surveying creates a background.   Surveying provides prior knowledge that counteracts tunnel vision and prepares you for reading. According to David P. Ausubel, a learning-theory psychologist, previewing the general content of a chapter creates *advance organizers*, which help students learn and remember material they later study closely.[7] These advance organizers become familiar landmarks when you go back to read the chapter in earnest. John Livingston Lowes, a professor of literature at Princeton University, described these landmarks as *magnetic centers* around which ideas, facts, and details cluster like iron filings around a magnet.

How does surveying compare to an athlete's pregame warm-up?

2. Surveying limbers the mind.   For an athlete, a pregame warm-up limbers the muscles as well as the psyche and brain. An athlete knows that success comes from the coordination of smoothly gliding muscles, a positive attitude, and a concentrating mind. The prestudy survey of a textbook achieves for the scholar what the pregame warm-up achieves for the athlete.

How does surveying overcome inertia?

3. Surveying overcomes mental inertia.   How often have you said, with impatience and exasperation, "C'mon. Let's get started!" Getting started is hard. According to Newton's First Law of Motion (also known as the Law of Inertia), "A body in motion tends to remain in motion; a body at rest tends to remain at rest." Many students find it difficult to open a textbook and begin to study. If you are one of them, use surveying to ease yourself into studying. Surveying does the job: It gets you started. (Figure 10.2 provides a mnemonic device that makes it that much easier to survey each textbook chapter systematically.)

Preparing for Lectures

What information can you use to help prepare for an upcoming lecture?

You can zero in on the upcoming lecture by marshaling the available information to provide a context for what the speaker will talk about. Of course, lectures aren't like textbook chapters; unless they've been written down or recorded already, you can't survey them in advance. But in most courses, there is enough available information supporting the lecture that it should enable you to effectively prepare for it. Each lecture can be viewed as a piece of a puzzle.

[7]John F. Wakefield, *Educational Psychology* (Boston: Houghton Mifflin, 1996), p. 368.

Figure 10.2
Surveying a Textbook Chapter

How Surveying TIES UP the Elements of a Textbook Chapter

A chapter's information and elements can become more meaningful if you can tie them all together somehow. Surveying the chapter before you begin reading it can help provide a way.

Title: Read the title of the chapter to get a general idea about its subject.

Introduction: Read the introductory paragraph to get a sense of the key ideas that will be covered.

Ending: Read the chapter's ending paragraph for a summary of its key ideas or a sneak preview of its conclusions or lessons.

Subheadings: Scan the major subheadings to build a framework for the chapter that extends from the introduction to the ending.

Unusual elements: Look for any unique or unusual elements that stand out, such as lists and boxes, and boldfaced, italicized, or underlined text.

Pictures: Glance at pictures, charts, illustrations, or any other graphical elements for a succinct summary of some of the chapter's important ideas or a vivid example of some of its concepts.

The more pieces you have in place, the more you know about the shape and size of the pieces that remain. The course syllabus, the notes from your last lecture, and related reading assignments can all function as these puzzle pieces as you prepare for a lecture.

Look Over the Syllabus

How can you use your course syllabus to prepare for an upcoming lecture?

Assuming that your instructor is sticking to the syllabus, you should be able to read the list of lecture topics to get a big-picture sense of where this latest lecture will fit in. Pay especially close attention to the title and description of the previous lecture, the upcoming lecture, and the one that will follow. Encourage active thinking about the lecture topics by transforming each title into a question and then answering your question in cases where the lecture has already been delivered or by speculating on the answer in cases where the lecture is still to come.

Review Your Notes from the Previous Lecture

Why is it helpful to prepare for an upcoming lecture by reviewing your notes from the previous lecture?

Each lecture will normally build on the concepts from the lectures that came before it. Most instructors will assume that you attended, understood, and can remember the previous lecture. After all, time will rarely permit a rehash of ideas that have already been fully explained. Although the upcoming lecture

will often have some ties to all the lectures that came before it, the bond will usually be strongest with the most recent one. In fact, in some courses, each lecture is like the next episode of a continuing story. To understand what's going on in Chapter 2 in a novel, you often must understand and remember Chapter 1. Lectures often work in a similar way.

Do the Assigned Reading

How do reading assignments relate to the upcoming lecture?

Some instructors will assign readings as background for an upcoming lecture. Others will give you readings designed to follow up on what you've just heard and learned in a lecture. In either case, surveying these readings can help provide advance organizers that will make it easier to understand and remember an upcoming lecture.

Starting with the Cornell System

What is the Cornell System?

All of the methodical preparation you've done will be wasted if you just wing it when you start to take notes. Instead of taking a chance on a haphazard, seat-of-the-pants method of taking notes, you need a proven note-taking system. The Cornell System, which was developed at Cornell University almost fifty years ago, has been embraced by countless colleges and universities in the United States and throughout the world. It can be used for taking separate notes, for marking your textbook, and even for annotating electronic texts. The system is flexible and far-reaching, but its secret is simple: Wide margins on the outside and the bottom of the text area are the key.

Taking Separate Notes

In what sense are notes more valuable than a textbook?

The notes you jot down can become a handwritten textbook. In fact, in many instances they are more practical, meaningful, and up-to-date than a textbook. If you keep your notes neat, complete, and well organized, they will serve you splendidly.

What are the principal components of Cornell-style note paper?

Although Cornell-style paper can be difficult to find at school or office supply stores,* you can easily use a pen and ruler to adapt standard loose-leaf paper to the task. First draw a vertical line down the left side of each page two-and-one-half inches from the edge of the paper; end the line two inches from the bottom of the sheet. This creates the *cue column*. Next draw a horizontal line two inches

*Special "law-rule" paper, available at some office supply stores, has an extra-wide margin similar to what the Cornell System recommends. However, it is slightly larger than standard letter-sized paper and lacks the summary area at the bottom of each page.

up from the bottom of the page. This is the border for your *summary area*. The large space to the right of the cue column and above the summary area is where you write your notes. Figure 10.3 shows a Cornell note sheet.

What are the cue column and summary area used for?

As you're taking notes, the cue column should remain empty, as should the summary area. But when the time comes to review and recite what you've jotted down, you'll use the cue column for questions to help clarify meanings, reveal

Figure 10.3
The Cornell Note Sheet

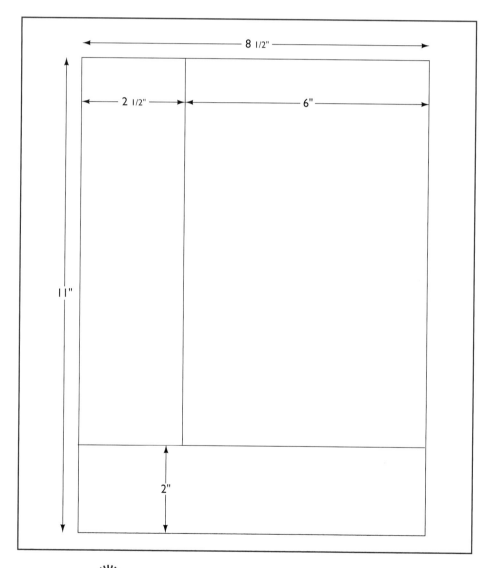

How does the Cornell System adjust to the demands of different courses?

Why is the outline format discouraged?

If outlines are a bad idea, what sort of note-taking format should you use instead?

How do sentences in your notes differ from traditional sentences?

relationships, establish continuity, and strengthen memory. The summary area will be used to distill a page's worth of notes down to a sentence or two.

The information that goes in the largest space on the page varies from class to class and from student to student. Different courses come with different demands. The format you choose for taking your notes and the ideas you jot down are almost entirely up to you. If you have a special way of jotting down your notes, you should be able to use it with the Cornell note sheet.

About the only format you should be wary of is the outline. As crisp and neat as they may look at a glance, outlines have a way of tying your hands and forcing you to squeeze information into an unforgiving framework. When you're taking notes—especially in a lecture—the last thing you want to be worrying about is Roman numerals. As Edward W. Fox, Cornell's great teacher, lecturer, and historian explained:

> Elaborate arrangements tend to confuse, and the traditional topical form, the use of Roman numerals, capital letters, Arabic numerals, and small letters, etc., with much indentation, has a fatal tendency to imply a logical analysis rather than elicit one.[8]

Outlines are the tail that wagged the dog. You should be concentrating on the information itself, not on its numbering scheme. Whatever works for you is best. You can take notes in sentence or paragraph form, in lists, as definitions, by adding drawings, or by using a combination of these formats.

Sentences.   Take key ideas from a lecture or reading and jot them down in your own words. If you're taking notes in a lecture, you probably won't have time to write out complete sentences. Instead, write telegraphically, leaving out articles such as *a*, *an*, and *the*, and abbreviating words you use often. Figure 10.4 provides an example.

Paragraphs.   Cluster related sentences in a block of text, often under a heading or label that serves to tie them together. As you see in Figure 10.5, these are not traditional paragraphs where one complete sentence flows smoothly to the next. Your sentences in paragraph-style notes will usually be telegraphic, and smooth transitions are not important. However, these paragraphs share one important thing with traditional paragraphs: All the sentences should relate to the same main idea.

[8]Edward W. Fox, *Syllabus for History* (Ithaca, NY: Cornell University Press, 1959). Reprinted by permission of the author.

Figure 10.4
Sentence Notes

What's animism?

Describe mana!

How to gain mana?

Who has mana?

Oct. 10 (Mon.) – Soc. 102 – Prof. Oxford

A. Animism
 1. Object has supernatural power
 2. Power called mana (not limited to objects)
  a. Objects accumulate mana
   Ex. Good canoe – more mana than poor one.
  b. Objects can lose mana
  c. People collect objects w/lots of mana
  d. Good person's objects collect mana
  e. People, animals, plants have mana, too.
   Ex. Expert canoe builder has mana –
    imparts mana to canoe
  f. Chief has lots of mana – dangerous to
   get too close to chief – mana around head.

Figure 10.5
Paragraph Notes

What is the Greek concept of a well-rounded person?

Nov. 6 (Mon.) – World Lit. 106 – Prof. Warnek

Greece

1. Unity = well rounded
 Early Greeks vigorous. Goal was to be well rounded: unity of knowledge & activity. No separate specializations as law, literature, philosophy, etc. Believed one person should master all things equally well; not only knowledge, but be an athlete, soldier, & statesman, too.

What do definition-style notes look like?

Definitions   Write a name or term, add a dash or colon, and then provide a succinct explanation or elaboration. Figure 10.6 provides an example.

How do you make items stand out in list-style notes?

Lists.   Start with a topic, name, term, or process, and then list phrases or telegraphic sentences that relate. Avoid numbering the items unless the numbers are relevant to the list. If you want to make the items stand out in your notes, consider beginning each with an asterisk or a bullet point. Figure 10.7 shows what these lists are apt to look like.

What is the advantage of using drawings in your notes?

Drawings.   Drawings and diagrams can succinctly sum up information that may be difficult to explain in words alone. A sketch can often convey locations or relationships more effectively than a sentence or two. Figure 10.8 shows the sort of diagram that a biology student might include in her notes.

Figure 10.6
Definition Notes

	Mar. 14 (Fri.) – Ed. 103 – Prof. Pauk
What are main types of note-taking formats?	<u>Types of note-taking formats</u> <u>sentence</u> - Notes written in sentences, but telegraphically: w/ abbrevs. for common wds. Articles ("a", "an", etc.) left out. <u>paragraph</u> - Like real paragraphs, clustered around main idea, but sentences telegraphic & transitions left off <u>definition</u> - name or term, followed by dash or colon and explanation <u>list</u> - word or phrase heading, followed by series of items. No numbers unless relevant. Use bullet pts. instead. <u>combination</u> - mix of other formats

Figure 10.7
List Notes

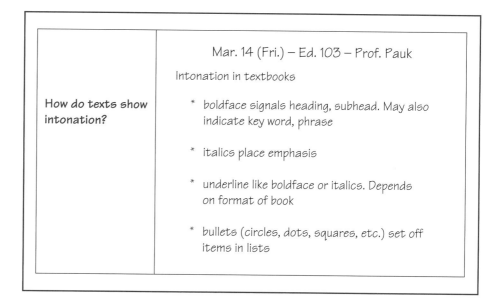

Mar. 14 (Fri.) – Ed. 103 – Prof. Pauk

Intonation in textbooks

How do texts show intonation?

* boldface signals heading, subhead. May also indicate key word, phrase

* italics place emphasis

* underline like boldface or italics. Depends on format of book

* bullets (circles, dots, squares, etc.) set off items in lists

Figure 10.8
Diagramming as a Study Aid

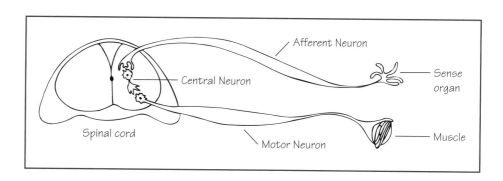

Afferent Neuron

Central Neuron

Sense organ

Spinal cord

Motor Neuron

Muscle

When will you need a combination of formats for your notes?

Combination.   Some chapters and a few lectures may fit into a single note-taking format, but it's unlikely that most will. Good note takers must remain flexible, shifting quickly from one format to another to capture key information as efficiently and meaningfully as possible. It's important to choose the right tool for the job. Figure 10.9 shows notes that combine several formats.

Online Study Center   www.college.hmco.com/pic/pauk9e

Figure 10.9
Notes That Use a Combination of Formats

	Mar. 14 (Fri.) – Ed. 103 – Prof. Pauk
	Organizational patterns
How do org. patterns help make books, lectures easier to follow?	Where is this going? Org. patterns provide guidance in lectures & texts. Tell you where author, speaker is headed. Learning common patterns can make it easier to follow both. Also, <u>signposts</u> (next, finally, thus) can provide clues about path.
What are movement patterns?	<u>Movement patterns</u> systematically travel through time, space, process. Can be easiest pattern to follow. Several types:
Examples?	* time or chronological pattern - events presented in order.
	* place or spatial pattern - info presented based on location or arrangement. Ex: descrip. of geog. features of U.S., outline of company setup
	* process pattern - steps or events lead to desired situation or product. Ex: recipe.

Marking Your Textbook

What happens to the key Cornell components when you choose to mark your text instead of taking separate notes?

Although the Cornell System can work as well with readings as it does with lectures, when you're taking notes for a textbook assignment, you also have the option of putting those notes directly on the pages of your book instead. When you choose to take notes directly in your textbook, the outside margin of the textbook page becomes the substitute for the cue column, and the spaces at the bottom or top of each page become the summary area. Of course, because a textbook page is already filled with text, you obviously can't put traditional notes where the text already is. What may at first seem like a disadvantage can actually be a great boon. Rather than jotting down your notes from scratch, you can mark the words or phrases in your textbook that make up the most important ideas.

Figure 10.10 contains twelve suggestions for marking textbooks. Notice especially the use of single and double underlines; the use of asterisks, circling, and boxing for important items; and the use of the top and bottom margins for long

Figure 10.10
A System for Marking Your Textbooks

EXPLANATION AND DESCRIPTION	SYMBOLS, MARKINGS, AND NOTATIONS
1. Use double lines under words or phrases to signify main ideas.	<u><u>Radiation can produce mutations</u></u> . . .
2. Use single lines under words or phrases to signify supporting material.	<u>comes from cosmic rays</u> . . .
3. Mark small circled numbers near the initial word of an underlined group of words to indicate a series of arguments, facts, ideas—either main or supporting.	Conditions change . . . ① <u>rocks rise</u> . . . ② <u>some sink</u> . . . ③ <u>the sea dashes</u> . . . ④ <u>strong winds</u> . . .
4. Rather than underlining a group of three or more important lines, use a vertical bracket in the margin.	had known . . . who gave . . . the time . . . of time . . .
5. Use one asterisk in the margin to indicate ideas of special importance, and two for ideas of unusual importance. Reserve three asterisks for principles and high-level generalizations.	* When a <u>nuclear blast</u> is . . . ** People <u>quite close</u> to the . . . ***The main <u>cause of mutations</u> . . .
6. Circle keywords and key terms.	The (genes) are the . . .
7. Box words of enumeration and transition.	[fourth,] the lack of supplies . . . [furthermore,] the shortage . . .
8. Place a question mark in the margin, opposite lines you do not understand, as a reminder to ask the instructor for clarification.	? | The lastest . . . | cold period . . . | about 1,000,000 . . .
9. If you disagree with a statement, indicate that in the margin.	Disagree | Even today . . . | Life became . . . | on land only . . . | 340 million years . . .
10. Use the top and bottom margins of a page to record ideas of your own that are prompted by what you read.	Why not use carbon dating? .... Check on reference of fossils found in Tennessee stone quarry.
11. On sheets of paper that are smaller than the pages of the book, write longer thoughts or summaries; then insert them between the pages.	Fossils Plants = 500,000,000 years old Insects = 260,000,000 " " Bees = 100,000,000 " " True Fish = 330,000,000 " " Amphibians = 300,000,000 " " Reptiles = 300,000,000 " " Birds = 150,000,000 " "
12. Even though you have underlined the important ideas and supporting materials, still jot brief cues in the side margins.	Adapt – _____ fossil – _____ layer – _____

notations or summaries. If some of these ideas appeal to you, work them into your marking system. Be sure to use them consistently so that you will instantly remember what they mean.

What advantage does textbook marking have over separate notes?

One key advantage of marking up your textbook directly is that your notes and your textbook travel together as a unit. Whenever you need clarification for a sentence or phrase you have marked, you have an entire book's worth of supporting material, including a table of contents, an index, and often a glossary, at your fingertips.

Of course, a potential disadvantage of textbook marking is that it doesn't require your complete concentration. Unlike taking separate notes, in which you have to consciously choose to add each idea, you can annotate your textbook without a true understanding of what you've marked. Drawing lines and boxes and inserting symbols and question marks can give you a false sense of accomplishment if you're not thinking deeply about what you read. It can also result in overmarking, which can undermine the original value of marking. When you mark your text, you need to do so sparingly, with both discipline and forethought. Keep in mind that the "you" who reviews the marked book will likely be more knowledgeable than the "you" who marked the book originally. Think ahead, so that weeks or months later when you look back at chapters you marked, your marks will still be meaningful and won't seem excessive.

How can you make sure your marks are meaningful and not excessive?

There is a simple but powerful way to manage your marking: recitation. Rather than marking each paragraph as you go, read it through completely and then recite its main idea in your own words. Then return to the paragraph and mark the words or phrases that express this main idea. This step will move you out of the realm of simple recognition and into recall. Recalling your notes is the way to help make information your own.

On the following pages are examples of appropriately marked textbook pages. Figure 10.11 shows how to organize a page using enumeration, that is, encircling words such as *first* and *second*. Write in numbers to identify salient points. The underlinings should be sparse and form the answers to the questions in the margins. This type of organization not only aids in comprehending and remembering the main points of the page, but also helps immensely when you're studying for an examination and time is short.

Annotating Electronic Text

How do you mark an electronic text?

These days, many of the texts we read are no longer printed pages. Instead, they take some electronic form, such as webpages, portable document format (PDF) files, word processor documents, or electronic slides from presentation software such as Microsoft PowerPoint. Any one of these formats can be printed out and then marked up as though they were pages from a textbook, although you may find that you don't have enough space for your marginal

Figure 10.11
Use of Enumeration in Textbooks

Source: John P. McKay, Bennett D. Hill, and John Buckler, *A History of World Societies*. Copyright © 2000 by Houghton Mifflin Company, Boston. Reprinted by permission.

MARITIME EXPANSION

Ming period Naval expeditions When? Who?	Another dramatic development of the Ming period was the series of naval expeditions sent out between 1405 and 1433 under Hong Wu's son Yong Lu and Yong Lu's successor. China had a
Naval history	strong maritime history stretching back to the eleventh century, and these early fifteenth-century voyages were a continuation of that tradition. The
Relative power?	Ming expeditions established China as the greatest maritime power in the world—considerably ahead
Portugal power when?	of Portugal, whose major seafaring reconnaissances began a half-century later.
Purpose of expeditions? Tribute system?? 2 motives? Contender – who?	In contrast to Hong Wu, Yong Lu broadened ①diplomatic and ②commercial contacts within the tribute system. Yong Lu had two basic motives for launching overseas voyages. First, he sent them in search of Jian Wen, a serious contender for the throne whom he had defeated but who, rumor claimed, had escaped to Southeast Asia. Second, he launched the expeditions to explore, to expand trade, and to provide the imperial court with luxury objects. Led by the Muslim eunuch admiral
Admiral? 1st expedition	Zheng He and navigating by compass, seven fleets sailed to East and South Asia. The first expedition (which carried 27,800 men) involved 62 major
Ship's size?	ships, the largest of which was 440 feet in length and 180 feet in the beam and had 9 masts. The
Sea route?	expeditions crossed the Indian Ocean to Ceylon, the Persian Gulf, and the east coast of Africa.
3 consequences?	These voyages had important consequences. They extended the ①prestige of the Ming Dynasty throughout Asia. Trade, in the form of tribute from as far as the west coast of southern India, greatly increased. ②Diplomatic contacts with the distant Middle East led to the arrival in Nanjing of embassies from Egypt. ③The maritime expeditions also led to the publication of geographical works.

Online Study Center   www.college.hmco.com/pic/pauk9e

cues if you simply print them out "as-is." However, there are adjustments you can make to accommodate Cornell-style margins.

How can you make room for Cornell margins on printed webpages?

Webpages. To add the space you need for note taking at the left and the bottom of each webpage, choose Page Setup from the File menu of your browser. Once you do, you should be able to change your browser's default margins to Cornell margins by typing the new dimensions into the appropriate text boxes. Enter 2.5 in the box for the left-hand margin and 2 in the box for the bottom. The text of the webpages will not be reduced. Instead it will be squeezed into the smaller text space to make room for the oversized margins.

Where do you put your markings on PDF files?

PDF files. Although portable document format provides excellent print-quality pages, it's not as flexible if you want to make room for oversized margins. You can't really squeeze the text this time. The best you can do is to resize it. You do this by fooling your printer into thinking that you are printing standard 8.5 × 11 sheets onto smaller sized paper. The paper size that comes closest to providing the proper margins you need on the side and the bottom is called "B5(JIS)," which shrinks 8.5 × 11 pages down to 7.15 × 10.11. Depending on the margins on the original document, this should give you just the right amount of space for the cue column and maybe a bit more than you need at the bottom for the summary space. The only other nonstandard aspect of this method is that the cue column winds up on the left-hand side instead of the right as if you were adding marginal jottings to a textbook that only had odd-numbered pages.

What are some ways that you can annotate presentation slides?

Presentation slides. Most presentation software is designed so the slides can be printed out in a way that allows room for notations. In addition, if the slideshow is editable, you may be able to add your notations onscreen without even printing out the slides.

How do you adjust word processor documents to accommodate Cornell markings?

Word processor documents. Of all the electronic documents you may want to annotate, word processor documents are probably the best suited and most flexible. If you prefer to handwrite your marginal jottings, you can change the margins in the document (just as you did with the webpages) to accommodate both the cue column and the summary space. With most word processing applications you do this by choosing Page Setup from the File menu, clicking on the tab for margins, and increasing the size of the left and bottom margins. When you print out the pages you should have ample room at both the left and the bottom of each printed page.

How can you type in your markings instead of jotting them down by hand?

Word processor documents also make it relatively easy to type your jottings onscreen instead of writing them down by hand. You do this by converting the text of your document into a one-column table, with one paragraph per row. Highlight the text of your document and then choose the item in the Table menu that converts your text to a table. Once you're satisfied that each paragraph occupies its own table row, go back and add an additional column to your table, just to the left of the original one. This should create a blank cell to the left of every paragraph in your document that you can use for typing in your marginal questions. Adding a summary area is a little trickier—particularly if you want to be sure that each summary winds up at the bottom of a page. To do so, highlight the last row on a page, choose Insert from the Table menu, and add a row below the one you've selected. Then select the newly created two-column row and choose Merge Cells from the Table menu. This should provide you with a summary space that spans the two columns of your note-taking table. To add a space to the next page of your notes, simply repeat the process.

Gathering Information

What can you do to be fully engaged as you take notes?

Whether you are taking notes on sheets of paper, making marks in your textbook, or typing your notes onscreen, you need to be fully engaged. To avoid drifting into the sort of robotic routine that adds little to learning, it is important to remain inquisitive as you take your notes, to keep alert for signs that will tip you off to the meaning of what you're reading or learning, to record things efficiently, and, as always, to stay flexible for the inevitable exceptions and special cases.

Being Inquisitive

What is the secret to being an active participant?

You can't really expect to do a good job of gleaning the most important information from a lecture or reading unless you are paying attention. And while getting enough sleep and sitting up straight can help promote alertness, the real secret to being an active participant is to maintain an inquisitive mindset. Formulating questions, whether silently or aloud, will unlock the meaning of information in a way that listening or reading passively just can't approach.

Ask Questions Both Silently and Out Loud During a Lecture

What are the roles of the speaker and listener in a lecture?

Although the communication may seem one-sided, both the speaker and the listener play important roles in a classroom lecture. The speaker's responsibility is to make points clearly. The listener's responsibility is to understand what the speaker says. If a speaker's message is not clear and the listener asks a clarifying question, both the speaker and the listener benefit. The speaker is encouraged and gratified to know that the audience is interested. The listener can concentrate on what the speaker has to say and feel good about raising a question that other, more timid members of the audience might have been hesitant to ask.

Why do questions often go unasked?

As vital as questions can be to comprehension, they often go unasked. A professor at the University of Virginia who conducted a survey found that 94 percent of her students had failed to understand something in at least one class lecture during the semester. Seventy percent of the students had not asked clarifying questions even though they knew they could. When she asked them why they had remained silent, they answered with such statements as "I was afraid I'd look stupid," "I didn't want to make myself conspicuous," "I was too proud to ask," and "I was too confused to know what question to ask." The way to dispel the fear of asking is to remember that the only dumb question is the one that is never asked. The way to dispel confusion is to acknowledge it by saying, "I'm confused about the last point you made" or "I'm confused about how the example pertains to your main point." In this situation, as in most, honesty is the best policy.

Formulate Questions as You Read

How do you ask questions when you're reading a book that can't talk back?

It's easy to see how questions can help clarify important points in a classroom lecture. After all, you usually have an expert right there who can sense your confusion and respond to the questions. Not so with a textbook assignment, where all you have are silent words on a printed page. Instead of approaching a textbook as a passive recipient of its information, build on the relationship you formed with the author or authors when you first surveyed the book and read over its prefatory material by constantly formulating questions as you read, by wondering out loud about issues or aspects that concern you, and by writing out questions that help you pinpoint and remember the most important information. The latter really serves as the foundation for taking notes and mastering them.

What's a good way to start asking questions as you read?

If asking questions as you read doesn't seem to come naturally at first, a good way to start is by reading the headings and subheadings in your assignment and turning them into questions. This is an important ice-breaker in a number of textbook reading systems, including the well-known SQ3R system (see Figure 10.12).

It doesn't take much to transform a typical textbook heading or subheading into an attention-getting question. For example, the main heading "Basic Aspects of Memory" could be turned into the question "What are the basic aspects of memory?" The technique is simple, but it works. Questions encourage interaction. Suddenly you will be reading with a purpose instead of just passively taking in information. And if your question is answered early in the discussion, simply ask another, based on what you have read.

Following the Signs

What signs help improve comprehension of lectures or readings?

Whether information is delivered in the form of a lecture or a textbook chapter, there are usually signs that help direct you down the road to comprehension. Both the intonation of the words and the way they are organized provide clues about the author or speaker's purpose and approach.

Figure 10.12

The SQ3R System

Source: Adaptation of "Steps in the SQ3R Method" (pp. 32–33) from *Effective Study*, 4th Edition, by Francis P. Robinson. Copyright 1941, 1946 by Harper & Row Publishers Inc. Copyright © 1961, 1970 by Francis P. Robinson. Reprinted by permission of the publisher.

THE SQ3R SYSTEM

S SURVEY
Glance through all the headings in the chapter, and read the final summary paragraph (if the chapter has one). This survey should not take more than a minute, and it will show you the three to six core ideas on which the discussion will be based. This orientation will help you organize the ideas as you read them later.

Q QUESTION
Now begin to work. Turn the first heading into a question. This will arouse your curiosity and thereby increase comprehension. It will bring to mind information you already know, thus helping you understand that section more quickly. The question also will make important points stand out from explanatory details. You can turn a heading into a question as you read the heading, but it demands conscious effort on your part.

R_1 READ
Read the paragraph or section to answer the question. Read actively.

R_2 RECITE
After you finish reading the paragraph or section, stop, look away from the book, and try to recite the answer to your formed question. If you cannot recite the answer correctly or fully, reread the section and try again.

R_3 REVIEW
When you have finished reading and reciting page after page, go back to the beginning of the chapter, glance at the headings and subheadings, and think briefly about the answers that you have already recited. Work your way in this manner to the end of the chapter. Now you should have ended with an integrated bird's-eye view of the entire chapter.

Online Study Center www.college.hmco.com/pic/pauk9e

Pay Attention to Intonation

How does intonation affect the meaning of words?

Consider the dramatic effect that intonation can have on the meaning of even a simple phrase, such as "Excuse me." Depending on the tone of voice, these two words can sound polite, tentative, argumentative, or downright resentful. In each case, the words are identical, but the delivery is different. If you pay attention only to the words when you're listening to a lecture or reading a textbook, but ignore their delivery, you may be missing a critical component of their meaning.

What are the three components of intonation?

Intonation in Lectures   Most college lecturers speak about 120 words per minute, which means that in a fifty-minute lecture you hear roughly 6,000 words. Listening for signals in a lecture is especially helpful because, unlike in reading, you don't have the luxury of retracing your steps if you discover that you're lost. In addition to words, intonation—variations in the lecturer's voice—is the most significant signal in spoken language. Intonation has three components: volume, pauses, and cadence.

Volume.   In general, the introduction of a crucial idea is preceded by a change in volume; the speaker raises or lowers his or her voice.

Pauses.   Pausing before and after main ideas sets these ideas apart from the rest of the lecture. Pauses achieve a dramatic effect and, on a practical level, provide note takers with extra writing time.

Cadence.   The rhythm of a lecturer's speaking patterns can be particularly helpful. Often, like the bulleted lists you find in textbooks, the speaker lists a series of important ideas by using a steady speaking rhythm, sometimes even beginning each idea with the same words or phrase. Whenever you detect these oral signals, your pencil should be moving steadily, adding these important points to your notes.

What does reading with intonation involve?

Intonation in Textbooks   Reading with intonation can make the words on your textbook page come alive. This doesn't mean reading out loud, but it does mean reading with expression. Intonation helps you combine individual words into meaningful mental "bites."

How does reading expressively help?

As your eyes move rapidly across the page, let your mind swing along each line with an intonation that can be heard by your "inner ear." By reading expressively, you will be supplying the important rhythm, stress, emphasis, and pauses that were taken out when the words were turned into written form. If at first you find it difficult to "hear" what you're reading, take a few minutes to actually read aloud in the privacy of your room. This should help to establish speech patterns in your mind and will ultimately result in what reading experts call "fluency," which is considered the key to reading with speed and accuracy.

How do type styles mimic the volume, pauses, and cadence of speech?

Adding your own intonation in this way can help impart meaning and expression to words that may otherwise seem to lack pizzazz. In addition, books provide another form of intonation that mimics the volume, pauses, and cadence of speech.

Open any textbook and you'll quickly discover that the words aren't all printed in the same size or the same style. The format may differ from text to text, but in general each book takes advantage of a variety of type sizes and styles to convey information. By noting these typographical differences, you can pick up on signals for organization and emphasis.

Boldface (thick, dark type) often signals a textbook heading or subheading. It may also be used to draw your attention to a specific principle, definition, or keyword within the text.

Italics (type that slopes to the right) places emphasis on a word or a phrase.

Underlining often performs the same functions as boldface and italics, depending on the format of the particular textbook.

• Bullets (small markers, often circular or square) set off the items in lists.

Size, color, and placement of type often call attention to headings and subheadings. Take note of words printed in larger type, in color, or on lines by themselves.

How can you learn the meaning of a book's typographical intonation?

You can usually crack a book's particular typographical code by skimming through it before you start reading. In addition, look for an explanation of format—especially if it is unconventional—in the book's introductory material.

Recognize Organizational Patterns

What role do organizational patterns play in lectures and textbooks?

Where are we going? And how are we going to get there? Those are both reasonable questions to ask when you're heading off on a journey. They're equally reasonable when you're reading an assignment or listening to a lecture. Luckily, both authors and speakers normally tell you where you're headed and how you're going to get there by using common organizational patterns to help arrange their information. Familiarize yourself with these patterns, and you should find things easier to follow. In addition, you can often navigate through information by noticing certain verbal signposts that commonly line the route. Simple words such as *next, thus*, or *finally* can provide valuable clues to the path that a chapter or lecture is taking.

What are movement patterns?

Movement Patterns   Authors or speakers will frequently move you systematically through time, through space, or through a process. Once you catch on, these patterns can be among the easiest to follow.

With the **time or chronological pattern**, events are presented in the order in which they occurred. This pattern can be recognized quickly from the author's or lecturer's use of dates and such phrases as *in previous years, the next day*, and *two years later*, which denote the passage of time.

Items in a **place or spatial pattern** are presented or discussed on the basis of their locations or their arrangement relative to one another. For example, an author might use a spatial pattern to describe the geographical features of the United States from the West Coast to the East Coast. This is often called a *geographical pattern*. It is also called a *topical pattern* when it is used to describe the organization of a corporation along the lines of purchasing, manufacturing, sales, and so forth. The progression from item to item is usually orderly and easy to follow: from left to right, from high to low, from north to south, and so on.

Steps or events in a **process pattern** are presented in an orderly sequence that leads to a desired situation or product. A recipe and the instructions for assembling a bicycle are examples of process patterns. They often include words such as *first*, *after this*, *then*, *next*, and *finally*. You'll frequently encounter this pattern in computer courses and the sciences, where the steps in a process are described in the order in which they must occur to put something together, run an application, or blend ingredients.

How are importance patterns organized?

Importance Patterns   A common way of organizing facts or information is by arranging them in terms of their relative importance.

In the **increasing importance pattern**, the most important or most dramatic item in a series is placed at the end. Each succeeding item is more important than the previous one, so a crescendo effect is created. Thus, this pattern is also called the *climactic-order pattern*.

In the **decreasing importance pattern**, the most important or most dramatic item in a series is placed at the very beginning. Such an organization grabs your interest immediately, so there is a good chance that you will stay with the writer or speaker all the way through. This pattern is commonly used in newspaper articles and is known by journalists as the *inverted pyramid pattern*.

What do causal patterns all share in common?

Causal Patterns   One thing leads to another in a number of patterns, most of which are variations on the well-known idea of cause and effect.

In the **problem–effect–solution pattern**, the writer or speaker outlines a problem (cause), explains its effect, and then often (though not always) maps out a solution.

The **problem–cause–solution pattern** inverts this approach. A predicament (effect) is introduced, followed by its antecedents (cause) and eventually by remedies. In short, the effect comes first this time, followed by the cause.

Of course, not all cause–effect patterns involve problems. In technical subjects, the generic **cause–effect pattern** is quite common. In this case, variables are defined and their result (effect) is explained. Meanwhile, in the social sciences, you'll often run into the **action–impact pattern**, where some sort of initiative is outlined, such as increased funding for education, followed by a result, such as a higher average income for employees who received a college education.

Regardless of the variation, phrases such as *as a result* or *consequently* will usually alert you to a causal pattern.

Comparison Patterns   Writers and speakers compare things, events, or people when they emphasize similarities, and contrast them when they emphasize differences. Individual characteristics may be compared or contrasted one at a time, or several characteristics may be discussed as a group. In either case, the pattern can be recognized from the various similarities or differences and from the use of words such as *similarly, likewise, conversely,* and *on the other hand.*

When do writers and speakers use comparison patterns?

Logical Patterns   In these patterns, a conclusion is either drawn or stated at the outset and then supported.

With the **inductive pattern**, a number of incidents are cited, and then a conclusion is arrived at. The main point will be something like this: "So, on the basis of all these facts, we come to this overriding principle, which is so-and-so."

With the **deductive pattern**, the reverse is true. Here, the principle or general statement is given first, and then the events or proofs are enumerated.

What do logical patterns have in common?

Signposts   Although identifying the precise organizational pattern can be extremely helpful, it isn't always easy or even possible. Some textbook chapters may defy easy organization, and some lectures can be rambling. In these cases, all is not lost. Keep in mind that your key goal while taking notes is to use cues and patterns to help arrange your thoughts and aid your search for meaning. Luckily, the signposts that often tip you off to a particular organizational pattern can still be helpful even if you have a tough time nailing down the overall arrangement. Table 10.1 lists some common signposts and the directions they're likely to point you in.

What should you do if you can't identify a precise organizational pattern?

Recording Efficiently

Depending on whether you're taking lecture notes or textbook notes, you may find that you are short on space, short on time, or both. Of course, if you scribble down information too quickly, your notes may be illegible. And if you're too choosy about what you record, you could be left with costly gaps in your information. The way to circumvent these problems and record legible, useful notes at a reasonable speed is to adopt the modified printing style, use telegraphic sentences, and record selectively.

YOUR Q

Table 10.1
Signposts

Categories and Examples	When you come across these words, immediately think . . .

Example Words
    specifically
    to illustrate
    for example
    for instance
    that is
	"Here comes an example. Must be double-checking to make sure I understood the point just made."

Cause-and-Effect Words
    consequently
    therefore
    as a result
    if . . . then
    accordingly
    thus, so
    hence
	"There's an effect word. Better check back when I have a chance to make sure I can find the cause now that I know what the effect is."

Enumeration Words
    the four steps . . .
    first, second, third
    next, finally
	"That's a lot of steps. I'd better be sure I'm keeping track of all of them and getting them in the right order."

Addition Words
    furthermore
    as well as
    along with
    in addition
    moreover
    also
    not only . . . but also
	"Seems there's always something else to be added. Must be worth remembering."

Contrast Words
    on the other hand
    in contrast
    conversely
    although
    however, despite
    whereas
	"Here comes the other side of the coin. Let's see how it differs from what's been said already."

Comparison Words
    likewise
    similarly
    comparatively
    identical
	"Lots of similar things, it seems."

Swivel Words
    however
    nevertheless
    yet
    but
    still
	"Looks like there's going to be a little bit of doubt or 'give back' on the point just made. Better pay attention to this qualifying remark."

(continued)

Table 10.1
continued

Categories and Examples	When you come across these words, immediately think . . .
Concession Words to be sure indeed though, although granted of course	"Okay! Here comes an argument or two from the opposing point of view."
Emphasis Words more important above all remember in other words finally	"Looks as though what's coming up is going to be important."
Repeat Words in other words it simply means that is briefly in essence as we've seen	"Here comes another explanation. Maybe I'll understand this one a little better."
Time Words before, after formerly, soon subsequently prior, during meanwhile	"Hmm! A time relationship is being established. Let's see: What came first, what came last, and what came in between?"
Place Words above below beyond adjacent to	"Okay! I'll put these ideas and facts not only in their proper places, but also in their proper relationship."
Summary Words for these reasons on the whole in conclusion in a nutshell to sum up in short finally	"Good. Now I'll get a simple wrap-up of the points that have been made. It's almost sure to be full of key ideas."
Test Words (lectures) This is important. Remember this. You'll see this again. Here's a pitfall.	"Sounds like a potential test item. Better be sure to pay close attention to it."

Use Modified Printing

What is modified printing?

Poor handwriting need not keep you from taking legible notes. The easy-to-master *modified printing style* combines the rapidity of writing with the legibility of printing. Your words still have a cursive look, but the periodic breaks between letters that are normally characteristic of printing prevent your writing from deteriorating into an unreadable blur.

$$a \; b \; c \; d \; e \; f \; g \; h \; i \; j \; k \; l \; m \; n \; o \; p \; q \; r \; s \; t \; u \; v \; w \; x \; y \; z$$

Figure 10.13 shows how modified printing looks in a typical paragraph.

Take Notes Telegraphically

What does it mean to take notes telegraphically?

The best way to take notes is telegraphically. Long before e-mail and the fax machine were invented, important business and personal messages were sent by telegraph. The sender paid by the word; the fewer the words, the lower the cost. A three-word message such as "Arriving three pm" was much less expensive than an eleven-word message: "I will arrive home promptly at three o'-clock in the afternoon." Of course, taking notes doesn't cost money, but it does cost time. To save time when you're taking notes, leave out unnecessary words such as articles (*a, an, the*), abbreviate words you use often (see Figures 10.14 and 10.15), and streamline definitions by using a colon (:) or a dash (—). Two examples of this telegraphic style are shown in Figure 10.16.

Figure 10.13
Modified Printing Style

> There are four advantages to using this modified printing style. First, it is faster than cursive writing; second, it is neater, permitting easy and direct comprehension; third, it saves time by precluding rewriting or typing; and fourth, it permits easy and clear re-forming of letters that are ill-formed due to haste.

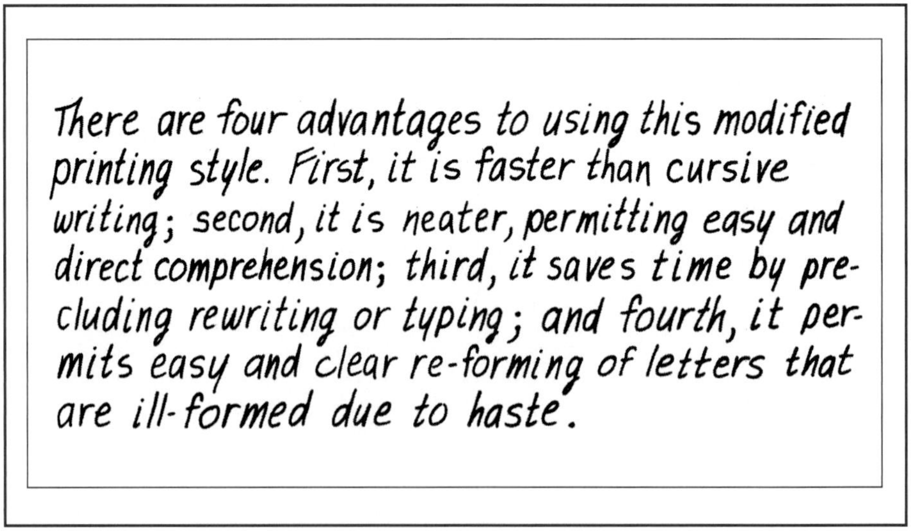

Figure 10.14
Examples of Technical Symbols

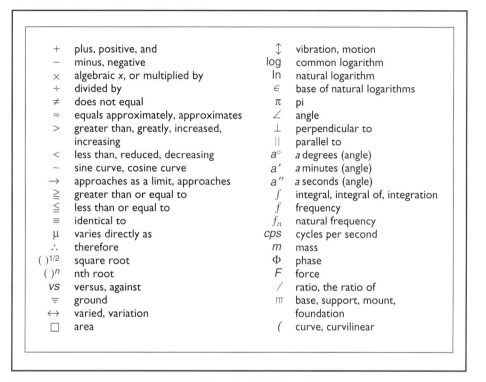

+	plus, positive, and	$\updownarrow$	vibration, motion
−	minus, negative	log	common logarithm
×	algebraic x, or multiplied by	ln	natural logarithm
÷	divided by	$\in$	base of natural logarithms
≠	does not equal	π	pi
≈	equals approximately, approximates	$\angle$	angle
>	greater than, greatly, increased, increasing	$\perp$	perpendicular to
<	less than, reduced, decreasing	$\parallel$	parallel to
~	sine curve, cosine curve	$a°$	a degrees (angle)
→	approaches as a limit, approaches	a'	a minutes (angle)
≧	greater than or equal to	a''	a seconds (angle)
≦	less than or equal to	$\int$	integral, integral of, integration
≡	identical to	f	frequency
μ	varies directly as	f_n	natural frequency
∴	therefore	cps	cycles per second
$()^{1/2}$	square root	m	mass
$()^{n}$	nth root	Φ	phase
vs	versus, against	F	force
≡	ground	/	ratio, the ratio of
↔	varied, variation	⊤⊤	base, support, mount, foundation
□	area	(	curve, curvilinear

Figure 10.15
Typical Technical Abbreviations

Source: Reprinted by permission from G. H. Logan, "Speed Notes for Engineers," *Product Engineering,* September 30, 1963. Copyright © 1963 by Morgan-Grampian, Inc.

anlys	analysis	pltg	plotting
ampltd	amplitude	reman	remain
asmg	assuming	rsnc	resonance
cald	called	rltnshp	relationship
cnst	constant	smpl	simple
dmpg	damping	smpfd	simplified
dmnsls	dimensionless	stfns	stiffness
dfln	deflection	systm	system
dfnd	defined	sgnft	significant
dstrbg	disturbing	ths	this
eftvns	effectiveness	trnsmsblty	transmissibility
frdm	freedom	thrtly	theoretically
frcg	forcing	valu	value
gvs	gives	wth	with
hrmc	harmonic	whn	when
isltr	isolator	xprsd	expressed
isltn	isolation		

Figure 10.16
Examples of Telegraphic
Sentences

<u>Lecture's words</u>

In marketing, we try to understand customers' needs and then respond to them with the right products and services. In the past, firms often produced goods first and tried to fit the customer's needs to the goods. Today's world-class marketers pride themselves on their customer orientation. We begin with the customer and build the product or service from there. A good example is McDonald's, the fast-food chain, which tailors its menus to local tastes and customs when it opens fast-food outlets in Moscow and other international locations.

Student's telegraphic sentences

Marketing understands customers' needs first.
- In past, firms produced goods first, then fit them to customers.
- World-class = having customer orientation.
- Ex. McDonald's in Moscow

<u>Lecture's words</u>

The US Patent Office has granted numerous patents for perpetual motion machines based upon applications with complete detailed drawings. Some years ago, though, the patent office began requiring working models of such a machine before a patent would be granted. Result: No patents granted for perpetual motion machines since that time.

Student's telegraphic sentences

Perpetual motion machine (drawings) = many patents.
Required working model = no patents since.

Take Notes Selectively

How do you take notes selectively?

With textbook note taking it's impractical to jot down every word. In lectures, it's impossible. Notes are not supposed to be a transcript. Your emphasis should be on the ideas, not the words. And you don't want all the ideas, either, just the key ones (as Figure 10.17 shows), along with any details or examples you need to make those ideas easier to understand.

Dealing with Special Cases

What should you do in special cases?

Not all note-taking scenarios are ideal. If you can't make it to a lecture or have difficulty taking notes when you do, you need an alternate plan. In the same way, there are factors that can throw a wrench into traditional textbook note taking.

Have a Backup Plan When You Can't Attend the Lecture

What's the best strategy if you have to miss a lecture?

If you know you'll be missing a class, supply a friend with a cassette or tape recorder and ask him or her to tape the lecture for you. Then you'll be able to take your own notes when you play the tape back.

Figure 10.17
Selective Note Taking

	Oct. 10 (Mon.) — Soc. 102 — Prof. Oxford

What's sympathetic magic?
 	
Describe contagious magic.
	A. Two kinds of magic
	   1. Sympathetic — make model or form of a person from clay, etc. — then stick pins into object to hurt symbolized person.
	   2. Contagious magic
	      a. Need to possess an article belonging to another person.
	      b. Ex. Fingernail clippings. By doing harm to these objects, feel that harm can be transmitted.

Use the Two-Page System for Fast-Moving Lectures

How can you cope with a lecturer who speaks too rapidly?

When you need to scramble to keep up with a fast-talking lecturer, try the two-page system. Lay your binder or notebook flat on the desk. On the left-hand page, record main ideas only. This is your primary page. On the right-hand page, record as many details as you have time for. Place the details opposite the main ideas they support. After the lecture, remain in your seat for a few minutes and fill in any gaps in your notes while the lecture is still relatively fresh in your mind.

Take a Different Approach for Supplemental Readings

What's the best approach to supplemental readings?

In many undergraduate courses, although assignments and lectures usually focus on a single textbook, instructors often assign additional readings to supplement the main text. You aren't usually expected to master such supplementary material as thoroughly as you master your primary text. Nevertheless, once the assignment has been made, you must cope with it. Here are some suggestions for doing so:

1. *Understand the assignment.* Try to figure out why the book was assigned. You might ask the instructor. If you find out, then you can skim the book, looking for pertinent material and disregarding the rest.
2. *Read the preface.* As you already know from earlier in this chapter, the preface provides inside information. It may tell you how this book is different from your textbook.
3. *Study the table of contents.* Notice especially the chapter titles to see whether they are like those in your textbook. If the chapters with similar titles contain the same information as the chapters in your textbook, read the chapters that do not duplicate your textbook's coverage. (Do this with topics covered in classroom lectures, too.)
4. *Find the pattern.* If you have not yet found an "angle," read the summarizing paragraph at the end of each chapter. Make brief notes on each chapter from the information thus gained. With these notes spread out before you, try to see the overall pattern. From the overall pattern, come up with the author's central thesis, principle, problem, or solution.
5. *Get to the point.* Don't put the book away with only a vague notion of what it is about. You must come up with something so definite that you can talk about it the next day or write about it two weeks later. Do not waste time on details, but be ready to answer general questions: What was the author's central approach? How was it different from that of your textbook? How was it the same? Look for the central issues around which everything else is organized.
6. *Have the courage to think big.* If you lack courage, you'll waste time on minor details that you won't remember. Select the big issues and concentrate on them.

Tying Things Together

Why is it a waste to end your note taking abruptly?

As a lecture draws to a close or a chapter comes to an end, there's a temptation to just pack up and move on. That may be understandable, but it can prove to be a great waste of an especially valuable time. At this point, the ideas from the lecture or reading are like wet clay. You have only a brief time to shape them into something meaningful. If you wait too long, they won't be nearly as pliable.

Finishing Readings

How do you conduct a quick overview of a reading assignment?

After you've completed a reading assignment, step back and quickly overview what you've just read. Here are two ways to do so:

1. *Reread the abstract, introduction, or summary.* Any of these three common elements provides a brief overview of what you've just read and puts the ideas you've picked up in an appropriate context.
2. *Reread the title and headings.* If the text doesn't include an obvious overview, create one yourself by rereading the title, headings, and subheadings. In combination, these elements can help you mentally organize the information you've just learned. Don't spend too much time doing this rereading. The primary purpose is to refresh your memory of the important points so that you'll be able to focus more carefully on them later. If you find you have questions, jot them down so you can ask them in class.

Leaving Lectures

What should you do at the end of a lecture?

The closing minutes can sometimes prove to be the most important part of an entire lecture. Speakers who do not pace themselves well may have to cram half the lecture into the last five or ten minutes. Record such fact-packed finales as rapidly as you can. After class, stay in your seat for a few extra minutes to write down as much as you can remember.

What should you do once you've left the lecture room?

As soon as you leave the lecture room, while walking to your next class, mentally recall the lecture from beginning to end. Visualize the classroom, the lecturer, and any chalkboard work. After mentally recalling the lecture, ask yourself some questions: What was the lecturer getting at? What was the central point? What did I learn? How does what I learned fit with what I already know? If you discover anything you don't quite understand, no matter how small, make a note of it and ask the instructor to explain it before the next class.

Online Study Center www.college.hmco.com/pic/pauk9e

What are the basic steps in taking lecture and textbook notes?

Summing Up

Despite some obvious differences, the core concepts that underlie taking lecture notes, taking textbook notes, and marking up your textbook are remarkably similar. If you are careful to devise a system and stick with it, to gather information actively, efficiently, and flexibly, and to pull things together conscientiously at the end of a note-taking session, the handful of steps below should put you in a powerful position to master your notes and make them your own.

How to Take Lectures Notes

Figure 10.18 is a flow chart of this process.

1. *Record*. Put the lecturer's ideas and facts (along with any relevant diagrams) in the six-inch column of your Cornell System note sheet.
2. *Remember*. As soon as class is over, take a moment to mentally recall the entire lecture from start to finish.
3. *Refine*. Looking over your note sheets, add words, phrases, and facts you may have skipped or missed, and fix any difficult-to-decipher jottings.

Figure 10.18
Taking Lecture Notes

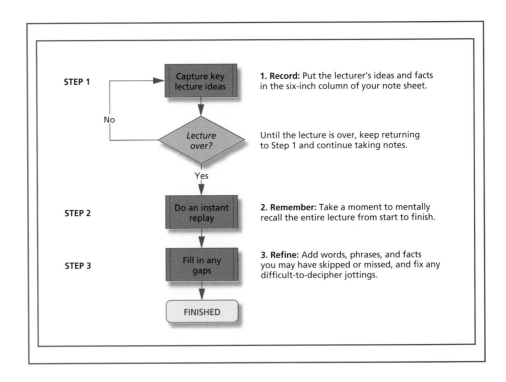

Figure 10.19
Taking Textbook Notes

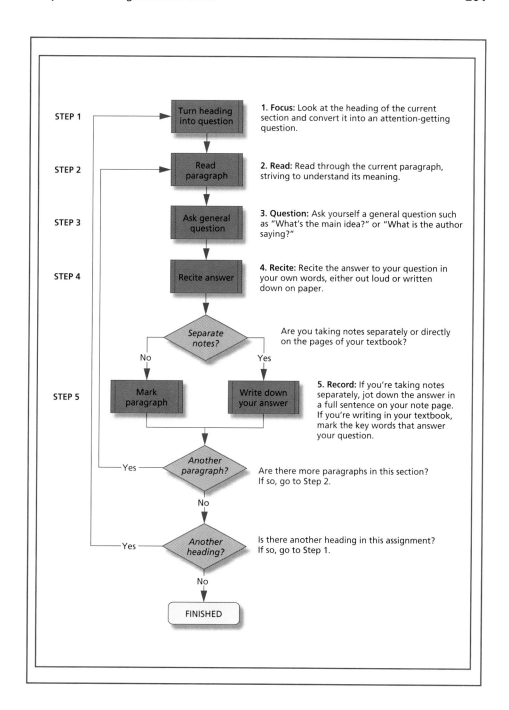

How to Take Textbook Notes

Figure 10.19 shows how this process works for textbook marking and separate notes.

1. *Focus.* As you read through each section, turn the headings and subheadings into attention-getting questions that help stimulate your thinking and your curiosity as you read on.
2. *Read.* Move through the assignment a paragraph at a time, striving to understand the meaning of the current paragraph.
3. *Question.* Before you move on to the next paragraph, take a moment to ask yourself, "What's the main idea?" or "What is the author saying?"
4. *Recite.* Recite the answer to the question you just asked, in your own words and preferably out loud.
5. *Record.* If you're marking your textbook, find the words or phrases in the paragraph that support your recited answer and mark them. If you're taking separate notes, jot down the answer you've just recited in the six-inch column of your Cornell System note sheet. Then repeat the entire process until you have completed the assignment.

FINAL WORDS

What is the final step that makes your note taking effective?

Despite indisputable benefits, taking effective notes can be difficult for many students. Of course, most students take some sort of notes when they attend lectures; and a smaller number do so when they're reading. But in each case, the students who take notes often come close but don't reach the point where their notes are truly effective. Taking effective notes requires work; it requires time; and it forces you to be actively engaged in what you're reading or listening to. This can be a little daunting, especially when you may already have a false sense of accomplishment from half-baked notes or markings. Take that final step. Cross that threshold and make your note taking truly effective. You'll be working harder initially, it's true. All new skills require a little extra effort at the outset. But the benefits you derive will materialize almost immediately when you begin to master the notes that you have taken and make your new knowledge permanent instead of just fleeting.

CHAPTER 10

HAVE YOU MISSED SOMETHING?

SENTENCE COMPLETION *Complete the following sentences with one of the three words listed below each sentence.*

1. Effective note taking requires building a background and creating a
   _____.

   context   summary   memory

2. Words such as *next, thus,* and *finally* often function as _____.

   signposts   diversions   intonation

3. The margin area at the outside of each page should be reserved for
   _____.

   reminders   questions   definitions

MATCHING *In each blank space in the left column, write the letter preceding the phrase in the right column that matches the left item best.*

_____ 1. TIES UP   a. Helps provide context for an upcoming lecture
_____ 2. Preface   b. Mnemonic for surveying a textbook chapter
_____ 3. Summary area   c. Provide clues for the organization of a chapter
                              or lecture
_____ 4. Telegraphic   d. Used for distilling a page's worth of notes
                              down to a few sentences
_____ 5. Two-page   e. The only note-taking format that is explicitly
                              discouraged
_____ 6. Outline   f. Often reveals a textbook's overall organiza-
                              tional plan
_____ 7. Signposts   g. System for taking notes in especially fast-
                              paced lectures
_____ 8. Syllabus   h. Note-taking style that employs only the most
                              essential words

TRUE-FALSE *Circle* T *beside the* true *statements and* F *beside the* false *statements.*

1. T F The first few pages of a textbook should usually be skipped.
2. T F Of all the electronic texts you annotate, word processor documents
         are probably the most flexible.
3. T F It's unlikely that a chapter or lecture will fit into a single note-taking
         format.

Online Study Center   www.college.hmco.com/pic/pauk9e

4. T   F   A sketch can rarely convey locations or relationships as clearly as a few sentences.

5. T   F   You're seldom expected to read supplemental materials as thoroughly as your textbook.

MULTIPLE CHOICE

Choose the word or phrase that completes each sentence most accurately, and circle the letter that precedes it.

1. To take notes effectively, you need
    a. a loose-leaf notebook.
    b. a system.
    c. sheets of unlined paper.
    d. several fundamental questions.

2. As you're taking notes, the cue column should
    a. remind you.
    b. get wider.
    c. remain empty.
    d. be filled.

3. One advantage of taking notes directly in your textbook is that
    a. your book is more valuable when you sell it at the end of the semester.
    b. your notes and your textbook can travel together as a unit.
    c. you can use a highlighter to single out important ideas and concepts.
    d. as the term progresses, your knowledge is likely to grow.

4. Surveying a textbook chapter can provide
    a. advance organizers.
    b. magnetic centers.
    c. familiar landmarks.
    d. all of the above.

5. Modified printing is
    a. speedy, like writing.
    b. neat, like printing.
    c. easy to learn.
    d. all of the above.

SHORT ANSWER   *Supply a brief answer for each of the following items.*

1. Discuss the principal components of the Cornell System.
2. Explain the various formats for taking notes.
3. Evaluate your options for annotating electronic texts.
4. Contrast the process of taking lecture notes with that of taking textbook notes.

IT'S YOUR Q

The Q System uses marginal questions to encourage active reading. You'll notice that most but not all paragraphs in this chapter are accompanied by marginal questions. Now it's your Q. Scan the chapter for any paragraph that is missing a question, reread the paragraph, establish the main idea, and then arrive at a question that elicits it. Use the questions in the surrounding paragraphs as models for your own marginal questions.

WORDS IN CONTEXT

From the three choices beside each numbered item, select the one that most nearly expresses the meaning of the italicized word in the quote. Make a light check mark (✓) next to your choice.

No amount of *sophistication* is going to *allay* the fact that all your knowledge is about the past and all your decisions are about the future.

—Ian E. Wilson (1941–), chairman, General Electric Corporation

| 1. *sophistication* | argument | refinement | discussion |
| 2. *allay* the fact | change | resolve | relieve |

There is always an easy solution to every human problem—neat, *plausible* and wrong.

—H. L. Mencken (1880–1956), American editor and critic

| 3. *plausible* | reasonable | smart | advantageous |

A committee is a *cul-de-sac* down which ideas are lured and then quietly strangled.

—Sir Barnett Cocks (1907–1989), English scientist

| 4. a *cul-de-sac* | trap | net | dead end |

 **Online Study Center**   www.college.hmco.com/pic/pauk9e

THE WORD HISTORY SYSTEM

Anecdote
unpublished notes

anecdote   an'-ec-dote' *n.* 1. A short account of an interesting or humorous incident. 2. Secret or hitherto undivulged particulars of history or biography.

Even among the ancient Greeks there were two kinds of stories—those given out publicly and those known only privately. The latter kind was called *an-ekdotos,* "not published." The word was formed by combining *a, an,* "not," and *ekdotos,* "given out." From this source comes French *anecdote* and thence English *anecdote,* which originally retained the Greek significance of "unpublished narratives." But an "unpublished narrative" especially about interesting things and famous people, has a ready market; so *anecdotes* are eagerly brought out on every occasion, and the word loses its original sense, coming to mean simply "a story," "an incident."

Reprinted by permission. From *Picturesque Word Origins* © 1933 by G. & C. Merriam Co. (now Merriam-Webster, Incorporated).

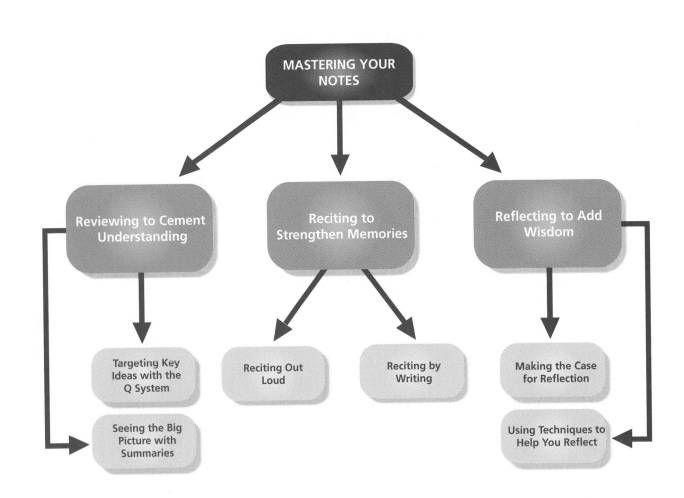

Mastering Your Notes

Order and simplification are the first steps toward the mastery of a subject— the actual enemy is the unknown.

Thomas Mann
(1875–1955),
German-American author

You've reached a crossroads. Now that you've conscientiously taken notes, you can let all that work go out the window and surrender to the unforgiving power of forgetting. Or you can put in extra effort and make what you've read and heard a permanent part of your knowledge. Congratulations. You've made the right choice. This chapter tells you how to take those notes and make them last by:

- **Reviewing to Cement Understanding**
- **Reciting to Strengthen Memories**
- **Reflecting to Add Wisdom**

How do you master your notes?   If you've taken notes thoroughly and conscientiously, you have every right to feel good about your efforts. But taking notes is not an end in itself. In fact, it is only the beginning. Far too many students jot down their notes and then forget about them until exam time rolls around. They leave them neglected in a desk drawer or repeatedly pass over their detailed textbook markings as they move on to subsequent chapters. This is a tragic mistake and a great waste of time and effort. The only way to take advantage of all the information you've jotted down or marked up and highlighted—to master information that you've worked so hard to understand—is to review it carefully, recite it regularly, and reflect on it deeply until it becomes a permanent part of your knowledge.

Reviewing to Cement Understanding

What's wrong with reviewing your notes just by looking them over?   Most students review their notes by reading them over and perhaps by asking themselves a question or two to see what they remember. This spot-check approach may be common, but it's also haphazard. A systematic approach not only makes your review worthwhile, but also enables you to gain a clear sense of how you're doing.

What do you gain by conducting an immediate review?   The purpose of the immediate review is to cement your understanding of what you've just read or heard. As you learned in Chapter 9, memory can be fleeting. Chances are that when you were taking notes, especially in a lecture, you were taking in information an idea at a time. You probably didn't have the opportunity to make sure you truly understood everything you'd marked or written down, and you almost certainly didn't have the chance to step back and see how things all fit together. That's where the immediate review comes in. By targeting key ideas with the Q System, you are able to verify that you understand your notes. And by pulling things together in summary, you gain a valuable big-picture perspective.

Targeting Key Ideas with the Q System

What is the Q System?   The left-hand margins of your Cornell System paper or the outside margins of your text should have remained blank up to this point. Here's your chance to put them to good use. At your earliest opportunity, move systematically through the notes you've just taken or the assignment you've just marked up, and come up with a question for each important idea. This is known as the Q System. Each question you write will provide a cue for the answer it addresses. Figure 11.1 provides a diagram of the Q System process.

Figure 11.1

Using the Q System to Review Your Notes

Whether you're reviewing text-book notes, lecture notes, or markings you've made directly in your textbook, the Q System is your best bet.

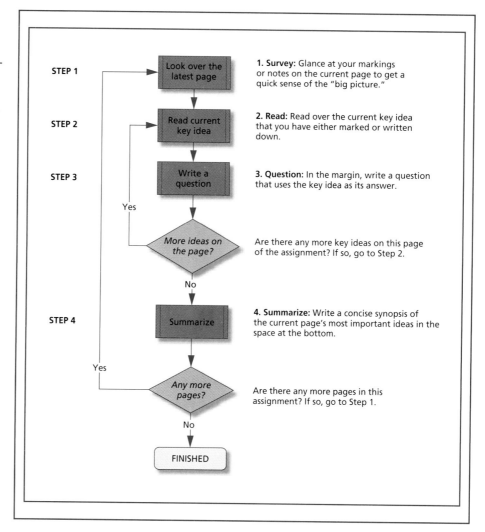

How do you arrive at Q System questions for each important idea?

When using the Q System, try to avoid formulating a question that can be answered with a simple yes or no. Aim instead for questions that prompt you to recall key information. Arriving at a suitable question is a little like playing the popular TV game show in which contestants are given the answers and asked to supply the questions. And it's almost identical to the process you went through as you were reading an assignment and converting the headings into questions. The only real difference is that this time you're using ideas from your notes or the lines you underlined in your textbook as the starting point. The goal is to pose a question whose answer most effectively sums up the entire key idea or paragraph. Jot (or type) the question down in the margin alongside the information it refers to. Figure 11.2 shows some marginal questions for a textbook passage.

What form should your marginal questions take?

Repeat the process of formulating questions and putting them in the margin as you systematically move through all the paragraphs in your text or notes from your note paper. It's OK to abbreviate your question, especially if you are short on space. (Figure 11.3 shows an excerpt from some classroom notes with abbreviated questions in the margins.) But be certain there's nothing ambiguous about what you've written down. After all, you'll want to be able to read these questions throughout the semester. A badly abbreviated question may make sense to you now, but it could leave you scratching your head later on. The same applies to your handwriting. Make sure you can read it. You may want to use the modified printing style (explained in Chapter 10) to help you write quickly and legibly.

Figure 11.2
Using the Q System with a Textbook Assignment

WRITING GOOD PAPERS IN COLLEGE

What 2 aspects lead to success?

The techniques of writing a good paper are easy to follow. You should remember two important aspects that lead to success. First, start work early on the paper. Second, if you have a choice, choose a subject that you are interested in or that you can develop an interest in.

What 3 elements might make up a paper?

Much of your work in college involves absorbing knowledge; when it comes to writing papers, you have the opportunity to put down on paper what you've learned about a subject, and perhaps your opinions and conclusions on the subject.

What's the key in choosing a topic?

Writing is an important form of communication. To communicate well you must have something you really want to say. So if you have a choice of topics, choose one that intrigues you. If it isn't one that everyone else is writing on, all the better.

If not sure of a topic, do what?

If you're not sure about your choice of topic, do a little preliminary research to see what's involved in several topics before you make a final decision. Remember the caution about allowing yourself enough time? Here's where it comes into play. Take enough time to choose a topic carefully.

Figure 11.3
Using the Q System with Classroom Notes

Sept. 10, 2007 (Mon.) – History 101 – Prof. A. Newhall

A. Some facts about Alaska

Who purchased Alaska? When?   Cost?

   1. William H. Seward, Sec. of State – fr. Russia in 1867 – $7,200,000.

Rough dimensions of mainland?

   2. Size – mainland: length = 1,500 mi. – width = 1,200 mi.

How long is the Yukon River?

   3. Yukon River – 1,979 mi. long

Name kinds of minerals?

   4. Minerals – oil, gold, silver, coal, chrome, iron, etc.

How are the forests?

   5. Forests – commercial timber = 85 billion board feet

Two most numerous fish?

   6. Fish – world's richest in salmon and halibut

Name several kinds of fur?

   7. Furs – seal, mink, otter, beaver, fox, etc.

What's the highest mt. in No. America?

   8. Mt. McKinley – 20,320 ft. – highest in No. America

When admitted as state?

   9. Statehood – Jan. 3, 1959 – 49th State

Who designed the state flag?

   10. State flag – designed by 13-year-old Benjamin Benson

What should you do if there's no space for your questions?

Properly ruled Cornell System note paper should provide plenty of room for your Q System questions. But if you've marked up your textbook and it has skinny margins, you have a handful of options to adjust for the limited space.

Try the Sticky Note Method

How does the sticky note method work?

Jot down the same sort of question that you would have written in the margin, but put it on a "sticky note" instead (use one sticky note per question). When you've finished writing the question, affix it near the paragraph it refers to. Because your sticky notes may come unstuck, it's often a good idea to put a circled number in the margin of your textbook next to the paragraph your question is intended for and to number your sticky note to match, adding the page number as well in case you renumber with each new page.

Online Study Center   www.college.hmco.com/pic/pauk9e

Use the Bookmark Method

What does the bookmark method involve?

One method that many students swear by is to jot their questions on slips of scrap paper that resemble extra-wide bookmarks (about two-and-a-half inches wide, the same dimension as the margin in Cornell System paper). Use one bookmark for each pair of facing pages, keeping a running list of the questions for the left-hand page on one side and putting the questions for the right-hand page on the other. Just as you did with the sticky note system, number each question and put a corresponding number in the margin alongside the paragraph it refers to. When you've written all of the questions for the two pages, you can lodge the slip in the book at just the right spot, the same way you would an ordinary bookmark.

Take Separate Notes

What is the advantage of using separate notes?

Of course, if your textbook doesn't offer an accommodating set of margins, it might be simpler to take separate notes. You'll miss some of the advantages of taking notes directly in your book (see Chapter 10), but you'll be able to carry the notes for your assignment (even stash them in a pocket or purse) without having to lug around the book.

What do you accomplish by writing marginal questions?

Regardless of the method you choose when using the Q System, you will be accomplishing something vital. The straightforward process of formulating questions should provide you with a thorough and immediate review of your material. Although it's possible to do so, it's unnecessarily difficult (not to mention pointless) to "fake" questions for each idea. Ask questions that truly get to the heart of the information. To be able to turn an idea into a meaningful question, you need to have a genuine grasp of that idea.

Seeing the Big Picture with Summaries

YOUR
Q

In the same way that questions from the Q System provide you with a better grasp of the important ideas from your notes, summaries help supply the context. It's surprisingly easy to get caught up in the details of your notes and lose the grand scheme of things in the process. Writing a summary is a sure-fire way to force yourself to think about and come to grips with the broader ideas, trends, lessons, and themes that run through notes like a thread. Summaries supply a straightforward answer to the question, "What is this page about?" This cut-to-the-chase aspect of summaries should be especially handy when you're studying for an exam or doing research for a paper and want to go straight to the key information in your notes without having to read through every note on every page to find it.

The Standard Summary

What is the standard system for writing summaries?

The standard system for summaries is to write one at the bottom of every page. Figure 11.4 shows an example. If you're taking notes directly in your textbook,

Figure 11.4
Summarizing a Page of Lecture Notes in Two Sentences

Psych. 105 – Prof. Martin – Sept. 14 (Mon.)

<u>MEMORY</u>

Memory tricky – Can recall instantly many trivial things of childhood, yet forget things recently worked hard to learn & retain.

Memory Trace
— Fact that we retain information means that some change was made in the brain.
— Change called "memory trace."
— "Trace" probably a molecular arrangement similar to molecular changes in a magnetic recording tape.

How do psychologists account for remembering?

What's a "memory trace"?

What are the three memory systems?

Three memory systems: sensory, short term, long term.
— <u>Sensory</u> (lasts one second)
   Ex. Words or numbers sent to brain by sight (visual image) start to disintegrate within a few tenths of a second & gone in one full second, unless quickly transferred to S-T memory by verbal repetition.

How long does sensory memory retain information?

How is information transferred to STM?

— Short-term memory [STM] (lasts 30 seconds)
   • Experiments show: a syllable of 3 letters remembered 50% of the time after 3 seconds. Totally forgotten end of 30 seconds.

What are the retention times of STM?

What's the capacity of the STM?

   • S-T memory — limited capacity — holds average of 7 items.
   • More than 7 items — jettisons some to make room.

How to hold information in STM?

   • To hold items in STM, must rehearse — must hear <u>sound</u> of words internally or externally.

What are the retention times of LTM?

— Long-term memory [LTM] (lasts a lifetime or short time).
   • Transfer fact or idea by
     (1) <u>Associating</u> w/information already in LTM.
     (2) <u>Organizing</u> information into meaningful units.

What are the six ways to transfer information from STM to LTM?

     (3) <u>Understanding</u> by comparing & making relationships.
     (4) <u>Frameworking</u> – fit pieces in like in a jigsaw puzzle.
     (5) <u>Reorganizing</u> – combining new & old into a new unit.
     (6) <u>Rehearsing</u> – aloud to keep memory trace strong.

Three kinds of memory systems are sensory, which retains information for about 1 second; short-term, which retains for a maximum of 30 seconds; and long-term, which varies from a lifetime of retention to a relatively short time.
   The six ways (activities) to transfer information to the long-term memory are associating, organizing, understanding, frameworking, reorganizing, and rehearsing.

Online Study Center   www.college.hmco.com/pic/pauk9e

you may find that there's more room to write at the top of each page than at the bottom. Either place is fine. Regardless of whether you're taking notes in your textbook or on separate sheets, don't pen an epic; you probably don't have the time, and you definitely don't have the room. Just come up with a concentrated sentence or two that efficiently pulls together the key information on the page. If space permits, it's a good idea to use complete sentences for your summaries. This reinforces your goal of articulately expressing what's important on the page. It can be a little too easy to disguise your confusion in an abbreviated sentence. Now is the time to make sure you grasp what you've written down or read. If you don't understand things at this stage, there's a good chance that they will grow murkier with time. Make the effort right now to see clearly. If you still don't understand, you have time to get help from a tutor or instructor. If you wait, it may be too late.

The Wrap-Up Summary

What is the approach for the wrap-up summary?

Rather than summarizing each page, you may choose to write a longer summary at the very end of your lecture notes or textbook assignment. Depending on the length or importance of the assignment, this method may be enough, but in general it's not recommended, at least not in isolation. Even if you write several paragraphs for your wrap-up summary, you probably can't expect to approach the level of insight and detail that you gain from summarizing each page. However, if the lecture is especially brief or the reading assignment is a supplemental one that doesn't require a great deal of attention (see Chapter 10), a wrap-up summary may suffice.

The Split-Level Summary

Why is the split-level approach best for summarizing your notes?

The best way to review and summarize your notes is to combine the standard summary with the wrap-up summary. Start with the standard summary, summarizing each page with a sentence or two. Then, rather than rereading all of your notes to arrive at a wrap-up summary, simply reread the summaries you've written for each page and come up with a summary of your summaries. This two-level approach makes your notes extremely useful and flexible. If you just need a reminder of what a single assignment or lecture was about, you can read the wrap-up summary. If you need more detail, you can go to the next level and read the summary on a particular page.

What else do questions and summaries provide besides an immediate review?

Formulating questions for each important idea in your notes and then coming up with summaries not only provides an extremely directed and effective means of review, but it also sets the stage for recitation, the most valuable technique you can use to help commit your notes to memory.

Reciting to Strengthen Memories

What is the role of reciting?

Now that you've added Q System questions (and brief summaries) to each page and conducted a thorough review in the process, how are you going to hold on to all that valuable information? After all, forgetting never lets up. It works continuously to expel from memory what you worked so hard to put there. Luckily, you can bring forgetting almost to a standstill by using the power of recitation.

How does reciting work?

Reciting forces you to think, and this thinking leaves a neural trace in your memory. Reciting promotes concentration, forms a sound basis for understanding the next paragraph or the next chapter, provides time for consolidation, ensures that facts and ideas are remembered accurately, and supplies immediate feedback on how you're doing. Moreover, experiments have shown that the greater the proportion of reciting time to reading time, the greater the learning. Students who spent 20 percent of their time reading and 80 percent reciting did much better than students who spent less time reciting and more time reading.

What is the process for reciting?

The process of reciting is relatively straightforward. Go back to the first page and cover it with a blank sheet of paper, exposing only your Q System questions. (If you used the sticky note method, you should still be able to obscure the text while reading your questions. If you chose the bookmark method, you can use your marker to cover the text. If your notes and Q System questions are in a computer file, open the file and then open another empty file and use it as an electronic version of a blank sheet of paper to cover your text.) Read the first question, and answer it in your own words. Slide the blank sheet down to check your answer. If your answer is wrong or incomplete, try again. Do this until you get the answer right. Go through the entire assignment this way. (See Figure 11.5 for a diagram of the entire process.) Your aim is to establish an accurate, crystal-clear impression in your memory, because that's what you want to return to during an exam. If the impression in your memory is fuzzy at this time, it will be even fuzzier three or four weeks later (see Chapter 9).

Reciting Out Loud

The traditional way to recite is out loud and in your own words. When you recite aloud, speak clearly so there's no mistake about what you are saying. Express the ideas in complete sentences, using the proper signal words. For example, when you are reciting a list of ideas or facts, enumerate them by saying *first*, *second*, and so on. Insert words such as *furthermore*, *however*, and *finally*. When you do so in oral practice, you will do so more naturally in writing during an

Figure 11.5
The Process of Reciting Your Notes

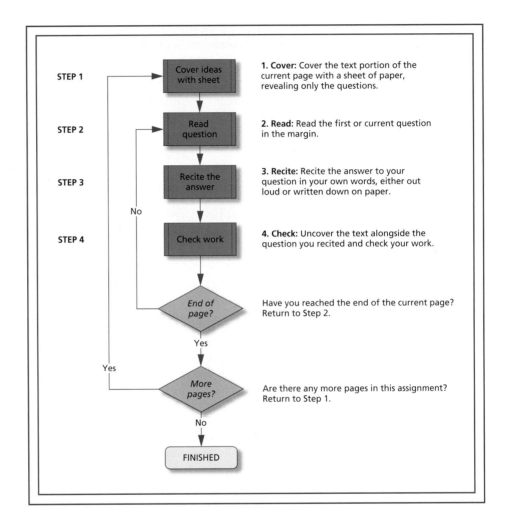

STEP 1 — Cover ideas with sheet — **1. Cover:** Cover the text portion of the current page with a sheet of paper, revealing only the questions.

STEP 2 — Read question — **2. Read:** Read the first or current question in the margin.

STEP 3 — Recite the answer — **3. Recite:** Recite the answer to your question in your own words, either out loud or written down on paper.

STEP 4 — Check work — **4. Check:** Uncover the text alongside the question you recited and check your work.

End of page? — Have you reached the end of the current page? Return to Step 2.

More pages? — Are there any more pages in this assignment? Return to Step 1.

FINISHED

exam. One of the best ways to recite out loud is in a group study or discussion (see Chapter 13), where there are people who can alert you right away should you answer your question incorrectly.

Reciting by Writing

How do you recite by writing?

If you are reluctant or unable to recite aloud, you can recite by writing out (or typing) your answers instead. This method is slower than traditional reciting, but it provides added benefits. Even more than reciting aloud, reciting by writing supplies solid proof that you can answer your questions. After all, you have a written record. And it provides excellent practice for essay and short-answer tests. To recite by writing, move through your notes a question at a time just as you would normally. But instead of speaking your answer, write it down on a sheet of paper. Then uncover the page and compare the answer you've just written with the one in your notes.

Reflecting to Add Wisdom

What is reflection?

After you learn facts and ideas through reviewing and reciting, take some time to mull them over. Use your innate sense of curiosity to speculate or play with the knowledge you've acquired. This is called reflection. To engage in reflection is to bring creativity to your learning. Ask yourself such questions as these: What is the significance of these facts and ideas? What principle or principles are they based on? What else could they be applied to? How do they fit in with what I already know? From these facts and ideas, what else can I learn? When you reflect, you weave new facts and ideas into your existing knowledge and create a fabric of genuine wisdom. History's greatest thinkers have relied on reflection for their breakthroughs. They make a strong case for reflection as a vital skill. With a technique or two to get you started, you can begin using reflection on your own to master your notes and gain lasting learning and genuine insight.

Making the Case for Reflection

What did Bethe say about reflection?

Professor Hans Bethe, Cornell University's famous nuclear physicist and Nobel Prize winner, talked about reflection as used by a scientist:

> To become a good scientist one must live with the problem he's working on. The problem must follow the scientist wherever he goes. You can't be a good scientist working only eight hours a day. Science must be the consuming interest of your life. You must want to know. Nothing matters more than finding the answer to the question or the problem you are engaged in.[1]

What is the connection between reflection and creativity?

Professor Bethe went on to say that students who go only as far as their textbooks and lectures take them can become proficient, but never creative. Creativity comes only with reflection. That is, seeing new material in the light of what you already know is the only road to original ideas, for having an idea is nothing more than discovering a relationship not seen before. And it is impossible to have ideas without reflecting.

[1]Interview with Professor Hans Bethe, May 19, 1960.

 **Online Study Center**   www.college.hmco.com/pic/pauk9e

What was Whitehead's position on reflection?

Alfred North Whitehead, famous British philosopher and mathematician, strongly advocated reflection. He, too, spoke about the knowledge that grows out of throwing ideas "into fresh combinations." He viewed reflection as taking what one already knows and projecting one's thought beyond familiar experience—considering new knowledge and ideas in the light of the old, and the old in the light of the new.

What was Schopenhauer's point about reflection?

The famous German philosopher Arthur Schopenhauer had exceptionally strong views on the importance of reflection.

> A library may be very large, but if it is in disorder, it is not so useful as one that is small but well arranged. In the same way, a man may have a great mass of knowledge, but if he has not worked it up by thinking it over for himself, it has much less value than a far smaller amount which he has thoroughly pondered. For it is only when a man looks at his knowledge from all sides, and combines the things he knows by comparing truth with truth, that he obtains a complete hold over it and gets it into his power.
>
> Reflections should not be left vague. Pursue the problem until ideas take definite shape. If you need more information, an encyclopedia or a standard book on the subject will often give you what you need to bring fuzzy ideas into focus.[2]

What is the connection between reflection and the subconscious?

The subconscious plays an important role in creative thinking and discovery. We have all had an exciting idea or even the solution to a problem suddenly flash upon us when we weren't consciously thinking about it. The great Hungarian physicist Leo Szilard came up with the solution to the nuclear chain reaction while crossing a London street. Archimedes arrived at the principle of displacement while sitting in his bathtub. The mind continues to work on concepts even when you aren't aware of it. The process that initiates much of this deep thinking is reflection.

Using Techniques to Help You Reflect

What is a big advantage of reflection?

A great advantage of reflection is its flexibility. It can be molded to fit your imagination. You can take it with you wherever you go and make use of it in spare moments. You can reflect while walking from one building to another, standing in line, waiting for a friend, or riding a bus.

What is a drawback of reflection?

But reflection's flexibility can also be a disadvantage if you're unsure of how to get started. This uncertainty prompts some students to skip over the reflection step completely. Although there are no specific reflection steps like those you might find for reviewing or reciting, there are a number of strategies you can use to ease into a reflective mindset.

[2]Essays of Arthur Schopenhauer, selected and translated by T. Bailey Saunders (New York: A. L. Burt, 1892), p. 321.

Use the Silver Dollar System

How does the Silver Dollar System work?

You can reflect on the information from your notes and make it more manageable by using the Silver Dollar System:

> Read through your notes and make an *S* in the margin next to any idea that seems important. Depending on the number of pages of notes you read, you'll probably wind up with several dozen *S*'s.
>
> Now read only the notes you have flagged with an *S*. As you go through these flagged notes for a second time, select the ideas that seem particularly important, and draw a vertical line through the *S*'s that are next to them. Your symbol will look like this: $.
>
> Make a third and final pass through your notes, reading only those ideas that have been marked $. Out of these notes, mark the truly outstanding ideas—there will be only a handful of them—with another vertical line so your markings look like dollar signs: **$**.

The Silver Dollar System stimulates reflection by helping you compare the relative weights of the ideas you have noted. It shows you at a glance which ideas are crucial to remember and which are not. The **$** sign alerts you to the truly important ideas, the "Silver Dollar" ideas that should receive most of your attention. Next come the $ ideas; they are worthy but shouldn't clutter up your memory if you have a lot to remember in a limited amount of time. Finally, the *S* ideas can be ignored. Although you flagged these as potentially important ideas, since then you've twice marked ideas that were even more important.

Rearrange Your Information

How is rearranging your information helpful?

You almost always gain insight when you look at information from a different perspective. If, for example, you've been studying countries geographically, you might want to consider grouping them by their systems of government or comparing them chronologically. You may want to group existing information under categories such as "pros" and "cons" or "before" and "after," depending on the nature of the information you are mastering.

Use Software

How can software be used to aid reflection?

Computer software can provide most of the benefits of manual rearranging but without the drudgery and time expense. Some computer programs can reconfigure in a split second information that would take hours to rearrange by hand. Both word processor and spreadsheet programs allow you to sort a table of information by one or more of its columns. More sophisticated tools found in many spreadsheet programs allow you to take an existing table and turn it into a brand new table that clusters the information in any number of ways of your choosing. Thus, if you had a table that listed all the presidents of the United

States, the years they took office, their political parties, and their states of birth, you would be able to see, for example, all the presidents from Ohio, all the presidents who were members of the Whig Party, or all the presidents who took office between 1800 and 1850. These clusters could trigger any number of reflective questions: What happened to the Whig Party? What other political parties no longer exist? Why are so many presidents from Ohio? Who was the first president from Ohio? Who is the most recent president from Ohio? Which state has produced the most presidents? How does the number of presidents between 1800 and 1850 compare with the number of presidents between 1900 and 1950? And so on. Because a computer performs it, the actual rearranging teaches you nothing. But the questions you ask as a result will stimulate reflection and strengthen your memories by allowing you to remember things in a variety of ways.

Put It in Context

Why is context an important factor in reflection?

Few ideas are meaningful when viewed in isolation. They need context to establish them in a realm that you can truly understand. For example, if you read about a scientific discovery from a certain time period, consider examining other events from the year the discovery was made or the place where the discovery occurred. Was this before or after the Civil War, the Second World War, the Vietnam War? Had the telephone, the radio, or the computer been invented? Were people traveling by horse, by car, or by jet? These investigations supply a basic background (see Chapter 9) that will often yield a deeper understanding.

Ask More Questions

Why is it helpful to ask additional questions?

In press conferences, the follow-up question is sometimes more insightful than the original question. If you've been using the Q System, each idea in your notes or paragraph in your reading assignment has an accompanying question. Come up with a follow-up to the original question and see if your notes or your text can provide the answer. If not, you might want to dig deeper for clues.

Think Visually

How can concept maps be used as a reflection tool?

Chapter 8 explains how concept maps can be used to work out problems, explore possibilities, and establish connections. These are exactly the sorts of issues that reflection addresses. Take the key concepts from your notes or from a chapter assignment, put them in ovals on a plain sheet of paper, and try numerous ways of arranging and connecting them. If you do, you will almost certainly learn something that wasn't clear to you when they were merely isolated words on a page.

Combine Textbook and Lecture Notes

How do you combine textbook and lecture notes?

Although the classroom lectures you attend should presumably relate to your reading assignments, you won't always see the connections clearly until you can actually place notes from both side by side. Using the format shown in Figure 11.6, jot down the most important information from a textbook assignment

Figure 11.6
Cornell System Format for Combining Lecture and Textbook Notes

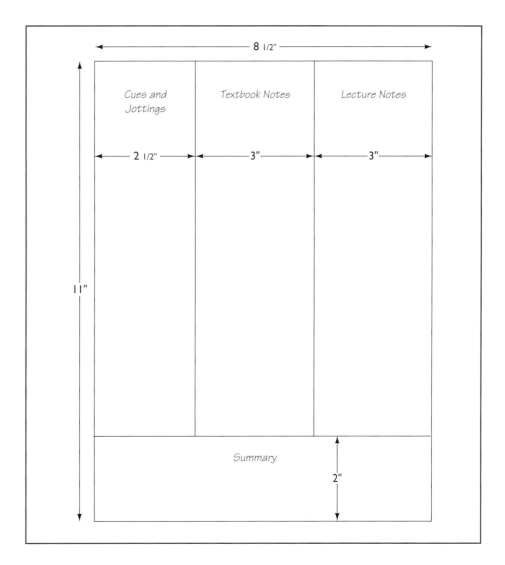

in the middle column of the three-column note sheet. Then add any lecture notes that deal with the same topic in the right column, alongside the textbook notes they pertain to. Finally, just as you did with your original notes, use the Q System to arrive at a question for which the textbook note *and* any related information from the lecture is the answer. It's impossible to predict in advance what you'll learn from this experience, but by combining two sets of notes you'll almost certainly arrive at an answer that is greater than the sum of the parts. This is the essence of reflection.

Online Study Center www.college.hmco.com/pic/pauk9e

FINAL WORDS

How do a scholar and a student differ?

There's a huge difference between proficiency and creativity. You can become proficient by studying your textbooks and lecture notes, but you will never be creative until you try to see beyond the facts, to leap mentally beyond the given. If your object is simply to tackle tests, pass your courses, and emerge from college with a degree and reasonably good prospects for employment, this book should serve you well. But if your aspirations aim higher, this book will serve you even better. The things that distinguish a scholar from a mere student are perpetual curiosity and an unquenchable thirst for learning. Reviewing and reciting should help you reach your modest goals. Reflection will enable you to reach for the stars.

HAVE YOU MISSED SOMETHING?

SENTENCE COMPLETION

Complete the following sentences with one of the three words listed below each sentence.

1. You can bring forgetting almost to a standstill with _____.

   summaries   recitation   questions

2. Creativity comes only with _____.

   practice   reflection   summaries

3. Ideas in your notes that you have marked with an *S* can be _____.

   saved   difficult   ignored

MATCHING

In each blank space in the left column, write the letter preceding the phrase in the right column that matches the left item best.

_____ 1. Reflection   a. Method that summarizes an entire assignment as well as each page

_____ 2. Recitation   b. System that allows you to reduce and reflect on your note sheets

_____ 3. Split-level   c. Used as an alternative to the traditional method of reciting your notes

_____ 4. Bookmark   d. Using your innate curiosity to mull over ideas

_____ 5. Rereading   e. Alternate Q System method when your textbook margins are too narrow

_____ 6. Silver Dollar   f. Provided when you add questions and summaries to your notes

_____ 7. Review

g. Mistakenly thought to be an effective method of reviewing

_____ 8. Writing

h. Repeating key information from memory and in your own words

TRUE-FALSE

Circle T *beside the* true *statements and* F *beside the* false *statements.*

1. T F Most students review their notes by reading them over.
2. T F When using the Q System, try to come up with yes-or-no questions.
3. T F It's OK to abbreviate your Q System questions.
4. T F If your notes are in a computer file, you will be unable to recite them.
5. T F Although reciting by writing is slower than traditional reciting, it provides added benefits.

MULTIPLE CHOICE

Choose the word or phrase that completes each sentence most accurately, and circle the letter that precedes it.

1. The primary purpose of an immediate review is to
   a. cement your understanding.
   b. spot-check your notes.
   c. look up words or terms you don't know.
   d. make sure your notes are legible.

2. If your textbook's margins are too narrow for Q System questions, you can use
   a. the sticky note method.
   b. the bookmark method.
   c. separate notes.
   d. all of the above.

3. Adding summaries to your notes helps you
   a. zero in on key ideas.
   b. gain a broader perspective.
   c. anticipate multiple-choice questions.
   d. include questions you couldn't fit in the margins.

Online Study Center www.college.hmco.com/pic/pauk9e

4. The traditional way to recite is
   a. out loud.
   b. in your own words.
   c. from memory.
   d. all of the above.

5. One strength and weakness of reflection is its
   a. cost.
   b. repetitiveness.
   c. flexibility.
   d. imagination

SHORT ANSWER   *Supply a brief answer for each of the following items.*

1. Elaborate on the role that questions play in the review process.
2. Explain the steps in the Silver Dollar System.
3. Discuss how reflection is important and why it is often overlooked.
4. Compare the differing approaches to summarizing your notes.

IT'S YOUR Q

The Q System uses marginal questions to encourage active reading. You'll notice that most but not all paragraphs in this chapter are accompanied by marginal questions. Now it's your Q. Scan the chapter for any paragraph that is missing a question, reread the paragraph, establish the main idea, and then arrive at a question that elicits it. Use the questions in the surrounding paragraphs as models for your own marginal questions.

WORDS IN CONTEXT

From the three choices beside each numbered item, select the one that most nearly expresses the meaning of the italicized word in the quote. Make a light check mark (✓) next to your choice.

It is a *capital* mistake to theorize before one has data.

—Sir Arthur Conan Doyle (1859–1930), British physician and novelist, author of Sherlock Holmes series

1. *capital* mistake   federal   criminal   major

A theory has only the alternative of being right or wrong. A model has a third possibility—it may be right but *irrelevant*.

—Manfred Eigen (1927–), Nobel Prize-winning German chemist

2. but *irrelevant*   unreliable   unrelated   dangerous

Economics is a subject *profoundly conducive* to *cliché, resonant* with boredom. On few topics is an American audience so practiced in turning off its ears and minds. And none can say that the response is ill advised.

—John Kenneth Galbraith (1908–2006), American economist

3. *profoundly*   completely   academically   abundantly

4. *conducive*   impartial   favorable   difficult

5. *cliché*   grasp   ridicule   trite phrase

6. *resonant*   complete   filled   echoing

THE WORD HISTORY SYSTEM

Arrive
to come to shore

arrive ar-rive′ *v.* 1. To reach a destination. 2. To achieve success or recognition.

Latin *ad* means "to" and *ripa* means "shore" or "sloping bank of a river." These two words combined are found in the Late Latin *arripare,* "to come to shore." Old French in the course of centuries changed the word into the form *ariver,* and Medieval (Middle) English borrowed it as *ariven,* meaning "to land." The meaning broadened from "going ashore" to mean reaching a point in any way. Today, when we *arrive* by automobile or airplane, it is interesting to think of the original meaning, "to come to shore."

Reprinted by permission. From *Picturesque Word Origins* © 1933 by G. & C. Merriam Co. (now Merriam-Webster, Incorporated).

Explaining Information

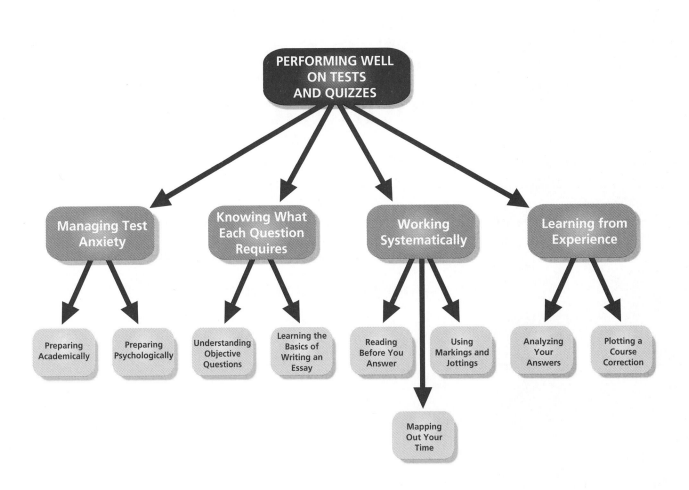

Performing Well on Tests and Quizzes

What is the answer? . . .
In that case, what is
the question?

Gertrude Stein
(1874–1946), American writer;
reportedly her last words

The real purpose of exams is to test your knowledge, not to try your patience. Yet when faced with the prospect of answering true-false, multiple-choice, matching, sentence-completion, or essay questions, many students would prefer to choose "none of the above." What they may not realize is that if they're well prepared, methodical, and thoughtful, then taking a test doesn't have to be traumatic. To show you how, this chapter looks at:

- **Managing Test Anxiety**
- **Understanding Each Question Type**
- **Moving Systematically Through the Test**
- **Learning from Experience**

What are the two basic categories of test questions?

Most of the test questions you'll be expected to answer in college fall into one of two categories: essay questions and objective questions. Essay questions take a broader view of a subject and generally emphasize your ability to recall and organize what you've learned and to write about it. Objective questions focus more on details and on your ability to recognize, rather than recall, them.

What does performing well on a test involve?

Performing well on a test involves managing test anxiety through preparation, understanding each question type, moving systematically through a test, and learning from experience.

Managing Test Anxiety

What is the simple cure for test anxiety?

The cure for test anxiety is simple but powerful: preparation. Advance preparation is like a fire drill: It teaches you what to do and how to proceed, even in a high-stress situation, because you've been through the procedure so many times that you know it by heart. To manage the anxiety that often arises at test time, you can prepare yourself both academically and psychologically.

Preparing Yourself Academically

To be prepared academically, start early, stay on top of your coursework, and organize yourself and your studying plan. Even if you're forced to cram for a test, do so as sensibly and methodically as you would if there were no time constraints.

Start Early

How can you get a head start on a course?

The pressure is almost nonexistent at the start of a new term. Take advantage of this calm before the storm. Get a head start in a course by picking up your textbooks, looking over your syllabus, and learning where and how to get academic help. Picking up your textbooks right away instead of waiting until the last minute will give you time to build a foundation of understanding. You'll be able to look through the text in a leisurely manner to get a sense of where the book and the course will be headed. In the same way that surveying your textbook gives you a sense of the book as a whole, reading the syllabus from start to finish at the earliest opportunity provides a valuable overview of the course and makes preparing for tests much easier. And finally, take a few minutes before the semester begins to find out where your campus tutoring service is located and how to arrange for a tutor. This information is often available on the campus website or in the materials you receive during orientation. Then, if you should find that you are struggling with a course and need help, all the research will have been done in advance. You'll be able to arrange for a tutor without delay rather than putting things off until the tutors' schedules are full and your situation has reached a crisis.

Stay on Top of Your Coursework

How do you stay on top of your coursework?

When the time comes to start focusing on an exam, you can seriously endanger your performance if you have to spend valuable time getting caught up. If you stay on top of your assignments throughout the semester—by taking notes as you read or listen and by mastering those notes at the earliest possible opportunity—they won't come back to haunt you when it's time to study for finals. Taken conscientiously throughout the semester, your Cornell-style notes will provide a valuable storehouse of knowledge and an excellent start in your preparation for upcoming exams. If you took notes using the Q System (see Chapter 11), you'll not only have used the powerful tool of recitation to embed your course's important ideas into your memory, but you will have already set up a format for your notes that allows you to study in a way that closely matches the format of your exams!

Organize Yourself

How can you organize yourself?

The work you put into preparing yourself academically by starting early and by keeping up with your classes and assignments can be best used if you make it a point to organize both your time and your notes.

What kinds of schedules help prepare you for exams?

Organize Your Time with Schedules   Scheduling is important throughout the term. Three-part scheduling plans (explained in Chapter 2) allow you to set aside time for reviewing material so that you won't get caught off guard by a quiz or test. As you near the end of a term or semester, scheduling your time becomes even more crucial. If you haven't been using schedules, now's a good time to start. If you have been, you probably feel on top of things already. In either case, it's a good idea to organize your time with a homestretch schedule especially designed to help you tie up loose ends and get you through that all-important last week before exams begin. When exam week arrives, devise another schedule that specifies when each of your tests takes place and that includes time for meals, sleep, and recreation, which are particularly crucial during exam week.

What items belong in a home-stretch schedule?

Make up a homestretch schedule.   Use the format in Figure 12.1 for your homestretch schedule. (This schedule uses the grid discussed in Chapter 2.) Start by filling in the time blocks that will be taken up by meals, sleep, job, and recreation. Next fill in your classes. Do not miss classes for any reason at this stage; you will want to hear the instructors' answers to students' questions about exams. Finally, fill in the time you will need to complete term papers and other assignments. Make sure you get them done before exam week. You don't want

Figure 12.1
Format for the Homestretch Schedule

	M	Tu	W	Th	F	Sat	Sun
7:00							
8:00							
9:00							
10:00							
11:00							
12:00							
1:00							
2:00							
3:00							
4:00							
5:00							
6:00							
7:00							
8:00							
9:00							
10:00							

unfinished business to interfere with your studying or distract your thinking during exams. Use any time remaining at the end of the week to study for your exams. Fill in the exact study times and subjects. Instead of writing "Study" in the time blocks, write exactly what you plan to study: "Study economics, chaps 1 to 10" or "Summarize sociology notes." Make a schedule that you'll be able to follow, and then be sure to follow it.

What items belong in an exam-week schedule?

Use an exam-week schedule.   Toward the end of the week before finals, make up a schedule for exam week. Fill in the times for your exams but be sure to leave time for meals, rest, and recreation. You must be in tiptop mental, emotional, and physical shape to do your best on the exams. Finally, leave a block of time immediately before each exam to review important information. The less time you allow between this last review and the exam, the less forgetting will take place. Review calmly and thoughtfully, and carry this calm, thoughtful behavior right into the exam room.

What is the best way to organize your notes?

Organize your notes with summary sheets.   The best way to organize your notes before an exam is by consolidating them into a set of summary sheets (a highly concentrated version of the notes), then reciting those sheets as you would your regular notes. But unlike your regular notes, your summary sheets should be limited to the truly important ideas from each lecture and reading. The process of reducing a semester's worth of notes to a handful of sheets provides a thorough, thoughtful review. If you have used the Silver Dollar System to pick out the main ideas and subideas from your notes, reducing those notes one step further should be relatively simple. Include only notes marked with a **$** in your summary sheets. If you haven't used the Silver Dollar System, you can narrow your notes all at once by employing it now, although the process may prove time consuming.

Figure 12.2 is an example of a standard summary sheet. It is indistinguishable from a regular Cornell note sheet except that it contains the most important ideas from several lectures, rather than just one, compressed into the same amount of space.

Encourage reflection with advanced summary sheets.   Although creating summary sheets of any kind gives you a chance to review your notes, devising advanced summary sheets also enables you to reflect on the information you have learned thus far. Reflection involves thinking about and applying the facts and ideas you've learned. By rearranging your notes into categories that you've chosen yourself, you are doing just that. Remember that "creativity comes only with reflection" (see Chapter 11). That's because reflection leads to *advantageous learning*—learning propelled by a burning desire to know something. You can't help being curious about your notes when you reorganize them for your summary sheets. The knowledge you gain from doing so not only provides excellent preparation for an exam but also remains with you long after the test is over.

Figure 12.3 shows an advanced summary sheet that represents more than ten pages of notes taken during two lectures. Notice how the points are categorized by century and are placed side by side for ease of comparison. The questions in the margin are appropriately brief; they hint at, but do not supply, each comparison.

Online Study Center   www.college.hmco.com/pic/pauk9e

Figure 12.2
A Standard Summary Sheet

<u>Steps in Writing</u>

What are four elements of college writing?

<u>Writing must have</u>: basic premise, logical development of ideas, support in paragraphs, good word choice

<u>Prewriting</u>

What are steps in prewriting?

Brainstorm about a subject — generate ideas
Narrow to a topic — use list or concept map
Focus on a basic premise — ask a meaningful question that makes a point
Plot a pattern — organize points into a framework

<u>Writing</u>

What is the basic structure?

Structure — use introduction, body paragraphs, and conclusion
— write body first

What should a body paragraph contain?

Body Paragraphs — begin each with topic sentence that supports basic premise (controlling idea)
— support points with good examples and detail

What is the purpose of introduction?
What does it reveal?

Introduction — first paragraph — states basic premise
Reveals: — topic of essay
— opinion about topic
— organization pattern you'll use

How do you conclude?

Conclusion — should leave reader with a feeling of completion
Either: summarize basic premise or main points — state your opinion

<u>Revising</u>

What are the two main facets of revising?

Strengthen support — data, examples, etc.
Edit for transitions, spelling, and grammar errors.

Figure 12.3
An Advanced Summary Sheet for Classroom Lecture Notes

Figure 12.4 shows an advanced summary sheet derived from textbook markings. The subcategories "Advantages" and "Disadvantages" were supplied by the student who took the notes. The material in each subcategory was originally scattered throughout the chapter.

Be a Study "Switch Hitter"

Baseball players who bat from both sides of home plate are more flexible than those who can hit only right-handed or left-handed. In the same way, you can often improve your test-taking average when you master the material in your notes from both directions instead of from just one. Use the Q System as you normally would to recall each important idea, but reverse the process from time to time by covering your questions, reading your notes, and then seeing whether you can remember the questions you wrote to accompany each important idea.

Online Study Center **www.college.hmco.com/pic/pauk9e**

Figure 12.4
An Advanced Summary Sheet from a Textbook Chapter

Economics 102 – Professor Maxwell

I. Single
Adv:
  1. freehand
  2. profits–his
Disadv:
  1. liable
  2. "venture capital"
	I. Single proprietorship
	       ADVANTAGES
	  1. Can do what desires
	  2. All profit goes to owner
	      DISADVANTAGES
	  1. All losses hurt owner (unlimited liability)
	  2. Commerical banks ordinarily will not provide "venture capital"

II. Partner–
Adv:
  1. common pool
  2. "vertical integration"
  3. "horizontal integration"
Disadv:
  1. death & change
  2. liable
	II. Partnership
	       ADVANTAGES
	  1. Pool wealth, profits, losses
	  2. "Vertical integration" = gain control of resources, become own wholesaler
	  3. "Horizontal integration" = buy out competitors; add products; improve products
	      DISADVANTAGES
	  1. Each time a member dies or leaves, a new partnership needs to be formed
	  2. Unlimited liability, even if own a small share

III. Corporation
Adv:
  1. legally formed
  2. stock–capital
  3. limited liability
  4. perpetual–board
Adv. to society:
  1. production–eff.
  2. continuation
  3. creates capital
  4. pays taxes
	III. Corporation
	       ADVANTAGES
	  1. Easy to form (legal permission needed)
	  2. Issue stock to raise capital; banker underwrites stock issue and sells to public
	  3. Limited liability – Corp., distinct from its owners; can sue and be sued
	  4. "Perpetual succession," or existence. Board of directors
	     ADVANTAGES TO SOCIETY
	  1. Technical efficiency – production of goods & services
	  2. Pool business risks – continuation of production
	  3. Creates further capital for expansion or finance new
	  4. It is taxed

What helps you master your material regardless of its order?

If you have time and want to make absolutely certain you know your material, write each important idea from your notes on the front of a separate index card, and jot your cue on the back. A stack of cards, instead of a few sheets of paper, enables you to constantly rearrange your notes, ensuring that you will be able to recall important information regardless of the order in which it's presented.

Cram Systematically

If you're forced to cram, how do you cram systematically?

Proper academic preparation usually eliminates the need for cramming. But if you find yourself unprepared for an exam, cramming is an unfortunate necessity. To cram systematically, the key words to remember are *selectivity* and *recitation*. Resist the temptation to try to learn everything. It's too late for that now. Instead, comb through your readings and lecture notes for only the essential facts, write them in your own words on summary sheets, and then use as much of your time as possible for remembering them. Don't make the mistake of reading and rereading this material. To make these notes your own, you must recite, recite, and recite. Begin by reading each fact you've chosen and devising a question you can jot down in the margin of your summary sheet for which that fact provides the answer. This will function as written recitation. Then, once you have a question for every idea, cover up the answers and test yourself by reading each question and reciting the answer from memory, again and again, until you know the information cold. By judiciously selecting the very top ideas and by using your own set of questions to help memorize them, you will have a chance of passing the exam. You may not remember much once the test is over, but for now the objective is to survive the battle so that you can come back next term and continue the war.

Preparing Yourself Psychologically

What role should psychological preparation play in getting ready for an exam?

When it comes to getting ready for an upcoming exam, there's no substitute for academic preparation. But even if you know your material inside out, there's still an advantage to be gained from putting yourself in the proper mindset. Some students who experience test anxiety claim that even when they've studied hard, they still freeze when the test is placed in front of them. Although academic preparation is essential, a little psychological preparation can help take the sting out of an exam. If you take time to find out all you can about the exam, get yourself acquainted with the test site or a similar site, and work at maintaining a positive attitude, you're more likely to escape the test-taking anxiety that plagues unprepared students.

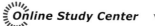

Find Out About the Exam

How can you lessen the fear of the unknown that contributes to test anxiety?

Fear of the unknown can be a great contributor to test anxiety. You can dispel some of this fear and its resulting anxiety by asking the instructor directly about the nature of the exam and by looking over previous exams for further clues. Asking the instructor seems so obvious that it's surprising how many students fail to do it. And yet, in many cases, instructors are not at all hesitant to discuss what the test will involve. Ask about the types of questions (objective, essay, or both), the length of the exam, and the materials (textbooks, notes, calculators) you'll be allowed to bring with you into the exam room. You can gain further clues about the nature of your upcoming exam by looking at exams from previous semesters and noting how the test was written and what the questions covered. When you do finally sit down to take the exam, you're less apt to be knocked off balance by surprises.

Get Acquainted with the Test Site

How can you get acquainted with the site where your exam will be held?

Exams may be held in auditoriums, large lecture halls, or ordinary classrooms. To be psychologically prepared for an exam, get acquainted with the site where the test will take place or with a similar location. A week or two before the exam, study for a few hours each evening at the site where you will be taking the test. Your familiarity with the room and the sense of control you feel while studying will help establish a link between working in this room and succeeding on the exam. If you can't study at the site of the test, you can still prepare yourself for the atmosphere of the test by studying in a quiet area, by practicing at a chairdesk if you know that's what you'll be sitting at for the exam, and by timing yourself as you work to get used to the challenge of performing under a deadline.

Maintain a Positive Attitude

How do you cultivate a positive attitude about an upcoming exam?

Of course, the ideas and strategies for managing stress (see Chapter 4) can be helpful throughout the semester. But often it's not until exam time that these techniques are truly put through their paces. It is essential to address the stress of a test with a can-do approach. Exam-anxious students often sabotage their own efforts by preparing themselves for failure. To counteract this inclination and cultivate an optimistic attitude, use deep breathing and progressive muscle relaxation to help you relax, use affirmative statements to counter any negative self-talk, and use visualization to help chart a course for your success. Take a moment to review Chapter 4 to find the techniques that will work best for you.

Knowing What Each Question Requires

What should you know before you take a test?

Even natural athletes can founder in competition if they don't know the rules. Although the most important things you can do to gear up for a test are to master your material and be psychologically ready for the challenge, you also need to be well acquainted with the rules of the game. Depending on the nature of your test or quiz, that means understanding objective questions, learning the basics of writing an essay, or both.

Understanding Objective Questions

Why are objective questions like pasta?

Objective questions are a bit like pasta in its various shapes. Each type may look different and many of us prefer one over another, but they're all basically made up of the same stuff. The primary ingredients of pasta are flour and water. The primary ingredients of objective questions are true statements and false ones. In the strictest sense, there are no real tricks for taking objective tests. The requirement for taking any test is basically the same: Know your material. Even so, it helps to understand how each question type works, to know the characteristics that will sometimes make it more complicated, and, finally, to be aware of certain rules and techniques that may not give you the answer, but can sometimes make answering a little easier.

True-False Leaves No Room for Ambiguity

How do true-false questions work?

The basic idea behind a true-false question is simple: Faced with a single statement, your job is to decide whether it's true. And when we say true, we mean true. The statement must be 100 percent true, not 50 percent or even 99 percent true. A partially true statement is still a false statement. Consider this example:

1. T F   In 1787, the year the United States ratified the Constitution, Washington, D.C., became the nation's capital.

The statement is false. Although the Constitution was ratified in 1787 and the nation's capital is Washington, D.C., the United States had no federal capital until 1790, when Congress chose Philadelphia. Washington didn't officially become the capital until June 10, 1800.

What makes true-false questions difficult?

Understanding What Makes Them Difficult   One word can be all it takes to turn a true statement into a false one. For example, consider the impact of a word like *always* on a true-false statement or how words like *no* and *not* can radically change a statement's meaning. Words like *always*, *no*, and *not* are known as qualifiers. Other qualifiers include *all, some, most, many, usually, never,*

Online Study Center   www.college.hmco.com/pic/pauk9e

and *none*. Simply adding one of these words can turn a true statement into a false one or a false statement into a true one. For that reason, you need to be extra sensitive to any qualifiers you encounter in a true-false statement.

Learning Techniques That Can Make Answering Them Easier

How can you make true-false questions easier?

Mark or circle each qualifier.   Qualifiers can have such a huge impact on the meaning of a true-false statement that it's crucial not to overlook them. As you read through each statement for the first time, underline or circle any quali-fiers. If you aren't sure whether a statement is true or false, try reading it with-out the qualifier or by swapping in a different qualifier. Comparing and contrasting the statements in this way can sometimes make it clearer whether the original was true or false.

Mark "True" if you're stumped.   Because instructors would rather leave true in-formation in your mind, they tend to stack true-false tests with more true state-ments than false ones. You shouldn't guess right away on a true-false question, but if you're stumped and pressed for time, the odds are in your favor if you choose true over false.

Be suspicious of longer statements.   Remember the importance of context, and re-member that true-false statements must be 100 percent true. Each word added to a true-false statement increases its chances of being false. All it takes is one incorrect word to make the statement false.

Multiple Choice Is a Cluster of True-False Statements

How do multiple-choice questions work?

A multiple-choice question normally begins with an incomplete sentence known as a *stem*, followed by a series of choices, known as *options*, for complet-ing that sentence. In a typical multiple-choice question, your job is to find the option that completes the stem and makes the resulting statement true. In that sense, a classic multiple-choice question is like a cluster of true-false state-ments, each one beginning the same way but ending a little differently.

> In 1787, the year the United States ratified the Constitution,
> a. George Washington became the country's first president.
> b. Washington, D.C., became the nation's capital.
> c. New Mexico was admitted to the Union.
> d. the country had no official capital.

In this question, connecting option (d) to the stem results in a true statement. Linking the stem to any other option results in a false statement.

What makes multiple-choice questions difficult?

Understanding What Makes Them Difficult   Multiple-choice questions inherit the aspect that makes true-false statements harder. Just as a qualifier

can transform a true statement into a false one (or vice versa), it can turn a correct option into a wrong one. In addition, because a multiple-choice question is more complex than its true-false ancestor, it acquires some additional aspects that can make it a little more difficult to answer.

Varying directions. Some multiple-choice directions tell you to pick more than one correct option; others ask you to mark the one option that is *incorrect*. Be sure to read the directions carefully and go over all the options before you mark your selection.

Divided context. Because each choice in a multiple-choice question is usually divided into stem and option, you have to mentally connect the two components to determine whether an option is correct. Correct answers aren't always obvious, even when you know your material.

Differing format. Most multiple-choice questions follow the incomplete stem and option format. In some cases, however, the stem may be made up of an entire sentence. A setup of this sort can take you by surprise if you're expecting a standard multiple-choice question, but in general this variation is easier because you don't have to work with a divided context.

Learning Techniques That Can Make Answering Them Easier

How can you make multiple-choice questions easier?

Use the true-false technique. If you know your material but have a mental block about the multiple-choice format, you can gain a new perspective by treating the question as a series of true-false statements instead. Construct each statement in your head (or on paper) and decide whether it is true or false. The true statement you find in the true-false statements you create should contain the correct multiple-choice option. Here's an example:

> Before becoming president in 1857, James Buchanan was
> a. married and divorced.
> b. secretary of defense.
> c. prime minister of Canada.
> d. secretary of state.

This question and its options can be thought of as four true-false statements:

1. T F Before becoming president in 1857, James Buchanan was married and divorced.
2. T F Before becoming president in 1857, James Buchanan was secretary of defense.

3. T F   Before becoming president in 1857, James Buchanan was prime minister of Canada.
4. (T) F   Before becoming president in 1857, James Buchanan was secretary of state.

Viewing the question this way can sometimes make it easier to spot the correct answer. The true statement you find in the true-false statements you create usually contains the correct multiple-choice option.

Discard foolish options.   Not all of the options in a multiple-choice question provide a plausible way of completing the stem. Some of the options are downright silly. If you spot one of these foolish options, known as *distracters*, you can eliminate it right away, and choose your answer from the options that remain. Any time you can reduce your possible choices in a multiple-choice question, you improve your odds of selecting the correct answer. In that sense, a foolish option can be considered a gift.

Do a double-check when you choose "all of the above."   You don't normally have to confirm that all of the options are correct when you choose "all of the above." You just have to verify two. If you are unsure whether one particular option is correct, but you know that the other two are, then you should have all the information you need to choose "all of the above."

Choose the middle number from a range of numbers. Test writers usually include at least one number lower than the correct answer and one number higher. Using this "rule," you can eliminate half the options in a four-option question. If you know the correct answer, then by all means pick that one. But if you're stumped by the question and have no other information to go on, you can increase your odds of guessing correctly by choosing a number in the middle.

Pick "all of the above" if you're in doubt. As the purpose behind a quiz or exam is not only to test but also to teach, "all of the above" becomes an attractive choice for the test maker because it allows a single question to convey several facts instead of just one. So, if you don't know the correct answer in a multiple-choice question and "all of the above" is an option, choosing "all of the above" can be a pretty safe bet.

Matching Is a Multiple, Multiple Choice

How do matching questions work?

Items in a matching test are usually divided into two columns and arranged in random order. Using a relationship that is normally explained in the directions, you systematically match the items in one column with the items in the other. (Consider the test shown on the following page.) Matching tests work

Groundbreaking Women of Science

Directions: Match the name of the scientist in the left-hand column with her discovery or distinction in the right-hand column by writing the proper letter in the space provided alongside each scientist's name. Use each item from the right-hand column only once.

Scientist	Discovery or Distinction
_____ **1.** Rachel Carson	a. Created the first programming language
_____ **2.** Mary Leakey	b. Devised the system for classifying stars by brightness
_____ **3.** Marie Curie	c. Garnered a Nobel Prize for her groundbreaking work in genetics
_____ **4.** Margaret Mead	d. Earned fame for children's books but gained respect as a mycologist
_____ **5.** Jane Goodall	e. First female physics instructor at Princeton University
_____ **6.** Grace Hopper	f. Invented the pie chart, although she is best known as a nurse
_____ **7.** Georgia Dwelle Rooks	g. First woman elected to the National Academy of Sciences
_____ **8.** Caroline Herschel	h. First American woman in space
_____ **9.** Florence Sabin	i. Founded the first hospital for African American women
_____ **10.** Florence Nightingale	j. Invented the compiler, a critical element in most computer programs
_____ **11.** Chien-Shiung Wu	k. Studied chimpanzees as a means of understanding human evolution
_____ **12.** Beatrix Potter	l. Popularized anthropology with her book *Coming of Age in Samoa*
_____ **13.** Barbara McClintock	m. Received two Nobel Prizes for her work on radioactivity
_____ **14.** Annie Jump Cannon	n. Uncovered fossils that helped unlock the origins of humankind.
_____ **15.** Sally Ride	o. Founded the contemporary environmental movement
_____ **16.** Ada Byron King	p. Teamed up with her brother to discover the planet Uranus

Answers: 1. o   2. n   3. m   4. l   5. k   6. j   7. i   8. p
9. g   10. f   11. e   12. d   13. c   14. b   15. h   16. a

like multiple-choice questions with an added dimension. You're faced with a *multiple* multiple choice. Instead of one stem and several options, you have several stems and several options.

What makes matching questions difficult?

Understanding What Makes Them Difficult   Answering a matching question is a bit like filling in a crossword or doing a jigsaw. If you make one mistake, it can sometimes lead to a chain reaction of errors. Therefore, you need to be confident that each match you make is correct before you move on to the next match.

Learning Techniques That Can Make Answering Them Easier

How can you make matching questions easier?

Mark off matches to avoid redundancy.   Each time you correctly match two items, cross them off or mark them with a circle or an X. If you're taking your test on a computer screen you might want to keep a running tally on a piece of scratch paper, crossing off the number and letter of each match you make. That way, when you move on to the next match, you'll have fewer items to read, and you won't be confused about which items you've chosen and which ones you haven't.

Match shorter items to longer ones.   In most matching tests, the items in one column are usually longer than the items in the other. For example, a typical matching test might contain a column of terms and a column of definitions. In cases like these, you can save yourself some time if you set out in search of matches for the longer items instead of the reverse. In other words, the column you keep reading and rereading contains the shorter items. That way you need to read each long item only once. It's a case of the dog wagging the tail instead of the other way around.

Sentence Completion Is Multiple Choice Without the Choice

How do sentence-completion questions work?

Sentence-completion questions work like multiple-choice questions without the choice. A typical sentence-completion question consists of a partial sentence and one or more blanks. Your job is to read the sentences and to use both context and recall to determine what words belong in the blanks.

What makes sentence-completion questions difficult?

Understanding What Makes Them Difficult   Unlike answering true-false, multiple-choice, and matching questions, answering a sentence-completion question requires recall instead of recognition. You have to extract the answer from your memory instead of picking it out from the exam page or computer screen. Recall is almost always better from a standpoint of learning, but it can be a little harder when you're taking a test.

Learning Techniques That Can Make Answering Them Easier

How can you make sentence-completion questions easier?

Try to clarify any ambiguity.   Sometimes a question seems to have two or more reasonable answers. In these cases, you may need to clarify the type of answer the question is seeking by raising your hand and asking a well-formulated, unambiguous question of your own to clear up the confusion.

Disregard the length of the blank.   With sentence-completion questions, the length of the blank is usually irrelevant. Use the context of the sentence not the length of the blank to help you arrive at your answer.

Treat some sentences as multiple questions. Even students who aren't influenced by the size of one blank when answering a sentence-completion question may become flustered by a question that has two blanks. If the blanks are side by side, the question may be calling for a person's name or a place name. Paying attention to the question's context should help you confirm whether this is the case. But if the blanks in a sentence-completion question are widely separated instead of side by side, the best way to treat them is as if each occurred in a separate sentence. There may or may not be a direct relationship between the missing words, so make sure that each filled-in word makes sense in its own part of the statement. Consider this example:

1. Although corn is second only to _____ as the most widely grown crop in the world, no one in Europe had even heard about corn until _____ returned from the New World.

   In the first portion of the sentence, the word *corn* indicates that you're dealing with a grain. If you had read your textbook carefully (or if you used your common sense), you'd know the answer is wheat. The second blank calls for a person's name: Columbus.

Learning the Basics of Writing an Essay

How do you write an effective essay?

To write an effective essay, you need to be able to understand each question with precision and provide a carefully constructed answer.

Understand Each Question with Precision

Why is it important to understand the questions precisely?

A precise question requires a precise answer. Read each question carefully so you understand exactly what it is asking. A good essay question is never vague or ambiguous. As you can see from Figure 12.5, words such as criticize, interpret, and describe have specific definitions. Therefore, if you have even the slightest uncertainty about what's being asked, don't hesitate to check with the instructor for clarification.

 *Online Study Center*   www.college.hmco.com/pic/pauk9e

Figure 12.5
Keywords in Essay Questions
This alphabetical list contains keywords encountered in the directions for essay questions, along with brief explanations of what each word means.

Key Word	Explanation
Apply a principle	Show how a principle works, through an example.
Comment	Discuss briefly.
Compare	Emphasize similarities, but also present differences.
Contrast	Give differences only.
Criticize	Give your judgment of good points and limitations, with evidence.
Define	Give meanings but no details.
Demonstrate	Show or prove an opinion, evaluation, or judgment.
Describe	State the particulars in detail.
Diagram	Show a drawing with labels.
Differentiate	Show how two things are different.
Discuss	Give reasons pro and con, with details.
Distinguish	Show main differences between two things.
Enumerate	List the points.
Evaluate	Discuss advantages and disadvantages with your opinion.
Explain	Give reasons for happenings or situations.
Give cause and effect	Describe the steps that lead to an event or a situation.
Give an example	Give a concrete example from the textbook or from your experience.
Identify	List and describe.
Illustrate	Give an example.
Interpret	State the meaning in simpler terms, using your judgment.
Justify	Prove or give reasons.
List	List without details.
Outline	Make a short summary with headings and subheadings.
Prove	Give evidence and reasons.
Relate	Show how things interconnect.
Review	Show main points or events in summary form.
Show	List your evidence in order of time, importance, logic.
Solve	Come up with a solution based on given facts or your knowledge.
State	List main points briefly without details.
Summarize	Organize and bring together the main points only.
Support	Back up a statement with facts and proof.
Trace	Give main points from beginning to end of an event.

Provide a Carefully Constructed Answer

What are the qualities of a carefully constructed answer?

For better or worse, an essay answer provides a kind of snapshot of your thinking processes. Depending on who is reading your essay, the instructor, a teaching assistant, or someone else, this may be the only glimpse the grader gets of who you are and what you know. That's why it's important that each essay is well organized, well supported, and neatly written.

What can you do to make sure your essay is well organized?

Be Sure the Path of Your Answer Is Easy to Follow   Essay exams are written in a hurry and are often read in a hurry. Graders usually have a lot of essays to read and seldom have the time or patience to untangle a convoluted answer. You have to be concise! Answer the question right at the start of the essay, choose a recognizable organizational pattern, use clear transitions, and wrap things up neatly with a summary. Wordy answers may be the refuge for unprepared students who hope to bury their ignorance under a heavy blanket of overstuffed sentences, but they seldom fool an experienced grader. This is no time for lavish flourishes or excessive subtlety. Clearly show what you know as soon as possible. Start with the question itself, turn it into the stem of your opening sentence, and complete it with your answer. (See Figures 12.6 and 12.7 for some examples of how to do this.) Then figuratively take your reader by the hand and lead him or her along the path of your essay by organizing your answer with a recognizable pattern such as decreasing importance or comparison/contrast (see Chapter 10). Make things that much easier to follow by inserting transitional words and phrases to act as signposts whenever you change direction or introduce evidence during the course of your essay.

Figure 12.6
A Paragraph-Length Essay

Question: Identify three of the theories psychologists have suggested to explain forgetting.

Answer: Three of the theories that psychologists have suggested to explain how forgetting occurs include fading theory, retrieval theory, and reactive interference theory. Fading theory defines memories as paths or traces in the brain. According to the theory, if these paths aren't used (recalled) regularly, they fade until they eventually disappear (are forgotten). Retrieval theory claims that memories never really disappear; they simply get lost or misfiled, like important information buried under piles of paper on a messy desk. Reactive interference theory says that your attitude or emotions can interfere with your memory. If you are bored with or bothered by information, there's a greater chance that you will forget it. In certain cases, evidence seems to support all these theories of forgetting. But they remain only theories. None of them can be proved conclusively.

Online Study Center   www.college.hmco.com/pic/pauk9e

**Figure 12.7
A Longer Essay Answer**

> *Question:*   Compare and contrast reciting and rereading as methods of study.
>
> *Answer:*   Although reciting and rereading are both common methods of study, reciting is superior to rereading as a way of mastering your material. Unlike rereading, reciting (1) gets you involved, (2) supplies motivation, and (3) provides you with feedback on your progress.
>
> 1. Reciting gets you involved by compelling you to extract the meaning out of each paragraph you read. In contrast, it's possible to reread an assignment without understanding it.
>
> 2. Reciting supplies motivation because it encourages you to understand what you've read. If you had trouble grasping the meaning of one paragraph, you may be determined to have an easier time with the next one. If you understood a paragraph, you'll be motivated to continue your progress. But if you simply reread your assignment, you'll have no such incentive to succeed.
>
> 3. Because you know right away whether you've understood each paragraph, reciting provides you with immediate feedback on your progress. Potential trouble spots in your reading are brought to your attention right away. With rereading, the first real feedback you get is delayed until the test or quiz.

Then finish things off with a summarizing conclusion that ties your points together and reminds the grader of the original answer that you wrote back at the beginning. These suggestions for organizing your essay become even more compelling when you learn how essays are actually graded. Figure 12.8 takes a brief behind-the-scenes look at an essay exam grading session.

What kind of support should you include in your essay?

Devote the Bulk of Your Essay to Supporting Your Answer   Instructors rarely include essay questions to learn how you *feel*. They want to find out how you *think* and what you *know*. The best way to make a good impression and earn a good grade is to write essays that are well supported. Back up your answer with solid evidence, support any general opinions, and steer clear of personal opinions. Provide examples, details, and further evidence for your initial answer and its major points. If you can support your answer with ideas or sources that your instructor has stressed in class, you would be wise to do so. An essay that incorporates some of the instructor's "pet ideas" is more likely to be viewed in a positive light. According to respected educator Hugo Hartig, author of *The Idea of Composition*:

> An alert student can easily identify these "pet ideas" and work them out carefully in his own words. The student who does this is prepared not only to see through

Figure 12.8
The Essay Grading Process

Behind the Scenes at an Essay Exam Grading Session

What happens after you finish your last essay, heave a sigh of relief, and hand in your exam? Although grading procedures may vary from school to school, here is how more than 200 examination booklets in a popular introductory history course are graded at one college.

The day of the exam, each grader in the history department has time to scan, but not to grade, the answer booklets. Then at a meeting the next day, each grader reads aloud what he or she thinks is the one best answer for each question. A model answer for each question is then agreed on by the staff. The essential points in the model answers are noted by all the graders for use as common criteria in grading the responses.

Unfortunately, simply listing all the essential points in your essay won t automatically earn you a superior score. During the reading of the answers, one grader remarks, "Yes, this student mentioned points five and six . . . but I think he didn t realize what he was doing. He just happened to use the right words as he was explaining point four."

These comments reinforce the importance of crystal-clear organization in your essay. You may also want to underline the main point of the essay so it s obvious and mark off your subpoints with dark numbers. Don t forget to include transitional words to show how you got from one idea to the next. Make sure that no one thinks you just stumbled on to the correct answer.

---

the instructor's questions quite readily, but he also knows exactly how to answer them, using the teacher's own methods of problem solving! Perhaps this is the very essence of grade-getting in any course that depends heavily on essay exams.[1]

Don't assume that even general opinions will unquestionably be accepted as fact. As Hartig explains,

If you make the statement: *"Huckleberry Finn* is a masterpiece of American literature," and do not give any good reason to show that the statement is true, you get a zero for the statement.[2]

And finally, unless asked for them specifically, keep your personal opinions out of your essay. Informed or uninformed, knowledgeable or ignorant, all of us

---

[1]Hugo Hartig, *The Idea of Composition* (Oshkosh, WI: Academia, 1974), p. 32.
[2]Ibid., p. 31.

Online Study Center   www.college.hmco.com/pic/pauk9e

have opinions. But that's not what the instructor is looking for. The purpose of essay exams, after all, is to see what you've learned and how you can apply it.

How can you improve your essay's appearance?

Pay Attention to Appearance as Well as to Content   In a carefully controlled experiment mixing neatly handwritten essay answers with others in which the handwriting was poor, instructors consistently gave better grades to the neater essays, even when they were word-for-word duplicates of the sloppy ones and graders were told explicitly to grade the essays *solely on the basis of their content*. The appearance of your essay has an unconscious effect on how it gets graded. Manage that appearance by writing legibly and on only one side of the sheet, by leaving ample space around each essay, and by avoiding careless errors. Writing in pen instead of pencil will make almost any handwriting look better. If your penmanship is less than it should be, start using the modified printing style explained in Chapter 10. Write on only one side of each sheet of paper so the writing on one side won't show through to the other. Leaving a little "breathing room" around the edges of your essay will not only make your answer look tidier, but it will also provide room for any grader's comments and give you space to insert any last-minute facts or ideas. Above all, keep your essay free of needless errors in grammar or spelling, which can be every bit as costly to your grade as sloppy handwriting. As Hartig observes:

> If you misspell common words, and make clumsy errors in sentence structure, or even if you write paragraphs that lack unity and coherence, many of your instructors are going to take it as a sure sign that you are sadly lacking in basic academic ability. Once a teacher thinks this about you, you will not get much credit for your ideas, even if they are brilliant.[3]

Working Systematically

Why are students tempted to rush through exams?

When an exam is handed out, some students have difficulty resisting the temptation to jump right in. Confident students are often anxious to "get down to business" and show what they know; apprehensive test takers want to get the whole thing over with as quickly as possible. At first glance, these behaviors seem reasonable because time is limited. But if you take a few moments to plan a systematic response to the test, you'll be a lot more efficient as a result. A little preparation saves you a lot more time than it uses. You can make the most of your test-taking experience if you read before you answer, map out your time wisely, and use markings or jottings to make taking a test more efficient and methodical.

[3]Ibid.

Reading Before You Answer

What causes some students to skip over the obvious step of reading?

It may sound silly to suggest reading through the test before you begin answering. After all, the advice seems obvious. But because of anxiety and time pressure, common sense is often a casualty, and many students skip the directions and even rush through the questions without paying attention to what they say. In the long run, cutting corners on these crucial elements of a test could cost you time and points. Take a few moments to read the directions before you make a single mark on your test and then read the questions carefully as well.

Read the Directions First

Why should you read the directions first?

Exam directions often contain vital instructions for answering the questions. They may establish the length of your answers (one paragraph, 300 words, five pages), the approach you should take (explain, compare, contrast, mark the two best options), the number of questions to be answered (say, half of the questions presented), or the overall time you've been allotted. If you miss such instructions, you may endanger your grade, waste a great deal of time, and even invite criticism for carelessness.

Read the Questions Carefully

Why is it important to read each test question carefully?

The text of a test question is usually very dense. If it's an objective question, it may be peppered with clauses, qualifiers, or negatives that can have a huge impact on its meaning. If it's an essay question, as we've already seen, whether it says *evaluate*, *enumerate*, or *interpret* can make a big difference in the instructor's expectations for your answer. For that reason, read each question carefully to pick up important details and context. If the questions are part of an objective test, you can read each question as you encounter it. If the questions are part of an essay test, it's best to read all of the questions before you write anything. This will give you a better sense of how to budget your time. If you have a choice among questions, you will be able to select those for which you are best prepared. If you have to answer every question, you'll know in advance which ones will require the most attention. And if several questions tackle different aspects of the same topic or issue, you'll be able to avoid including information on one answer that should have been saved for another.

Mapping Out Your Time

How can you map out your time?

Once you've carefully read over the directions and questions and jotted down any thoughts you may have, you should be able to get a realistic sense of how much time remains for answering the questions. Using this as a starting point, divide the time you have left by the number of questions to figure out roughly how much time you can spend on each question in order to complete the test.

Stick as close to your time plan as you can, but don't become overly anxious or rigid about doing so.

Answer the Easiest Question First

A good way to get a head start is by tackling the easiest question first. Nothing inspires confidence and clear thinking more than answering one question right away. If the first question has you stumped, don't let it deflate your morale and throw off your time plan. Just pick an easier question and build on the momentum that you get from answering it to your satisfaction.

Keep Your Schedule Flexible

How do you keep your schedule flexible?

Of course, even with an easy question under your belt, your time schedule still may not go exactly as planned. It's important to keep your schedule flexible by developing strategies to deal both with a time shortage and a time surplus. If time is running out, zero in on any remaining easy questions and tackle them first. If you've got essay questions remaining, outline the key points you were trying to make in any unfinished questions. Instructors sometimes award partial credit when you can demonstrate that you know the material. If you finish early, use the surplus time to your advantage by going over your exam and re-checking your answers, especially any you were uncertain about. If you've answered essay questions, use any extra time to double-check your spelling and grammar, and, if necessary, insert words, phrases, and examples that may make your answers clearer.

Using Markings and Jottings

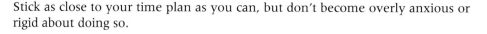

What should you jot on your question sheet?

In some exam settings, the most underused piece of paper is the question sheet itself. Except in tests in which the question and answer sheet are the same, in tests in which writing on the question sheet isn't allowed, or when the test is onscreen instead of on paper, you can often use the question sheet as a helpful scratch pad as you're progressing through the test. You can use the back of the sheet to jot down important ideas you want to remember. You can use the front to annotate questions, cross off certain items, and to highlight any questions that deserve extra attention.

Make Notes on the Back of Your Exam Sheet

What sort of notes should you jot on the back of your exam?

In the few minutes before you begin an exam, your brain may be buzzing with information you want to include or remember. Before you begin reading the test, unburden your mind by quickly jotting on the back of the exam sheet the ideas, facts, and details you think you may forget. Almost like a summary of your summary sheets, these jottings act as cues for the Silver Dollar ideas you gleaned from your lectures and readings (see Chapter 11). Furthermore, the action of writing these notes involves you in the exam immediately. But remember: You are graded for what you write on the front of the exam, so don't spend more than a minute or so jotting down reminders on the back.

What sort of cue should you add to each question?

Jot a Cue Beside Each Question   As you read through each question, underline or circle important words that provide clues for answering that question. With objective questions, these will likely be the qualifiers and negatives that can make a simple question more complex. With essay questions, these will be words such as *contrast*, *demonstrate*, *summarize*, or any other word or phrase that provides insights into the type of answer that is expected. If the directions ask for an essay answer, you may also want to keep track of any keywords or key phrases that come to mind by jotting them in the margin. Later, when you begin writing, use these jottings and those on the back of the exam sheet to help organize your answer.

What sorts of choices should you cross off?

Cross Off Choices You've Used or Eliminated   If you're answering objective questions, you can cross off any multiple-choice options you've been able to eliminate or cross off the items in a matching question that you've already used. If you're taking an essay test and are expected to answer only some of the questions, cross off the questions you don't plan to answer. Then, as you answer the questions that remain, you can cross them off as well. In each case, whether you're answering essay questions or objective questions, crossing off items will help to simplify your job and provide the same sort of sense of accomplishment you get when you cross an item off a to do list.

What kinds of questions should you mark?

Put a Mark Next to Questions Requiring Special Attention   Annotating certain questions with a circle or a check mark can make it easier to distinguish them from the rest of the questions in the test. Which questions you choose to mark depends on your purpose. If you're taking an essay test in which you have to answer only some of the questions, you might want to mark the questions you plan to complete. If you've answered an objective question but you're not confident about that answer, you could add the mark to remind you to go back and double-check your response if you have time. Regardless of the marking strategy you use, it should make taking a test a bit more efficient and methodical.

Learning from Experience

What should you do with a test once it's been returned to you?

Once a test or quiz is over, whether you did well or you did poorly, the urge to "move on" or to "put it behind you" can be strong. Don't give in to temptation. The test is more than just a score. It's an informative record of how you

perform on a variety of topics and question types. Before you stash the test in a desk drawer or worse, take a few minutes to systematically survey the results. To get the most out of returned exams, analyze your answers and then, based on your analysis, adjust your strategy for taking future tests.

Analyzing Your Answers

What can you learn from your test?

Unless you earned a perfect score, you missed some questions and answered others correctly. On some questions, particularly essay questions, your answer may be accompanied by comments from the grader. You can learn something valuable from your mistakes, from your correct answers, and especially from any comments on your test.

What questions should you ask yourself as you analyze your mistakes?

Examine Your Mistakes   Look over any objective questions you missed and if the answer hasn't been provided for you, see if you can figure out what it was supposed to be. If the answer is provided, try to discover why you didn't choose it. Was it a case of failing to recall a detail or fact? Misunderstanding an important idea or concept? Or did you misinterpret the wording of the question? Seeking the correct answer in this way will encourage you to reflect on your answers. This reflection should help to strengthen your memory of the correct information, so it will be more readily available the next time you should need it.

Inventory Your Correct Answers   Oddly enough, wrong answers probably provide more information, but you can learn from your correct answers as well. Take an inventory of the questions you answered correctly. Is there a pattern you detect? Do you perform better on multiple-choice questions than on true-false? Are you better at essay questions than objective questions? Do you remember dates but forget names? Are you good at details but bad at concepts? Once again, these questions encourage reflection and help you to arrive at some conclusions that you can use in preparing for future tests.

Why are the grader's comments valuable?

Pay Close Attention to Comments   Carefully look over any comments that the instructor or grader has added to your test sheet. What did she or he like? Dislike? Some instructors may not clearly articulate their standards or preferences in class but will convey them in comments on a test paper, especially in the case of essay questions. Analyze these comments and see if you can draw some conclusions about the instructor's expectations for test answers.

Plotting a Course Correction

What similarities do students and navigators share?

Navigators at sea, on land, in the air, and even in space share some qualities in common: They all point their craft toward a destination and then carefully map out a route designed to get them there. That's how it's supposed to work in theory at least. But in real life, the wind may shift, a road could be closed, a storm might blow in, or an engine could lose power. It's a rare route that doesn't require some sort of adjustment along the way. Navigators rely on constant feedback to determine whether a course correction is needed. In the same way, tests are your feedback as you head toward your academic goals. Depending on your own specific analysis of the test you've just taken, you may need to place greater emphasis on mastering the type of information you missed, gaining additional practice on types of questions you seem to struggle with, or working at moving through your tests more methodically. And if none of these strategies seems as though it will help to get you back on track, it might be a good idea to make an appointment to get your instructor's perspective or arrange to have a tutor provide you with the extra assistance you require.

FINAL WORDS

Exams don't have to be situations of stress. They can actually be times of great triumph. Know your material, know your test site, and know as much as you ethically can about the content of the upcoming test. But above all, know yourself. Learn to distinguish a natural sense of excitement from a damaging feeling of doom. Keep in mind that some of the world's greatest actors still feel nervous when they first walk on stage. But these actors quickly settle down when they realize the obvious: They know their lines and they know their abilities. Like an accomplished actor, with preparation and confidence you can overcome your initial hesitation and be a star.

HAVE YOU MISSED SOMETHING?

SENTENCE COMPLETION   *Complete the following sentences with one of the three words listed below each sentence.*

1. One of the most obvious but overlooked sources of information on an up-coming exam is your _____.

    instructor   textbook   intuition

2. In a test question, the qualifiers should be _____.
    avoided   circled   defined

3. Key points in an unfinished essay should be _____.
    outlined   combined   deleted

MATCHING   *In each blank space in the left column, write the letter preceding the phrase in the right column that matches the left item best.*

_____ 1. Introduction   a. Allows for late additions as well as for instructor's comments

_____ 2. Context   b. Is provided when you read the entire question

_____ 3. "Switch hitting"   c. Statement that starts off a multiple-choice question

_____ 4. Homestretch   d. Schedule that ties up loose ends as exam week approaches

_____ 5. Reflection   e. Often provide specifics on how each question should be answered

_____ 6. Directions   f. Should be left off to ensure that your essay gets right to the point

_____ 7. Space   g. Added benefit that comes from creating advanced summary sheets

_____ 8. Stem   h. Mastering possible test material from both sides

TRUE-FALSE   *Circle* T *beside the* true *statements and* F *beside the* false *statements.*

1. T F If you've been using the Silver Dollar System, creating summary sheets should be relatively easy.

2. T F By finals week, the bulk of your exam preparation should be completed.

3. T   F   For a statement to be marked true, it must be entirely true.

4. T   F   The length of the blank dictates the size of the answer in a sentence completion question.

5. T   F   The appearance of your essay will have no influence on your grade.

MULTIPLE CHOICE

Choose the word or phrase that completes each sentence most accurately, and circle the letter that precedes it.

1. During exam week, it is OK to skip
   a. meals.
   b. sleep.
   c. recreation.
   d. none of the above.

2. Deep breathing has been shown to produce feelings of
   a. relaxation.
   b. fatigue.
   c. anxiety.
   d. resentment.

3. A multiple-choice question can be viewed as a series of
   a. stems.
   b. qualifiers.
   c. true-false statements.
   d. decoys or distracters.

4. Jotting down notes on the back of the test sheet
   a. gets you involved right away.
   b. is usually not permitted in an essay exam.
   c. takes time that could be better spent.
   d. will often gain you partial credit.

5. Keywords in an essay question should be
   a. paraphrased.
   b. circled.
   c. discussed.
   d. replaced.

 *Online Study Center*   www.college.hmco.com/pic/pauk9e

SHORT ANSWER   *Supply a brief answer for each of the following items.*

1. Outline ways you can prepare for the atmosphere of an upcoming exam.
2. Point out the difference between regular and advanced summary sheets.
3. Compare and contrast the four basic types of objective questions.
4. How should opinions be treated in an essay answer?

IT'S YOUR Q

The Q System uses marginal questions to encourage active reading. You'll notice that most but not all paragraphs in this chapter are accompanied by marginal questions. Now it's your Q. Scan the chapter for any paragraph that is missing a question, reread the paragraph, establish the main idea, and then arrive at a question that elicits it. Use the questions in the surrounding paragraphs as models for your own marginal questions.

WORDS IN CONTEXT

From the three choices beside each numbered item, select the one that most nearly expresses the meaning of the italicized word in the quote. Make a light check mark (✓) next to your choice.

We hold these truths to be *self-evident*, that all men are created equal, that they are *endowed* by their Creator with certain *unalienable* rights, that among these are life, liberty, and the *pursuit* of happiness.

—Thomas Jefferson (1743–1826), third president of the United States

1. *self-evident*	genuine	effective	obvious
2. *endowed*	provided	developed	established
3. *unalienable* rights	lawful	intrinsic	earned
4. *pursuit*	enjoyment	search	goal

Diplomacy is the art of saying "nice doggie" until you can find a rock.

—Will Rogers (1879–1935), American actor and humorist

5. *diplomacy*	trickery	cleverness	tact

There is nothing *sinister* in so arranging one's affairs as to keep taxes as low as possible.

—Judge Learned Hand (1872–1961), American jurist

6. Nothing *sinister* illegal   easy   evil

Capitalism is *humanitarianism.*

—Margaret Thatcher (1925–), former prime minister of Great Britain

7. *capitalism*   development free enterprise democracy

8. *humanitarianism* philanthropy impermanent materialistic

THE WORD HISTORY SYSTEM

Deliberate
weighed in the scales

deliberate de-lib'-er-ate *adj.*
1. Done with or marked by full consciousness of the nature and effects; intentional. 2. Arising from or marked by careful consideration. 3. Unhurried in action, movement, or manner, as if trying to avoid error.

A *deliberate* decision is one based upon a weighing of the facts and arguments involved—and that is the literal meaning of the word. *Deliberate* is derived from Latin *deliberatus,* past participle of the verb *deliberare,* from *librare,* "to weigh." *Librare* comes from *libra,* "a balance" or "pair of scales."

Reprinted by permission. From *Picturesque Word Origins* © 1933 by G. & C. Merriam Co. (now Merriam-Webster, Incorporated).

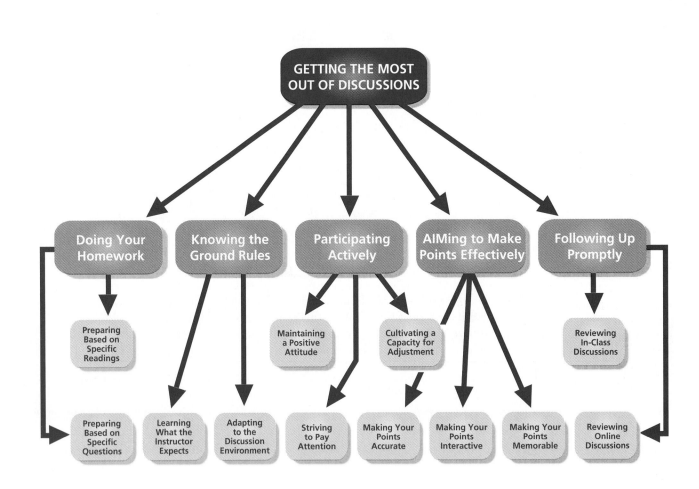

Getting the Most Out of Discussions

*The most fruitful and
natural exercise of our
mind, in my opinion,
is discussion.*

Michel de Montaigne
(1533–1592), French essayist

Do you want to raise the stakes for recitation? Do you want to do some high-quality reflection on the ideas you've learned from your lectures and texts? Some of the most valuable learning you can do comes from what is often the least valuable part of your overall grade. And yet, online or in class, discussions are a precious tool in the pursuit of knowledge. This chapter explains how to get the most out of discussions by:

- **Doing Your Homework**
- **Knowing the Ground Rules**
- **Participating Actively**
- **Making Points Effectively**
- **Following Up Promptly**

Why are discussions not given more respect?

Discussions, whether held in class or online, are perhaps the most underappreciated component of any course. Why are discussions unsung? Part of it may be because their bearing on your grade—if they are graded at all—is relatively small. It may also be because discussions involve the significant participation of "ordinary people"—you and your classmates—instead of the "experts" who write textbooks or deliver lectures.

What are the benefits of discussions?

The potential benefit from discussions in fostering true understanding and long-lasting knowledge is huge. Discussions can breathe life into dormant ideas. They encourage active learning, allow for a kind of recitation that rivals most solitary study, and, perhaps most important, provide an opportunity to reflect on ideas through the perspectives of multiple minds instead of simply your own. That's why it's vital to treat discussions with the respect they deserve.

How do you get the most out of discussions?

To get the most out of a discussion, approach each one well prepared, make sure you're familiar with any ground rules your instructor has laid out, remain fully engaged throughout, make any points of your own as effectively as possible, and finally, review each discussion while it is still fresh in your mind.

Doing Your Homework

What can you do to prepare for discussions in general?

The good thing about preparing for discussions is that, for the most part, if you've been keeping up with your assignments and reciting and reflecting on your textbook and lecture notes, then you should be well prepared already. Of course, sometimes you learn a little more about the scope of the discussion. Perhaps the instructor has set specific guidelines, such as "Read Chapter 5 and be prepared to discuss it on Monday," or has supplied one or more specific questions designed to start a discussion going. In either case, you can focus your study so you are better prepared for the discussion.

Preparing Based on Specific Readings

YOUR
Q

If the instructor suggests that the discussion will revolve around a specific chapter or section, take your notes from that portion of the text and use them to create summary sheets similar to those discussed in Chapter 12. If you are more visually inclined, take a blank sheet of paper and write down some of the assigned text's important names, terms, and concepts and then draw connectors between those items that are related. Annotate the connectors with brief explanations of each relationship. Your annotations might include words and phrases such as "worked with," "discovered," "invented," "opposed," and "led to." The resulting map should give you a "big picture" sense of what's important in the reading.

Preparing Based on Specific Questions

How should you prepare
if you are given the discussion
questions in advance?

If the instructor has given you one or more questions that will serve as the basis for the discussion, it's a bit like preparing for a live-action essay test. Search back into your notes for material that relates to the question or questions. Consolidate that material into summary sheets or create a concept map that pulls together all the important names, terms, and concepts onto a single sheet and then draw connectors between related items. In either scenario, you should be able to use the resulting summary sheet or concept map as a "cheat sheet" during the discussion, regardless of whether it's in class or online.

Knowing the Ground Rules

What are the ground rules
for discussions?

To get the most out of class discussions, it helps to know the ground rules. That means learning the instructor's expectations and getting acquainted with the specific discussion environment.

Learning What the Instructor Expects

What should you know about
your instructor's expectations
for discussions?

Instructors' expectations for discussions can vary widely. However, you can usually get a better handle on the role discussions play in a specific class by learning the percentage of your grade that will come from the discussion part of the course and by reading any guidelines the instructor may have provided for taking part in discussions.

Find Out the Grade Percentage

How does it help to know the
number of points allocated for
discussions?

If you haven't done so already, check the class syllabus or the course website to see how your instructor has divided up the components that make up your semester grade. Discussions—sometimes just called "class participation"—often account for the smallest percentage of your grade, but not always. With the increasing popularity of online discussions, some instructors are placing added emphasis on your ability to carry on a discussion based on what you've read in your text or learned in a lecture. At any rate, it can be risky or reckless to take this part of your class for granted. Even in cases in which the instructor doesn't officially award any points for discussions, your ability to successfully articulate key ideas from the course in a discussion may color the instructor's overall perception of your performance. Besides, discussions provide an excellent "dress rehearsal" for essay tests and can sometimes serve as an early warning sign if you are struggling with the concepts in your class.

Online Study Center   www.college.hmco.com/pic/pauk9e

Read Any Guidelines

What is the value of knowing the instructor's discussion guidelines?

Some instructors like to keep the guidelines for the class participation portion of your grade rather vague so they have the flexibility to give you extra points (or take them away) at their own discretion. Others are very specific about the criteria they use for awarding your discussion or participation grade. Check to see if your instructor has provided some guidelines for discussion performance. This can provide a goal you can aim for and may also alert you to any specific discussion dos and don'ts as far as the instructor is concerned.

Adapting to the Discussion Environment

What should you do to adapt to your discussion environment?

It wasn't all that long ago when class discussions could be understood to take place in only one environment: the classroom. But things have changed. More and more colleges and universities are conducting class discussions online. That doesn't mean that in-class discussions don't still exist. They definitely do. Some instructors may have moved their discussions online, but others continue to hold them in the classroom. Still others go with a mixture of both.

What are some key differences between classroom discussions and online ones?

Many of the guidelines for discussions hold true whether you're discussing something face to face or keyboard to keyboard. But there are some conspicuous differences between the real and online discussion worlds, and just as knowing your audience is important if you're a writer or a speaker, understanding your environment is essential if you're taking part in a discussion. Figure 13.1 compares the classroom and online discussion environments.

Learn the Ropes If You're New to Discussion Software

Although the basic design for many online discussions is similar, their superficial appearance can sometimes be quite different. As a result, it's best to learn the basics of your class's particular discussion software so that you can become familiar with its layout and capabilities.

- *Follow the demo or tutorial.* Depending on the course management software you are using, there may be an interactive demo (demonstration) or tutorial available that will walk you through the functions you are most likely to use in an online discussion.
- *Get assistance from a fellow student.* If you're new to discussion software or uncomfortable using it, you may be able to find a friend at school or someone else in your class who can help you with the basics.
- *Contact your campus learning lab or skills center.* If your campus uses discussion software, it's likely that the entire school has adopted the same program. If so, someone at the learning lab or skills center should be able to help you out.

	Classroom Discussions	Online Discussions
How can I keep track of the key points in a discussion?	Your notes, ears, and memory are your only real means of navigating an in-class discussion.	Threaded messages provide a helpful visual representation for organizing related comments.
What are some suggestions for planning the points I'm going to make?	Although writing cue cards or using regular notes can sometimes be helpful, delivering prewritten comments verbatim will sound awkward and obvious to all.	With asynchronous discussions, you can take your time. It's recommended but not essential to have some notes prepared in advance.
How should I handle any sources in my comment?	Paraphrasing a source is usually preferable to reading a direct quotation, although you must still be sure to attribute it.	Cutting and pasting quotations from your text or notes is usually permitted, but you must be certain to provide attribution.
What factors can affect the meaning of my message?	For better or worse, your posture, facial expression, and tone of voice are all elements of your message.	Without spoken or visual cues, careful phrasing and proper context are crucial if you don't want to be misunderstood.
When is it best to contribute my comment?	Wait for an opening. Participants aren't supposed to talk at once or interrupt each other during a classroom discussion.	Contribute when you can. Simultaneous posting is common although it can sometimes have the same effect as when letters (or e-mail messages) cross in the mail.
What happens to my comments once I've made them?	In-class comments are ephemeral. Impressions of what you said may linger, and your ideas may be retained in the notes of others, but your exact words are fleeting.	Your comments can be read and reread by others for days and weeks after you first posted them. Great insights and glaring errors are immortalized. So be careful!
What if I make a point that someone has already made?	If you've been paying attention, the chances of accidentally repeating someone else's point are quite small. Redundancy provides a sure indication that you haven't been participating actively.	The risks of inadvertently repeating a point that has already been made are greater than in a classroom discussion. Try to be sure you've read all earlier comments before posting.

Figure 13.1
How Classroom and Online Discussions Compare

- *Ask your instructor.* If you can't figure out your discussion software on your own and have been unable to get help from a tutorial, a fellow student, or someone at the learning lab, check with your instructor. But before you do, carefully check the instructor's syllabus or website to make sure they don't already provide advice or instructions for learning the software or a link to a site that will provide help. If no help is available, your instructor should be willing to provide some assistance. But if you ask the instructor for help that she or he has already provided elsewhere, you may start class off on the wrong foot.
- *Don't delay in getting assistance.* If your class uses discussion software, try to test it out at your earliest opportunity so you can seek help promptly if you need it. The longer you wait, the harder it may be to get help.

Online Study Center www.college.hmco.com/pic/pauk9e

Participating Actively

How have online discussions changed the guidelines for good listening?

"Online discussions have changed *everything*." Breathless claims such as this often seem to accompany the introduction of new media or methods. Granted, as we've seen, there are obvious differences between carrying on a discussion in a classroom and participating in one on a computer screen. But just as the evolution from pen to typewriter to personal computer hasn't altered the basic rules for writing, online discussions haven't changed the fundamental guidelines for good listening, even when that "listening" is *e-listening* and is done with the eyes instead of the ears. Figure 13.2 presents a short quiz to help you learn where you stand as a listener. Although originally designed for analyzing "standard" listening, you'll see that the questions are just as relevant online as they are in the classroom. All you need to do is recognize the habits of a poor listener as well as the techniques used by a good listener. Then, knowing the good techniques, apply them without exception in all your daily activities. You can make a fresh and immediate start today by referring to Figure 13.3, which lists the ten most important keys to effective listening.

Being a good listener or e-listener means being fully engaged in what goes on in a lecture or discussion. It is a conscious activity that grows out of three basic skills: *a*ttitude, *a*ttention, and *a*djustment. These skills are known collectively as *triple-A listening.*

A₁: Maintaining a Positive Attitude

Why do you need a positive attitude to listen effectively?

You can take many steps to improve your listening, but the primary prerequisite to effective listening is a positive mental attitude. A positive attitude sets the stage for the open-mindedness that is essential to learning and comprehension. As businessman and author Kevin J. Murphy says in *Effective Listening*, "Minds are like parachutes; they only function when open."[1] You must walk into the classroom or log on to a threaded discussion convinced that you will acquire new information and insights and learn things of real value. No matter how diligently and conscientiously you reflect on information on your own, it's unlikely that you will be able to rival the benefits you gain from the exciting ideas and multiple perspectives that good discussions can provide.

What can you do to help cultivate a positive attitude?

Cultivating a positive attitude isn't always easy. But it is worth the effort. If you're struggling to do so, try finding areas of interest in what others have to say, judge the content of their points instead of the delivery, and hold your fire if you're inclined to lash out at those things you don't agree with.

[1]Kevin J. Murphy, *Effective Listening: Hearing What People Say and Making It Work for You* (New York: Bantam Books, 1987), p. 28.

Figure 13.2
Listening Habits

Source: Adapted from Ralph G. Nichols and Thomas R. Lewis, *Listening and Speaking*, p. 166. Originally published by William C. Brown Group, 1954. Reprinted by permission of the authors.

How often do you find yourself engaging in these ten bad habits of listening? Check the appropriate columns.

How often do you ...	Almost always	Usually	Sometimes	Seldom	Almost never	Score
Decide that the topic is boring?						
Criticize the speaker?						
Overreact by disagreeing?						
Listen only for bare facts?						
Outline everything?						
Fake attention?						
Yield to distractions?						
Avoid listening to tough technical information?						
Let emotion-laden words arouse personal antagonism?						
Waste thought speed by daydreaming?						
Total score						

Column group header: **Frequency**

Tally your score as follows:

Almost always	2
Usually	4
Sometimes	6
Seldom	8
Almost never	10

Interpret your score as follows:

Below 70	Need training in listening
70 to 90	You listen well
Above 90	Extraordinarily good listener

Figure 13.3
Ten Keys to Effective Listening

Source: Reprinted by permission of Unisys Corporation.

Keys to Effective Listening	The Poor Listener	The Good Listener
1. Find areas of interest	Tunes out dry topics.	Seizes opportunities: "What's in it for me?"
2. Judge content, not delivery	Tunes out if delivery is poor.	Judges content, skips over delivery errors.
3. Hold your fire	Tends to enter into argument.	Doesn't judge until comprehension is complete.
4. Listen for ideas	Listens for facts.	Listens for central themes.
5. Be a flexible note taker	Is busy with form, misses content.	Adjusts to topic and organizational pattern.
6. Work at listening	Shows no energy output, fakes attention.	Works hard; exhibits alertness.
7. Resist distractions	Is distracted easily.	Fights or avoids distractions; tolerates bad habits in others; knows how to concentrate.
8. Exercise your mind	Resists difficult expository material; seeks light, recreational material.	Uses heavier material as exercise for the mind.
9. Keep your mind open	Reacts to emotional words.	Interprets emotional words; does not get hung up on them.
10. Thought is faster than speech; use it	Tends to daydream with slow speakers.	Challenges, anticipates, mentally summarizes, weighs the evidence, listens between the lines to tone of voice.

How can you find areas of interest in "boring" ideas?

Find Areas of Interest

It doesn't take any talent to brand someone else's ideas as "boring." Anyone can do that. Discussions are a cooperative activity. Do your part by remaining engaged. You can usually find some aspect of another person's comments that appeals to your personal interests.

What if you can't find anything that interests you?

Of course, you can't always immediately find something that captures your interest. Remember the James-Lange theory from Chapter 4? Although we usually think that emotions trigger physical reactions (when you're happy, you smile), a number of recent studies have turned this idea on its head. In other words, smiling can sometimes make you happy. In the same way, acting interested in something that doesn't immediately interest you can sometimes lead to genuine interest! Pay close attention to what's being posted or said, take notes vigorously, and show interest by your facial expression, even if you are by yourself and sitting at the computer. In time real interest may emerge where none existed.

Judge Content, Not Delivery

What's the most important aspect of a discussion comment?

Listeners are sometimes terribly rude or downright cruel to people whose delivery fails to measure up to some preconceived standard. Keep in mind that great thinkers aren't always excellent writers or orators. The most important aspect of a comment is its content, not the way it's delivered. Try to approach each comment with a humane attitude. Concentrate on the substance of the remark instead of how it's expressed. If you do, you'll emerge with a positive self-image. You will also learn something.

Hold Your Fire

What should you do if someone writes or says something you don't agree with?

In college you're bound to be exposed to ideas that are different from or even contrary to those you hold. When this happens, your knee-jerk reaction may be to speak up immediately to defend your position. Hold your fire! Try to fully grasp the differing viewpoint even if you strongly disagree with it. If you shift all your focus to rebutting a point you don't agree with, you'll be unable to concentrate on the rest of the remark. In a war of words of this type, understanding is often the first casualty.

A₂: Striving to Pay Attention

Why is attention important?

Attention is the path that will lead you into the wonderful state of concentration. Without concentration there is no focus, and without focus there is almost no learning. If you pay attention and concentrate, you will become an active listener able to synthesize new information with facts and ideas you've already known.

How can you build anticipation?

Attention often thrives on anticipation. Before a discussion, look over your notes from the latest lecture and your most recent textbook assignment. Once the discussion starts, let your mind dart ahead (during pauses) to anticipate what's coming next. You'll be alert, engrossed in the material, and concentrating 100 percent.

Online Study Center   www.college.hmco.com/pic/pauk9e

What should your attention be focused on?

Of course, as we learned in Chapter 3, you cannot attain concentration by concentrating on concentration. Your attention must focus on the discussion, not on the act of concentration itself. Deep cognition, or deep thinking, is vital. Whether you hear a discussion or read it online, the words enter your working memory, where they have to be swiftly processed into ideas to avoid getting dumped from your memory altogether. Active participation ensures the words' survival. If you process them into ideas, those ideas will be stored in your long-term memory in a flash.

How can you foster the kind of attention that leads to concentration?

You can foster the kind of attention that leads to concentration by focusing on ideas instead of facts, by working to stay fully engaged, by tuning out distractions, and by using the natural lag between speech and thought to forge ahead in your mind in order to consider the current point and anticipate the next one.

Listen for Ideas

What's the drawback of listening for facts instead of ideas?

Don't imitate the detective who says, "The facts, ma'am, just stick to the facts." Sure, facts are important. And it's true that they're often what you'll be tested on. But facts in isolation don't hold together well. In order to organize information both in your notes and your memory, look to the ideas that lie behind the facts. Strive to uncover the principle or idea that each fact is supporting. Try to see how the pieces of the puzzle fit into the big picture.

Work at Listening

How do you work at listening?

Listening isn't a passive activity; it requires true participation. Good listeners are fully engaged, outwardly calm, but inwardly dynamic; and they sit toward the front of the classroom. While taking notes, the listener may nod in agreement or look quizzical when the presentation becomes unclear. These sorts of gestures aren't just for effect. Such activity actually promotes comprehension and learning by the listener and provides encouragement to the speaker.

Resist Distractions

There are distractions aplenty in the classroom: antics of other students, whispering, the speaker's dress and mannerisms, outside noise, and outside views. In some classes, students may actually be browsing the Web or sending instant messages while the lecturer is speaking! The best way to resist distractions and maintain your concentration is to rivet your eyes on the speaker when you have a chance and focus on taking notes the rest of the time. You may also want to consider sitting close to the front. The level of distraction tends to increase as you move farther away from the instructor, especially in large lecture halls.

Use Your Thought Speed

How can you take advantage of thought speed?

In a race of ideas, thought is swifter than spoken words and even speedier than typed ones. Most of us can grasp the gist of a point faster than someone can express it. This "thought speed" leaves a bit of a lag during which your mind is apt to wander. Rather than using this time to daydream or to dart off on mental side trips, devote it to thinking more deeply about what has just been typed or said. Mentally enumerate the ideas that have been expressed and summarize them until it's time to shift your focus back to the comments. Keep alternating in this fashion throughout the discussion.

A₃: Cultivating a Capacity for Adjustment

Why is adjustment so important to active participation?

Even though the discussion may start out with a very specific topic or question, you still need to be mentally limber enough to follow its inevitable twists and turns. You can't simply tune out the parts that don't fit with your expectations. You have to be able to "roll with the punches." That's why adjustment is such an important component of active participation. You can cultivate your capacity for adjustment by remaining flexible while taking notes, by exercising your mind through exposing it to complex or different ideas, and by keeping your mind open to ideas and information that you may initially want to tune out.

Be a Flexible Note Taker

What is the key to being a flexible note taker?

Flexibility in note taking depends on informed participation. Informed participation means being able to identify the organizational patterns used by discussion participants. Organizational patterns are easily recognizable if you know their basic structures in advance. (Several of the most common organizational patterns are described in Chapter 10.) Once you have detected a pattern, you'll have a framework you can use to anticipate the form of the message and adjust the way you record your notes. Similarly, when someone suddenly shifts gears and adopts a different pattern, a flexible note taker should be able to adjust accordingly.

Exercise Your Mind

How can you exercise your mind to become a better listener?

From time to time, try to sit in on discussions of topics you know very little about or that you may consider to be "over your head." When you do, make a serious effort to follow the chain of thoughts and ideas. True, some parts may be unintelligible to you, but you're bound to understand other parts of it. Such participation can be hard work, but in the same way that hard work at a gym can strengthen your muscles, the hard work of following strange or difficult ideas will strengthen your will to concentrate and your power to persist.

Keep Your Mind Open

What can you do to prevent highly charged words from interfering with your participation?

It is hard to believe that a single word or phrase can cause an emotional eruption. But all of us can be susceptible to these reactions from time to time. In class such words can raise the blood pressure or even trigger an outburst. Online they can prompt nasty messages commonly known as *flames*. Notorious

Online Study Center www.college.hmco.com/pic/pauk9e

hot-button words include *activist, fundamentalist, liberal, conservative, evolution, creationism, feminist, abortion, pro-life,* and *free market*. Dealing with highly charged language is similar to dealing with a fear or phobia. Often, the emotional impact of the words can be decreased through a frank and open discussion. Don't be so inflexible as to totally shut out opposing ideas, as incendiary as they may seem at first. Genuinely listen to the other point of view. You might learn something that you didn't know before.

AIMing to Make Points Effectively

What should you do to truly be part of a discussion?

You can't truly be part of a discussion if you aren't participating actively. But even if you're conscientiously maintaining a positive attitude, working hard to pay attention, and nimbly adjusting to the discussion's unexpected twists and turns, you're unlikely to add anything to your grade until you take advantage of your active participation and chime in yourself.

How can you add something valuable to a discussion?

But how do you do it? You can't just jump recklessly into the fray. There's a real risk that a callous or careless contributor will do more to harm her or his grade than someone who rarely pipes up. To earn a good grade from your instructor, the respect of your classmates, and to truly add something valuable to a discussion, whether in-class or online, your AIM should be to make your points Accurate, Interactive, and Memorable.

Making Your Points Accurate

What do you need to make sure your discussion points are accurate?

On one level, the expectations for the points you make in discussions are not all that different than those for essay answers you write. They need to be well supported and well expressed.

Make Sure Your Comments Are Well Supported

How can you make sure that your comments are well supported?

A discussion comment typically begins with some sort of assertion that is then fleshed out with facts. Sometimes the instructor will jump-start a discussion with an assertion of her or his own or a quotation from a respected source and then look to you and your classmates to explore its implications. Other times, you may introduce the assertion yourself. Unlike in essays, opinions are usually acceptable in discussions, but they still need to be backed up with material from your lectures or readings. It's legitimate to say either "I think Martin Luther King would be appalled by the state of the world if he were living today" or "I think Martin Luther King would be pleased by the state of the world if he were living today" as long as you can support your contention with evidence, examples, facts, and reasons.

Make Sure Your Comments Are Well Expressed

How are comments best expressed in online or class-room discussions?

Even the best-supported assertions can still suffer if they are poorly expressed. Poorly expressed statements in a discussion—like bad handwriting in an essay—have a way of undermining otherwise good ideas. In online discussions, that means you should write in clear, complete, properly punctuated, grammatical sentences with words and names spelled correctly. Because most online discussions are asynchronous, don't be in such a hurry to respond that you post something sloppy. If your course management software doesn't include a spell-checker, type your comment in a blank document of your word processor and then do a spell-check before pasting it in to the discussion. If you are making your comments in the classroom instead of online, it still pays to think in terms of the written word. Try to visualize the sentences as you are saying them, ending each with a period and including transitions to make your argument easier to follow. Simply visualizing such structures will almost automatically transform you into a thinking-on-your-feet kind of speaker instead of a shooting-off-your-mouth one. In sum, you'll be thinking rather than just rambling. When you come to the end of your point, a summarizing sentence—ending with a period—will be impressive.

Making Your Points Interactive

How are discussion points interactive?

The emphasis on well-supported, well-expressed points may share something in common with essay answers, but discussions are fundamentally different in one crucial respect. They're interactive. Each comment you make should connect in some way to the others, and each person who participates in the discussion should be part of the group instead of acting as a lone wolf.

Keep the Comments Connected

What can you do to connect your comments to the rest of the discussion?

Skillfully integrate your comments into the general discussion by keeping to the topic at hand, steering clear of loose threads, and refraining from being a rubber stamp.

1. *Stay on topic.* Your comments may be interesting and even important, but if they're off the subject, they're irrelevant to the current discussion. Save them for the appropriate forum. If you're taking part in an online discussion, you may be able to start a new topic thread or add your comment to another existing discussion, but don't gum up the current one with needless detours or digressions. They don't reflect well on your ability to think in a clear and disciplined fashion.

2. *Avoid loose threads.* Even if your comment is on topic, it shouldn't just dangle freely. Work to weave it into the overall fabric of the discussion by referring specifically to other comments and then by supporting, refuting, or refining them.

 *Online Study Center* **www.college.hmco.com/pic/pauk9e**

3. *Don't be a rubber stamp.* "Me too" adds nothing to a discussion. If you agree with another comment, that's fine. But cite specific information from lectures or readings that explains why you concur. Above all, be sure to avoid making a point that has already been made. Redundancy provides a sure sign to your classmates and, more important, to your instructor, that you haven't been paying attention.

Keep the Others in Mind

What steps can you take to keep the other members of the discussion in mind?

Just as you want to make sure that your discussion comments fit into the topic at hand, it's also important that you make an effort to keep your classmates in mind by tying in their comments, treating them with sensitivity, keeping your voice down, and pausing for effect.

1. *Tie in the comments of others.* Even if the instructor started things off, it's good to try to relate your comment to the points made by several other classmates. Beginning your comment with a phrase such as "Although I share Anil and Julie's concerns, I am more inclined to agree with Juan that . . ." will help to make it clear that you have not only read or listened to the other comments but that you have actually *thought* about them.
2. *Be a diplomat.* There's a difference between being forceful and being rude. Don't let strong opinions overwhelm your ability to be civil and respectful. Be especially careful to steer clear of sarcasm, which may grant you a moment of supremacy but can lead to some long-term resentment. This can be tricky in online discussions in which you don't have the benefit of your facial expressions or your tone of voice to help make your intentions clear. Play it safe and make your comments constructive and straightforward.
3. *Turn the volume down.* Obviously, you need to be heard, but yelling isn't going to make your point any clearer. Let your choice of words, not their volume, provide the oomph in your assertion. Similarly, when posting to an online discussion, refrain from posting messages in all capital letters, which is considered to be the typographical equivalent to yelling.
4. *Take a breath.* Pauses not only give you a second to collect your thoughts and come up with a good opener, but if you're participating in a classroom discussion, the brief, unanticipated silence can actually stimulate the interest of the others. Most people view it as a signal that something important is coming.

Making Your Points Memorable

What helps to make your discussion comments memorable?

The interactive nature of discussions often provides insights and perspectives that couldn't be gained from individual study. But if your contributions are going to be a key part of the process and—from a practical standpoint—if they are going to earn you suitable recognition from your instructor and a superior grade, you need to ensure that your contributions are memorable by striving to make them easy to follow and fresh.

Make Your Points Easy to Follow

How can you make your points easy to follow?

We've seen how a clear organizational pattern makes it easier to follow another person's point. When it's your turn to contribute to the discussion, it helps to return the favor. State your point succinctly at the outset. Don't make others have to read between the lines to figure out what you are saying. Then elaborate on your point by using a clear and obvious organizational pattern. If you have a series of facts to support your original point, enumerate them by preceding each supporting fact with a number and by introducing your last supporting fact with the word "Finally." If you're comparing and/or contrasting your point with points made by others, begin each comparison with an obvious phrase, such as "Just as" or "In the same way" or "Like," and introduce each contrasting point with phrases such as "Unlike" or "In contrast to" or "On the other hand." A succinctly stated main point and clearly structured support supply an easy-to-follow framework that will make your comments more valuable and memorable.

Make Your Points Fresh

What is it that makes discussion comments seem fresh?

Good instructors seldom want their students to behave like walking, talking versions of their lectures or readings. This robotic approach may be a simple test-passer but it rarely fosters genuine learning. That's why, in all but the most rigorous courses, instructors place a premium on fresh insights, not on rote regurgitation. In short, they are seeking creativity. You can do only so much to analyze ideas in different ways on your own. Even though it may have several facets, your thinking generally comes from a distinct perspective. Because they represent the meeting of many minds, discussions expose you to a wide variety of perspectives and provide an extraordinary opportunity for reflection. And, as Nobel Laureate Hans Bethe reminds us (see Chapter 10), creativity comes only with reflection.

Following Up Promptly

Why is it important to promptly do a follow-up?

A good discussion may be full of fresh ideas, but those ideas will have a short shelf life if you don't make a concerted effort to reinforce them in your memory. As the Leon and Clyde episode (see Chapter 9) made all too clear, even brilliant insights can fade quickly if you don't do something to fix them in your memory.

 **Online Study Center**   **www.college.hmco.com/pic/pauk9e**

Reviewing In-Class Discussions

Why are in-class discussions so easy to forget?

Discussions that take place in the classroom are especially susceptible to the ravages of forgetting. Ideas and facts spend such a brief time in your working memory that a key point at the beginning of a classmate's comment could be gone without a trace before she or he is even finished talking! And because class discussions are more interactive than regular lectures, you may not be able to take notes as thoroughly as you'd like.

What's wrong with taping discussions?

Some students try to solve this problem by tape recording class discussions. This is a mistake on a number of levels:

- *It's a waste of time.* The discussion will take twice as long because you'll be compelled to replay the entire tape once you're home.
- *It's an invitation to inattention.* Recording a discussion can discourage you from remaining fully engaged because you're aware—whether consciously or not—that you can go back and catch what you missed in class by listening to the tape.
- *It's a technical gamble.* Unless you have a very good tape recorder or a number of microphones, you may not be able to make out all of the comments when you go back and listen to them on your tape.

Your best strategy for following discussions is to use the two-page system (explained in Chapter 10). With the main points on one page and important details on the other, you should be able to reconstruct a lot of what went on in the discussion, providing you are careful to review your notes right away while you're still able to fill in some of the missing pieces. You can further improve your memory of the discussion by labeling each point in your notes with the name of the person who made it. Associating each idea with a name and a face will strengthen its memory. Finally, because all the comments won't be coming from the same part of the classroom, you can use the loci method (see Chapter 9) to trigger memories of the points that came from various parts of the room.

Reviewing Online Discussions

What are the drawbacks to reviewing online discussions?

Asynchronous online discussions aren't as susceptible to your forgetting them as are discussions that are held in a classroom setting. That's because the threads retain a record of everything that's been "said" during the course of a discussion. But online discussions have their own special drawbacks. Depending on the nature of your course management software, most of the important discussion points are at least one click away, hidden beneath a hyperlinked thread title that may not be especially informative. Also, an online discussion that is many threads deep can result in a snakelike string of links that can be intimidating to approach.

What's the best strategy for reviewing online discussions?

Your best strategy for reviewing online discussions is to do so on an ongoing basis, rather than waiting until the discussion is over. Each time you read a message, try to determine its main point right away, just as you would with a paragraph in your textbook. Then type or jot down that point. If the messages are grouped in threads, try to summarize all the comments in each thread, just as you would summarize a page of your notes (see Chapter 11). Most discussion programs automatically change the color of a link after you've read its associated message. If you make a point to capture the main idea right away, the color change will not only tell you that it's a message you've read, but also that it's one you've taken notes for. That knowledge should make a dense page of threads a little less intimidating and should actually provide encouragement as you get a visual sense of the progress you've made. Also, it should make reviewing an online discussion much easier. Instead of having to painstakingly reread each thread, you should be able to conduct a thorough review of the discussion without even logging on.

FINAL WORDS

What is an unexpected outcome of some class discussions?

Like tests, quizzes, and papers, discussions provide an opportunity to take your knowledge and explain it—in short, to show what you know. But unlike the other three, which are essentially solitary activities, discussions require interaction with others. This not only encourages insight and reflection as we've seen, but it can also result in something unexpected: friendship. This underscores the motivation for treating other participants with respect. After all, the person you're agreeing (or disagreeing) with may start out as just a classmate and wind up as a good friend.

HAVE YOU MISSED SOMETHING?

SENTENCE COMPLETION   *Complete the following sentences with one of the three words listed below each sentence.*

1. The number of colleges and universities using online discussions is
   _____.

   increasing   decreasing   stagnant

2. When you participate actively in a discussion, your attention often thrives
   on _____.

   appearance   anticipation   agreement

3. Posting a message in all capital letters is generally considered to signify
   _____.

   agreement   disagreement   yelling

MATCHING   *In each blank space in the left column, write the letter preceding the phrase in the right column that matches the left item best.*

_____ 1. Content   a. Provides a tool for discussion preparation

_____ 2. Sarcasm   b. Should be provided when you cite sources during a discussion

_____ 3. Concept map   c. Much more important than delivery when it comes to discussion comments

_____ 4. Attribution   d. Leads to a state of concentration

_____ 5. Redundancy   e. Often indicates that you haven't been paying attention to the discussion

_____ 6. Thought   f. Can provide an effective means of drawing attention to your comments

_____ 7. Attention   g. May provide a brief moment of supremacy but can often lead to resentment

_____ 8. Pauses   h. Moves at a faster rate of speed than writing or speech

TRUE-FALSE   *Circle* T *beside the* true *statements and* F *beside the* false *statements.*

1. T F   Discussions are often the most appreciated component of a course.
2. T F   Discussions can provide an excellent "dress rehearsal" for essay tests.
3. T F   Many of the guidelines for discussions apply whether the discussion is in class or online.

4. T F Simultaneous posting is rare in online discussions.
5. T F Your comments on an online discussion can normally be read for days after you've posted them.

MULTIPLE CHOICE

Choose the word or phrase that completes each sentence most accurately, and circle the letter that precedes it.

1. Discussions
   a. encourage active learning.
   b. allow for superior reciting.
   c. provide reflection from many perspectives.
   d. all of the above.

2. In-class discussion comments are usually
   a. brief.
   b. ephemeral.
   c. archived.
   d. required.

3. With in-class discussions, the meaning of your message can be affected by your
   a. facial expression.
   b. tone of voice.
   c. posture.
   d. all of the above.

4. Flexibility in note taking depends on
   a. your handwriting.
   b. the content of the discussion.
   c. informed participation.
   d. whether the discussion takes place in class or online.

5. When you disagree with a discussion comment,
   a. begin rehearsing your rebuttal.
   b. automatically decide he or she is misinformed.
   c. take his or her stand as a bias.
   d. make a note of it, but keep on taking notes.

SHORT ANSWER　　*Supply a brief answer for each of the following items.*

1. Discuss strategies for preparing for discussions.
2. Contrast the environments for in-class and online discussions.
3. Explain the relationship between discussions and reflection.
4. Enumerate the elements of AIM, the mnemonic for making effective discussion comments.

IT'S YOUR Q

The Q System uses marginal questions to encourage active reading. You'll notice that most but not all paragraphs in this chapter are accompanied by marginal questions. Now it's your Q. Scan the chapter for any paragraph that is missing a question, reread the paragraph, establish the main idea, and then arrive at a question that elicits it. Use the questions in the surrounding paragraphs as models for your own marginal questions.

WORDS IN CONTEXT

From the three choices beside each numbered item, select the one that most nearly expresses the meaning of the italicized word in the quote. Make a light check mark (✓) next to your choice.

Failure! There is no such word in all the bright *lexicon* of speech, unless you yourself have written it there! There is no such thing as failure except to those who accept and believe in failure.
—Orison Swett Marden (1906–1975), American lawyer

1. *lexicon* of speech　　　expressions　　　idioms　　　dictionary

In the depth of winter, I finally learned that within me there lay an *invincible* summer.
—Albert Camus (1913–1960), French novelist, essayist, and dramatist

2. an *invincible* summer　　　fiery hot　　　unbeatable　　　intense

The gambling known as business looks with *austere* disfavor upon the business known as gambling.
—Ambrose Bierce (1842–1914), American author

3. with *austere* disfavor　　　stern　　　enormous　　　particular

Calculate
from the counting stones of
Romans

calculate   cal'-cu-late' *v.*
1. To ascertain by computation;
reckon. 2. To make an estimate
of; evaluate.

The Romans had no adding machines. Even the art of writing was known
to comparatively few persons. So they did their adding and subtracting with
the aid of little stones used as counters. The Latin word for the little stone
used in this way was *calculus*, diminutive of *calx*, meaning "limestone."
From *calculus* the verb *calculare*, "to calculate," was formed, and its past
participle, *calculatus*, is the immediate origin of English *calculate*.

Reprinted by permission. From *Picturesque Word Origins* © 1933 by G. & C. Merriam Co. (now
Merriam-Webster, Incorporated).

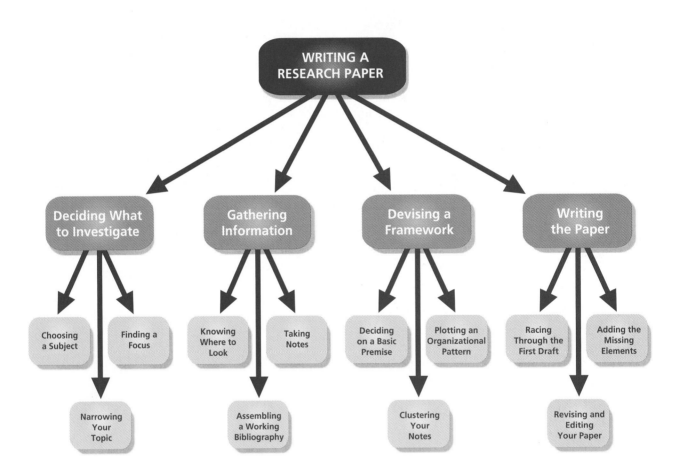

Writing a Research Paper

From the time it is assigned until the day it is due, a research paper can occupy your mind like no other type of assignment. Although writing a research paper can be time consuming, it doesn't have to be overwhelming if you take the process one step at a time. To give you a head start in the art of the research paper, this chapter provides a calm and well-organized system for

- **Deciding What to Investigate**
- **Gathering Information**
- **Devising a Framework**
- **Writing the Paper**

How does writing a research paper compare to studying your notes?

Writing even a modest research paper can take a lot of effort. Yet though the task is long, the skills it requires aren't sophisticated, and most of them aren't new. In fact, writing a paper isn't much more difficult than reading about a subject in detail, taking notes on your reading, organizing your notes, and reciting—all the activities you undertake to prepare for a test or quiz. The difference is that instead of reciting out loud, you put your recitation on paper in a form that makes what you've learned readable for others. If you realize that writing a paper is not much different from studying your notes, and if you systematically decide what to write about, gather information, devise a framework, and then do the actual writing, you may even find that writing papers can be a most absorbing way to learn about a subject.

Deciding What to Investigate

What are the steps in finding a suitable topic?

Finding a suitable topic is often the biggest stumbling block in research. It's essential that you know how to choose a topic easily and efficiently. There are three steps in the process of selecting a topic: Begin with a general subject that interests you, narrow it down, and then sharpen it even further by finding a focus. If you follow these steps, you'll wind up with a topic that is both interesting and specific.

Choosing a Subject

What type of subject should you choose?

In most cases, you'll be selecting a topic from a broad subject area. Because you'll be spending a great deal of time on the subject, your best bet is to choose one you are interested in or can develop an interest in. And if it isn't a subject that others are researching, then so much the better.

If you aren't sure what subject to select, do some preliminary research. Although you can sometimes get ideas by surfing the Web, the best place to do your preliminary research is still the library, where you'll have access to a variety of reference sources, both bound and computerized, a chance to browse through the section of the library stacks that matches your area of interest, and an opportunity to talk to a reference librarian, who will introduce you to an array of possible topics.

Suppose you are fascinated by natural disasters and want to learn more about them. But the subject "natural disasters" includes scores of topics: droughts, floods, tornadoes, hurricanes, volcanoes, and earthquakes, to name just a few. How can you do justice to them all? Obviously, you can't. You must narrow your topic.

Narrowing Your Topic

How do you narrow your topic?

Selecting a topic that interests you is just the beginning. The most common criticism of a research paper is that its topic is too broad. A Cornell professor of English suggests this method for narrowing your topic: Put your subject through three or four significant narrowings, moving from a given category to a class within that category each time. This method is similar to the Silver Dollar System (see Chapter 11), which enables you to select the most important ideas from your notes.

For example, if you select natural disasters as the topic for a ten- to fifteen-page research paper, you have to narrow the scope of your topic before you can cover it in adequate depth. Three narrowings will probably reduce the subject down to a manageable size, although four may be necessary.

General Topic: Natural Disasters
First narrowing: earthquakes
Second narrowing: earthquake prediction
Third narrowing: scientific developments in earthquake prediction
Fourth narrowing: computer simulations in earthquake prediction

How can you use concept maps to help you narrow your topic?

Concept maps, which are explained in Chapter 8 and are similar to those at the beginning of each chapter, can be used to "visually" narrow a topic. Write your general subject on a blank sheet of paper and circle it. Next write down subtopics of your general subject, circle each, and connect them with lines to the general subject. Then write and circle subtopics of your subtopics. At this point, you may have a suitably narrow subject. If not, keep adding levels of subtopics until you arrive at one. (See Figure 14.1.) The advantage of narrowing your topic with a concept map is that you provide yourself with a number of alternate topics should your original topic choice prove unworkable.

Finding a Focus

What is the purpose of finding a focus for your topic?

Once you've narrowed your topic, give your research direction and purpose by developing a compelling question about that topic. The information you gather from your research can then be used to develop an answer. For the topic "The use of computer simulations in earthquake prediction," you might ask, "How helpful are computer simulations in earthquake prediction?"

Why is posing a research question important?

Whether you actually arrive at a definitive answer to your research question isn't crucial. The important thing is to focus your research efforts on answering the broad question.

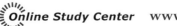

Figure 14.1
Using a Concept Map to Narrow a Topic

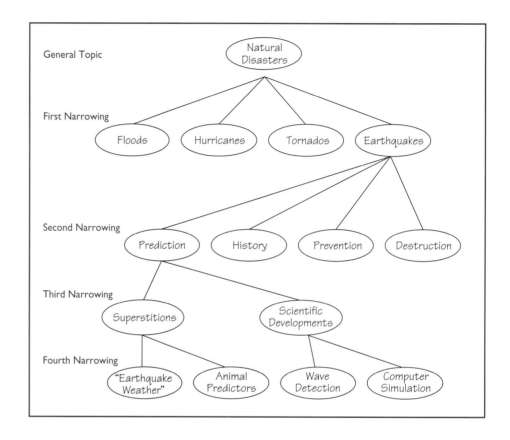

Gathering Information
=====================

What does gathering
information require?

The next step in your research is to begin gathering information. That requires knowing where to look (and knowing what you're looking for), assembling a working bibliography, and then taking detailed notes.

Knowing Where to Look

Where should you look to find material for your paper?

Unless you're using firsthand information—from interviews or experiments—nearly all your material will come from the library (although depending on the nature of your topic, some of it may be found on the Web as well). During this stage of your investigation, the library's most valuable resources will be the reference librarian, indexes, periodicals, and books.

Get Help from the Reference Librarian

How can a reference librarian help?

Before you begin your research, as well as any time during the process when you hit a snag, seek out the reference librarian. Although librarians may not be experts on your particular subject, they *are* experts at using the library's research tools. Librarians can often suggest indexes or databases you may not have heard of, sources you didn't think to consult, and searching strategies you didn't try.

Consult Periodical Indexes

Why is it helpful to consult periodical indexes first?

It's wise to consult the articles that relate to your paper topic before you begin to delve into books. Not only do periodicals frequently provide the most recent information on a subject; sometimes they supply the *only* information. In addition, articles often include important names and titles that relate to your subject and occasionally provide a valuable overview of your topic. There are several general and specific indexes—both computerized and bound—for periodicals.

How do computerized magazine indexes work?

Using Computerized Indexes   Most libraries use computerized magazine indexes that enable you to type in the name of a subject, author, or title and receive a list of relevant articles. You should also be able to customize your search with keywords and/or Boolean searching.

Keyword search.   Unless you know the title of a specific article, keywords usually provide the most direct route to the kinds of articles you are seeking, especially when searching by subject isn't convenient or fruitful. For example, if you want information about Gregg Toland, the cinematographer who worked with Orson Welles on the movie *Citizen Kane*, you may come up empty if you use the subjects "Toland" or "Citizen Kane" in your search. The database simply may not have enough articles on these topics to justify a separate subject heading. If, however, you search for articles under a broader subject, such as "Motion pictures—American," you may have to scan through hundreds of citations before you find appropriate ones. With a keyword search, by contrast, you can type in a word (or name) such as "Toland," and the computer will reply with every article in its database that contains the keyword you have typed.

What is a Boolean search?

Boolean search.   A Boolean search enables you to narrow your search by combining two or more keywords. Suppose you need information about the Detroit Lions football team. If you searched under the subject "Detroit," "Football," or "Lions," you would have to scan thousands of citations that have nothing to do with your particular topic. But by searching for titles that contain all three keywords—"Detroit," "Football," and "Lions"—you are likelier to pinpoint articles that deal directly with your topic. Depending on the type of search engine you're using, you may need to specify that you want your result to include *all*

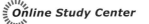

the keywords, instead of one or more. Sometimes this is done by inserting the word AND between the keywords: "Detroit AND Football AND Lions" Most search screens, whether they're specific to your library or available on the Web, will include a button that says "Advanced Search" or something similar. Clicking on this button should provide you with more information about the search engine's rules and capabilities.

What is the most useful bound index?

Use Bound Indexes   Despite the abundance of computerized options for searching periodicals, some bound indexes remain. The most useful of these is the *Readers' Guide to Periodical Literature*. Each volume lists by author and subject all the articles that appeared in several dozen magazines during a given year. To locate articles on your topic, consult the years in which you think those articles may have been published. Each entry in the *Readers' Guide* gives you the information you need to locate the appropriate journal or magazine.

What kinds of articles have their own indexes?

Your paper topic may pertain to a subject that has its own index. For example, if you are doing research in psychology, you can refer to several indexes that deal specifically with psychology and that include journals and magazines that aren't listed in the *Readers' Guide*. A number of other subjects, such as business and education, have their own indexes. In addition, large newspapers such as the *New York Times* publish indexes of their articles.

Consult Book Indexes

What are your search options in book indexes?

Although some libraries may consolidate their search tools, books usually have their own indexes. Like the traditional card catalogs that came before them, computer-based catalogs usually allow you to search for a book based on its subject, title, or author. In addition, most computer catalogs include advanced commands similar to those used with the periodical index that allow for keyword and Boolean searching. Many college libraries now allow you to search their collections from any browser. If yours works this way, you can get a head start on compiling a list of possible references before you even set foot in the library. That should put you in a more knowledgeable position should you need to ask the reference librarian for additional assistance.

How can you make your search more efficient if your library still uses a card catalog?

If for some reason your library still has just a paper card catalog, you can sometimes use the Internet to help make your search more efficient. Start by conducting an Internet search either from home or at the library to come up with an extensive list of possible sources, taking advantage of the keyword searching that you wouldn't be able to use in a card catalog. You won't be able to search your library's specific holdings, of course, but you will be able to arrive at a pretty good list of books in print on your subject. Then, with a printout of your list, go to your library's card catalog and see which books are actually available. This hybrid search should make your time at the card catalog more efficient.

Assembling a Working Bibliography

What is a working
bibliography?

As you discover books, magazines, newspapers, journals, and websites that relate to your research, add them to a *working bibliography*—a list of promising sources that you plan to consult. Be generous in compiling your list. It's better to check out several references that do not help than to miss a good one because its title isn't appealing.

How should you list the
references for a working
bibliography?

Instead of listing all these references on a large sheet of paper, you can use a separate index card for each reference. Then later on, if you decide that a particular reference doesn't help, you can simply throw away its card.

What information belongs on
the front of each bibliography
index card?

Figure 14.2 provides an efficient format for putting your bibliography on index cards. On the front of the card, record the following information:

For sources you find at a library, write the library's name on your card.

A short title of your subject. A title will make it easier to locate a particular card and will aid in clustering your information.

A unique identifier. For books (and some periodicals) that will usually be the library call number. For sources you found on the Web, that will be the URL (Web address).

The reference information—that is, the author, title, publishing data, and any page references—in exactly the form that you plan to use it in the bibliographical portion of your paper. This ensures that you will include all the essential parts of the reference and that typing your paper will be much easier.

Olin Library	Theories of Memory	Bottom-up and top-down theories of memory described in Chapter 18.
Q 360 .C33	Campbell, Jeremy	Refers back to previous chapters and is difficult to read in spots. Provides solid summary of the two theories.
	Grammatical Man. New York: Simon & Schuster, Inc., 1982.	Uses simple, vivid examples to explain difficult points.

Index Card with Data   **Reverse of an Index Card with Comments**

Figure 14.2
Working Bibliography: Index Card Method

Online Study Center   www.college.hmco.com/pic/pauk9e

What information belongs on the back of each bibliography index card?

On the back of the card, jot down your assessment of the reference. If the source doesn't seem useful, then briefly explain why. If the source appears helpful, jot down how. Then when you have a chance to take another look at the article or book, you'll know why you thought it would or would not be useful. And if you shift the focus of your paper, you'll be able to determine whether sources you had eliminated should now be consulted and whether previously promising sources will no longer be of help.

Taking Notes

What qualities should you strive for in the notes that you take?

Using your bibliography as a springboard, you can investigate your sources and begin taking notes. There's no getting around it—taking notes is time consuming. But if your notes are easy to use, neat, brief, and accurate, then the bulk of your paper will be written by the time you have completed the note-taking step.

Make Sure Your Notes Are Easy to Use

How can you make sure your notes are easy to use?

To make your notes easy to use, jot each note on a separate piece of paper rather than writing them one after the other on regular-sized sheets. Index cards are commonly used for notes, although you can use slips of paper instead. Whether you use cards or slips, you will be able to rearrange them easily and often because each note is separate.

Why are paper notes superior to those taken on a computer?

Assuming you're going to write your paper on a computer, it can be tempting to take your notes on one as well. Resist the temptation. Here's why. Although software has been developed that mimics many of the characteristics of index cards, the fact is that there's no program currently available that's as flexible and as portable as a simple stack of cards or paper slips. As you're organizing your paper, you're going to want to be able to shuffle your cards easily and arrange them in stacks on the desk or table in front of you. You may want to be able to quickly shift a card from one stack to another, suddenly write a new card or slip, or tear one up and toss it in the trash. Some programmers have written thousands of lines of computer code to simulate these actions, but their programs cost money and don't work nearly as well as ordinary pieces of paper. It's also true that you can "write" your cards on a computer and then, depending on your printer, print them out on ordinary index cards or on special (expensive) index card paper, but this maneuver just complicates a relatively simple process. You could also conceivably just type your notes into one or more computer files and then shift them around by cutting and pasting or dragging and dropping. But there is lots of information on a regular note card that would get in the way if you had to include it in a document file along with the text of each card.

What else can you do to make your notes easy to use?

Another way to make your notes easier to use is by conscientiously identifying each card or slip. In the top left corner, write the author's name or the title of the source you consulted. Then at the bottom right, jot down the specific page on which you found the information. With these two markings on every note card, you can easily verify or add to any information you've gathered for your paper. In addition, you'll have all the information you may need for your citations (see Figure 14.3).

Keep Your Note Cards Neat

Detailed notes are useless if you can't read them. Write your notes neatly the first time, even if it takes a little longer to do so. Use the modified printing system (see Chapter 10) to write quickly but legibly, and write in pen, instead of pencil, to avoid smears and fading.

Keep Your Note Cards Brief

Why should you keep your note cards brief?

Brevity is the secret behind a useful note card. If a note card contains several key ideas instead of just one, you're going to find it harder to organize your paper when the time comes. Get to the heart of the matter with each note you take. Make your notes concise, yet sufficiently detailed to provide accurate meaning.

What is one simple way to limit the length of each note card?

One simple way to limit the length of each note card is by abbreviating common words. For example, use *w/* instead of "with," *co.* instead of "company," and *govt* in place of "government." Develop your own abbreviations for words you commonly use. For example, if you're doing research on earthquakes, you may want to use *RS* to stand for "Richter scale" and *tct plates* to abbreviate "tectonic plates." Be careful not to go overboard with abbreviations, however. Abbreviating words may save you time to begin with, but you don't want to waste that time later trying to decipher your unfamiliar shorthand.

Figure 14.3
Detailed Note Written on One Side of an Index Card

Campbell

Hemispheres of a normal brain are connected by a bundle of fibers called the corpus callosum.

(p. 240)

Online Study Center www.college.hmco.com/pic/pauk9e

Strive for Accuracy

What steps can you take to ensure that your notes are accurate?

Because you're dealing in facts, you must make certain that the information you jot down is accurate. It's relatively easy to remember as you're taking notes who said what and which of the thoughts you are writing down are your own and which are the thoughts of the author. But between the time you fill your last note card and the moment you write the first line of your paper, you're liable to forget these crucial details. To counteract forgetting and to ensure the information in your paper is accurate, distinguish clearly on your note cards between quoted ideas and paraphrased ideas and between the writer's thoughts and your own.

How should you treat quotations that you add into your notes?

Copy Quotations Carefully　When you quote from a book or an article, make sure that you do so carefully. Place quotation marks on your card around the exact words you copied from the reference. Compare your version with the original quotation to make sure you copied it correctly. Don't change the wording or the spelling of the author's quotation. If you find a misspelling or a grammatical error in the quotation, you may use the bracketed notation [sic] to make it clear to your reader that you're aware of the mistake.

What should you do if you leave out part of a quotation?

If you leave out a section or even one word from a quote, use three ellipsis points (. . .) to indicate the omission. If the words you left out came at the end of a sentence, add a period before the ellipses.

What is the purpose of an ellipsis?

The purpose of an ellipsis is to leave out information that doesn't relate to the point you are using the quotation to support. An ellipsis should not be used to rearrange a quotation simply to suit your needs. Ellipses are intended to abbreviate a quotation, not alter its meaning.

What happens if you come up with your own ideas as you're taking notes from a source?

Mark Thoughts of Your Own　Some of your best ideas may occur as you're taking notes. Put these thoughts on paper right away, but do so on a separate card or slip marked "my idea" or something similar. That way you'll be sure not to confuse your original ideas with the ones you've encountered in your reading.

What should you do with notes that paraphrase material you've found in a source?

Paraphrase What You Read　Although it is important to distinguish your original ideas from the ones you have read, there's nothing wrong with paraphrasing—expressing someone else's ideas in your own words—as long as you give proper credit to the source. If you paraphrase as you take notes, you'll often be able to transfer what you've written in your notes to your draft without changing a word.

Devising a Framework

How can you devise a framework for your paper?

You can devise a solid framework for your paper out of a pile of disconnected notes by deciding on a basic premise, clustering your notes under a handful of main ideas, and plotting out a clear and logical organizational pattern.

Deciding on a Basic Premise

What is a paper's premise and how can you arrive at one?

In the same way that choosing a focus helped provide direction for your research, deciding on a basic *premise* from the notes you now have lays the foundation for your paper's organization. Potential arguments, apparent similarities, and possible theories all have a way of rising to the surface in the process of taking notes. Any of these can be used to form a basic premise, which is the fundamental approach that underlies your paper. If a premise doesn't become obvious to you as you're taking notes, go back over the information and ask yourself some hard questions. For example:

Where is this paper heading?
What are the ramifications of the information I've assembled?
What point is most important?
What am I saying?
What do I want to say?
If there's a choice of viewpoint—for or against a question, for example—which view has the most evidence to support it?

If you've done a good job of research, you should be able to decide now what you want to say in your paper, and you should have the evidence in your notes to support that view.

Clustering Your Notes

How does the paper's premise influence the way you cluster your notes?

The paper's basic premise should act as a magnet for clustering your notes, which enables you to draw out the most important ideas from the dozens and perhaps hundreds of notes you have written. In most cases, a research paper should incorporate fewer than seven main ideas. These ideas will form the framework for your paper. The cards or slips that remain won't be wasted but will be used as support for the more important ideas. Of course, if a note isn't important enough to be considered a main idea and doesn't provide support for the main ideas, that note should be left out of your paper.

Online Study Center www.college.hmco.com/pic/pauk9e

How do you decide on the most important ideas in your notes?

Choosing the main ideas and clustering your research notes require selectivity, the same skill you used not only in narrowing your original paper topic, but in studying conventional notes as well (see Chapter 11). In fact, if you find it difficult to pick out a handful of main ideas from a pile of notes, apply the following three-step system to help pinpoint the pillars that will form your paper's supports.

1. Read through your notes and pick out those cards or slips that seem more important than the others.
2. Now that you have two piles of notes instead of one, pick up the smaller pile and repeat the process, pulling out the most important notes and using them to make up a third pile.
3. Finally, pick up the third pile, which by now should contain only a dozen or so cards or slips, and find four or five ideas that seem to be the most important ones. These ideas will be the basis of your premise and of the pattern for your paper.

Plotting an Organizational Pattern

What are the factors that influence how you plot an organizational pattern?

Your basic premise and personal choice largely determine the pattern your paper will follow. You could use any of the organizational patterns listed in Chapter 10 as the framework for your paper. The time pattern or the process pattern is appropriate for most college papers. For some papers, however, you may be required to develop an argument. A good pattern for such papers is to begin with a statement of your premise and then support it with logical examples that build to a conclusion. This kind of organization affords more flexibility than the others.

What techniques can you use to help arrive at a pattern for your paper?

You may need to experiment with several patterns before you arrive at a framework that adequately accommodates the information you want to include in your paper. Don't be discouraged by the inevitable period of trial and error. There's no one "correct" way of plotting your paper. You may feel most comfortable using a traditional outline. Or you may find the process of mapping easier and more enjoyable.

How can you use mapping to come up with your paper's organization?

To map out your research paper, use the notes that contain your paper's main ideas and sub-ideas (or jot these ideas down on small slips of paper). On a clear surface such as a desk or a tabletop, shift these ideas around like checkers on a checkerboard, clustering them in various ways, according to the premise of your paper.

How does your paper's pattern influence the way you create your map?

If you're planning to structure your paper using the time or process pattern, arrange your ideas so they follow logically from the earliest to the latest or from the start of the process to the end. If you're structuring your paper as an argument, decide which of the major points should be made first; then arrange the remaining points in an order that will make your argument smooth, logical, and easy to follow.

What sorts of patterns do the maps that begin this book's chapters normally use?

The chapter maps in this book provide examples of the process and argument patterns. The map in this chapter, for example, uses the process pattern, spelling out in order the steps for writing a research paper. The map for the text's Chapter 3, in contrast, develops an argument; it asserts a premise—staying focused involves eliminating distractions and cultivating concentration—and then goes on to explain the role of each.

What should you do with the notes that deal with minor points in your paper?

When you arrive at an arrangement that incorporates your information and makes logical sense, you have found a suitable pattern for your paper. Once you have arranged the cards or slips that contain your major points in an effective order, repeat the procedure by arranging the notes that contain your minor points. Think of each major point as a premise in itself. Then arrange the minor points that support a major point in a clear and effective way.

What happens if you find gaps in the organization of your paper?

If, as you arrange your notes, you find gaps in your organization, you may need to create new categories or perhaps even return to the library or the Internet to take more notes.

How can you make it easier to turn your notes into your paper?

Finally, with all points arranged to your satisfaction, go back and number your note cards or slips according to the order in which they'll appear in your paper.

Writing the Paper

What steps are involved in actually writing your paper?

You already have most of your paper worked out—information, sources, organization. Now all you have to do is put your data into sentences and paragraphs and work up a first draft of your paper. Once that is accomplished, allow yourself plenty of time to go back and revise and edit what you've written, add the missing elements, and type the final copy.

Racing Through the First Draft

**YOUR
Q**

The best way to start writing is simply to write. Pausing with your pen poised over an empty page or with your fingers resting idly on a keyboard waiting for inspiration to strike is a useless endeavor. Inspiration, like concentration, seldom comes when you call it. Once your hands are engaged in the physical motions of writing, your brain will follow.

How should you handle alternatives that occur to you as you're writing?

Write your first draft as rapidly and spontaneously as possible. To ensure continuity, record your thoughts as they go through your mind. Don't stop to ponder alternatives. Although you will probably write too much, don't be concerned; it's easier to cut than it is to add.

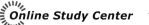 *Online Study Center*   www.college.hmco.com/pic/pauk9e

What is the procedure for moving through your notes as you write your draft?

In your first draft your goal is simply to transfer information from your notes to your paper or computer screen. Take each card or slip in order and write. Start with major point one. State what it is, and then use supporting evidence to show why it is so. As you use a reference from the card, note the card number on your paper. You can put the footnotes in later, taking the exact information from the card. Continue to write, following your organized and numbered notes.

Once you've finished your first draft, what should you do next?

Only after you've completed your first draft should you step back and take a look at what you've written. If you typed your draft using a computer, either print out a hard copy so you can jot down your comments or use the word processing program's comment function to insert any thoughts directly into your text. Regardless of the form your first draft takes, go over it carefully in search of possible changes, adding words or phrases and highlighting paragraphs you want to move or remove.

How should you handle any comments, insertions, or deletions that you've added to your draft?

While your annotations are still fresh in your mind, produce a clear copy that incorporates all your changes. Don't wait before adding in these corrections. If you delay even a day, you may lose a lot of time trying to recall exactly what you meant by some of your comments. And if you update your draft while it's still fresh, you may find that you do some spontaneous revision.

What should you do with your draft once you've updated it?

Once you have made these changes, put your draft aside for a while. To gain objectivity about what is in the paper and what is still missing, you need a cooling off period of at least a day. When you return to your paper, you'll then more easily spot errors and weaknesses in your writing.

Revising and Editing Your Paper

What should you be trying to accomplish in later drafts of your paper?

The hardest part of writing a research paper is completing the first draft. From that point on, you'll be refining what you've already written. In the next drafts—and you may write two, three, or even four drafts before you are satisfied with your paper—you'll focus on strengthening supporting evidence and fine-tuning technical details such as transitions, grammar, and spelling.

Strengthen Supporting Evidence

What are the guidelines for supporting the points in your paper?

Students often state a main point and then go on to something else without supporting it. The kinds of evidence you need to support a major point are statistics, quotations from other published works, facts, examples, comparisons and contrasts in views, expert opinion, and description. If you make statements and follow them up with generalities, you will not convince your reader that your main point is true. Use what you have collected on your cards to support your points. Using examples, Figure 14.4 shows the steps you can take to develop a major point.

**Figure 14.4
Strengthening Supporting
Details**

1. **State your point clearly.**
   The two sides of the human brain perform distinct functions.

2. **Develop the point beyond a brief statement.**
   According to the theory of brain laterality, the left hemisphere of the brain handles analytical thinking, while the right hemisphere is the home of abstract thought.

3. **Support with data from authorities and with statistics.**
   Drs. Michael Gazzaniga and Roger Sperry found that the cerebral hemispheres process information differently (add reference here). Subsequent research determined that the brain's left and right sides contrast information that is symbolic and conceptual versus information that is nonsymbolic and directly perceived.

4. **Illustrate with examples.**
   For example, if you were to add up a column of numbers, you would probably be using the left side of your brain. But if you were sketching a picture, you would be engaging the right side.

What should you do if you can't find enough evidence to support one of your main points?

Why won't padding work to make your paper longer?

Be sure that all the main points are supported equally with this kind of evidence. If you can't find enough evidence to support one point, perhaps it's not a major one. You may need to reorganize the structure of your paper to include that point under one of the other major points.

Avoid padding. You may be tempted to add words or to rephrase a point to make the paper longer. Such padding is obvious to the reader, who's looking for logical arguments and good sense, and will not improve your grade. If you haven't enough evidence to support a statement, leave it out or get more information.

Fine-Tune Technical Details

What are some of the technical details in your paper that may require fine-tuning?

Although awkward transitions, clumsy grammar, and poor spelling may not affect the basic meaning of your paper, they do affect the reader's perception of how you have thought about your topic and what you have written.

Provide Transitions   In writing your paper, consider how to help your readers move easily from one main point to the next. If they feel that there's no connection, they will find it hard to follow the logical sequence that you have established in your own mind. You must therefore use transitional words and phrases to make your paper easy to follow. (See Chapter 10 for a list of these words.) Check carefully for transitions, and insert them where they are needed.

What should you do if you aren't sure whether your paper is grammatically correct?

Correct Grammar   Students who use the English language correctly get their ideas across to other people more clearly and forcibly than do those who stumble over every sentence. Moreover, students who apply the rules of grammar in

their papers earn better grades. If you are unsure about these rules or careless with them, your meaning may get lost. If you feel that you could use a review of grammar, there are good texts that provide answers for most of your grammatical questions. Some of them are even fun to read.

Here's a brief list of some popular books on English grammar:

Casagrande, June. *Grammar Snobs Are Great Big Meanies: A Guide to Language for Fun and Spite*. New York: Penguin, 2006.

Diamond, Harriet, and Phyllis Dutwin. *Grammar in Plain English*, 4th ed. New York: Barron's Educational Series, 2005.

Glenn, Cheryl, et al. *Hodges' Harbrace Handbook*, 15th ed. Belmont, Calif.: Thompson Learning, 2004.

O'Conner, Patricia. *Woe Is I: The Grammarphobe's Guide to Better English in Plain English*. New York: Riverhead Books, 2003.

Shertzer, Margaret D. *The Elements of Grammar*. New York: Macmillan Publishing, 1996.

Strumpf, Michael. *The Grammar Bible: Everything You Always Wanted to Know About Grammar But Didn't Know Whom to Ask*. New York: Holt, 2004.

How can you remedy the spelling problems in your paper?

Check Spelling   If your spelling problems are not severe, you will find a dictionary helpful. If your spelling is poor, look for one of the paperback books that list the most commonly misspelled words. If you cannot recognize that you are spelling words incorrectly, have someone who is good at spelling read your paper and mark, not correct, the words that are wrong. Then look up and insert the correct spellings. If you do this conscientiously over a period of time, you will improve your spelling.

What are the pitfalls of relying on a spell checker?

Of course, if you are writing your paper using a computer, you can use a spell-checking program to pinpoint your spelling mistakes. The spell checker compares each word you have typed with the words stored in its dictionary and calls your attention to words that don't appear there. Although the computer can catch many of your spelling errors, it isn't infallible. The size of the dictionary is limited, and the spell checker is unable to recognize words that are spelled correctly but used incorrectly (such as *there* instead of *their*).

Adding the Missing Elements

What elements will make your paper complete?

Having revised and edited your writing, you can now add the missing elements that will make your paper complete. Because your paper is a research paper, you must give credit for your information by including citations and a bibliography. In addition, the paper will need a title, an introduction, and a conclusion.

Give Credit Where It's Needed

What should you do to properly credit your paper?

To avoid any appearance of plagiarism and to demonstrate the depth of your research, attribute quoted or paraphrased material and include a bibliography.

What constitutes plagiarism?

Don't Plagiarize Plagiarism is stealing other people's words and ideas and making them appear to be your own. It need not be as blatant as copying whole passages without giving credit. If you paraphrase something from already published material and do not cite your source, you're guilty of plagiarism even though you may have no intention of stealing. Simply rearranging sentences or rephrasing a little without crediting is still plagiarism.

How do instructors detect plagiarism in a paper?

Those who grade papers are quick to notice a change in writing style from one of your papers to another or from one part of your paper to another. Your writing is like your fingerprints—individual. If you try to use another's work, his or her style will not match the rest of your paper, and the difference will be obvious. If you stole some sentences or paragraphs outright, your theft will be easy to detect, especially if you took from material that is available on the Internet. (A Web-savvy instructor or teaching assistant can usually just type a suspicious phrase into a search engine and quickly locate its original source.) Instructors may give you the benefit of the doubt if they cannot prove where you got plagiarized material. But if they can—and doing so is usually not difficult—plagiarism can be grounds for expulsion from college. In a world where the written word is a major product, stealing it from someone else is a serious offense.

What approaches can you take to credit quoted or paraphrased material in your paper?

Include Citations Avoid plagiarism by crediting material you've quoted or paraphrased to its source. You may include a credit right after the quoted material, within the body of the paper, in a format like this: (Jones 2003, p. 264). This citation refers to page 264 of the work by Jones that was published in 2003 and is listed in your bibliography. Or you can use a superscript 1 and cite the full source at the bottom of the page or in a complete listing at the end of the paper. Credits that appear at the bottom of the page are called *footnotes*. Figure 14.5 shows a format for footnotes and for credits at the end of the paper. References are numbered in the order in which they appear in your paper. Other forms are given in handbooks on English usage.

Figure 14.5
Format for Footnotes and End-of-Paper Credits

> 1. Richard Webster, *Why Freud Was Wrong* (New York: Basic Books, 1995), pp. 136–154.
> 2. Glenn Alan Cheney, *Journey to Chernobyl* (Chicago, Ill.: Academy Chicago Publishers, 1995), p. 107.

Online Study Center 　www.college.hmco.com/pic/pauk9e

What should go into your bibliography?

Supply a Bibliography The bibliography lists the sources you cite in your credits and may include other books or published material that you read as background for the paper but did not quote. A bibliography is not "notes," "endnotes," or "sources." It is a listing of the books that you used in preparing the paper, and you should use the correct title for this listing. When you compile the bibliography, use the index cards you prepared earlier. Each entry should include enough information so that a reader can identify the work and find it in a library or on the Web.

What format should you use for your bibliography

Entries are listed alphabetically by author. Different bibliographic forms are used in different fields of study. Either select a standard form from a handbook on English usage, or follow the form used in one of the journals on your subject.

Ask your reference librarian to assist you in finding the style manual for a specific field such as biology, chemistry, law, mathematics, physics, psychology, and so forth.

The following three widely used general style manuals will provide you with a form for your citations and bibliography:

Gibaldi, Joseph. *MLA Handbook for Writers of Research Papers*, 6th ed. New York: The Modern Language Association of America, 2003.

The Chicago Manual of Style. 15th ed. Chicago: University of Chicago Press, 2003.

Publication Manual of the American Psychological Association, 5th ed. Washington, D.C.: American Psychological Association, 2001.

No matter what form you use, follow it consistently for every entry in your bibliography. Figure 14.6 shows a common bibliographic form.

**Figure 14.6
Format for a Bibliography**

Bibliography

Carlson, Karen J., Eisenstat, Stephanie A., and Ziporyn, Terra. *The Harvard Guide to Women's Health*. Cambridge, Mass.: Harvard University Press, 1996.

Field, Shelly. *100 Best Careers for the 21st Century*. New York: Macmillan, 1996.

Hanke, Steve H. "The Stagnation Myth," *Forbes* 157 (April 22, 1996): 145–146.

Krefetz, Gerald. *Read and Profit from Financial News*. 2nd ed. Dearborn, Mich.: Dearborn Financial Publishing, 1995.

Maughan, Jackie Johnson, ed. *Go Tell It on the Mountain*. Mechanicsburg, Pa.: Stackpole Books, 1996.

Quammen, David. *The Song of the Dodo*. New York: Scribner, 1996.

Wertheimer, Neil, ed. *Total Health for Men*. Emmaus, Pa.: Rodale Press, 1995.

Choose a Suitable Title

How do you choose a title for your paper?

It is often a good idea to wait until you have written the paper before you decide on a title. Although the title should reflect the content of the paper, you can give it an interesting twist or perhaps make use of part of a quotation that seems particularly appropriate. Of course, there's nothing wrong with a straightforward title. In many cases, a no-nonsense title that gets straight to the point is your best choice.

Write an Introduction

What sort of information should go into your paper's introduction?

The paper's premise serves as the basis of the introduction. In revising your paper, you can expand on this premise and come up with the introduction in its final form. In addition to stating your premise, the introduction explains how you plan to support it and can include an apt example, anecdote, or quotation. Choose any of these devices carefully; they must be right on target. If you're not sure they will contribute to the paper, then write a straightforward statement.

State a Conclusion

Why do you need a conclusion for your paper?

Don't end the paper without a concluding passage. If you do, your readers will be left dangling, wondering what happened to you and the rest of the paper. Let them know they have come to the end.

What is the primary purpose of a conclusion?

By now, all your major points should have been made and adequately supported. The primary purpose of your conclusion is to restate or summarize your basic premise. In addition, you may want to use your premise to draw a related conclusion. For example, if your premise states that alcohol is one of the country's leading causes of death and your paper has supported that contention with data and examples, you may choose to conclude with some suggestions for dealing with the problem of alcohol abuse:

Taxes on alcoholic beverages should be increased.
Beer, wine, and liquor companies should be made to subsidize alcohol treatment programs.
Americans must overcome their tendency toward self-destructive, addictive behavior.
Alcohol education should begin at the elementary school level.

How does the conclusion differ from the rest of your paper?

Although the rest of your paper should be backed up with information you discovered through research, the conclusion affords you the opportunity to state your own opinion and draw a personal conclusion. In general, of course, the kind of conclusion you write depends on the paper and the subject. In most cases, the conclusion need not be long and involved. But be certain you include one.

Printing the Final Copy

What are the guidelines for printing out your final copy?

All the time and energy you have spent on your research paper should be reflected in the appearance of the final copy. Make it neat, clean, and attractive.

1. Use only one side of white paper. Although instructors seldom specify, most assume that your paper will be printed on 8-1/2 × 11–inch sheets.
2. Leave a generous margin at the top and bottom of each page and a margin of 1-1/2 inches on both sides to provide room for the instructor's comments.
3. Type your paper or have someone type it for you. Of course, if you've composed your paper on a computer, simply print it out. Handwritten papers are time consuming to produce, difficult to read, and are rarely accepted.
4. Set up long, direct quotations (of five or more lines) in block style—that is, single-space and indent the lines from both sides about a half inch or five spaces. Omit the quotation marks when you block a quotation in this way—the block setup shows that you are quoting.
5. Proofread your final copy. Go over it carefully to catch spelling errors and other minor flaws. Don't rely entirely on a spell checker. This is a very important step.

FINAL WORDS

How is writing a research paper like running a marathon?

Even the most experienced writers can find writing a research paper to be a challenge. After all, unlike taking notes, answering test questions, participating in a discussion, or even writing an essay, writing a paper can take weeks and even months. If the other components that make up your semester grade can be considered sprints, writing a research paper is the marathon. But if you take a hint from the long-distance runner by working systematically and pacing yourself throughout, when you finally reach the finish you'll have something that you can be proud of.

My First Research Paper
By Walter Pauk

Registration was like a game of chess. The smart students made their moves early. Some lined up before dawn, while others used the university's new computerized system to register from home. They registered early, not especially to get the best courses, but to avoid being "stuck" with one—the one taught by Professor Wilbur Hendricon.

The word on the grapevine was that this was a course to be avoided by the faint of heart. The chances of being forced into Professor Hendricon's course were slim but still too terrifying to take a chance. Professor Hendricon had, as the students said, "a special deal with the administration." He could handpick twenty-five students for his class, but had to take another ten at general registration.

This unusual procedure was a compromise. It came about this way: Professor Hendricon had originally taught only graduate courses; but ten years ago he decided that he would like to teach one section of English 105. So Professor Hendricon suddenly proclaimed to the dean that he would take twenty-five first-year students and turn them into scholars.

The dean was faced with a dilemma. On the one hand, the proud and sensitive Hendricon might take a negative answer as a rude rebuff. Also, the dean thought, "If he resigns, I will have to answer to the president." Hendricon was the university's brilliant light and other universities eagerly tried to woo him. On the other hand, a positive answer would be a blow to the morale of the other members of the English Department, who had no choice but to take their usual thirty-five students per class. The dean consulted her colleagues and persuaded them to accept the compromise. Needless to say, I was one of the unlucky ten.

Right from the very first day in class, I could see how well Hendricon had chosen. The twenty-five were geniuses. I later discovered that they all had straight As in high school and that they were clustered at the top of the scholarship list. Furthermore, they excelled in language and literature, while my strengths were in mathematics and music. Math skills and musical talent did not count for much in an English course.

At first I thought Professor Hendricon's legendary standards might just be rumor, but after the first test any hopes evaporated. We unfortunate ten compared notes and found our grades in the 30s and 40s. But no one questioned Professor Hendricon's honesty and sincerity. Our papers were filled with notations, symbols, and helpful comments. We did, however, question his standards. They were not for us mere mortals. Six of the ten transferred to other sections of the course immediately; the other three students transferred after the second test. Everyone knew that transferring was possible. The other instructors expected to get all ten of us in their classes within the first few weeks of term. In this way, morale was preserved, because administratively, at least, all the classes started out with thirty-five students each.

Perhaps it was the lemming instinct in me or perhaps it was Hendricon's appeal, but I decided to hang in. On the day after the last date for changing classes, I took my usual seat. The other twenty-five students, who usually chatted loudly until Professor Hendricon entered the door, were strangely silent today. You see, in all these past ten years, not one of the unchosen had ever stayed in Hendricon's class. Everyone knew this.

We could hear Hendricon's brisk but firm footsteps drawing closer to the open door. The pace was faster than usual. We saw the toe of his left foot puncture the blank space of the doorway. The blood was pounding at my temples. My breathing was fast and shallow. Hendricon always walked straight to the lectern, put down his notes, and said, "Good afternoon" to the class. As he entered today, he glanced at me with a curious look. He did not greet the class as usual. He just lectured, but more seriously. I could not keep my mind on the lecture. No one could. It seemed that I had spoiled the atmosphere of this select club. Why had I not been less foolhardy?

On Monday, however, the class resumed its normal pace and atmosphere. I was present but not accepted. The chosen twenty-five sat in a solid square. I sat outside the square, separate but linked like an appendix. But that did not bother me, for I was really fascinated by Professor Hendricon. He was a great teacher. I took copious notes and studied the assignments carefully. I occasionally forgot myself and spoke out during discussions. I worked hard on tests and examinations, but they were never quite up to standard. I could usually understand the ideas and concepts, but time always ran out. I needed more time to think. But I was not discouraged because I was enjoying the course and learning a lot.

It was just after the Christmas holidays that Professor Hendricon announced it. "It" was the research paper—3,500 words and counting for one-third of the final grade. I should have been petrified because I could not write, and yet, I was glad. This was my chance to raise my present hard-earned average of 62.7% to the necessary 70.

This would be the first instance where I would have an advantage over the students—I would have the advantage of time. I needed time. Time is the great equalizer; time is democratic. We all receive the same amount of it every morning. No distinction is made between the genius and the plodder. This is what I told myself; it helped me feel a little better.

There should not have been any excitement because everyone knew about the Hendricon paper. It was indeed another factor that encouraged the rush to register early for other courses. The paper was not due until after the late winter break—almost two months off. But still, there were groans and whisperings. I could hardly hear the professor's caution against plagiarism. "Use both the primary text as well as secondary critical sources," he instructed against a background of restless inattention. Very few paid attention to his next point about thinking carefully before choosing a topic. I somehow caught, "Once you have decided on your topic, it should be narrowed three or four times." What did he mean by this?

After the others had left, I edged up to Professor Hendricon, who was gathering up his lecture notes, and asked about the idea of narrowing the topic. He said, "If, for example, you were doing a history course, and you chose as your topic the 'Civil War,' you would be almost sure to fail. You simply could not do justice to such a large topic—dozens of books would be necessary to cover that subject, not an undergraduate research paper. Even a second narrowing of the topic to the 'Battle of Gettysburg,' a major engagement in the war, would still be too broad. A third stage of narrowing such as the 'Battle of Cemetery Ridge' would be more manageable, but your focus might not be sufficiently defined yet. So perhaps a further narrowing to the 'Tactical Importance of Cemetery Ridge' might be necessary. This would be an aspect of the original broad topic on which adequate information could be found to write an in-depth paper."

I was so excited about writing the term paper that I went straight to the library, eager and determined to find an interesting topic on which to use this technique of narrowing. I was surprised to find the cavernous library so empty of students. But of course, there would be time during "reading week" and the late winter break—there was no pressure yet. I went directly to the reference librarian, who showed me how to use the various special reference books. Another librarian, who joined us, had an interesting idea. She said, "If you choose a subject area carefully in your first year, and continue throughout your university years to research and write in that area, you could probably become quite an expert." This idea intrigued me.

Over the next few days I brainstormed possible topics for my paper. First, I scrutinized Professor Hendricon's course outline, mulling over his lecture themes and the prescribed authors and texts. Then I returned to the library to peruse reference books such as encyclopedias, surveys of literature, and biographical dictionaries. I developed a list of nineteen topics that interested me. I reflected on these over the weekend and after careful deliberation rejected fourteen of them.

The remaining five topics I decided to discuss with Professor Hendricon. He seemed happy to see me. In about five minutes we eliminated two. As far as the other three were concerned, he suggested that I talk about each with professors who were experts in the respective areas.

These talks were especially stimulating. I got to know three new professors from whom I received not only useful insights about narrowing the topics, but also details of important sources and prominent authorities as well. After thinking through the suggestions made by these professors, I settled on the area that was most appealing to me.

I arranged another session with Professor Hendricon to inform him of my decision and to obtain advice on the direction my assignment should take. We discussed the precise purpose of my paper, and, over a cup of tea, we juggled words and finally formulated a challenging question to launch my research. I emerged from his Dickensian study aglow with inspiration and enthusiasm. The stern and serious Hendricon of the lecture hall had a warm and sensitive side that few students had glimpsed.

So, with the topic narrowed and a clear sense of direction established, back to the library I went to search for sources and to start my research. With the first week over I was surprised to find none of the class in the library. During the first term I had learned how to use the library's computerized catalog. Why not explore other searching opportunities offered by the computer system, such as using a keyword to locate titles relevant to the focus of my research? I was amazed at the wealth of material available through the computer catalog, and soon I had an impressive list of titles in my working bibliography. Gaining confidence, I decided to use the CD-ROM databases and discovered several periodical articles pertaining to my research question.

I gathered some of my sources and began taking notes on pages of notebook paper. The reference librarian, ever helpful, wandered over and asked if I knew the advantages of recording my notes on index slips. Without waiting for an answer, she said that the ability to categorize my notes would ensure a much more efficient research system. Her specific suggestions were these:

- Record only one point, or a small cluster of related points, on one card.
- Record only information that is relevant to the purpose of your research.
- Use only one side of the card.
- Each card should indicate the author and page numbers of the source.
- Enclose all verbatim notes in quotation marks.
- Most notes should be paraphrased or summarized.
- Whenever you have a thought or insight of your own, jot it down and enclose it with brackets to signify "my own."

Noticing that I had no slips, she darted to her desk and pulled out the bottom drawer and thumped several rubber-banded stacks of cards on my table. "These are old cards left over when we converted the catalog to a computer system. They are used on only one side. You are welcome to use them for your research notes."

The card method intrigued me and now that I had a wide-ranging list of sources, I was eager to get started on the research. I worked steadily in the library for the next two weeks, averaging two to three hours a day. It was surprisingly easy jotting down important information and ideas on cards and indicating the sources and page numbers. Rather than waste time writing out the author's name or the title on each card, I used a simple coding system to identify each source. I did not have a written outline. I had tried to prepare one after formulating my question, but I could not anticipate the material I would find. I also sensed that it would be too restricting. However, although I did not have an outline, it would be unfair to say that I selected the material for my note cards haphazardly. I selected material that had a bearing on my specific question. Once I immersed myself in the research, I began to sense what was relevant and what was not.

After two weeks, I had a shoebox full of cards. I was ready to start structuring and drafting the paper. During the course of the research I had sketched out a tentative list of sections that might serve as an outline. I stepped back from my intense two-week spell of research to reflect on the provisional outline. Keeping the research question uppermost in my mind, I modified the sections so that they would provide a structure around which I could shape my answer. Next, I read through all my note cards and moved them into categories corresponding to my outline. Having notes on each card that pertained to only one idea permitted me to place the cards in separate categories. If I had put two different notes on one card, I would have had to rewrite the information onto two separate cards now. I was glad that I had a system. It was like playing a card game.

My outline required further modification because not all the cards fitted the major sections. I added another section to accommodate some of the cards, while a number of cards simply did not fit into any of the sections. So, with the cards in categories, I started to follow the second step of the librarian's advice. I began to shift the piles of cards into an order that seemed logical for my paper. It was surprisingly easy to reorder the piles of cards so that there was a logical flow in the sequence of the sections.

With the categories of cards spread out before me, I began to study each category independently to create a detailed outline. As I wrestled with sections, subsections, and supporting material, I began to see where I had gaps in data and weak spots in the argument. My detailed outline revealed plainly the areas in which my paper lacked balance and completeness. My work was cut out for the next few days since I needed specifics that the paper at that point lacked. I was glad that each card carried a reference to the source, so that I could locate not only the source but the precise page as well.

After a few hours of additional research in the library, I was able to augment my note cards. I felt that the more complete I could make my collection of cards, the more effective the first draft would be. I remembered Professor Hendricon's advice: "If you do not gather enough first-class material, you will have trouble writing a major paper." I used some of the new research information to revise and refine my detailed outline.

Finally, I was satisfied with my outline. Then I began to write the first draft. It surprised me to see how easy it is to write a long paper once the material is placed in order. I actually enjoyed the process. It took four days of writing in my spare time to complete the draft. I preferred writing my first draft in longhand because I seemed to think more clearly when writing rather than typing. On each day, I concentrated on writing one of four major parts of the paper. When I had finished, I immediately read it over and it sounded good to me—so good that I knew I would be able to enjoy the late-winter holidays—a wonderful reward. First, I had to type up my draft on the computer, and after backing it up, I printed a copy. I proudly left the copy on my desk to "cool" while I went home for the holidays.

On the last day before we departed for our week's holiday, Professor Hendricon did his duty as a teacher to remind us to work on our papers because they were due five days after our return to campus. The students fidgeted, a nervous laugh or two mingled with some of the spontaneous whispering, but no one said anything. I thought to myself that I had not seen any of the chosen twenty-five in the library; but then they could have been there at other times. Also, the thought struck me that they loved to discuss every moot point and debate hypothetical issues. They seemed to excel at writing creative papers, often at the last minute, with information they already had in their heads. Perhaps a research paper that demanded hard and dogged work was just too rigorous for their creative souls. Well, I just thought these thoughts and was a bit ashamed at my suspicious mind.

Even though I was still failing Professor Hendricon's course, the warm feeling generated by my completed draft provided the tone that I needed to enjoy my holidays. I had a good rest.

I arrived back on campus on Friday to avoid the weekend traffic. That evening, feeling proud of myself, I casually picked up my draft and, to extract the maximum amount of satisfaction from my accomplishment, I began reading. By the time I had finished page 3, my smile had vanished, and by page 10 fear had gripped me. The development of my thesis, which sounded so smooth upon completion, was now disjointed and repetitious and some paragraphs were meaningless. How could that be?

I pacified myself after the initial shock by realizing that I still had seven days, while many of the other students in the class had not even started their papers. Most of them would only arrive back on campus on Sunday evening, and that would leave them but a scant five days. As I pondered how to fix up my research paper, I realized, for the first time, the truth of the words that I had discarded as "teachers' preachings": "No paper should ever be handed in unless you have revised it. For the revision to be effective, you must always put your paper away for a few days so that you will lose some familiarity with it. Then, when you reread it, you will be better able to spot the weaknesses and the rough sections. Once these are spotted, revise, revise, revise."

My paper was certainly rough. I recalled the steps for revising: First, look through the draft to make sure the ideas are understandable and supported by details and examples. Second, make sure the organizational plan for the paper is clear and that the sections follow in logical sequence. Third, check for consistency of style, and, finally, ensure that the mechanics such as spelling and hyphenating are correct. I discovered that I had scattered throughout the paper bits of interesting information—interesting but not always pertinent. I added some of the misplaced material to the introduction and eliminated the rest. It was tough to throw away these gems that I had worked so hard to extract from my sources, but I heard ringing in my ears: "Good writers don't put everything down that is interesting. Remember the iceberg with its nine-tenths underwater and only one-tenth showing above the surface. This submerged part—your background work—gives the iceberg its strength and power."

After weeding out the irrelevant material, I concentrated on the structure of the paper and discovered that it, too, was a bit vague. Parts of the general statement that should have been at the beginning were in the body of the paper. So I sharpened the introduction by stating the thesis and then broke it down to the five main points that I had planned to establish and support. By the time I had reworked the introduction, I really knew for the first time what I was attempting to do. I was shocked to realize that my own understanding of what I was trying to do had not been clear. By the time I went to sleep on Sunday, I had hammered out a clear statement of what I was trying to establish and support.

Monday rolled around all too soon. The vacation was over. There was a lot of activity on campus as students accelerated into a faster tempo of study. Papers were due, final examinations hovered on the horizon, and most plans to complete work during the holidays had fallen through. Hendricon reminded the class of the Friday deadline. There was no whispering this time, just grim silence. I, too, contributed to the silence. I had to write not only a passing paper, but a paper good enough to earn an 85 if I was to raise my average to the passing grade of 70. I had, perhaps, counted too heavily on time and technique. Time was running out and technique was not holding up. But I still had a chance. Most of the chosen twenty-five, I was sure, had not even started.

I worked hard to strengthen the body of the paper by realigning my main sections in the same order as in the statement of thesis in the introduction. I made sure that each main section led off with a brief paragraph that introduced the section. Then I grouped the supporting information in a number of separate paragraphs all focused on the central idea of the section. As I worked through the other sections, checking the paragraph structure, I was surprised to discover that some of the supporting materials were still widely scattered even though I had carefully laid out a sequence when I grouped my note cards. By moving some of the information to more appropriate sections, I was able to eliminate repetition. I reworked each main section, especially those that seemed vague or hastily composed. Occasionally, I dug back into my collection of note cards when an idea needed additional support.

On Tuesday I fashioned a concluding summary that was not repetitious, synthesizing the thesis and key points in such a way to show mastery of the material. After dinner I printed a copy of the complete paper. I was immensely relieved and satisfied when I fell asleep that evening.

After the 9 o'clock class on Wednesday, I was free to devote the whole day to the final editing of the essay. I first read the entire paper aloud, checking for style. By reading aloud I could better detect redundant words, vague phrases, and awkward-sounding sentences. I corrected the flawed sentences so that they flowed smoothly and naturally. As part of the editing process, I made frequent use of a dictionary and a thesaurus to ensure that the vocabulary was precise. Also, I worked on internal transitions to give my paragraphs and sentences better cohesion. After I had edited the printed copy, I corrected the computer version and saved it carefully. I was meticulous in backing up each version in the event that my computer malfunctioned.

i woke early on Thursday, excited to see the final copy in print at last, and printed out my "magnum opus." I was so eager to start proofreading that I toyed with the possibility of skipping my morning lectures. But with final examinations looming, common sense won out! After lectures, I gobbled my lunch down and headed for my room and my prized paper. I proofread it meticulously, from title page to bibliography. All my thoroughness had paid off—not a single error was apparent. I was flushed with that warm feeling of satisfaction that the completion of a creative assignment brings.

This was it. This was the day! I never heard such an outpouring of incidents to a professor from frantic, frightened students who tried so hard to look and act sophisticated. "The library is so full, you can't find a table to write on." "Two other students are working on the same topic as I am and I cannot get hold of the sources." "My computer crashed." "My printer overheated and seized up." "I'll need more time, because all the typists in town are busy, and they can't get to mine until after the weekend."

Hendricon was calm but exceedingly serious. He looked around the room solemnly, making no attempt to answer any of the excuses. After a moment, he held up his hand for quiet and went on with his lecture as if nothing had happened. There was deep silence that hour. Professor Hendricon was always good, but he was especially good that day. He talked hard and earnestly. Most of the students sat glumly, motionless and glassy-eyed. Only a few had the discipline to take notes. For some reason, the professor's words seemed to be aimed at me. He was trying to make scholars of us, as well as mature men and women. About half the students handed in papers that day. Spurred by the announcement, "Five points a day will be deducted on all late papers," the rest were in on the following Monday. I was pleased and proud that mine was in on time.

With only two and a half weeks to go, Professor Hendricon lectured hard and fast, determined to complete his schedule of topics. By now, I had reconciled myself that failure was a possibility. Though I still wanted to pass the course, I was not too worried about it. I was just glad to have had the opportunity to attend Professor Hendricon's class.

On the last day of class, Professor Hendricon strode in with our research papers. "Before I hand them back to you," he said, "I want to talk about them both generally and specifically." He continued, "A few of the papers were excellent, a few poor, and the majority mediocre. The excellent ones were creative and imaginative in their use of technique; but the poor ones seemed as if they had been put together artificially and mechanically with scissors and paste."

That last remark hit me. Of course, I should have known that Professor Hendricon would be quick to see the artificial way my paper was put together: how I took notes on cards; distributed them in piles; mechanically shifted stacks of cards around; made an outline last, not first; filled gaps by digging out more material; mechanically revised; looked up words; read aloud to detect faulty intonation—all done like a "hack" in mechanical and piecemeal fashion. The rest of the class had real talent—they were truly gifted. In four or five days, they were able to write down their thoughts directly, fully developed, like true artists. And like true artists, they made good with one chance, whereas I had dozens of chances to write and rewrite.

As Professor Hendricon continued to talk about "scissors and paste," he suddenly picked up a paper to illustrate a point. I was shocked. I could tell it was my paper. I just couldn't stand the embarrassment. All I wanted to do was to get out of that room, fast! Then I suddenly realized that though I knew it was my paper, no one else did. So I steeled myself. Professor Hendricon read one paragraph after another. He jumped to the first part of the paper for a paragraph, then to the end for another. Then I noticed that the rest of the class was listening attentively, and though Professor Hendricon's voice was excited, it was kindly. As I calmed and composed myself, I heard, "Note the smooth rhythm of the prose and the careful choice of words. This is what I mean by scholarship. The technique is discernible. Yes! But put together with a scholar's love, and care, and time."

P.S. You guessed it! I passed the course.

HAVE YOU MISSED SOMETHING?

SENTENCE COMPLETION   *Complete the following sentences with one of the three words or phrases listed below each sentence.*

1. Give your research purpose, direction, and focus by developing a
   _____ about your topic.

scientific	fascinating	compelling
discovery	misconception	question

2. When you are using the Web or a library's computerized indexes, a Boolean search enables you to narrow your search by _____.

using a prominent	combining	using a full sentence
keyword	multiple keywords	

3. As you discover magazines and books that relate to your research, add them to a working bibliography that is _____.

in your notebook	on separate cards	kept by the reference
	or slips	librarian

MATCHING   *In each blank space in the left column, write the letters preceding the phrase in the right column that matches the left item best.*

_____ 1. Index cards   a. Can help you find a suitable topic

_____ 2. Spell checker   b. Synopsis found at the beginning of some journal articles

_____ 3. Abstract   c. Can be used to plan your paper visually

_____ 4. Index   d. More flexible than a computer for taking notes

_____ 5. Ellipses   e. Primary source for most of your paper's information

_____ 6. Concept map   f. Good starting point in the search for books or magazines

_____ 7. Preliminary research   g. Helpful but not infallible tool for correcting your paper's errors

_____ 8. Library   h. Indicate that part of a quotation has been omitted

Online Study Center   www.college.hmco.com/pic/pauk9e

TRUE-FALSE

Circle T *beside the* true *statements and* F *beside the* false *statements.*

1. T F Three or four narrowings should reduce your general topic to a suitable size.
2. T F The *Readers' Guide* is the best-known bound periodical index.
3. T F A computerized catalog usually enables you to search by subject, author, title, or keyword.
4. T F Paraphrasing is permitted in a research paper.
5. T F A conclusion isn't always necessary in a research paper.

MULTIPLE CHOICE

Choose the word or phrase that completes each sentence most accurately, and circle the letter that precedes it.

1. The basic skills for writing a research paper are similar to those for
   a. writing a novel or short story.
   b. preparing for a test or quiz.
   c. taking notes during a lecture.
   d. doing none of the above.

2. The most common criticism of research papers is that they are
   a. too broad.
   b. too long.
   c. poorly written.
   d. carelessly researched.

3. A research librarian is an expert on
   a. most research paper topics.
   b. the proper form for footnotes.
   c. use of the library.
   d. all of the above.

4. Your notes will be easier to use if you
   a. recopy them so they are easy to read.
   b. copy all your information verbatim.
   c. jot down each note on a separate card or slip.
   d. fit them on as few pages as possible.

5. You can avoid plagiarism by including
   a. quotation marks.
   b. citations.
   c. a bibliography.
   d. all the above.

SHORT ANSWER

Supply a brief answer for each of the following items.

1. Explain the role of selectivity in writing a research paper.
2. How can Boolean searching be used to pinpoint references?
3. How can concept maps be used in organizing a research paper?

IT'S YOUR Q

The Q System uses marginal questions to encourage active reading. You'll notice that most but not all paragraphs in this chapter are accompanied by marginal questions. Now it's your Q. Scan the chapter for any paragraph that is missing a question, reread the paragraph, establish the main idea, and then arrive at a question that elicits it. Use the questions in the surrounding paragraphs as models for your own marginal questions.

WORDS IN CONTEXT

From the three choices beside each numbered item, select the one that most nearly expresses the meaning of the italicized word in the quote. Make a light check mark (✓) next to your choice.

No one wants advice—only *corroboration*.

—John Steinbeck (1902–1968), American novelist

| 1. only *corroboration* | cooperation | agreement | confirmation |

Incomprehensible jargon is the *hallmark* of a profession.

—Kingman Brewster Jr. (1919–1988), president of Yale University and U.S. ambassador to Britain

2. *incomprehensible*	self-evident	unfathomable	foreign
3. *jargon*	lingo	shorthand	writing
4. the *hallmark*	direction	identification	standard

If you do good, people will accuse you of selfish *ulterior motives*. Do good anyway.

—Dr. Robert Schuller (1926–), American evangelist

5. *ulterior*   monetary   hidden   self-serving

6. *motives*   advantages   profits   reasons

A team should be an *extension* of the coach's personality. My teams were *arrogant* and *obnoxious*.

—Al McGuire (1928–2001), American basketball coach

7. *extension*   mirror-image   counterpart   continuation

8. *arrogant*   haughty   excitable   high-spirited

9. *obnoxious*   tough   noisy   nasty

THE WORD HISTORY SYSTEM

Curfew
cover the fire for the night

curfew cur'-few *n.* A regulation requiring certain or all people to leave the streets or be at home at a prescribed hour.

In the Middle Ages, peasants were required to cover or to extinguish their fires at a fixed hour in the evening announced by the ringing of a bell called the "cover-fire," French *couvre-feu*. The Norman French used the word in England, where it was adopted as *curfu*, modern *curfew*, meaning the hour and the signal for citizens to retire to their homes, or, as now, for the closing of a public place or the cessation of an activity for the night.

Reprinted by permission. From *Picturesque Word Origins* © 1933 by G. & C. Merriam Co. (now Merriam-Webster, Incorporated).

Appendix: Answers

Chapter 1 Knowing What You're Aiming For

HAVE YOU MISSED SOMETHING?

Sentence completion: 1. destination   2. experience   3. action

Matching: 1. f   2. d   3. e   4. g   5. h   6. a   7. c   8. b

True-false: 1. F   2. T   3. F   4. T   5. F

Multiple-choice: 1. d   2. a   3. c   4. c   5. a

WORDS IN CONTEXT: 1. perseverance   2. natural gift   3. high aptitude   4. vagrants   5. gorge   6. rewards

Chapter 2 Using Time and Space Effectively

HAVE YOU MISSED SOMETHING?

Sentence completion: 1. game plan   2. daytime   3. term

Matching: 1. g   2. f   3. d   4. b   5. h   6. c   7. a   8. e

True-false: 1. F   2. F   3. F   4. T   5. T

Multiple-choice: 1. b   2. b   3. b   4. c   5. d

WORDS IN CONTEXT: 1. strength   2. sorrowfully   3. death   4. worth   5. inexplicable   6. associated   7. included

Chapter 3 Staying Focused

HAVE YOU MISSED SOMETHING?

Sentence completion: 1. thinking   2. steady   3. distraction

Matching: 1. g   2. h   3. a   4. b   5. c   6. d   7. e   8. f

True-false: 1. T   2. T   3. F   4. F   5. F

Multiple-choice: 1. a   2. b   3. b   4. d   5. c

WORDS IN CONTEXT: 1. corruptive   2. orderly   3. refinement   4. unappealing   5. despicable

Chapter 4 Managing Stress

HAVE YOU MISSED SOMETHING?

Sentence completion: 1. stressors   2. value   3. saturated

Matching: 1. f   2. g   3. b   4. e   5. a   6. h   7. d   8. c

True-false: 1. T   2. T   3. T   4. T   5. F

Multiple-choice: 1. c   2. c   3. b   4. c   5. d

WORDS IN CONTEXT: 1. stressed   2. gibberish   3. insinuations   4. untalkative   5. average people   6. nullified

Chapter 5   Improving Your Reading

HAVE YOU MISSED SOMETHING?

Sentence completion: 1. concept   2. fixations
3. phrases

Matching: 1. c   2. e   3. h   4. a   5. d   6. g   7. f
8. b

True-false: 1. F   2. T   3. T   4. T   5. T

Multiple-choice: 1. c   2. b   3. b   4. a   5. b

WORDS IN CONTEXT: 1. unfeeling   2. disdainful
3. component   4. irritating

Chapter 6   Strengthening Your Vocabulary

HAVE YOU MISSED SOMETHING?

Sentence completion: 1. self-esteem
2. convenience   3. familiarity

Matching: 1. d   2. c   3. g   4. f   5. a   6. b   7. h
8. e

True-false: 1. T   2. T   3. T   4. T   5. F

Multiple-choice: 1. d   2. d   3. b   4. b   5. b

WORDS IN CONTEXT: 1. given new life   2. absolute
3. rewards

Chapter 7   Zeroing In on Information That's Valuable

HAVE YOU MISSED SOMETHING?

Sentence completion: 1. questions
2. hierarchically   3. "the wall"

Matching: 1. d   2. a   3. h   4. b   5. f   6. g   7. e
8. c

True-false: 1. T   2. T   3. F   4. F   5. T

Multiple-choice: 1. d   2. a   3. a   4. b   5. c

WORDS IN CONTEXT: 1. damaging force   2. unseen
3. decreased value   4. inordinate   5. peculiarities
6. cautious   7. outdated

Chapter 8   Learning Through Multiple Channels

HAVE YOU MISSED SOMETHING?

Sentence completion: 1. sequentially
2. intelligence   3. symmetrical

Matching: 1. c   2. f   3. e   4. h   5. a   6. g   7. d
8. b

True-false: 1. F   2. T   3. T   4. T   5. T

Multiple-choice: 1. b   2. c   3. b   4. a   5. d

WORDS IN CONTEXT: 1. impresario   2. delegate
3. briefness   4. abundantly

Chapter 9   Defending Your Memory

HAVE YOU MISSED SOMETHING?

Sentence completion: 1. selectivity   2. DRAM
3. reciting

Matching: 1. c   2. e   3. g   4. h   5. a   6. d   7. f
8. b

True-false: 1. T   2. T   3. T   4. F   5. F

Multiple-choice: 1. b   2. b   3. b   4. b   5. c

WORDS IN CONTEXT: 1. new ideas   2. reword
3. possessed   4. disasters

Chapter 10   Taking Effective Notes

HAVE YOU MISSED SOMETHING?

Sentence completion: 1. context   2. signposts
3. questions

Matching: 1. b   2. f   3. d   4. h   5. g   6. e   7. c
8. a

True-false: 1. F   2. T   3. T   4. F   5. T

Multiple-choice: 1. b   2. c   3. b   4. a   5. d

WORDS IN CONTEXT: 1. refinement   2. relieve
3. reasonable   4. dead end

Chapter 11   Mastering Your Notes

HAVE YOU MISSED SOMETHING?

Sentence completion: 1. recitation   2. reflection
3. ignored

Matching: 1. d   2. h   3. a   4. e   5. g   6. b   7. f
8. c

True-false: 1. T   2. F   3. T   4. F   5. T

Multiple-choice: 1. a   2. d   3. b   4. d   5. c

WORDS IN CONTEXT: 1. major   2. unrelated
3. abundantly   4. favorable   5. trite phrase
6. filled

Chapter 12   Performing Well on Tests and Quizzes

HAVE YOU MISSED SOMETHING?

Sentence completion: 1. instructor   2. circled
3. outlined

Matching: 1. f   2. b   3. h   4. d   5. g   6. e   7. a
8. c

True-false: 1. T   2. T   3. T   4. F   5. F

Multiple-choice: 1. d   2. a   3. c   4. a   5. b

WORDS IN CONTEXT: 1. obvious   2. provided
3. intrinsic   4. search   5. tact   6. evil
7. free enterprise   8. philanthropy

Chapter 13   Getting the Most Out of Discussions

HAVE YOU MISSED SOMETHING?

Sentence completion: 1. increasing
2. anticipation   3. yelling

Matching: 1. c   2. g   3. a   4. b   5. e   6. h   7. d
8. f

True-false: 1. F   2. T   3. T   4. F   5. T

Multiple-choice: 1. d   2. b   3. d   4. c   5. d

WORDS IN CONTEXT: 1. dictionary   2. unbeatable
3. stern

Chapter 14   Writing a Research Paper

HAVE YOU MISSED SOMETHING?

Sentence completion: 1. compelling question
2. combining multiple keywords   3. on separate
cards or slips

Matching: 1. d   2. g   3. b   4. f   5. h   6. c   7. a
8. e

True-false: 1. T   2. T   3. T   4. T   5. F

Multiple-choice: 1. b   2. a   3. c   4. c   5. d

WORDS IN CONTEXT: 1. confirmation
2. unfathomable   3. lingo   4. identification
5. hidden   6. reasons   7. continuation
8. haughty   9. nasty

Index